Artificial Intelligence in Performance-Driven Design

Artificial Intelligence in Performance-Driven Design

Theories, Methods, and Tools

Edited by

Narjes Abbasabadi
University of Washington
Seattle, USA

Mehdi Ashayeri
Southern Illinois University Carbondale
Carbondale, USA

WILEY

Copyright © 2024 by John Wiley & Sons, Inc. All rights reserved.

Published by John Wiley & Sons, Inc., Hoboken, New Jersey.

Published simultaneously in Canada.

No part of this publication may be reproduced, stored in a retrieval system, or transmitted in any form or by any means, electronic, mechanical, photocopying, recording, scanning, or otherwise, except as permitted under Section 107 or 108 of the 1976 United States Copyright Act, without either the prior written permission of the Publisher, or authorization through payment of the appropriate per-copy fee to the Copyright Clearance Center, Inc., 222 Rosewood Drive, Danvers, MA 01923, (978) 750-8400, fax (978) 750-4470, or on the web at www.copyright.com. Requests to the Publisher for permission should be addressed to the Permissions Department, John Wiley & Sons, Inc., 111 River Street, Hoboken, NJ 07030, (201) 748-6011, fax (201) 748-6008, or online at http://www.wiley.com/go/permission.

Trademarks: Wiley and the Wiley logo are trademarks or registered trademarks of John Wiley & Sons, Inc. and/or its affiliates in the United States and other countries and may not be used without written permission. All other trademarks are the property of their respective owners. John Wiley & Sons, Inc. is not associated with any product or vendor mentioned in this book.

Limit of Liability/Disclaimer of Warranty: While the publisher and author have used their best efforts in preparing this book, they make no representations or warranties with respect to the accuracy or completeness of the contents of this book and specifically disclaim any implied warranties of merchantability or fitness for a particular purpose. No warranty may be created or extended by sales representatives or written sales materials. The advice and strategies contained herein may not be suitable for your situation. You should consult with a professional where appropriate. Further, readers should be aware that websites listed in this work may have changed or disappeared between when this work was written and when it is read. Neither the publisher nor authors shall be liable for any loss of profit or any other commercial damages, including but not limited to special, incidental, consequential, or other damages.

For general information on our other products and services or for technical support, please contact our Customer Care Department within the United States at (800) 762-2974, outside the United States at (317) 572-3993 or fax (317) 572-4002.

Wiley also publishes its books in a variety of electronic formats. Some content that appears in print may not be available in electronic formats. For more information about Wiley products, visit our web site at www.wiley.com.

Library of Congress Cataloging-in-Publication Data:

Names: Abbasabadi, Narjes, editor. | Ashayeri, Mehdi, editor.
Title: Artificial intelligence in performance-driven design : theories, methods, and tools / edited by Narjes Abbasabadi, University of Washington, Seattle, USA, Mehdi Ashayeri, Southern Illinois University Carbondale, Carbondale, USA.
Description: First edition. | Hoboken, New Jersey : Wiley, [2024] | Includes bibliographical references and index.
Identifiers: LCCN 2024006963 (print) | LCCN 2024006964 (ebook) | ISBN 9781394172061 (paperback) | ISBN 9781394172085 (adobe pdf) | ISBN 9781394172078 (epub)
Subjects: LCSH: Artificial intelligence—Industrial applications. | Engineering design—Data processing.
Classification: LCC TA347.A78 A85 2024 (print) | LCC TA347.A78 (ebook) | DDC 620/.0042028563—dc23/eng/20240314
LC record available at https://lccn.loc.gov/2024006963
LC ebook record available at https://lccn.loc.gov/2024006964

Cover Design: Wiley
Cover Image: Courtesy of Narjes Abbasabadi and Mehdi Ashayeri

Set in 9.5/12.5pt STIXTwoText by Straive, Chennai, India

Contents

List of Contributors *xi*
Introduction *xiii*

1 Augmented Computational Design *1*
  Introduction *1*
  Background *2*
    Relevance of AI in AEC *2*
    Historical Context *3*
    Design as Decision-Making *5*
    AI for Generative Design *7*
  Framework *9*
    Design Space Exploration *11*
    Spatial Design Variables *13*
    Statistical Approaches to Design *14*
  Demonstration *15*
    Case Study *15*
    Methodology *16*
  Results *21*
    BBN Validation Results *21*
    Toy Problem *22*
  Discussion *22*
  Outlook *25*
  Acronyms *26*
  Notations *27*
  References *28*

2 Machine Learning in Urban Building Energy Modeling *31*
  Introduction *31*
  Urban Building Energy Modeling Methods *32*
    Top–Down Models *33*
    Bottom–Up Models *33*
  Uncertainty in Urban Building Energy Modeling *36*
    Epistemic Uncertainty *36*
    Stochastic Uncertainty *36*
    Addressing Uncertainty *37*
  Machine Learning in Urban Building Energy Modeling *39*

Supervised Learning *39*
Unsupervised Learning *44*
Reinforcement Learning *46*
Machine Learning-Based Surrogate UBEM *47*
Conclusion *49*
References *50*

3 A Hybrid Physics-Based Machine Learning Approach for Integrated Energy and Exposure Modeling *57*
Introduction *57*
Materials and Methods *59*
Data, Data Sources, and Dataset Processing *59*
Methodology *61*
Results *70*
Physics-Based Simulation *70*
Data-Driven Computation (Prediction) *70*
Discussion *73*
Conclusion *74*
Acknowledgment *75*
References *75*

4 An Integrative Deep Performance Framework for Daylight Prediction in Early Design Ideation *81*
Introduction *81*
Background *83*
Daylight Simulation *84*
Deep Learning Models *85*
DL-Based Surrogate Modeling *85*
Verification Methods *85*
Research Methods *86*
Data Acquisition *86*
Model Training *88*
Results and Validation *88*
Discussions of Results *90*
Conclusions *94*
References *94*

5 Artificial Intelligence in Building Enclosure Performance Optimization: Frameworks, Methods, and Tools *97*
Building Envelope and Performance *97*
Artificial Intelligence and Building Envelope Overview *97*
Optimization Routes and Building Envelope *98*
Optimization Frameworks *99*
Optimization Methods *99*
Machine Learning and Building Envelope *101*
Artificial Neural Network *101*
Convolutional Neural Network *105*

Recurrent Neural Network *105*
Generative Adversarial Networks *106*
Ensemble Learning *107*
Discussions on Practical Implications *108*
Summary and Conclusion *109*
References *110*

6 Efficient Parametric Design-Space Exploration with Reinforcement Learning-Based Recommenders *113*
Introduction *113*
Methodology *115*
  Section 01: Clustering Design Options *116*
  Section 02: Reinforcement Learning-Based Recommender System *120*
Design Dashboard *123*
Discussion *124*
Conclusion *125*
References *126*

7 Multi-Level Optimization of UHP-FRC Sandwich Panels for Building Façade Systems *129*
Introduction *129*
Building Façade Design Optimization *130*
Methodology *134*
  Midspan Displacements and Thermal Resistivity of UHP-FRC Panels *136*
  Energy Performance of the UHP-FRC Panels at the Building Level *141*
  Life Cycle Cost Analysis of the UHP-FRC Panels *142*
  Surrogate Models *145*
  Multi-objective Optimization Algorithm *147*
Results and Discussion *148*
  Surrogate Models *148*
  Pareto Front Solutions *151*
Conclusion *152*
References *153*

8 Decoding Global Indoor Health Perception on Social Media Through NLP and Transformer Deep Learning *159*
Introduction *159*
Literature Review *161*
  Social Media and Urban Life: Theories, Challenges, and Opportunities *161*
  Methods for Computing Social Media Data in Environmental Studies *163*
Materials and Methods *168*
  Data Query *168*
  Text Preprocessing *169*
  Text Tokenization *169*
  Text Summarization *170*
  Generating Co-occurrence Matrix *170*
  Sentiment Analysis and Classification *170*

Visualizations   *171*
  Embedding Visualization   *171*
  Attention Score Visualization (Attention Map) and Interpretation   *172*
Results and Discussion   *173*
Conclusion   *178*
References   *179*

9 Occupant-Driven Urban Building Energy Efficiency via Ambient Intelligence   187

Introduction   *187*
Occupancy and Building Energy Use   *191*
  Definitions   *191*
Occupant Monitoring Methods   *193*
  Occupant Monitoring Via Observational Studies   *194*
  Occupant Monitoring via Experimental Studies   *195*
Occupant-driven Energy Efficiency via Ambient Intelligence   *196*
  Ambient Intelligence Advancements and Applications   *196*
  AmI-Based Energy Efficiency Feedback (EEF) Systems   *197*
  Energy Efficiency via AmI Systems and Digital Twins Technology   *201*
Conclusion   *202*
References   *203*

10 Understanding Social Dynamics in Urban Building and Transportation Energy Behavior   211

Introduction   *211*
Methodology   *213*
  Modeling Framework   *214*
  Explanatory Model   *214*
  Data   *215*
Results and Discussion   *219*
  Effects of Occupancy and Socio-economic Factors   *219*
  Variable Importance (VI)   *219*
  Lek's Profile   *219*
Conclusion   *226*
References   *227*

11 Building Better Spaces: Using Virtual Reality to Improve Building Performance   231

Introduction   *231*
Applications of Virtual Reality in Building Performance   *233*
  Virtual Reality for Improving Building Design through Integrated Performance Data   *233*
  Virtual Reality for Building Design Reviews and Education in Architecture and Engineering   *236*
  Virtual Reality for Research on Building Occupant Comfort and Well-Being   *240*
Conclusion   *243*
References   *245*

12 Digital Twin for Citywide Energy Modeling and Management *251*

Introduction *251*

Urban Building Energy Digital Twins (UBEDTs) *252*
  Definition and Conceptualization *252*
  Implications for Citywide Energy Management *254*

Enabling Technologies *256*
  Twining Technologies *256*
  Urban Digital Twin (UDT) and Data Sources *258*
  Artificial Intelligence (AI) and Digital Twin *260*
  Relationship Between IoT, Big Data, AI–ML, and Digital Twins *261*
  Interoperability Technologies *262*

Maturity Levels *263*

Architecture *265*
  Data Acquisition Layer *266*
  Transmission Layer *266*
  Modeling and Simulation Layer *266*
  Data/Model Integration Layer *269*
  Service/Actuation Layer *269*

Challenges in Implementing Citywide Digital Twins *269*
  Data Quality and Availability *270*
  Required Smart Infrastructure and Associated Cost *270*
  Interoperability *270*
  Data Analysis *271*
  Cybersecurity and Privacy Concerns *271*

Conclusion *272*

References *272*

Index *277*

List of Contributors

Narjes Abbasabadi
Department of Architecture
School of Architecture
College of Built Environments
University of Washington
Seattle
WA
USA

Bahram Abediniangerabi
Department of Civil Engineering
The University of Texas at Arlington
Arlington
TX
USA

Md Shariful Alam
Department of Architecture
University of Washington
Seattle
WA
USA

Mehdi Ashayeri
School of Architecture
College of Arts and Media
Southern Illinois University Carbondale
Carbondale
IL
USA

Shervin Azadi
Eindhoven University of Technology
Eindhoven
The Netherlands

Nan Bai
Delft University of Technology
Delft
The Netherlands

Anil Baral
Department of Civil Engineering
The University of Texas at Arlington
Arlington
TX
USA

Daniel Bolojan
School of Architecture
Florida Atlantic University
Fort Lauderdale
FL
USA

Kynthia Chamilothori
Human-Technology Interaction
Industrial Engineering and Innovation Sciences
Eindhoven University of Technology
Eindhoven
The Netherlands

Pooya Darghiasi
Department of Civil Engineering
The University of Texas at Arlington
Arlington
TX
USA

Tomás Méndez Echenagucia
Department of Architecture
University of Washington
Seattle
WA
USA

Farshad Kheiri
School of Architecture
Southern Illinois University Carbondale
Carbondale
IL
USA

Atefe Makhmalbaf
School of Architecture
The University of Texas at Arlington
Arlington
TX
USA

Pirouz Nourian
University of Twente
Enschede
The Netherlands

Azadeh Omidfar Sawyer
School of Architecture
Carnegie Mellon University
Pittsburgh
PA
USA

Mohsen Shahandashti
Department of Civil Engineering
The University of Texas at Arlington
Arlington
TX
USA

Roy Uijtendaal
Nieman Raadgevende Ingenieurs
Utrecht
The Netherlands

Shermeen Yousif
School of Architecture
Florida Atlantic University
Fort Lauderdale
FL
USA

Introduction

Narjes Abbasabadi[1] and Mehdi Ashayeri[2]

Department of Architecture, School of Architecture, College of Built Environments, University of Washington, Seattle, WA, USA
School of Architecture, College of Arts and Media, Southern Illinois University Carbondale, Carbondale, IL, USA

Artificial intelligence (AI) has emerged as a ubiquitous force in today's world, asserting its influence across an expansive spectrum of human endeavors. AI, as defined by Margaret A. Boden in *AI: Its Nature and Future*, "seeks to make computers do the sorts of things that minds can do" (Boden 2016). At its core, AI endeavors to engineer computational entities capable of performing tasks traditionally associated with human cognition and to facilitate a synthetic replication of human abilities such as communication, learning, perception, problem-solving, and reasoning. In pursuit of this, the discipline is methodically segmented into distinct yet interconnected subfields, for example: machine learning (ML), which learns from data to enable informed decision-making; natural language processing (NLP), which deciphers and constructs human language; computer vision (CV), which interprets visual data; and robotics, which imparts autonomy to machines for task execution. These diverse subfields underpin AI's quest to forge machines that operate with a semblance of human intelligence, enhancing human capacities and spearheading a revolution in technological innovation.

The history of AI unfolds from Blaise Pascal's 17th-century mechanical calculator through the 19th-century programmable machine of Charles Babbage and Ada Lovelace, arriving at the 20th century where the formalization of neural networks by Warren McCulloch and Walter Pitts, and Alan Turing's machine intelligence, sets the stage for AI's theoretical and practical evolution. Alan Turing's seminal work, "Computing Machinery and Intelligence," is central to AI's philosophical underpinnings, which posits the critical inquiry, "Can machines think?" and introduces the Turing Test as a measure of a machine's capability to exhibit intelligence indistinguishable from human intelligence (Turing 1950). Turing's work has significantly influenced the computational cognition and the trajectory of AI evolution, underscoring Turing's enduring legacy in shaping the ongoing discourse in computing technology.

The term "Artificial Intelligence" was coined in 1956, around the time of the seminal Dartmouth Conference, and has since become the standard bearer for a field characterized by rapid growth. It has navigated through the vicissitudes of "AI winters" and resurgences, marked by significant milestones. This journey includes the triumphs of chess-playing computers such as IBM's Deep Blue, the widespread adoption of digital assistants such as Siri, Alexa, and Google Assistant, and the development of advanced generative models in the 21st century, particularly those in the realm of deep learning enabling the generation of text, images, and other forms of media to open up new possibilities for creativity, automation, and problem-solving. Moreover, the integration of AI with big data has catalyzed significant breakthroughs across various domains, with ML and deep learning technologies becoming intertwined with the ability to process and learn from vast datasets and enable complex predictive models. In addition, it led to significant advances in autonomous systems, including self-driving cars, drones, and robotics, as well as in NLP technologies like GPT, and biologically impactful models such as DeepMind's AlphaFold. Today, as AI navigates ethical landscapes and quantum futures, it stands not only as a testament to the relentless human pursuit of creating machines that mirror and extend our cognitive faculties but also as a beacon for the untapped capabilities of intelligent systems and continuously expanding the horizons of computational and cognitive potential.

While data-driven approaches using AI have shown their power to solve challenges across many domains, particularly science and engineering, their full potential within the built environment, specifically architectural discipline, remains largely underexplored. AI innovations and advancements in sensing technologies, real-time global information exchange, and open data initiatives have influenced our cities and increased our ability to better understand and solve interconnected built environment problems. These advancements, combined with predictive information modeling and intelligence across scales, present opportunities to address multi-scale crucial issues—from mobility and energy to environmental quality and human well-being—potentially enabling cities to be transformative stages. The integration of AI and big data into urban and building modeling workflows facilitates enhancing the accuracy, efficiency, scalability, and accessibility of complex models and enabling a deeper understanding and more nuanced solutions to multifaceted problems. Particularly, the convergence of AI and big data with built environment technologies presents a transformative opportunity for performance-driven design and planning, promising more accurate, faster, and actionable insights that could lead to improved decision-making. In this light, AI emerges as a catalyst for reimagining the future of built environments, driving performance-driven design toward greater social and environmental sustainability.

This book, *Artificial Intelligence in Performance-Driven Design: Theories, Methods, and Tools*, serves as an interdisciplinary exploration of the utilization of AI, specifically ML, in the domain of performance-driven design and modeling within the context of the built environment. This work delves into the theoretical foundations and methodological frameworks that underpin the application of AI techniques in performance-driven exploration. Notably, it places a particular emphasis on the multi-scale modeling of diverse facets such as energy flows, environmental quality, and human systems. This book examines relevant examples showcasing the integration of AI and big data into modeling and design workflows to enhance their accuracy, efficiency, scalability, and accessibility in complex models. Moreover, it explores conceptual frameworks and computational tools that harness AI's potential in physics-based simulation frameworks, facilitating the integration of physics-based modeling, optimization, and automation procedures, showcasing how AI can streamline decision-making processes in performance-driven design.

Across the various chapters in this book, ML and its application to the built environment offers an array of methodologies tailored to distinct learning paradigms, each leveraging data to enhance design, planning, and operational efficiencies. Fundamentally, ML is categorized into several core approaches: supervised learning, which employs labeled datasets to instruct algorithms on pattern recognition and outcome prediction, is essential for tasks such as predicting building energy consumption and classifying buildings by energy efficiency levels. This approach has become fundamental for developing predictive models that inform sustainable architectural practices. Conversely, unsupervised learning leverages unlabeled data to discover latent patterns and correlations, enabling applications like the clustering of buildings according to energy usage or the application of dimensionality reduction techniques to distill complex data into actionable insights. Reinforcement learning broadens this spectrum by focusing on the iterative process of decision-making through direct interaction with environments, proving pivotal in scenarios such as the optimization of building façades, building and urban layouts, traffic management, and the operational dynamics of smart grids. Additionally, generative algorithms introduce the capability to synthesize new data samples based on predefined parameters, expanding the creative scope within performance-driven design and planning. Together, these applications underscore the transformative potential of AI and ML in redefining the built environment, pushing the boundaries of traditional architectural paradigms toward more efficient, responsive, and sustainable outcomes.

Deep learning, as a branch of ML and AI, stands at the forefront of technological advancements, transforming the built environment sector. Categorized by neural networks designed to mimic the complex processing layers of the human brain, deep learning surpasses traditional data analysis techniques by its capacity to learn from and interpret vast amounts of data autonomously. This capability enables the identification of complex patterns and relationships within data, significantly enhancing accuracy in predictive analytics, image processing, and autonomous system controls. Deep learning's advanced analytical prowess is particularly beneficial in predictive modeling for various performance metrics, such as energy consumption, and in enhancing automated and optimized design processes. By employing deep learning, designers, planners, and researchers in the built environment are equipped with powerful tools for driving innovation, improving sustainability, and responding to complex design and planning challenges. The integration of deep learning signifies a major advancement in utilizing data for creating smarter, more efficient, and sustainable solutions within the built environment. It also highlights the broad potential of AI and ML technologies to transform and improve how we develop built environments.

The book also explores the integration of intelligent systems and digital twin technology throughout the lifecycle of the built environment. It underscores its transformative potential in enhancing our comprehension and management of built environments. Intelligent systems, augmented with AI capabilities, contribute to real-time monitoring, analysis, and adaptation of building systems to optimize performance. Digital twins, virtual replicas of physical structures and systems, serve as powerful tools for monitoring prediction, and decision support. The integration of AI within these paradigms augments their utility, leading to more informed design and operational decisions that can enhance the sustainability, efficiency, and user experience of the built environment. Through the integration of intelligent systems and digital twins, AI emerges as a catalyst for enhancing our understanding and management of the complexities inherent in contemporary built environments.

Presented herein is a synopsis, capturing the essence and intellectual journey offered by each chapter:

Chapter 1 presents methodological reflections on the necessity and utility of AI in generative design. It also offers a concise history of significant AI developments, establishing a groundwork for understanding architectural design as a series of decision-making processes. This chapter sets the stage for perceiving architectural design as a sequence of decision-making steps. It explores how AI can augment generative design by addressing numerous decisions for achieving specific outcomes or performance indicators. The essence of performance-based generative design lies in creating statistical or simulation-based links between these decisions and their consequences for mapping and navigating through intricate decision landscapes. The chapter further investigates the potential of AI in refining decision-making in architectural design, particularly in mapping and navigating complex design environments.

Chapter 2 explores the integration of ML into urban building energy modeling (UBEM), which is key for quantifying and understanding city-wide energy dynamics. It underscores ML's role in enhancing UBEM's predictive and optimization capabilities, focusing on improved accuracy and efficiency. The chapter reviews current UBEM methods, their strengths, limitations, and inherent uncertainties, showing how ML helps overcome these challenges. It explores various ML paradigms—supervised, unsupervised, and reinforcement learning—and their specific algorithms, as well as ML-based surrogate modeling for more accurate, efficient, and uncertainty-reduced urban energy consumption estimates. This integration aims to advance urban energy modeling facilitating more efficient, informed decision-making in urban development.

Chapter 3 introduces a hybrid approach, combining ML and urban big data analytics with physics-based performance simulation, for the integrated modeling of indoor air quality, operational energy, and ambient airflow in urban buildings. It aims to optimize design by focusing on both climate and health considerations. A pilot was conducted on a large office building prototype in a densely populated urban setting. This approach utilized advanced simulation tools, including computational fluid dynamics (CFD), energy modeling, and artificial neural networks (ANNs). The results demonstrated the framework's effectiveness in evaluating building performance strategies and understanding natural ventilation and indoor air quality. Compared to traditional methods, this hybrid model significantly enhances simulation speed and accuracy. It offers valuable insights for architects and engineers in the early design stages, enabling the integration of occupant health with energy efficiency, contributing to decarbonization efforts.

Chapter 4 investigates the fusion of AI with performance-driven design strategies, focusing on developing an automated, accurate daylight performance simulation method. As part of broader efforts to automate environmental assessments in design, it introduces "Deep Performance" (DP), a deep learning-based method for creating a surrogate model. This model, trained on vast datasets of building plans and daylight meshes, predicts architectural features and daylight distribution. The DP method showcases notable efficiency, being 600 times faster than traditional simulations, and achieves 90% accuracy. The shift from simulation-based to prediction-based approaches is transformative, enabling designers to integrate real-time environmental metrics into generative design systems. Early incorporation of daylight analysis in design decisions aids in exploring passive strategies and optimizing layouts and envelope designs. Ultimately, this research aims to empower environmentally efficient and cost-effective designs in the built environment through advanced, data-driven solutions.

Chapter 5 reviews the role of AI in optimizing building enclosure performance, a critical aspect influencing a building's overall efficiency. Building enclosures significantly affect thermal, daylighting, acoustics, and indoor air quality performances, yet their complex design and varying environmental factors make optimal solutions challenging. AI automates the design and evaluation process, enhancing information synthesis and decision-making. As a result, architecture has increasingly incorporated AI and computational optimization into building enclosure design. It provides an overview of AI frameworks, methods, and tools, with a focus on ML algorithms, especially neural networks, and optimization methods like metaheuristic algorithms. These are specifically discussed in the context of designing and analyzing building envelope performance, showcasing their potential for improving sustainable building practices.

Chapter 6 introduces a reinforcement learning-based recommender for efficient exploration in parametric design. Parametric designs, while flexible, often overwhelm designers with numerous alternatives. Traditional optimizers such as genetic algorithms focus mainly on quantitative outcomes, neglecting aesthetic preferences. The proposed framework integrates a reinforcement learning recommender to navigate these vast design spaces effectively. A case study on a mid-rise apartment building demonstrates this. This approach learns from user interactions, suggesting designs that align with both performance and aesthetic choices. It streamlines the decision-making process, enabling designers to explore high-performing solutions with personal design preferences within a vast array of options.

Chapter 7 explores multi-level optimization of ultra-high-performance fiber-reinforced concrete (UHP-FRC) sandwich panels for building façades using AI, optimizing energy efficiency, structural performance, and construction cost. It analyzes design optimization at building and assembly levels, focusing on façade system variables for building performance and panel-specific criteria. A surrogate-based optimization framework is proposed, providing Pareto efficient solutions across panel displacement, building energy use, and life cycle cost. Illustrated with a case study of an office building, the study employs a genetic algorithm for optimization. The results underscores the importance of holistic design considerations, preventing suboptimal performance in isolated areas. The methodology offers insights into optimizing multi-layer façade systems from various perspectives.

Chapter 8 delves into decoding global indoor health perceptions on social media, utilizing NLP and transformer deep learning techniques like the RoBERTa algorithm. It examines digital media's impact in urban studies, reviews social media's role in environmental health research focusing on air quality, and identifies methodological gaps. The study analyzes occupant feedback on the X platform (formerly Twitter), exploring how stay-at-home orders during the pandemic's first year affected indoor air quality perceptions, compared to 2019 baseline data. The findings reveal a significant increase in negative perceptions in 2020. This research underscores the importance of social media analytics in shaping environmental health strategies and emphasizes the need to prioritize indoor air quality in design of urban buildings and policy-making. Particularly in the context of global events such as pandemics, this focus is crucial for enhancing overall urban resilience.

Chapter 9 explores occupant-driven urban building energy efficiency, enhanced by ambient intelligence (AmI). It acknowledges the role of human factors—occupancy, behavior, and socioeconomic dimensions—in achieving urban decarbonization goals across a building's lifecycle, including design, construction, operation, and retrofit. Advances in digital technologies and data-driven approaches, including sensing, computing, and AI, offer new opportunities to understand and reduce energy use in buildings. The chapter reviews energy monitoring methods and systems that encourage positive occupant behaviors, highlighting the benefits of real-time monitoring through AI and IoT-powered AmI systems. These systems aim to support adaptable, user-centered environments and improve occupancy data for future scenario modeling. Emphasizing a holistic approach, it advocates for developing digital twins to supplement models, incorporating occupants in the feedback loop through a socio-technical approach. This spans across building lifecycle stages, encompassing design, planning, policymaking, and operation.

Chapter 10 investigates the complex interplay of social contexts in urban building and transportation energy use. It focuses on how human dynamics, including social determinants of public health (SDPH), mobility, and occupancy, shape urban energy consumption. The research introduces a novel urban energy model using ANNs, augmented with Garson, Lek's profile, and Partial Dependence Plot (PDP) methods, for an in-depth analysis of energy behaviors across Chicago. Validated through diverse public datasets and cross-validation, this model integrates building and transportation energy use, emphasizing the significance of human dynamics. The findings reveal a pronounced link between SDPH status, mobility, occupancy, and urban energy behavior, identifying household income as a crucial factor. The study underscores the need for a comprehensive evaluation of various urban energy determinants to achieve decarbonization goals in cities, advocating for the use of advanced technologies and detailed analytical approaches to fully understand urban energy use behaviors.

Chapter 11 explores enhancing building performance through virtual reality (VR), particularly in the early design phase. It underscores the importance of initial design decisions in shaping the built environment, individual experiences, and addressing climate change and resource depletion. While metrics for energy consumption and occupant comfort are well-established, qualitative aspects such as aesthetic experience lack established metrics. In light of energy challenges, effective communication and collaboration among stakeholders are vital. The chapter explores VR's potential and limitations for investigating both quantitative and qualitative design aspects. It reviews existing studies on VR's application in building performance, spanning visualization, design, education, and research. Additionally, it identifies current limitations and research gaps in VR usage for building performance, aims to support future research and technological advancements, and emphasizes its value in early building design stages.

Chapter 12 delves into the use of digital twins for citywide energy modeling and management, a critical tool for understanding and reducing urban carbon emissions. It explores and conceptualizes urban building energy digital twins (UBEDTs), offering a comprehensive examination of its definition, conceptual framework, architecture, maturity levels, and enabling technologies such as twinning, AI, ML, and interoperability solutions. The study also addresses the limitations of UBEDT development and implementation. By providing an in-depth understanding of UBEDTs, the chapter aims to enhance their adoption in urban building decarbonization efforts. This investigation not only bridges a significant gap in existing literature but also highlights UBEDTs' potential, especially in utilizing AI-driven techniques. The findings equip researchers and policymakers with insights to foster innovation and progress in urban building energy systems and management.

References

Boden, M.A. (2016). *AI: Its Nature and Future*, 1e. Oxford, United Kingdom: Oxford University Press.

Turing, A.M. (1950). Computing Machinery and Intelligence. *Mind* 49: 433–460.

1

Augmented Computational Design

Pirouz Nourian[1], Shervin Azadi[2], Roy Uijtendaal[3] and Nan Bai[4]

[1] *University of Twente, Enschede, The Netherlands*
[2] *Eindhoven University of Technology, Eindhoven, The Netherlands*
[3] *Nieman Raadgevende Ingenieurs, Utrecht, The Netherlands*
[4] *Delft University of Technology, Delft, The Netherlands*

Introduction

The core of the performance-driven computational design is to trace the sensitivity of variations of some performance indicators to the differences between design alternatives. Therefore, any argument about the utility of artificial intelligence (AI) for performance-based design must necessarily discuss the representation of such differences, as explicitly as possible. The existing data models and data representations in the field of architecture, engineering, and construction (AEC), such as computer aided design (CAD) and building information modelling (BIM), are primarily focused on geometrical representations of building elements and facilitating the process of construction management. Unfortunately, the field of AEC does not currently have a structured discourse based on an explicit representation of decision variables and desired outcomes. Specifically, the notion of design representation and the idea of data modeling for representing "what needs to be attained from buildings" is rather absent in the existing literature.

This treatise proposes a systematic view of the differences between design alternatives in terms of decision variables, be they spatial and nonspatial. Based on such an explicit formulation of decision variables, we set forth a framework for building and utilizing AI in (architectural) generative design processes for associating decision variables and outcomes of interest as performance indicators in a reciprocal relationship. This reciprocity is explained in terms of the duality between two quintessential problems to be addressed in generative design: the evaluation of design alternatives (mapping) and the derivation of design alternatives (navigation).

Starting with an explicit representation of a design space as an ordered pair of two vectors, one denoting decision variables and the other performance indicators, we put forth a mathematical framework for structuring data-driven approaches to generative design in the field of AEC. This framework highlights two major types of applications for AI in performance-driven design and their fusion: those capable of augmenting design evaluation procedures and those capable of augmenting design derivation procedures. Moreover, we introduce the

Artificial Intelligence in Performance-Driven Design: Theories, Methods, and Tools, First Edition.
Edited by Narjes Abbasabadi and Mehdi Ashayeri.
©2024 John Wiley & Sons Inc. Published 2024 by John Wiley & Sons Inc.

reciprocity between "flows" and "manifolds" as an intermediary notion for going beyond the so-called form-function dichotomy. Discussing these notions necessitates the introduction of a mathematical foundation for the framework rooted in multivariate calculus.

The main advantage of this explicit formulation is to enhance the explainability of AI when utilized in generative design by introducing meaningful and interpretable latent spaces based on the reciprocal relationship between manifolds and flows. The balance of predictive/deterministic power and interpretability/explainability is discussed in the concrete context of an illustrative example.

This chapter will introduce a chain of key concepts, starting with the notion of decision-making in design, the nature of design variables, the specifics of spatial decision variables, the notion of design space, and the two dual actions in the exploration of design spaces: mapping and navigating.

While the introduced framework is quite general, a particular class of Probabilistic Graphical Models (PGM), Bayesian Belief Networks (BBN), is introduced to provide a concrete illustrative example of the utility of AI in AEC. For a deeper insight into this particular approach to data-driven design, the readers are referred to two classical books on PGM: Pearl (1988) & Koller and Friedman (2009). The illustrative example is a BBN trained to make a data-driven replica of the building energy model used by the Dutch government in order to obtain a rough meta-model to be used in mass-scale policy analysis, such as advising the government on the relative utility of energy transition subsidies and planning measures. This example is chosen not because the BBNs are the most advanced models or the most accurate models for approximating such large functions. Instead, the choice is rather pragmatic in that this model has proven to be promising from the stance of predictive power while retaining a basic level of theoretical interpretability and intuitive appeal.

The chapter is structured as follows: we first present a historical context to establish the necessity of such a data-driven generative design framework; continue with conceptualizing and mathematically formulating the structure of the framework, dubbed as Augmented Computational Design (ACD); present an illustrative example demonstrating the utility of the framework; and conclude with a discussion on its outlook, open questions, and avenues for further research.

Background

Here, we revisit the utility of AI for data-driven generative design by highlighting some key gaps of knowledge in the field of AEC and briefly mentioning overarching frameworks in computational design and AI that can address these gaps.

Relevance of AI in AEC

The earliest attempts to enhance accountability and predictive power in computational design can be traced back to the notions of Scientific Architecture (Friedman 1975) and The Sciences of the Artificial (Simon 2019). Both of these seminal books explicitly discuss the necessity of forming some kind of a specific spatial and configurative form of design knowledge, the core of which boils down to being able to explicitly represent the main subject matter of spatial design as "spatial configurations." One of the first phenomenological and systemic descriptions of design processes explicitly referring to the notion of performance is the "Function, Behaviour, Structure" framework of Gero and Kannengiesser (2004), in which the overused notions of form and function are elaborated in terms of expected and required behavior/functionality from a system (dubbed as the function), its design as a form or configuration (dubbed as structure), and its performance (dubbed as behavior). The framework explicitly discusses the idea of design as a process of generating the representation of a spatial structure, and the difference between desired behavior and the actual behavior of the structure is discussed as the performance drive for the process. What can be observed in this phenomenological framework, predating most recent advancements in computational design, is the fundamental belief about the innate necessity of creativity in terms of the cognitive capability of designers for proposing structures capable of working as desired, based on some kind of tacit knowledge. Congruently, an anthropological description of design processes refers to the age-old duality between the form (structure) and function (purpose) of designed artifacts, and the fact that [in the absence of explicit knowledge and representation schemes], as Kroes (2010) has put it, designers are traditionally trained to produce solutions (draw them) through a "logical leap" often without even understanding or paying any attention to the design requirements or supposed levels of quality attainment. Suppose, we wanted to evaluate (compare) two different alternative designs for a hospital (Jia et al. 2023), or a home, the question is: How do we want to represent the designs digitally for a computer to evaluate them? Let us discuss an analogous example: if we wanted to compare two pieces of music in terms of their beauty, it would be very straightforward to digitize their notations and feed them to a machine, because the musical notation is already discretized (digitized), regardless if it is written on paper or etched on the cylinder of an old-fashioned winding music box (Zeng et al. 2021). However, doing the same, such as comparing two buildings, would be a much more difficult challenge, especially because there is currently no (discrete/textual) notation for spatial design that can capture the features of spatial configurations.

Instead of the extensive emphasis on the product of architecture as the shapes of buildings, we turn our attention to the processes of design and put a lens of "design as [discrete] decision-making" on the debate to avoid the common reduction of design to the production of design drawings. This view forms the basis of the generative design paradigm, as extensively articulated by Nourian, Azadi, and Oval (2023) and Veloso and Krishnamurti (2021). Similarly, the challenges, opportunities, and promising ways of utilization of AI, particularly deep-learning and generative models, for goal-oriented design explorations have been discussed extensively in Regenwetter, Nobari, and Ahmed (2022) and Regenwetter and Ahmed (2022).

Historical Context

In this section, we first give a very brief history of the most important and relevant developments in AI. Then, we lay the foundation for a formulation of architectural design as a matter of decision-making. We discuss the mathematical implications of this paradigmatic frame for generative design, elaborate on the notion of decision-making and the duality of derivation and evaluation problems, and discuss two statistical approaches to design: a possibilistic approach utilizing Fuzzy Logic or Markovian Design Machines and a probabilistic approach utilizing BBNs or Diffusion Models.

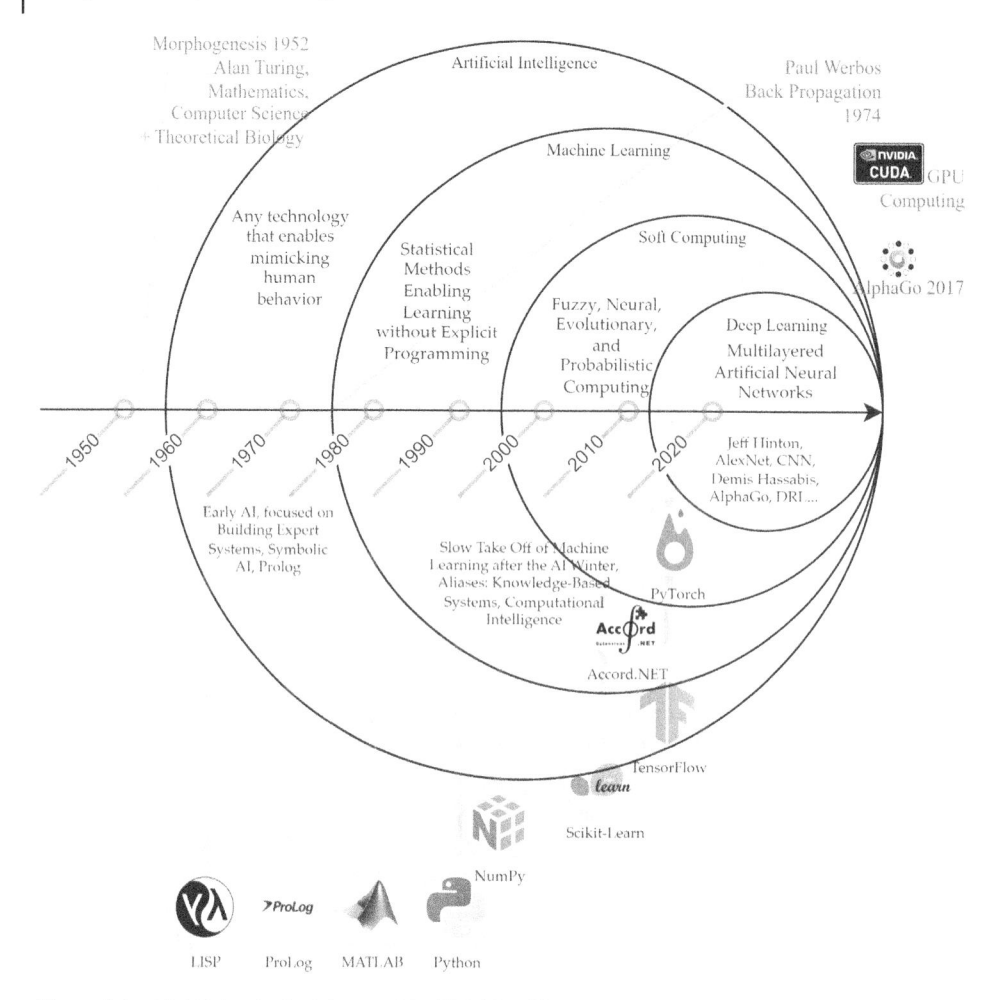

Figure 1.1 Highlights in the history of Artificial Intelligence.

We are currently witnessing an era of exponential success in the field of AI that has been evolving for more than 50 years (See Figure 1.1). Meanwhile, it is common knowledge that progress is slow in terms of innovation and scientific knowledge development in the field of AEC.

As extensively argued by Simon (1973) and Azadi and Nourian (2021), once an unambiguous language is adopted for discussing the classification of problems, we can see that many of the problems in AEC can be adequately (and possibly painstakingly) dealt with through conventional mathematics, physics, and computer science. In other words, the utility or the necessity of employing AI for dealing with problems that can be dealt with through conventional mathematical or computational procedures is not only pointless from a resource-efficiency stance but also questionable from the point of view of interpretability, transparency, and explainability. To assess the potential applications of AI in AEC regarding these questions, we highlight the history of AI (see Figure 1.1) and refocus on its scope (see Figure 1.2), at least as it could possibly pertain to AEC.

Once a problem is adequately formulated, two major determinants can be considered as to whether it would be sensible to apply AI or not: whether the data schemata of the problem

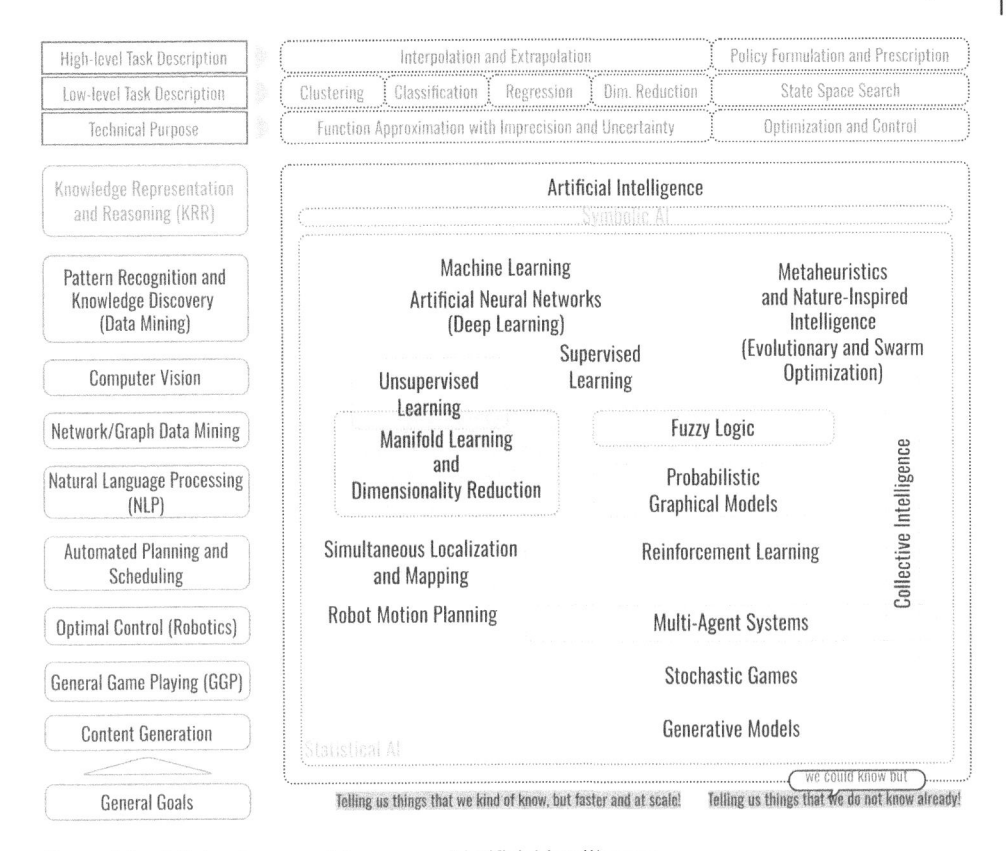

Figure 1.2 A Euler diagram of the scope of Artificial Intelligence.

are structured (vectorized) or unstructured (textual/visual), and whether the underlying associations between the inputs and outputs can be modeled through first principles (governing laws of physics, typically stated in differential equations), stochastic processes, or agent-based models. If the problem data are unstructured or the conventional modeling approaches do not have the capability of capturing the complex associations between the inputs and the outputs of interest, especially when interpretability can be sacrificed over the necessity of predictability, utilizing AI is quite sensible. The example that we discuss in this chapter may seem somewhat questionable according to these points; however, on the other hand, it is too overwhelmingly large and complex that no conventional approach can deal with it at the aimed level of abstraction. In this case, the ambition of the project is on such a high level of abstraction in policy analysis that the inaccuracies and ambiguities of the purely data-driven approach can be justified because of the insights that can be gained from the meta-statistical model.

Design as Decision-Making

The commonly overstated notions of difficulty or the ill-defined nature of design problems, as explained by Simon (1973), can be attributed to the fact that most design tasks are expected to produce a very concrete geometric description of an object to be built (the form), given only a very abstract description of what the object is supposed to be used for, how it should work, and what would be desirable for it to achieve, all of which are often described quite vaguely (the function), by Kroes and Meijers (2006).

Hillier was one of the few shrewd theorists who understood that, at least after the separation of structural design from architecture in the 19th century (Giedion 2009), what distinguishes building buildings from architecture is the art and science of configuring spaces, as stated in "Space is the Machine," (Hillier 2007). Once one realizes that the so-called architectural form is not only a single shape of an iconic object but also a set that includes the shapes of spaces and, eventually, the constituent segments of a building, we can distinguish the superior importance of spatial configurations. As obvious as it may sound, it seems to be necessary to emphasize that architectural design is not merely about sculpting a shape but configuring spaces to accommodate some human activities. This involves some puzzling tasks, such as packing, zoning, and routing spaces of various functions, which we hereinafter refer to as the task of configuring buildings (Azadi and Nourian 2021). For problems of shape and configuration to be transformed into decision problems, they need to be rigorously discretized. In short, we can call a massing problem a shape problem and a zoning problem a configuration problem.

The mainstay of the generative design paradigm is a rigorous reformulation of a design problem as a discrete topological decision problem rather than a geometrical problem (Nourian, Azadi, and Oval 2023). Therefore, discretization is the process of breaking down the integrated design problem into multiple smaller yet interdependent decision problems. An example of such discretization can be a voxel grid that provides a non-biased and homogeneous representation of spatial units, each of which poses a decision problem of function allocation (Nourian et al. 2016; Soman, Azadi, and Nourian 2022).

Moreover, to ensure the correspondence of these discrete decisions, we need to include the topological information about their neighborhood to represent their spatial interdependencies, similar to topology optimization (O'Shaughnessy, Masoero, and Gosling 2021). At the limit, such discretization can also be used to model a continuum of solutions and provide a frequency-based or spectral representation system, similar to the study by Marin et al. (2021), for spatial design, much like the musical notation that is based on notes.

Additionally, it is important to note that design decisions have a strong spatial dimension; however, they can include the social dimension to represent the preference of stakeholders and enable consensus-building (Bai et al. 2020). Given a view of design as a matter of decision-making, we can readily see two important types of practical questions that will shed light on the relevance of AI for decision-making:

1. How to map/learn the associations of hundreds or thousands of constituent choices of a compound design decision (function approximation and dimensionality reduction for ex-ante assessment of the impact of decisions)?
2. How to navigate a gigantic decision space with thousands of choices and their astronomically large combinations with a few important consequences in the picture?

The proposed notion of design as decision-making makes a point of departure for the rest of the chapter in that it highlights two equally essential problems of significance that can be tackled by AI and their duality: First, evaluation problems can be portrayed as mapping problems in Machine Learning (ML) and Deep Learning, where the approximation power of Artificial Neural Networks (ANN) can be exploited in regression and classification settings. Second, derivation problems can be portrayed as navigation problems in generative models, concerned with navigating from a low-dimensional representation of performance indicators toward disaggregated design decisions.

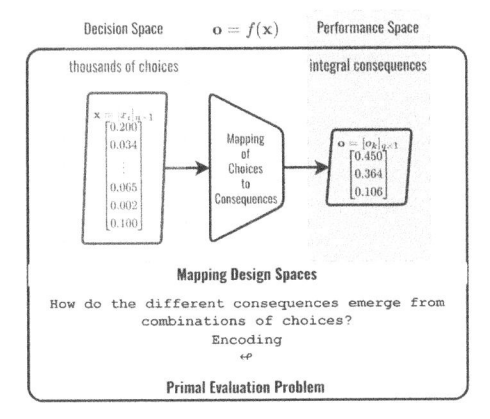

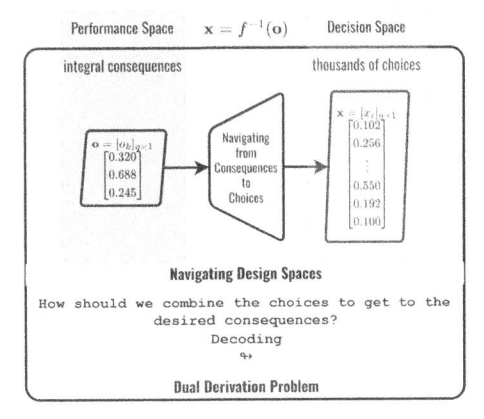

Figure 1.3 The duality of evaluation and derivation problems in generative design.

Encapsulating the complex and often nonlinear associations of many design decisions with a few outcomes of interest or performance indicators is here dubbed as a mapping problem. Inverting this map, as an approximated function (e.g. in the form of an ANN), can thus be viewed as an enhanced or augmented form of design, where the designer is navigated toward many small decisions just by pointing toward certain data points within a low-dimensional performance space (see Figure 1.3). It must be apparent that a navigation problem in this sense is much harder to solve, almost always impossible in the absolute sense, due to an arbitrarily large increase in information content and thus a combinatorial explosion of possibilities.

AI for Generative Design

Given the formulation of main generative design tasks as *mapping* and *navigating*, we focus on a particular set of AI methods that are distinguished for their relevance for these tasks in high-dimensional design decision spaces. More specifically, within the spectrum of generative design methods (Nourian, Azadi, and Oval 2023), we focus on data-driven *mapping* and *navigating* strategies. As shown in Figure 1.4, for brevity, we will only focus on the data-driven approaches to design on the right-hand side of the spectrum. Despite the other possible applications of (different kinds of) AI in this generative design spectrum, such as Reinforcement Learning in Policy-Driven design (playing design games), approximation of evaluation functions in topology or shape optimization, and Expert Systems in grammatical design, our framework here is focused on the statistical AI paradigm. So we only discuss the purely data-driven approaches to generative design.

Two subtle issues must be noted here: first, instead of discussing the utility of the wondrous application of generative models for the entertainment industry, we shall reflect on how the generative processes based on diffusion or dimensionality reduction can be controlled for attaining high-performance designs in an explainable manner. Second, model-driven approaches to performance-based generative design (topology optimization in particular) based on first principles, are already utilizing something important from the realm of nature-inspired computing called Hebbian Learning, which is already in the scope of (statistical) AI. This point, although important, generally interesting, and relatively unknown, falls outside the scope of this chapter.

A Spectrum of Generative Design Methodologies & Generative Models for Content Generation

Knowledge ←——— Performance-Based (Associative) ———→ Data

Model-Driven

- Topology Optimization & Shape Optimization
- Mathematical Derivation from Governing Equations

$f(\mathbf{x})$

White Box Models

Analytical/Differential

- Numerical Methods
- Partial Differential Eq.
- Multivariate Calculus

Mostly out of scope of AI

Data-Driven

- Generative Models & Bayesian/Markovian Probabilistic Graphical Models
- Systematic Data Collection & Black-Box Training

$f(\mathbf{x})$

Black Box Models

Statistical-Probabilistic

- Diffusion Processes
- Markov Chains
- Manifold Learning

Within the scope of AI

Generative Design Methods → Computational Design Practice

Mathematics

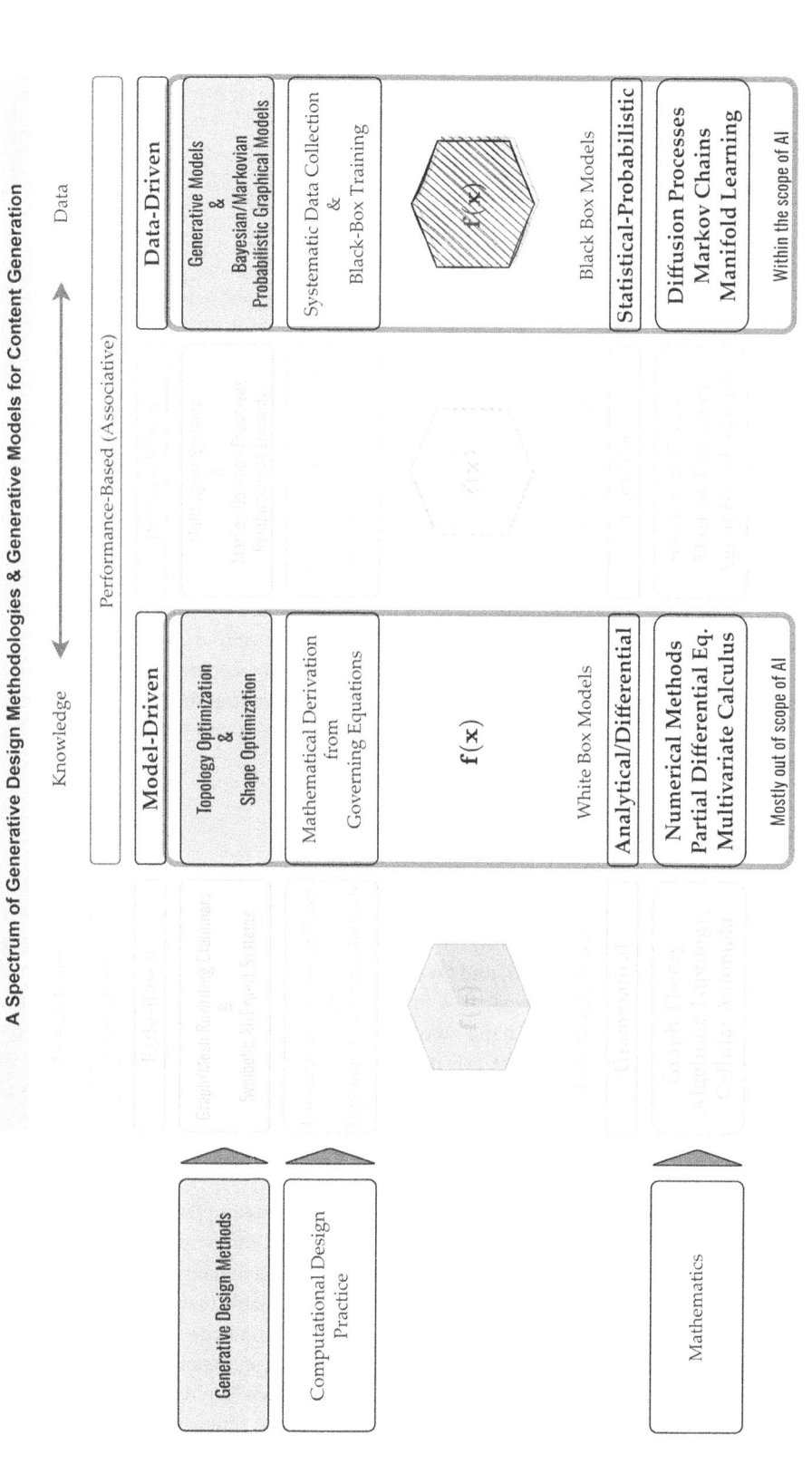

Figure 1.4 The spectrum of generative design methods and their relation to AI methods.

Framework

The emphasis on the decision-making approach to design entails that design tasks can be formulated as a set of (typically unstructured) questions about the form and materialization/construction of an object (a building) to be answered. In this chapter, we focus on the questions that pertain to form.

We propose a mathematical framework for generative design that relates multiple strands of work together. We use *design space* for referring to an ordered pair of two vector spaces: a decision space containing vectors or data points representing design configurations in the form of $\mathbf{x} \in (0, 1]^n$ and a performance/quality space containing vectors or data points representing combinations of outcomes of interest in the form of $\mathbf{o} \in [0, 1]^q$.

The mathematical lens that we shall put on the issue is to redefine both of these notions to provide a much more specific and workable idea for discussing the utility or futility of applying AI to design problem-solving. It is hopefully easy for the reader to accept that a regular discretization of so-called *design space* (which is an unfortunately common misnomer, but here somewhat pragmatically useful) provides a straightforward and simple discretization of design decisions as vectors in the form of $\mathbf{x} := [x_i]_{n \times 1} \in (0, 1]^n$ or $\mathbf{x} \in \{0, 1\}^n$, where n is the number of discrete cells in the design space, in which virtually any conceivable shape can be constructed at a certain level of resolution. Without loss of generality, the decision variables are not necessarily spatial and can be assumed to be relativized float variables within the range of minimum and maximum admissible parameter values of the functions that together result in the shape and configuration of a building. Even if a multicolor (multi-label, multi-functional) space is the subject of the design problem, then multiple categories/colors of such vectors can be seen together as a matrix of decision variables, in which rows of the matrix have to add up to 1 (see Figure 1.5).

Once this terminology is established, it is easy to observe that, in ML terms, the problem of performance-based design can be seen as two problems that are dual to one another: a multivariate regression problem for figuring out an approximation function that can map a few outputs to many inputs (referred here as mapping or the evaluation problem), and a pseudo-inversion problem for finding the combination of inputs that could result in desired output data points (referred to here as navigation or the derivation problem), as shown in Figure 1.3.

When approached as a data-driven problem-solving task, both problems are somewhat hard and impossible to solve in the absolute sense of the word, unless we think about them as loss minimization or approximation problems. The navigation/design problem is much harder than the mapping/evaluation problem. The main idea here is to advocate for training (fitting) meta-models (neural networks), to sets of sampled pairs of inputs and outputs, to first approximate a complex design space as a map between decision data points and performance data points, and then find the pseudo-inverse of this map or navigate it in the reverse direction to identify designs (decision data points) that perform in a desired way. In other words, mathematically, we look at the performance-based design process as a pairing between a decision space and a performance space, where a map is conceptualized as a function $f : (0, 1]^n \mapsto [0, 1]^q$ such that $\mathbf{o} = f(\mathbf{x})$. The pseudo-inverse map is thus dubbed as $f^{-1} : [0, 1]^q \mapsto (0, 1]^n$, such that $\mathbf{x} = f^{-1}(\mathbf{o})$.

For brevity and generalizability to nonspatial design problems, we will focus on massing problems, and exclude colored configuration problems out of the picture momentarily (see Figure 1.5 for the distinction).

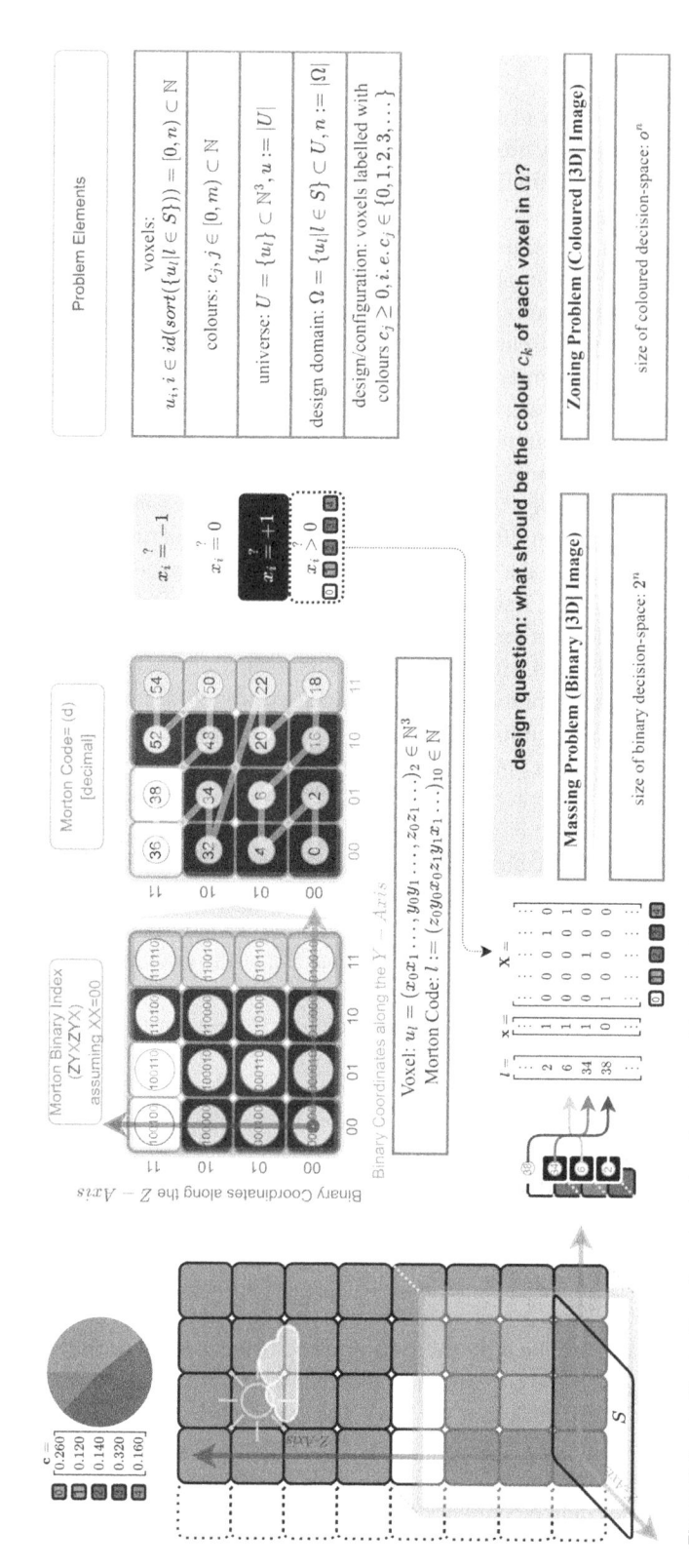

Figure 1.5 An illustrative discrete design domain and its associated decision space distinguished for shaping/massing and zoning/configuring problems.

Furthermore, by considering two abstract and high-level descriptions of a design task in our proposed regular discretization frameworks, we can formulate two mathematical tasks:

- Mapping Design Spaces: Approximating the function that models the associations between the many input design variables and a few outcomes of interest.
- Navigating Design Spaces: Approximating the inverse function that guides the generation of valid configurations in the decision space given desired data points in the performance space.

Design Space Exploration

Here, we explain the mathematical meaning of the two dual problems that, together, can be called design space exploration tasks: mapping and navigation.

Mapping

The problem of mapping associations between a large set of independent input decision variables and dependent output performance indicators is key to performance-driven design. Any explainable and accountable design methodology should have the capacity to guarantee the attainment of some quality or performance indicators. From a mathematical and statistical point of view, we might prefer to have an explainable and interpretable model of such relations that can be fitted into our data, or ideally, a simulation model to predict outputs from input data. However, in some cases, especially where a multitude of diverse quality/performance indicators are involved, and when one does not have an established basis for simulation modeling, statistical (data-driven) modeling seems to be the only option. And so, when the complexity of the model passes a certain threshold of nonlinearity and a multitude of inputs and outputs, we might prefer to trade interpretability for predictive power. That is exactly where ANNs as families of adjustable nonlinear functions stand out as viable function approximators. Training a network is practically a matter of minimizing a loss/error function by adjusting the parameters of a family of functions that are set out by the so-called architecture/structure of the ANN.

Even though this approximation is inherently nonlinear and global, it is illuminating to think of an alternative (locally) linear approximation based on the Jacobian Matrix. Suppose that $\mathbf{o} = f(\mathbf{x}) := [f_k(\mathbf{x})]_{q \times 1} = [f_k([x_i]_{n \times 1})]_{q \times 1}$ is a vector of multiple scalar functions of vector input variables. Then a basic idea of approximation is to approximate this function locally around an input data point by its Jacobian. This matrix operator gives the basis for a hyperplane equation that provides the n-dimensional Euclidean tangent space of the underlying function, similar to a multivariate regression hyperplane, although the latter would be fitted to the entire dataset.

Note that the ML task here would be a multivariate regression task in this case, that is, predicting the dependent given the independent variables. To understand the difficulty of the mapping, consider that the Jacobian matrix $\mathbf{J} := \left[J_{k,i} \right]_{q \times n} = \left[\dfrac{\partial f_k}{\partial x_i} \right]_{q \times n} = \left[\nabla^T f_q \right]_{q \times 1}$ would just provide the best local linear approximation of an otherwise globally nonlinear map from $\mathbb{R}^n$ to $\mathbb{R}^q$, that is, n decision variables to q quality criteria or performance indicators.

The Jacobian approximation is numerically computable provided the underlying function is smooth and differentiable. For brevity, as commonly done, we have omitted the fact that the Jacobian can be evaluated at a certain input data point and that it is expected to be the best linear approximation of the function in question in the vicinity of that point. If we abbreviate the notation for the Jacobian as such a functional, then we can denote the approximate linear function at any given data point as follows, using the first-order Taylor Series expansion: $\mathbf{o}(\mathbf{x})\big|_{x \sim x_o} \simeq \mathbf{J}(\mathbf{x_0})(\mathbf{x}-\mathbf{x_0})$, or simply put, as $\mathbf{o} \simeq \mathbf{Jx}$, if we assume $\mathbf{x}$ to represent the vector of differences between the input data point with the center of the neighborhood.

The Jacobian approximation is also illuminating for another important reason: it allows us to approximate the Jacobian in a different sense, that is, in the sense of dimensionality/rank reduction using the Singular Value Decomposition (SVD) to see a clearer picture of the main factors playing the most significant roles in attaining the outcomes of interest; in other words, identifying the input variables to which the outcomes of interest are most sensitive. Even though we do not explicitly perform this operation in our demonstrative example using the SVD, it is still illuminating to see what SVD can do for this insightful approximation and dimensionality reduction for two reasons:

1. The SVD approximation of the Jacobian allows us to make a cognitive and interpretable map of the most important causes of the effects of interest.
2. The SVD approximation of the Jacobian allows us to conceptualize a pseudo-inverse function to navigate the design space from the side of performance data points.

The SVD (low-rank) approximation of the Jacobian matrix can be denoted as below:

$$\mathbf{J} := \mathbf{U}\Sigma\mathbf{V}^T$$

where, $\mathbf{U}_{q \times q} := [\mathbf{u}_k]_{1 \times q}$ and $\mathbf{V}_{n \times n} := [\mathbf{v}_i]_{1 \times n}$ are orthogonal matrices (i.e. $\mathbf{UU}^T = \mathbf{I}_{q \times q}$ and $\mathbf{VV}^T = \mathbf{I}_{n \times n}$), and Σ is a matrix of size $q \times n$ with only $p = min\{q, n\}$ nonzero diagonal entries denoted as σ_c and called singular values, which are the square roots of the eigenvalues of both $\mathbf{J}^T\mathbf{J}$ and $\mathbf{JJ}^T$, sorted in descending order, see Martin and Porter 2012.

$$\mathbf{J} \simeq \sum_{c \in [0,r)} \sigma_c \mathbf{u}_c \mathbf{v}_c^T$$

where $r \leq p$. It must be noted that the sum is not meant to be exhaustive; instead, the sum of the first significant terms achieves the purpose of dimensionality reduction of the decision space by showing a low-dimensional picture of the correlations between decision variables and their performance consequences. So, instead of decomposing the Jacobian up to p, we can choose to have a lower-dimensional approximation up to some arbitrary smaller number r.

Navigation
Navigating a high-dimensional design space from the side of the performance space toward the decision space for deriving design decisions (see Figure 1.3) is a very challenging task, almost always impossible in the absolute sense of solving the equation $\mathbf{Jx} = \mathbf{o}$, if the decision variables $\mathbf{x}$ are the unknowns.

It is easy to see that the Moore-Penrose pseudo-inverse of the approximated Jacobian matrix can be computed as a matrix of size $n \times q$ by easily using the SVD factorized matrix:

$$\mathbf{J}^\dagger := \mathbf{V}\Sigma^\dagger\mathbf{U}^T$$

where, $\mathbf{\Sigma}^{\dagger}$ is simply formed as a diagonal matrix of size $n \times q$ with the reciprocals of the singular values. Similarly, the approximate pseudo-inverse of the Jacobian can be computed as:

$$\mathbf{J}^{\dagger} \simeq \sum_{c \in [0.r)} \sigma_c^{-1} \mathbf{v}_c \mathbf{u}_c^T$$

However, in the same way, a minimal-loss approximate solution exists for such equations when the matrix is rectilinear, $\mathbf{J}^{\dagger}\mathbf{o}$ is expected to be the least-square solution to the linearized Jacobian approximation of a navigation problem. Even though the system might theoretically have a solution, the odds of finding a unique solution are practically very skewed toward having an indeterminate system with many more inputs than outputs, and thus the system will have many approximate solutions rather than a unique exact solution.

This is of course in line with the intuition of most human beings about the inherent difficulty of design problems for which there is no unique solution. Note that in all these theoretical treatments, we implicitly assumed that all data points within the decision space correspond to valid designs, whereas, in reality, it might be more difficult to ensure finding valid solutions (feasible in the sense of complying with constraints), rather than good solutions. In other words, constraint solving tends to be more difficult than optimization within a feasible region of the decision space.

Spatial Design Variables

If the question of the design problem directly pertains to the shape of the configuration of an object, we can still construct decision variables to be handled within the proposed framework for mapping and navigating design spaces.

The idea of bringing spatial decision variables in a generative design process is to consider first the nature of the objects being designed as manifolds, that is, locally similar spaces (homeomorphic) to Euclidean spaces of low dimensions (2D planes or 3D hyperplanes), but globally more complex, possibly having holes, handles, and cavities (shells). Three types of these manifolds are of special interest for generative design, such as those that conduct walk flows (explicit or implicit pedestrian corridors in buildings and cities), light flows (rays of sunlight, sky-view, or other visibility targets), and force flows in structures. Our conceptual framework proposes that these flows are conducted within spatial manifolds, as below:

1. Walkable Space Manifolds (2D): Conduct walks (accessibility questions)
2. Air Space Manifolds (3D): Conduct light rays (visibility questions)
3. Material Space Manifolds (3D): Conduct forces (stability questions)

This consideration allows us to see that the way this object is supposed to function is largely determined by how this manifold is configured in that the way the manifold in question conducts the flows of walks in a walkable floor space, flows of light rays in a visible air space, or flows of forces in a reliable material space. Thus, we can highlight the specific concept of flow in a network representation, which is dual to the discrete representation of a manifold, as an unambiguous alternative intermediary instead of any vague notion of function to study and measure.

Apart from mathematical elegance, this approach also provides multiple computational advantages that are very much in line with the recent advancements in the field of generative models in AI. In a nutshell, the discrete representation of the so-called design space provides a workable representation of not only all possible forms but also some inherent functional properties of the represented manifold that should logically determine how it could function as a building or a structure. The manifold representation can be mathematically denoted as a polygon mesh of vertices, edges, and faces $\mathcal{M} = (V, E, F)$ (for a two-manifold), or a polyhedral mesh of vertices, edges, faces, and cells $\mathcal{M} = (V, E, F, C)$ that can have a dual graph representation in the form of $\Gamma = (N, \Lambda)$.

This description should principally sound natural if we articulate the purpose of a design task as follows: finding the ideal form (configuration and shape) of a manifold to conduct some flows in a desirable pattern. In this way, we are diverting our attention from the containers of space (the building) into what it contains (i.e. the space and its spatial configuration). This change of focus allows us to see the direct correspondence between the so-called form and function of a design or, better put, the form (i.e. configuration and shape) and the expected quality/performance of a spatial configuration.

In what follows, we will go much beyond the vector data inputs consisting of only numerical variables, especially in the context of our illustrative example. In fact, without loss of generality, the ideas of mapping and navigating design spaces in an approximate sense go beyond decision variables pertaining to continuous decision variables and those pertaining to the spatial configuration and geometric shape of spatial manifolds. The same ideas can be applied to design problems that are about decision-making in a much more general sense, as discussed above. Note that the illustrative example that we have demonstrated at the end of the chapter has a heterogeneous mix of spatial and mostly nonspatial decision variables as well as a mix of categorical and numerical decision variables.

Statistical Approaches to Design

Among the statistical approaches to design, we can distinguish the possibilistic approaches from the probabilistic ones.

- Probabilistic approaches: BBN, Variational Auto-Encoders (VAE), and Diffusion Models
- Possibilistic approaches: Markovian Design Machines and Fuzzy Design (see MAGMA below)

Possibilistic Approach

The essence of the possibilistic approach to design using a multivalued or nonbinary logic framework for making design decisions, typically in the sense of making discrete choices about discrete segments of space; for example, the Markovian Design Machines of Batty (1974), the Spatial Agents Academy of Veloso and Krishnamurti (2020), and Multi-Attribute Gradient-Driven Mass Aggregation (MAGMA) through Fuzzy Logic, as introduced briefly in Nourian (2016) and Soman, Azadi, and Nourian (2021). Both of these methodologies apply nonbinary logic from a possibilistic point of view, in the sense that they take design inputs that are valued in the range of [0, 1] but treat them as possibility measures rather than probability measures. The two big ideas behind these two methods are the utilization of Markov Chains, Markov Decision-Processes, and Fuzzy T-Norms for coping with uncertainty and human-like reasoning in simulated negotiations between spatial agents.

Probabilistic Approach

The probabilistic models briefly mentioned here are all related to the concept of conditional probability, the Bayes' theorem, and (generalized) stochastic processes that resemble Markov

Chains (Weng 2021; Nourian 2016). In a nutshell, the core of these models is about updating some posterior probabilities, indicating beliefs about the truth of some statements by prior probabilities multiplied by the likelihood of compelling evidence, scaled by the probability of the existence of the evidence. When probabilistic neuron-like nodes in PGM are combined, these new posterior probabilities or probability distributions can be fed into other layers of a network to create ANN architectures. A basic idea here is to gradually reduce the dimensionality of input data into an abstract low-dimensional representation (encoding, or mapping, albeit into a typically unintuitive and interpretable latent space), and then gradually use the inverse of the forward diffusion-like processes to denoise a vector in the low-dimensional hidden space. The latter process is called denoising or decoding, and it matches our description of navigation processes, albeit without direct control of the meaning of the latent space vectors. A breakthrough in this domain can come from enhancing the explainability of the latent space low-dimensional representations. This idea, however interesting, falls way outside the scope of this short treatise. Therefore, here we only provide a theoretical minimum for understanding the demonstrative example (i.e. a shallow BBN).

Demonstration

In this section, we will present a demonstration of the utility of the proposed framework to indicate how a discrete decision-making approach can facilitate generative design processes. As a disclaimer, it must be noted that this example is not chosen for technical reasons related to AI but rather due to its real, societal, and environmental importance for policy analysis concerning energy transition planning actions at the country level and sustainability strategies at the building level.

Case Study

Understanding the energy performance of architectural designs is crucial in ensuring a sustainable future. Building Energy Modeling (BEM) is a multipurpose approach used by designers and policymakers for checking building code compliance, certifying energy performance, subsidy policymaking, and building management. The Dutch government has recently introduced the NTA 8800 calculation model for quantitatively determining the energy performance and code compliance of buildings ("NTA 8800" 2022). The NTA 8800 aims to provide a transparent, verifiable, and enforceable building energy performance model, based on the European Energy Performance of Buildings Directive (EPBD), the European Committee of Standardization (CEN), and the Dutch Normalization Institute (NEN) published standards ("Nen 7120+C2:2012/A1:2017 NL" 2017). These regulations describe methods to calculate the energy performance of buildings, set energy requirements for new buildings, and make agreements about energy label obligations in existing buildings. The NTA 8800 only concerns building-related measures, as expressed in the EPBD, Annex A (Union 2021).

The NTA 8800 document has been implemented as an MS Excel tool by the Dutch government (commissioned by Nieman B.V. consultants). This calculation model translates the public European standard document into a calculation tool. The calculation tool is not publicly available, and it is not documented. Since we were given temporary and bounded access to this model, we chose to approximate it and construct a meta-model. The model consists of

269 unique input parameters about the spatial and technical building design configurations, based on which the model returns three scalar response values about the energy performance of the building design: BENG 1 (maximum permissible energy demand in kWh/m^{2}y), BENG 2 (maximum permissible primary energy consumption in kWh/m^{2}y), and BENG 3 (minimum permissible share of renewable energy use as a percentage). The acronym BENG refers to national performance indicators for Nearly Zero-Energy Buildings (Bijna Energie Neutrale Gebouwen in Dutch).

The NTA 8800 model has three main limitations: (1) it can only process and compute information about a single specific scenario at a time; (2) it returns scalar values about the energy performance that is untraceable to input parameters; and (3) missing input values could result in errors or nonrealistic response values. These three limitations make the model impractical for designers and policy analysts, particularly in the early stages of design. This impracticality is because, in conceptual design and policy analysis, designers need to (1) explore and iterate various options simultaneously; (2) need feedback on the degree of influence of each design decision; and (3) cannot provide detailed information yet about later-stage design choices, such as the technical systems.

The framework of ACD is particularly useful here as it allows us to relate the aggregated performance changes of the few NTA 8800 outputs of interest to the changes in the many design decision parameters of its input. In this particular case, we adopt a probabilistic meta-modeling (function approximation) approach based on the methodology suggested by Conti and Kaijima (2021).

Methodology

Meta-Modeling

Meta models are models that describe the structure, behaviors, or other characteristics of related models, providing a higher-level abstraction for constructing and interpreting complex numerical models that approximate more sophisticated models often based on simulations. A meta-model serves as a simplified, computationally efficient *model of the model* (Conti and Kaijima 2021), also referred to as a surrogate model (Kleijnen 1975). The process of creating a meta-model is referred to as meta-modeling (Gigch 1991). Some alternative meta-modeling techniques include interpolation methods, such as spline models (Barton 1998), polynomial regression (Kleijnen, n.d.), or Kriging (Ankenman, Nelson, and Staum 2010).

Within the ACD framework, such meta-models provide structured ways to perform the two most important tasks of the generative design: *mapping* and *navigation*.

In general, a standard meta-model can be described as: $\mathbf{o} = \mathbf{f}(\mathbf{x}) \simeq \mathbf{g}(\mathbf{x})$, where $\mathbf{o}$ is the aggregated simulation response, $\mathbf{f}$ denotes a computational simulation-based model conceptualized as a vector function, and $\mathbf{g}$ is the approximated model function (see Figure 1.3.) With this notation, the objective of meta-modeling is to build $\mathbf{g}$ in such a way that it produces reasonably close values of $\mathbf{o}$. In the case of ACD, meta-modeling can be adopted as a methodology of design *mapping* that provides a differentiable and ideally reversible $\mathbf{g}$ that can be used in the *navigating* process. In other words, the meta-modeling should structurally relate the choices and consequences in such a way that the choices can be derived from the desired consequences; hence, providing a data-driven basis for generative design. The next part demonstrates a probabilistic meta-modeling approach to navigation tasks in high-dimensional design decision spaces, based on the methodology introduced by Conti and Kaijima (2021).

Bayesian Belief Networks

A BBN is a kind of PGM that is effectively an ANN in the form of a Directed Acyclic Graph (DAG) with neuron-like nodes that can compute Joint Probability Distributions (JPDs) from input probability distributions or discrete Probability Density Functions (PDF), which is then attributed to an output probability distribution through a Conditional Probability Distribution (CPD) computing posterior probabilities/beliefs through the Bayes' theorem, hence the name Bayesian. The set of edges in a BBN forms the model architecture or structure that represents the particular probabilistic dependencies between discrete probability distributions attributed to the starting and ending nodes (Figure 1.6). This structure is typically set by the modeler based on their knowledge of the process, while the CPDs (transition probability matrices) are learned from experimental data. BBNs can help us semiautomatically reason about uncertain knowledge or data (Peng, Zhang, And Pan 2010). This makes it possible to perform probabilistic inference, such as computing the JPDs of some outputs (effects) given some inputs (causes). The name of these ANN comes from the idea of updating beliefs or hypotheses posterior to observing evidence; more precisely, utilizing Bayes' theorem for updating conditional probabilities in network structures, in a fashion similar to modeling and evaluating Markov Chains, with the difference that Markov Chains operate as uni-partite networks, each neuron in a BBN is a bipartite network coupled with an outer product calculator.

The neurons in a BBN consist of two layers. The first layer can be dubbed as a presynaptic layer that combines input discrete probability distributions (through an outer product) and forms a JPD and then flattens the JPD to form a vector-shaped probability distribution. The second, that is, the synaptic layer is a CPD, practically a rectangular probability transition matrix that maps this flattened JPD to the output probability distribution. A BBN then consists of such neurons connected in a DAG. Training a BBN means finding the entries of the CPD in such a way as to minimize the loss in the recovery of the output probability distribution from the input distributions. The appeal of BBNs is twofold: first, they allow the inclusion of expert knowledge and intuition into the network's architecture, and second, training of the network makes the network adapted to the objective data. In this case, we limit the architecture of the network to a single layer of neurons to keep the network invertible.

Workflow

Research by Conti and Kaijima (2018) illustrates the four process steps involved in developing a BBN meta-model. In this use case, we alter this methodology as creating a BBN with all

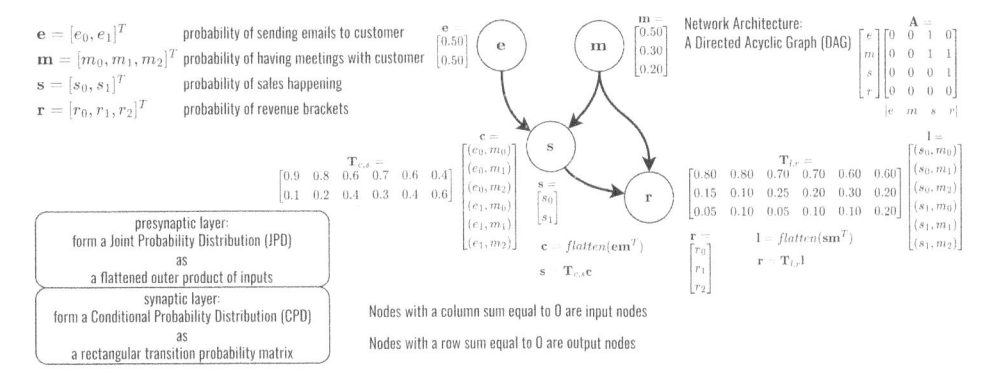

Figure 1.6 An illustrative example of a Bayesian Belief Network, eliciting the nature of nodes and the network architecture, an example inspired by Beaumont et al. (2021).

269 input parameters is infeasible. We add an intermediary step of sensitivity analysis to identify the most influential input parameters before constructing the BBN. Thus, we follow these steps in order (see Figure 1.7): (1) sample the input parameter space, (2) run simulations to generate the output values, (3) sensitivity analysis and selection of influential input parameters, (4) train the BBN, and finally, (5) evaluate the model's robustness. As highlighted by Conti and Kaijima (2021), it is important to model a shallow BBN as a complete bipartite graph connecting all input nodes to all output nodes, effectively limiting the topology to two layers. This would allow us to make a reversible approximation that can be used to derive the necessary input configuration for any desired performance output. Additionally, the fixed values can also include some of the input variables turning them into design constraints.

Step 1: Sampling the Parameter Space
We need to set up a Design of Experiment (DoE), to generate simulation data to study the relationships between various input variables and output variables (Hicks 1964). This experiment involves running several simulations at randomized input configurations (Sacks et al. 1989). Before running the simulation, it is important to carefully select a sampling method, to determine these input configurations, since the chosen strategy influences the quality of the meta-model (Fang, Li, and Sudjianto 2005). Since it is assumed that the decision space is unknown, the intention is to be as inclusive of all regions of the decision space as possible. The sampling algorithm should generate a well-varied response dataset that captures all the information about the relationships between the input parameters and responses. In this study, 20,000 quasi-random input samples were generated based on Sobol's sequences (Sobol' 1990) to ensure sample homogeneity.

Step 2: Run NTA 8800 Simulation Model
Vectorization is an important part of the ACD; we represent decision variables and outputs of interests as vectors (See Section Framework) Each sample point can be interpreted as a vector of scalar input values, **x**. Each batch of such vectors is fed into the NTA 8800 model to generate the vector of corresponding building performance outputs, **o**. After running the primary simulation model for the sampled input data points, the response data is collated and linked to the input samples to form an input–output dataset for regression modeling (as in ML).

Step 3: Sensitivity Analysis
The creation of a meta-model from 269 parameters, each with scalar input values, requires a simulation of all possible combinations (the number of options to the power of 269). Even limiting the number of options for each parameter to two, results in an immense number of possible combinations, calculated at 5.39×10^{80}. To contextualize the magnitude of this number, it is more than the estimated number of atoms in the observable universe.

The sheer magnitude of this number makes storage and training of BBNs infeasible. Therefore, in this study, we use global sensitivity analysis to apportion the uncertainty in outputs to the uncertainty in each input factor over their entire range. This allows us to remove the parameters with the lowest influence on energy performance. The sensitivity analysis method is implemented in the workflow based on the SALib library (Herman and Usher 2017).

This results in a meta-model with 15 parameters instead of 269, making it feasible to store and train the BBN; however, reducing the accuracy and scope of the model. However, the

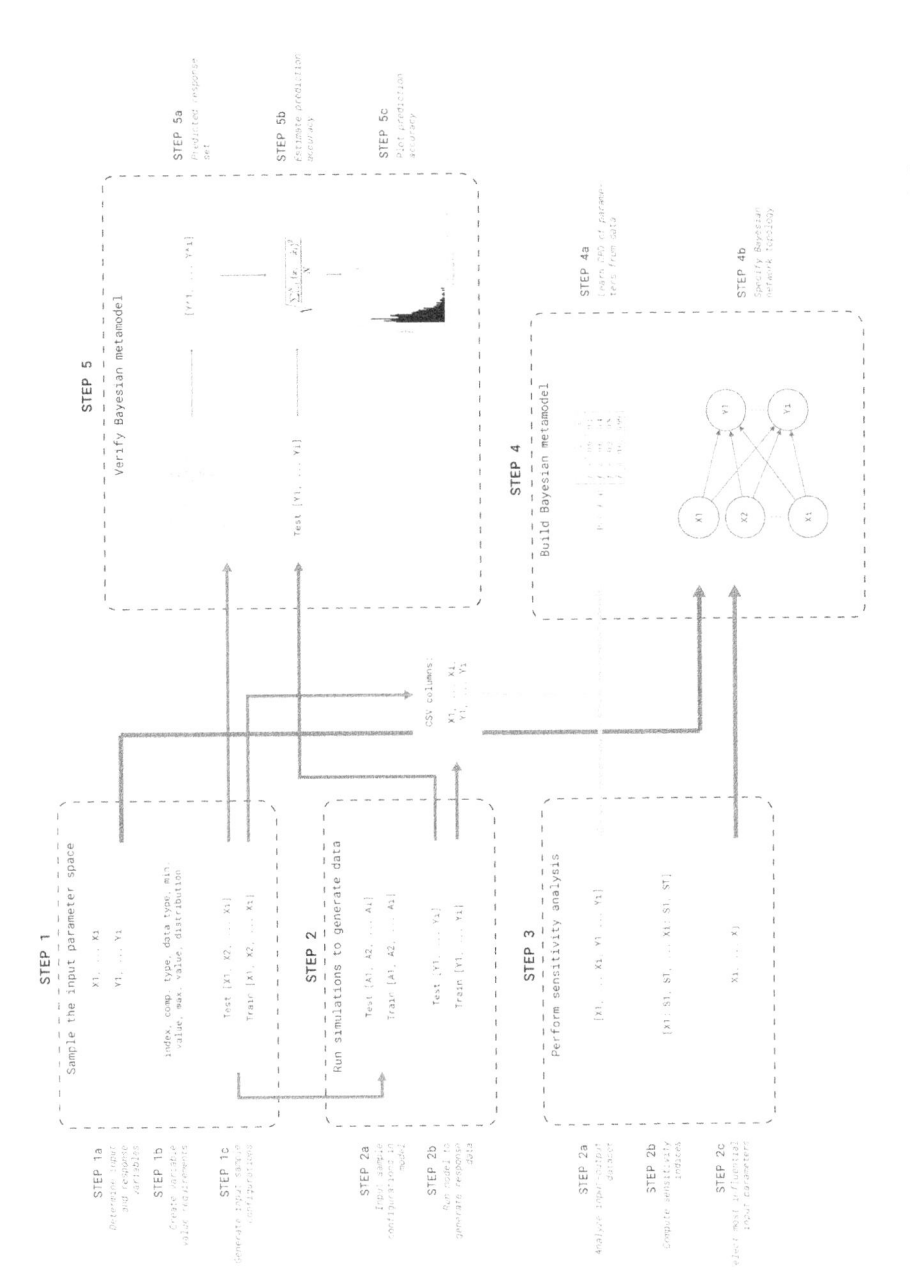

Figure 1.7 Overview of the workflow adopted from the framework. Source: Adapted from Conti and Kaijima (2018).

most influential 15 parameters are responsible for 90.45% to 92.30% of the final energy performance score. Hence, we decided on the inclusion of the 15 specific parameters to construct the BBN meta-model.

Step 4: Build a BBN Meta-model
Building a BBN meta-model is a process of associating the probabilistic relationships of inputs and outputs. These relationships may be characterized by a high degree of nonlinearity and possibly multiple interactions and correlations between model parameters. Consequently, there are two main steps in this process: (1) learning the network topology as a DAG structure and (2) estimating the CPD attributed to the neuron-like nodes of the network.

In this demonstration, we adhere to a particular network topology to ensure the reversibility of the trained model (Conti and Kaijima 2021). Accordingly, this BBN has only two layers: one corresponding to the input and one corresponding to the output. However, effectively, only a single layer of neurons operates in the middle of these two layers. In this case, the selected parameters from the sensitivity analysis results are represented by the input nodes, and the BENG 1, BENG 2, and BENG 3 parameters are the output nodes (see Figure 1.8). Therefore, we skip the topology learning step in the conventional BBN modeling because the topology of this particular network is assumed to be a complete bipartite DAG. In particular, we use the *pgmpy* Python package to model the network topology (Ankan and Panda 2015).

The next step is to estimate the CPDs for the nodes from the input–output dataset. The CPDs for the nodes can be directly learned from the input–output simulation data generated in steps 1 and 2, using the Maximum Likelihood algorithm. Additionally, we discretize each variable range into a fixed number of intervals. All numerical input distributions generated using a space-filling approach, such as Sobol's sequence or Latin Hypercube, are sampled based on continuous ranges, and should therefore be discretized. Discretization is done by dividing the parameter interval over a fixed number of ranges between the minimum and maximum values.

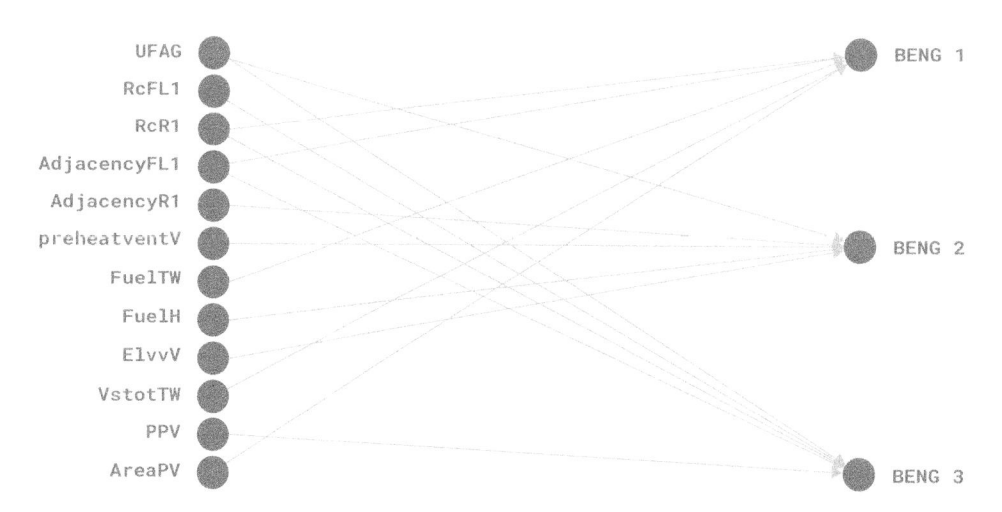

Figure 1.8 The single layer BBN: Right: BENG 1, BENG 2, and BENG 3 parameters are the output nodes; Left: Most sensitive input parameters as input nodes.

Step 5: Validating the Meta-Model

To assess how our trained BBN approximates the original NTA 8800 model, we use a cross-validation approach in combination with Normalized Root Mean Square Error (NRMSE) and Mean Absolute Percentage Error (MAPE) (James et al. 2013). The cross-validation splits the generated input–output dataset (step 2) into a *training set* and *testing set* before building the BBN (step 3). The BBN is trained on the *training set* and assessed based on the *testing set*. However, to obtain a more reliable estimate of the model's performance, the dataset is split into several subsets or folds, with each fold used as both a training set and a testing set. This research adopts a k-fold cross-validation technique, where k refers to the number of groups that the data set is split into. We set $k = 10$ based on experimentation to ensure a low bias and a modest variance. The model is then trained on $k-1$ of the folds, and the remaining fold is used for testing. This process is repeated k times, with each fold used for testing once. The model's performance is then evaluated by averaging the performance across all k runs.

Following the approach suggested by Conti and Kaijima (2021), we computed the mean difference of the predicted and actual output values and normalized the RMSE values by dividing standard deviation to achieve NRMSE.

To calculate the accuracy of the meta-model, it is recommended to use multiple metrics to get a comprehensive evaluation of the model's accuracy. Hence, NRMSE is combined with the MAPE metric. MAPE measures the average absolute percentage difference between predicted and actual values. It is a measure of the magnitude of the errors in the model's predictions. Lower NRMSE and MAPE values indicate better model performance. The larger the error between the two, the higher the NRMSE and MAPE values will become. Therefore, the NRMSE and MAPE results will indicate how dispersed the prediction data is compared to the actual model response.

Results

This section presents the numerical results obtained from the experiment of NTA 8800 meta-model.

BBN Validation Results

Here, we elaborate on the results of the cross-validation technique in combination with NMSRE and MAPE based on the test dataset ($s = 1100$). The interpretation of what is considered an acceptable NRMSE and MAPE score depends on the specific problem and the context in which the meta-model is being used. In general, it is recommended to compare the NRMSE and MAPE scores of the meta-model with the baseline models and state-of-the-art models in the field. This can provide a benchmark for what is considered acceptable performance in the specific context of the problem.

In our case, the BBN does not compete with other models but rather competes with consulting building energy specialists in estimating building energy performance in the early design stages. However, to assess the proficiency of our model in capturing the underlying relationships using solely the 15 selected parameters, we employ the following benchmarks: The NRMSE values should be in the range of $(0.20\%, 0.60\%)$ for the baseline, and in the range of $(0.10\%, 0.30\%)$ for state-of-the-art (Bui et al. 2021) models. The MAPE values should be in the range of $(0.10, 0.30)$ for the baseline, and in the range of $(0.05, 0.15)$ for state-of-the-art models (Khan et al. 2021).

The NRMSE for the trained BBN are 0.82%, 1.52%, and 0.47% for BENG 1, BENG 2, and BENG 3, respectively. This indicates that, except for the BENG 3 indicator, the model's predictions are not accurate enough. The MAPE values for the trained BBN for BENG 1, BENG 2, and BENG 3 are 0.35, 0.28, and 0.33, respectively. This indicates that the predictions of the model are on the upper threshold of being acceptable as baseline models. The absolute prediction difference can be seen in Figure 1.9.

Toy Problem

Here, we present a test case that demonstrates the effectiveness of the BBN meta-model in building design. The study involves two toy problems that showcase the advantages and utilization of the meta-model. The toy problems address two common design challenges that cannot be solved using the currently available tools, such as the NTA 8800. The first problem involves predicting the BENG 1 energy performance of a typical Dutch dwelling during the early design stage. The spatial characteristics of the building are fed to the meta-model. As output, the meta-model returns a range and the confidence level of that range.

In this toy problem, the meta-model predicts the BENG 1 value to be within the range of $(0-50)$ kWh/m^2. y, with a 100% confidence level (see Figure 1.10). To validate this result, we cross-checked the predicted result with the final configuration of the dwelling using the original NTA 8800 model. The NTA 8800 model returns a value of 39.8 kWh/m^2. y, confirming the prediction capability of the meta-model.

The second problem reverses the first problem and involves the ex-ante determination of the most probable design configuration that satisfies a specific energy performance goal. In this example, the BENG 3 value of a typical Dutch dwelling design (35%) does not satisfy the minimal requirements (50%). Since this problem arises in the final design stage, some input parameters can no longer be changed. In this case, architects and engineers are limited to modifying only the area (AreaPV) and power (PPV) of the PV panels. Since the minimum required performance goal for BENG 3 is 50%, we set the goal value to a range of 60–80%. Given the binning approach employed, it should be noted that the AreaPV value of 5 depicted in the figure corresponds to a range of [40,50]m^2, while the PPV value of 5 corresponds to a PV Power range of [200,250] W/m^2. Accordingly, the meta-model advises increasing the PV area to [40,50] m^2, and the PV power to [200,250] W/m^2 (See Figure 1.10).

This discretization allows a clearer representation of the recommended parameter values within the specified ranges, facilitating the interpretation and practical implementation of the BBN meta-model outputs. Since these ranges are the maximum of both scales: the meta-models advise can be interpreted as maximizing the PV area and PV power to reach the goal BENG 3 value of 60% to 80%.

Discussion

In the end, to validate this result, we finish the loop by calculating the final configuration of the dwelling with the original NTA 8800 model. The NTA 8800 returns a value of 71%, confirming the reverse inference capability of the meta-model. These results, illustrated in a simple and digestible example, show how the BBN meta-model is capable of providing valuable insights and assisting architects and engineers in navigating the multidimensional decision space.

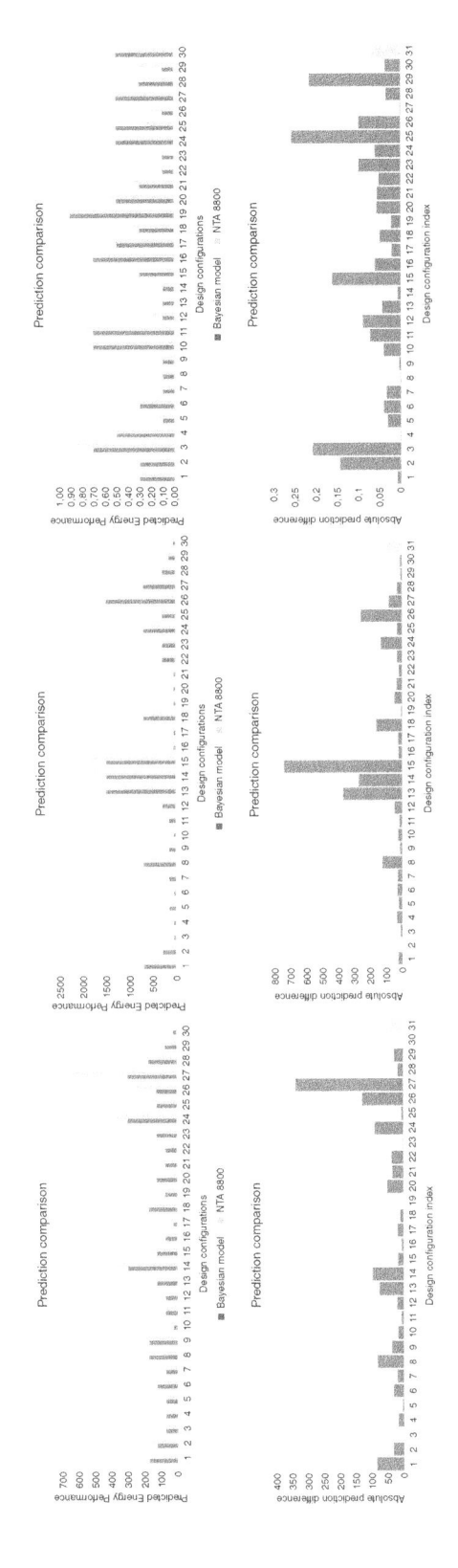

Figure 1.9 Histogram of BBN prediction and NTA 8800 outputs (top) and their comparison (bottom) for BENG1, BENG2, and BENG3, in order from left to right.

1 Augmented Computational Design

AreaPV

		1	2	3	4	5
PPV	1	0.033	0.038	0.039	0.041	0.044
	2	0.036	0.040	0.041	0.044	0.045
	3	0.044	0.043	0.041	0.039	0.045
	4	0.044	0.039	0.038	0.043	0.047
	5	0.047	0.047	0.047	0.047	**0.048**

Figure 1.10 Output Recommendations of the BBN Meta-model for Achieving BENG 3 Compliance.

By using the numerical DoE and Sensitivity Analysis, we are effectively conducting a dimensionality reduction task, similar to the low-rank SVD as introduced before. As mentioned earlier, the mention of this particular approach of ACD was to illustrate the utility of the framework with a concrete example in a societally relevant context where a ML approach to modeling can help make an otherwise very complicated simulation procedure to be approximately scaled up massively for policy analysis. Here, we discuss the potentials and shortcomings of the model and note the issues with this large-scale black-box approximation that require further investigation.

The existence of categorical variables in the inputs of the BBN limits the general applicability of ACD as it affects the smoothness and differentiability of the underlying function that is being approximated. However, for pragmatic reasons, we have ignored this issue to demonstrate the idea in a large-scale case.

Validation results

Compared to the NTA 8800, the Bayesian meta-model is capable of capturing the most important relationships between inputs and outputs. However, the difference between the meta-model's predictions and the NTA 8800 predictions can be rather high. This means that there is a large difference between the output of the meta-model and the NTA 8800. The NRMSEs of BENG 1 (0.82%) and BENG 2 (1.52%) show that the BBN is able to follow the NTA 8800 to some extent but is far from accurate, as NRMSE is greater than 0.5%. On the other hand, the model could predict BENG 3 (0.47) relatively accurately. This insufficient accuracy was expected as we have dictated a particular topology on the BBN while learning the network structure is an important step in constructing BBNs. This decision was made to enable the model to function in a bidirectional way: inference and reverse inference (i.e. evaluation and derivation in the terminology of our ACD framework).

Forward Inference

The trained BBN is now capable of inferring the outputs of interest given certain input configurations. This inference uses the learned CPDs to predict the most likely values for the outputs. In this way, we can predict the energy performance of buildings, in a quick and intuitive way for ex-ante assessment based on a certain design configuration. In particular, this inference demonstrates the potential of a mapping described in Section 3.

Backward Inference
Since our BBN had only two layers in its network, it can be reversed. This means that, instead of presenting evidence to it, we can present the desired performance values and ask for the derivation of the particular configuration of inputs that will produce such an output. This can be done through the *Variable Elimination* module of the *pgmpy* (Ankan and Panda 2015). The same is also true for a combination of given inputs–outputs, meaning that evidence can be given for both inputs and outputs of the BBN. In such cases, the given inputs can also function as design constraints. The reverse inference demonstrates how we can utilize probabilistic models to navigate a decision space as explained in Section 3.

Augmenting
The Bayesian meta-model is capable of representing the input–output relationships in a bidirectional and probabilistic format, illustrating a complete example of mapping and navigating processes. However, the use of a subset of the most influential variables of the NTA 8800 limits the navigation to decision space made of the selected variables. Nevertheless, this selection was necessary to manage the computationally resource-intensive task of learning. Therefore, BBN does not compete with, or mimic the NTA 8800 model; rather, it complements it by increasing its accessibility and providing navigation capabilities. The result is a model that can augment the designers' intuition or experience and enhance the level of accuracy even in otherwise vague processes of policy formulation; for example, in assessing the potential efficacy of alternative subsidies and incentives for building renovation aimed at sustainable energy transition.

Outlook

The ACD framework and its constituent concepts can be best positioned within the context of performance-driven computational design and generative design. In particular, the idea of approximating complex and nonlinear functions for estimating measurable performance indicators from configurations of decision variables, even if referring to nonspatial decision variables, is generalizable to all areas of computer-aided design. However, such surrogate models are not to replace simulation models based on first principles, as they cannot match their transparency and explainability. Nevertheless, in cases where one needs to estimate the effects of design decisions on human factors, ergonomics, or combinations of many different types of governing equations, an estimation model trained from actual data can be of utility in that it provides a basis for comparisons in the absence of analytical knowledge. In other words, the utility of ANNs for *mapping* associations between decision data points and performance data points is apparent.

The *navigation* problem, on the other hand, is much harder, philosophically, technically, and mathematically for being solved in any sense. The real advantage of an AI framework in dealing with a design space navigation problem can be attained if the latent space of the model reveals interpretable information or if it is at least coupled with a sensible low-dimensional space. If the latent space of, for example, an Auto Encoder (Marin et al. 2021) is understandable as a low-dimensional vector space (as an endpoint of the *mapping* and the start point of the *navigating* processes), it can be used not only to guide the navigation process but also to gain insight into which design variables are more important in determining the attainment levels of outcomes of interest. In other words, even though it appears that in the mapping process, the information content of the decision data points is gradually reducing, one can think of this process as a distillation of an elixir from a large data point that makes the information richer from a human perspective.

In light of this, the major advantages of the proposed framework are twofold: First, it provides an elegant framework for applying AI in computational design in the presence of many complex quality criteria; and second, it provides an elegant framework for designing spatial manifolds very much like the methodology of electrical engineering in designing electronic circuits and systems for signal processing. The latter point requires much more space for discussing the theoretical minimum for such an approach to design from a signal processing standpoint. In short, however, we can briefly mention that the idea of defining a central representation of a configuration as a discrete manifold provides for directly modeling the functionality of the spatial manifold with respect to the flows of walks, light rays, or forces not only from the point of view of spatial movement but also much more elegantly and efficiently in the frequency or spectral domain (which can be attained using Discrete Fourier Transform or Spectral Mesh Analysis). One fundamental idea of analog circuit design from a signal processing point of view is that of designing passive "filters," whose properties can much better be understood in the so-called frequency domain analyses put forward by Fourier and Laplace transforms of the so-called transfer functions of the Resistor, Self-Induction Loop, Capacitor (RLC) circuits. This approach to circuit design can be traced back to the ideas and propositions of Oliver Heaviside (1850–1925), a self-educated pioneer of electrical engineering. Arguably, this frequency-based outlook, relating to the spectrum of eigen frequencies of vibration of shapes (also identifiable as a spectral approach), has revolutionized the formation of the field of electronics and thus contributed significantly to the development of AI as we know it today. Identifying spectral latent spaces and associating them with low-dimensional performance spaces and latent spaces of ANNs is a topic that calls for further theoretical research and computational experimentation.

Acronyms

Acronym	Term
ACD	Augmented Computational Design
AEC	Architecture, Engineering, and Construction
AI	Artificial Intelligence
ANN	Artificial Neural Networks
BBN	Bayesian Belief Networks
BEM	Building Energy Modeling
BENG	Bijna Energie Neutrale Gebouwen: Nearly Zero-Energy Buildings
BIM	Building Information Model
CAD	Computer-Aided Design

Acronym	Term
CEN	Comité Européen de Normalisation: European Committee of Normalization
CPD	Conditional Probability Distribution
DAG	Directed Acyclic Graph
DoE	Design of Experiment
EPBD	European Energy Performance of Buildings Directive
JPD	Joint Probability Distributions
MAPE	Mean Absolute Percentage Error
MAGMA	Multi-Attribute Gradient-Driven Mass Aggregation
ML	Machine Learning
NEN	Nederlandse Norm: Royal Dutch Standardization Institute
NRMSE	Normalized Root Mean Square Error
NTA 8800	Nederlandse Technische Afspraak (Dutch Technical Agreement)
PDF	Probability Density Functions
PGM	Probabilistic Graphical Models
SVD	Singular Value Decomposition
VAE	Variational Auto-Encoders

Notations

Notation	Name	Definition
$\mathbf{x}$	Design/decision space	$\mathbf{x} \in (0,1]^n$; each x_i corresponds to a single spatial decision variable
$\mathbf{o}$	Performance space	$\mathbf{o} \in (0,1]^q$; each o_k corresponds to an objective or outcome of interest
$\mathbf{o} = f(\mathbf{x}) := [f_k(\mathbf{x})]_{q \times 1}$	Map from design to performance	$f:(0,1]^n \mapsto [0,1]^q$; representing a meta-model that approximately maps the decision space to the performance space
$\mathbf{x} = f^{-1}(\mathbf{o})$	Map from performance to design	$f^{-1}:[0,1]^q \mapsto (0,1]^n$; pseudo-inverse of a meta-model that approximately maps the performance space to the decision space
$\mathbf{J} := [J_{k,i}]_{q \times n}$	Jacobian matrix of f	$\left[J_{k,i}\right]_{q \times n} = \left[\dfrac{\partial f_k}{\partial x_i}\right]_{q \times n} = \left[\nabla^T f_q\right]_{q \times 1}$
$\mathbf{U}_{q \times q} := [\mathbf{u}_k]_{1 \times q}$	Matrix of left singular vectors	$\mathbf{U}\mathbf{U}^T = \mathbf{U}^T\mathbf{U} = \mathbf{I}_{q \times q}$; ordered by importance
$\mathbf{V}_{n \times n} := [\mathbf{v}_i]_{1 \times n}$	Matrix of right singular vectors	$\mathbf{V}\mathbf{V}^T = \mathbf{V}^T\mathbf{V} = \mathbf{I}_{n \times n}$; ordered by importance
$\mathbf{\Sigma}_{q \times n} := [\mathbf{u}_k]_{1 \times q}$	Matrix of singular values	$\mathbf{\Sigma}$ is an $q \times n$ rectangular diagonal matrix with non-negative real numbers on the diagonal ordered by importance, i.e. singular values σ_c, $c \in [0, \min\{q, n\})$

References

Ankan, A. and Panda, A. (2015). Pgmpy: Probabilistic Graphical Models Using Python. In: *Proceedings of the 14th Python in Science Conference (Scipy 2015)*, vol. 10. Citeseer.

Ankenman, B., Nelson, B.L., and Staum, J. (2010). Stochastic Kriging for Simulation Metamodeling. *Operations Research* 58 (2): 371–382. https://doi.org/10.1287/opre.1090.0754.

Azadi, S. and Nourian, P. (2021). GoDesign: A Modular Generative Design Framework for Mass-Customization and Optimization in Architectural Design. In: *Towards a New, Configurable Architecture*, vol. 1, 285–294. Novi Sad, Serbia: CUMINCAD.

Bai, N., Azadi, S., Nourian, P., and Roders, A.P. (2020). Decision-Making as a Social Choice Game. In: *Proceedings of the 38th eCAADe Conference*, vol. 2, 10.

Barton, R.R. (1998). Simulation Metamodels. In: *1998 Winter Simulation Conference. Proceedings (Cat. No.98CH36274)*. IEEE https://doi.org/10.1109/wsc.1998.744912.

Batty, M. (1974). A Theory of Markovian Design Machines. *Environment and Planning B: Planning and Design* https://doi.org/10.1068/b010125.

Beaumont, P., Horsburgh, B., Pilgerstorfer, P. et al. (2021). CausalNex [Computer software]. https://github.com/quantumblacklabs/causalnex.

Bui, V., Le, N.T., Nguyen, V.H. et al. (2021). Multi-Behavior with Bottleneck Features LSTM for Load Forecasting in Building Energy Management System. *Electronics* 10 (9): 1026. https://doi.org/10.3390/electronics10091026.

Conti, Z.X. and Kaijima, S. (2018). A Flexible Simulation Metamodel for Exploring Multiple Design Spaces. In: *International Association for Shell; Spatial Structures (IASS)*. https://doi.org/10.13140/RG.2.2.23313.53600.

Conti, Z.X. and Kaijima, S. (2021). Explainable ML: Augmenting the Interpretability of Numerical Simulation Using Bayesian Networks. In: *The Routledge Companion to Artificial Intelligence in Architecture*, 315–335. Routledge.

Fang, K.-T., Li, R., and Sudjianto, A. (2005). *Design and Modeling for Computer Experiments*. Chapman: Hall/CRC https://doi.org/10.1201/9781420034899.

Friedman, Y. (1975). *Toward a Scientific Architecture*. First American Edition. Cambridge, Mass: MIT Press.

Gero, J.S. and Kannengiesser, U. (2004). The Situated Function–Behaviour–Structure Framework. *Design Studies* 25 (4): 373–391.

Giedion, S. (2009). *Space, Time and Architecture: The Growth of a New Tradition*. Harvard University Press.

van Gigch, J.P. (1991). *System Design Modeling and Metamodeling*. Language of Science: Plenum https://books.google.nl/books?id=M5mD0ZZcwaEC.

Herman, J. and Usher, W. (2017). SALib: An Open-Source Python Library for Sensitivity Analysis. *The Journal of Open Source Software* 2 (9): 97. https://doi.org/10.21105/joss.00097.

Hicks, C.R. (1964). *Fundamental Concepts in the Design of Experiments*. New York: Holt, Rinehart; Winston.

Hillier, B. (2007). *Space Is the Machine: A Configurational Theory of Architecture*. Space Syntax.

James, G., Witten, D., Hastie, T., and Tibshirani, R. (2013). *An Introduction to Statistical Learning: With Applications in R*, Springer Texts in Statistics. Springer New York https://books.google.nl/books?id=qcI_AAAAQBAJ.

Jia, Z., Nourian, P., Luscuere, P., and Wagenaar, C. (2023). Spatial Decision Support Systems for Hospital Layout Design: A Review. *Journal of Building Engineering* 106042.

Khan, A.N., Iqbal, N., Ahmad, R., and Kim, D.-H. (2021). Ensemble Prediction Approach Based on Learning to Statistical Model for Efficient Building Energy Consumption Management. *Symmetry* 13 (3): 405. https://doi.org/10.3390/sym13030405.

Kleijnen, J.P.C. (1975). A Comment on Blannings Metamodel for Sensitivity Analysis: The Regression Metamodel in Simulation. *Interfaces* 5 (3): 21–23. https://doi.org/10.1287/inte.5.3.21.

Kleijnen, J.P.C. (n.d.). Low-Order Polynomial Regression Metamodels and Their Designs: Basics. In: *International Series in Operations Research and Management Science*, 15–71. Springer US https://doi.org/10.1007/978-0-387-71813-2_2.

Koller, D. and Friedman, N. (2009). *Probabilistic Graphical Models: Principles and Techniques*. In: *Adaptive Computation and Machine Learning*. Cambridge, MA: MIT Press.

Kroes, P. (2010). Engineering and the Dual Nature of Technical Artefacts. *Cambridge Journal of Economics* 34 (1): 51–62.

Kroes, P. and Meijers, A. (2006). The Dual Nature of Technical Artefacts. *Studies in History and Philosophy of Science* 37 (1): 1–4.

Marin, R., Rampini, A., Castellani, U. et al. (2021). Spectral Shape Recovery and Analysis Via Data-Driven Connections. *International Journal of Computer Vision* 129 (10): 2745–2760. https://doi.org/10.1007/s11263-021-01492-6.

Martin, C.D. and Porter, M.A. (2012). The Extraordinary SVD. *The American Mathematical Monthly* 119 (10): 838–851.

Nen 7120+C2:2012/A1:2017 NL. 2017. *NEN*. https://www.nen.nl/nen-7120-c2-2012-a1-2017-nl-229670.

Nourian, P. (2016). *Configraphics: Graph Theoretical Methods for Design and Analysis of Spatial Configurations*. TU Delft Open https://doi.org/10.7480/isbn.9789461867209.

Nourian, P., Azadi, S., and Oval, R. (2023). Generative Design in Architecture: From Mathematical Optimization to Grammatical Customization. In: *Computational Design and Digital Manufacturing* (ed. P. Kyratsis, A. Manavis, and J. Paulo Davim), 1–43. Cham: Springer International Publishing https://doi.org/10.1007/978-3-031-21167-6_1.

Nourian, P., Gonçalves, R., Zlatanova, S. et al. (2016). Voxelization Algorithms for Geospatial Applications: Computational Methods for Voxelating Spatial Datasets of 3D City Models Containing 3D Surface, Curve and Point Data Models. *MethodsX* 3 (January): 69–86. https://doi.org/10.1016/j.mex.2016.01.001.

"NTA 8800." 2022. *Gebouwenergieprestatie (EPG)*. https://www.gebouwenergieprestatie.nl/bepalingsmethode.

O'Shaughnessy, Connor, Enrico Masoero, and Peter D. Gosling. 2021. "Topology Optimization Using the Discrete Element Method. Part 1: Methodology, Validation, and Geometric Nonlinearity." Preprint. engrXiv. https://doi.org/10.31224/osf.io/c6ymn.

Pearl, J. (1988). *Probabilistic Reasoning in Intelligent Systems: Networks of Plausible Inference*. Morgan kaufmann.

Peng, Y., Zhang, S., and Pan, R. (2010). Bayesian Network Reasoning With Uncertain Evidences. *International Journal of Uncertainty, Fuzziness and Knowledge-Based Systems* 18 (05): 539–564. https://doi.org/10.1142/s0218488510006696.

Regenwetter, L. and Ahmed, F. (2022). Towards Goal, Feasibility, and Diversity-Oriented Deep Generative Models in Design. *arXiv* http://arxiv.org/abs/2206.07170.

Regenwetter, L., Nobari, A.H., and Ahmed, F. (2022). Deep Generative Models in Engineering Design: A Review. *Journal of Mechanical Design* 144 (7): 071704. https://doi.org/10.1115/1.4053859.

Sacks, J., Welch, W.J., Mitchell, T.J., and Wynn, H.P. (1989). Design and Analysis of Computer Experiments. *Statistical Science* 4 (4): https://doi.org/10.1214/ss/1177012413.

Simon, H.A. (1973). The Structure of Ill Structured P Coblems. *Artificial Intelligence* 21.

Simon, H.A. (2019). *The Sciences of the Artificial, Reissue of the Third Edition with a New Introduction by John Laird*. MIT press.

Sobol', I.'y.M. (1990). On Sensitivity Estimation for Nonlinear Mathematical Models. *Matematicheskoe Modelirovanie* 2 (1): 112–118.

Soman, A., Azadi, S., and Nourian, P. (2022). DeciGenArch: A Generative Design Methodology for Architectural Configuration via Multi-Criteria Decision Analysis. In: *Proceedings of eCAADe 2022*, forthcoming. Education; research in Computer Aided Architectural Design in Europe. https://www.overleaf.com/project/60f1ae165edde605561c28e1.

Union, European (2021). Proposal for a Directive of the European Parliament and of the Council on the Energy Performance of Buildings (Recast). *Lex - 52021PC0802 - En - EUR-Lex* https://eur-lex.europa.eu/legal-content/EN/ALL/?uri=CELEX%3A52021PC0802.

Veloso, Pedro, and Ramesh Krishnamurti. 2020. "An Academy of Spatial Agents: Generating Spatial Configurations with Deep Reinforcement Learning." In *eCAADe: Anthropologic - Architecture and Fabrication in the Cognitive Age*.

Veloso, P. and Krishnamurti, R. (2021). Mapping Generative Models for Architectural Design. In: *The Routledge Companion to Artificial Intelligence in Architecture*, 29–58. Routledge.

Weng, L. (2021). What Are Diffusion Models? *Lilianweng.github.io*, July. https://lilianweng.github.io/posts/2021-07-11-diffusion-models/.

Zeng, M., Xu, T., Wang, R. et al. (2021). MusicBERT: Symbolic Music Understanding with Large-Scale Pre-Training. *In ACL-IJCNLP 2021*: https://www.microsoft.com/en-us/research/publication/musicbert-symbolic-music-understanding-with-large-scale-pre-training/.

2

Machine Learning in Urban Building Energy Modeling

Narjes Abbasabadi[1] and Mehdi Ashayeri[2]

[1] *Department of Architecture, School of Architecture, College of Built Environments, University of Washington, Seattle, WA, USA*
[2] *School of Architecture, College of Arts and Media, Southern Illinois University Carbondale, Carbondale, IL, USA*

Introduction

Addressing climate change targets and fostering low-carbon urban areas is crucial, as cities are responsible for approximately two-thirds of worldwide energy consumption and greenhouse gas emissions (IPCC 2014). An accurate representation of urban building energy dynamics is key for informed energy-driven planning, design, optimization, and policy evaluation (Reinhart and Davila 2016; Kontokosta and Tull 2017; Mostafavi, Farzinmoghadam, and Hoque 2017; Happle, Fonseca, and Schlueter 2018; Schiefelbein et al. 2019). Urban Building Energy Modeling (UBEM) stands as a key element in the domain of urban energy management, offering invaluable insights into the energy dynamics of cities and the multifaceted aspects of the built environments. Urban energy modeling endeavors to bridge the gap in data by generating essential quantitative energy information and strategies for energy reduction using various methods, including physics-based or data-driven models (Reinhart and Davila 2016; Keirstead, Jennings, and Sivakumar 2012). However, despite significant efforts, existing urban energy modeling tools are constrained in presenting a realistic energy model due to methodological uncertainties (Fonseca and Schlueter 2015; Reinhart and Davila 2016; Kontokosta and Tull 2017; Silva et al. 2017). The complexity of urban building systems, involving multifaceted factors such as urban building characteristics, technology parameters, and dynamic factors such as human behavior and microclimate aspects, further complicates energy modeling. Additionally, data scarcity and extensive modeling efforts hinder urban-scale modeling (Mostafavi, Farzinmoghadam, and Hoque 2017; Happle, Fonseca, and Schlueter 2018; Schiefelbein et al. 2019). Hence, the challenge remains in devising an accurate and efficient approach to large-scale urban energy modeling.

Today, our capacity to comprehend and address interconnected challenges in the built environment has expanded significantly. This is primarily attributable to the increasing availability of high spatiotemporal resolution data from big data, sensor networks, the emergence of smart cities, and open data initiatives. Coupled with advances in AI, computational tools, multisensory technologies, and data-driven approaches have demonstrated their prowess in tackling myriad challenges across various industries, particularly in the fields of

---

Artificial Intelligence in Performance-Driven Design: Theories, Methods, and Tools, First Edition.
Edited by Narjes Abbasabadi and Mehdi Ashayeri.
©2024 John Wiley & Sons Inc. Published 2024 by John Wiley & Sons Inc.

science and engineering (Montáns et al. 2019). However, these tools have yet to be comprehensively harnessed within the realm of energy-efficient built environments. This presents an unprecedented opportunity for conceptualizing a transformative approach to advance UBEM. Investing in this unparalleled opportunity provides the foundation for an approach that can yield more reliable and efficient models, offering a crucial contribution to scaling up energy efficiencies, a global imperative of utmost urgency.

The integration of machine learning (ML) in UBEM has the potential to enable data-driven approaches that enhance both the accuracy and efficiency of energy modeling (Abbasabadi and Ashayeri 2019). In addition, ML enables data-driven decision-making by harnessing historical energy consumption data and developing predictive models that estimate future energy demands. This capability is invaluable in both the design and retrofit scenarios, as it guides architects and engineers in optimizing the energy needs of buildings, from layout and materials to systems and operations. In retrofit scenarios, it helps identify areas with the highest energy consumption, allowing for targeted and cost-effective upgrades. ML optimizes energy use in real-time through adaptive control systems, allowing for the dynamic adjustment of building systems based on occupancy, weather, and other factors. It also supports the efficient integration of renewable energy sources, such as solar panels or wind turbines, in both new building designs and retrofit projects. It also results in increased sustainability, lower environmental impact, and reduced energy costs.

This chapter provides a review of ML in the UBEM domain. By delving into the fundamental principles of ML and its practical applications in the UBEM field, we aim to provide a foundation for understanding the profound impact of this approach. Moreover, we will undertake a critical review of existing UBEM methods, shedding light on their inherent strengths and limitations. By recognizing these characteristics, we discuss the opportunities that emerge from the integration of ML technologies into UBEM. Throughout this chapter, we will explore the various applications of ML in the realm of UBEM. From predictive models that extract energy consumption patterns to optimization that aids urban energy management. This approach unites the precision of data-driven simulations with the fundamentals of physics-based models, thereby enhancing accuracy while reducing uncertainties in modeling various aspects of urban energy use.

Urban Building Energy Modeling Methods

There are two major approaches for UBEM including top–down and bottom–up (Abbasabadi and Ashayeri 2019) (Figure 2.1):

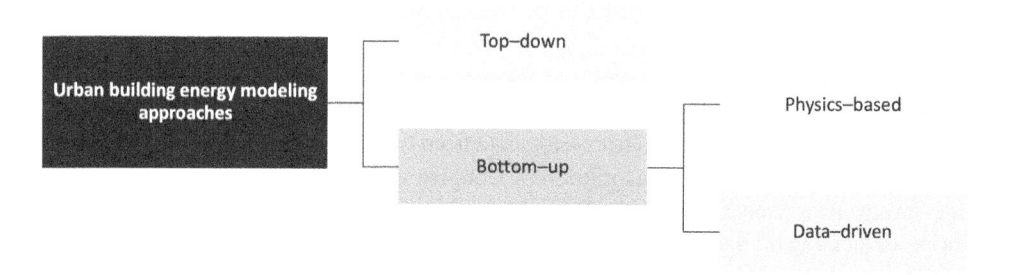

Figure 2.1 Urban Building Energy Modeling Approaches.

Top–Down Models

Top–down models take a macroscale perspective when analyzing urban energy use (Abbasabadi and Ashayeri 2019). They treat the entire built environment of a city as a collective energy user and rely heavily on historical aggregated energy data for analysis (Swan and Ugursal 2009). One notable strength of top–down approaches is their consideration of macroeconomic and socioeconomic effects, making them valuable for long-term studies (Swan and Ugursal 2009). Researchers employing top–down models often explore the relationships between urban energy use and variables such as macroeconomic indicators, demographics, and technology adoption. For instance, examining the influence of economic and demographic factors, such as population and Gross Domestic Product (GDP) per capita, on yearly electricity use (Bianco, Manca, and Nardini 2009), or investigating building energy consumption through a macroeconomic approach and how macroeconomic factors affect urban building energy use (Lin and Liu 2015) are examples of top–down approach. Despite these advantages, top–down models have significant limitations. Their reliance on aggregated data for energy use estimation can lead to generalizations that compromise their accuracy for detailed urban energy supply–demand (Swan and Ugursal 2009; Davila and Reinhart 2011).

Bottom–Up Models

In contrast to top–down models, bottom–up approaches localize energy use studies and consider urban attributes at the microscale, focusing on individual buildings or clusters of buildings (Shorrock and Dunster 1997). This microscale framework relies on extensive data to estimate the energy consumption of each user. In contrast with the *top–down* statistical approaches that employ econometric or technological methods that use aggregated data with low spatiotemporal resolution and generalize the status quo, *bottom–up* approaches consider energy determinants and their interactions (Swan and Ugursal 2009; Kavgic et al. 2010). The *bottom–up* UBEM approaches are classified into two major groups: data-driven and physics-based methods (Abbasabadi and Ashayeri 2019). (Figure 2.2).

Data-driven methods are developed based on statistical techniques, and recent works lean toward employing more promising ML algorithms. Data-driven UBEMs harness extensive datasets sourced from government, utilities, or local providers to establish mathematical relationships between end-user characteristics and energy consumption. When a comprehensive set of variables is included, data-driven models can offer a more precise representation of urban operational energy than urban-scale physics-based simulation approaches (Hsu 2015; Kontokosta, Bonczak, and Duer-Balkind 2016; Paula Guillaumet, Rosas-Casals, and Travesset-Baro 2018). These models employ statistical and ML techniques to uncover these relationships, enabling the estimation of individual end-users' energy usage. The most prevalent data-driven models employ statistical and ML-based methods to model energy usage in urban buildings and transportation. These models "learn" from patterns in energy data, utilizing a training dataset to establish mathematical relationships between energy use and influencing factors, such as building characteristics, urban attributes, and occupancy features. This process involves two key steps: (1) identifying statistical patterns in the data, and (2) making predictions based on these patterns. In a study by Abbasabadi et al. (2019), an introduced data-driven framework for UEUM in

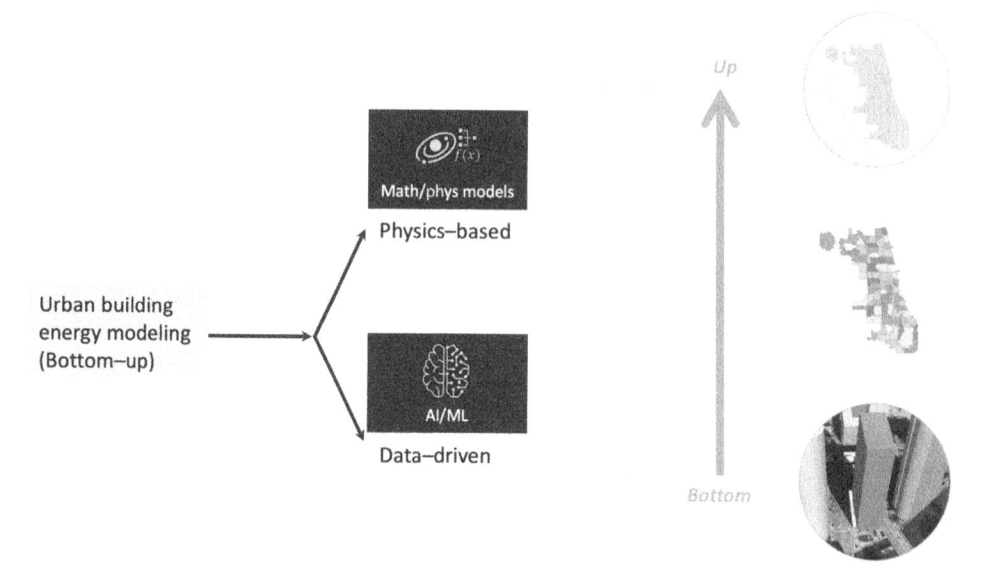

Figure 2.2 Bottom–up Urban Building Energy Modeling Approaches.

Chicago was introduced. The study assessed various ML algorithms and demonstrated the accuracy of each model, followed by monitoring their performance (Figure 2.3).

Physics-based methods, also known as engineering simulations, rely on the thermodynamics of energy systems (Swan and Ugursal 2009; Reinhart and Cerezo Davila 2016; Sola et al. 2018). The physics-based modeling is rooted in mathematical representations of real-world physical phenomena and principles, employing fundamental laws and equations from physics to predict system behavior under various conditions. These models use simulation techniques and engines, thermodynamic principles, and data encompassing construction, climate, and system aspects to estimate energy consumption at an urban scale. To achieve computational efficiency, urban energy modeling is simplified by obtaining geometric and physical data from geographic information system (GIS) and city geography markup language (CityGML) (Biljecki et al. 2015; Mastrucci et al. 2014). CityGML is used for storing and sharing 3D city models. It represents urban environments' physical characteristics and semantic information in a standardized way, supporting different levels of detail for various urban building features. Nongeometric data, such as heating, ventilation, and air conditioning (HVAC) and construction systems, are assumed based on building typologies called "archetypes" (Davila, Reinhart, and Bemis 2016), grouping buildings with similar characteristics and systems. These archetypes are then converted into simplified thermal shoebox models for urban-scale energy simulation (Dogan and Reinhart 2013). This reduced-order approach, although based on various assumptions regarding temporal and spatial characteristics, comes in two main variations: aggregating workload reduction (e.g. prototypical, sample, and distribution methods) and load forecasting simplification (Li, Quan, et al. 2015; Heidarinejad et al. 2017; Shamsi et al. 2017). While utilizing a highly detailed representation of all buildings in urban-scale modeling is computationally inefficient, reduced-order models may exhibit differences in results, yet they are useful for exploring different scenarios (Figure 2.4).

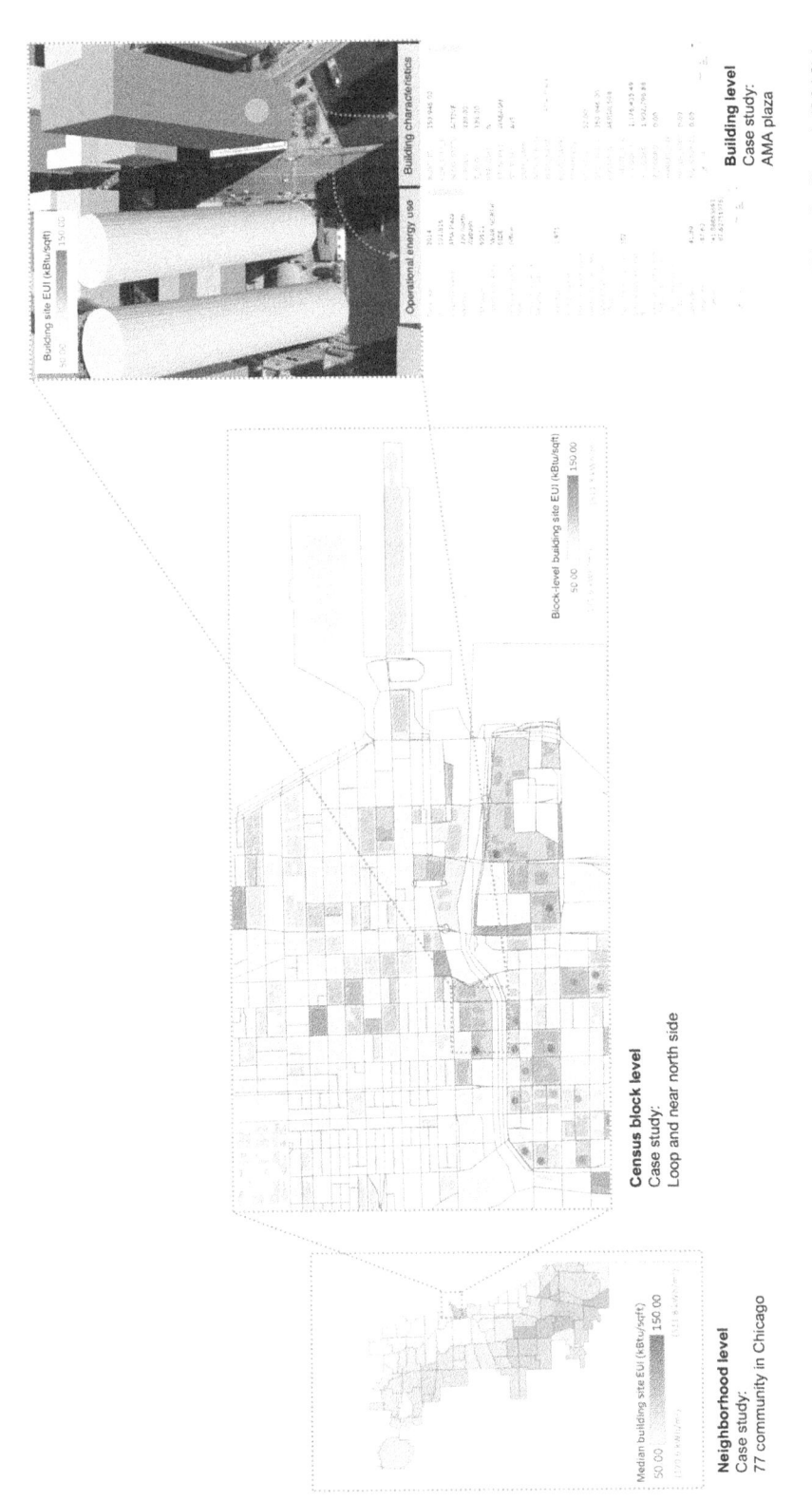

Figure 2.3 Data-driven Modeling: An integrated data-driven framework for urban energy use modeling (UEUM). Chicago, IL. Source: Abbasabadi et al. (2019)/ with permission of Elsevier.

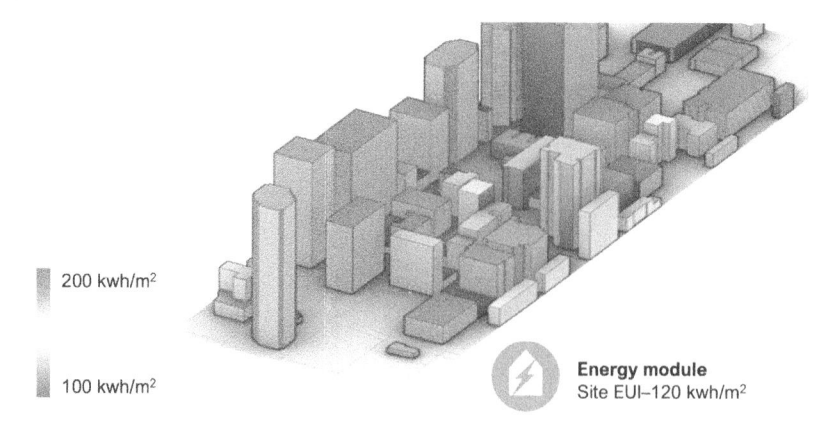

Figure 2.4 Physics-based modeling: Analysis and optimization of building energy systems at the neighborhood and city levels. Dallas, TX Energy model.

Uncertainty in Urban Building Energy Modeling

Uncertainty is an inherent and critical aspect of UBEM, stemming from various sources that impact the accuracy and reliability of energy predictions and assessments. Understanding and quantifying uncertainty are essential for improving the accuracy of models and decision-making processes in the urban energy domain. The two primary categories of uncertainty in UBEM are epistemic uncertainty and stochastic uncertainty.

Epistemic Uncertainty

Epistemic uncertainty arises from limited knowledge or incomplete information regarding input parameters and system components in urban building energy models. This form of uncertainty often stems from several factors, including inadequate or inaccurate data, reliance on model assumptions, and challenges associated with parameter estimation. Incomplete, inconsistent, or error-prone data for input parameters can lead to uncertainties in the model's outputs. Model assumptions as another common source of epistemic uncertainty happen when models rely on assumptions that do not precisely reflect real-world complexities. Parameter estimation is another source, as estimation methods contribute to uncertainty when the values of model parameters are challenging to ascertain with precision. Addressing epistemic uncertainty requires improving data quality, refining models, and minimizing reliance on assumptions, encompassing enhancements in data collection methods, parameter estimation techniques, and a reduction in assumptions, collectively reducing this form of uncertainty in UBEM.

Stochastic Uncertainty

Stochastic uncertainty arises from the inherent variability within system components and processes. In urban settings, the behavior of building energy systems is influenced by random factors, resulting in uncertainties within the model's output. Key sources of stochastic uncertainty include weather, climate, microclimate, occupant behavior, and technological variability. Weather conditions, which significantly impact energy consumption and generation, exhibit inherent stochastic patterns, introducing uncertainty into energy models. Occupancy and occupant behavior and actions within buildings, such as heating and cooling preferences, lighting usage, and appliance selections, contribute to variability and uncertainty. Technological variability such as the performance of energy systems, renewable energy sources, and building materials may also exhibit variability. Managing stochastic uncertainty typically often employs probabilistic modeling techniques, such as Monte Carlo simulations or stochastic optimization, to account for the probabilistic nature of these variables.

Data-driven and physics-based approaches have their own limitations and uncertainties involved. These uncertainties pose challenges in achieving reliable and accurate urban building energy simulations. The bottom–up physics-based models–which may be powerful for single-building simulations and assessing different energy-saving strategies–have limitations for large urban-scale modeling because of extensive time and computational requirements and, therefore, mostly rely on simplified and universal archetypes that are not representative of actual variations of building dynamics and energy systems in a city (Li et al. 2015; Chen, Hong, and Piette 2017; Nutkiewicz, Yang, and Jain 2018). The limitations in available archetypes are due to oversimplifying real-world features and complexities, such as geometric and semantic representation of buildings and urban context, which leads to epistemic uncertainty, spatiotemporal representation of microclimate condition, and occupancy and occupant behavior technological variation and making stochastic uncertainty. These limitations have a significant impact on the design and optimization of building energy use and energy systems.

These limitations have a significant impact on the design and optimization of the built environment; therefore, addressing them is crucial. Yet, bringing accurate urban building semantic information and truly incorporating dynamic factors such as microclimates and human systems is an overlooked area in urban-scale building energy modeling. In addition to a lack of a holistic approach to consider dynamic urban energy determinants, the existing models have limitations in terms of sufficient information, data resolution, and methodological approach (Fonseca and Schlueter 2015; Reinhart and Cerezo Davila 2016; Kontokosta and Tull 2017; Silva et al. 2017; Happle, Fonseca, and Schlueter 2018). In previous urban energy models, the data was limited and often acquired from low-resolution aggregated datasets or partial and sparse experimental data used to validate a specific hypothesis, leading to often neglecting significant factors.

On the other hand, bottom–up data-driven energy modeling approaches, which are built upon using actual energy data with a higher spatial resolution, offer the potential to quantify uncertainty and more accurately represent urban energy use (Hsu 2015; Kontokosta, Bonczak, and Duer-balkind 2016; Guillaumet et al. 2018a; Sohn and Dunn 2019). These models, however, heavily rely on the availability, granularity, and quality of supporting data, particularly due to lack of local occupancy and disaggregated building energy data at the individual building level. Therefore, data-driven models are considered less cost-effective when data availability is limited. Additionally, these models face limitations in investigating "what if" scenarios, as they lack the flexibility of physics-based simulation platforms to modify and test different energy strategies.

Addressing Uncertainty

Enhancing the reliability of UBEMs necessitates a multifaceted approach, encompassing the mitigation of both epistemic and stochastic uncertainties. This entails several key strategies: first, data enhancement is pivotal, involving the improvement of data collection and validation processes through the integration of advanced technologies, such as remote sensing and the widespread adoption of Internet of Things (IoT) systems, which substantially enhance data accuracy and coverage. Second, in managing stochastic uncertainty, probabilistic modeling techniques are crucial as they enable the seamless incorporation of randomness into energy predictions, accommodating the inherent variability within urban energy systems. Third, sensitivity analysis provides valuable insights by identifying the input parameters that contribute most significantly to uncertainty, guiding targeted data enhancement efforts to optimize model accuracy. Lastly, scenario analysis, which considers uncertainty within a spectrum of scenarios, empowers decision-makers by providing a range of potential outcomes, thereby enhancing the robustness of the decision-making process. This comprehensive approach equips urban energy researchers and professionals with the tools needed to effectively navigate and address the multifaceted uncertainties within UBEM, ultimately contributing to more accurate and reliable energy predictions and better-informed urban energy management practices.

UBEM introduces uncertainty due to unknown or partially known factors, such as building geometry, end-use, envelope materials, age class, and HVAC system performance. This lack of data leads to multiple assumptions, converting physics-based models into black-box models. Geospatial data in GIS-compatible formats such as shapefiles and geoJSON describe buildings' spatial distribution and geometry. Higher Levels of Detail (LoD) are essential for more accurate building energy simulations. The use of standardized building archetypes is common in UBEMs, where predefined shapes, materials, and occupancy patterns are employed. This simplifies modeling but fails to represent realistic day-to-day variations and randomness in occupant behavior, which are crucial for accurate simulations. Stochastic models, including Monte Carlo, Markov Chains, or ML, can address this by incorporating randomness in occupant behavior (Prataviera et al. 2022). However, the availability of occupancy data varies, with mobile phone tracking methods and environmental sensors being recent data sources. In the context of UBEMs, the hybrid data-driven and physics-based approaches are promising in leveraging the benefits of both engineering physics-based and ML-based techniques and enabling more efficient and accurate UBEMs (Abbasabadi and Ashayeri 2019). The engineering physics-based procedure enables "what-if" scenario analysis, while data-driven through leveraging ML techniques can resolve data scarcity issues for the problem.

A study by Prataviera et al. (2022) aimed to enhance the reliability of UBEMs by addressing input parameter uncertainty and data quality challenges. It integrates physics-based UBEMs with uncertainty and sensitivity analysis, employing regional/national energy consumption statistics. This approach identifies key input parameters, characterizes their uncertainties via forward uncertainty analysis and sensitivity analysis, and generates stochastic load profiles for heating and cooling. Validated on buildings in Verona and a Milan district, the method significantly improves heating load profiles, reducing peak load overestimation from 80% to 25% and energy calculation deviation from 18% to 10%. These results underscore the importance of considering parameter uncertainty for reliable urban simulations. The microclimate variables, such as local temperature, wind speed, wind pressure, and solar irradiation, also play a key role in defining boundary conditions that affect a building's interaction with its environment and energy models. Another study by Sun et al. (2014) leverages emerging statistical methods and theories from engineering statistics, particularly those related to uncertainty quantification (UQ), to address the uncertainty in microclimate variables within building energy models.

In conclusion, a profound comprehension of uncertainty within UBEM is indispensable for making well-informed decisions in urban energy planning and design. The mitigation of both epistemic and stochastic uncertainties, achieved through improved data quality, advanced modeling techniques, sensitivity analysis, and scenario assessments, can lead to more precise and dependable urban building energy predictions.

Machine Learning in Urban Building Energy Modeling

ML involves the scientific exploration of algorithms and statistical models employed by computer systems to execute particular tasks without the need for explicit programming (Mahesh 2019). ML enhances data handling and interpretation by teaching machines to extract meaningful insights autonomously. ML is in high demand across industries due to the wealth of available datasets. Its primary goal is autonomous learning from data, with researchers employing various approaches to enable machines to learn independently, particularly when dealing with large datasets. In the context of UBEM, AI models primarily rely on ML techniques and algorithms refer to a set of computational techniques, and mathematical models that enable systems to learn patterns, relationships, and insights from data related to urban building energy consumption (Abbasabadi and Ashayeri 2019). These methods and algorithms are designed to assist in understanding, predicting, and optimizing energy use in urban environments. ML techniques fall into the following key categories (Figure 2.5):

Supervised Learning

Supervised learning is one of the most common and fundamental types of ML. In this paradigm, the algorithm is provided with labeled training data, consisting of input features and their corresponding correct output or target. The primary goal is for the model to learn mapping from inputs to outputs. Supervised learning can be further categorized into regression, where the model predicts continuous values, and classification, where it predicts discrete class labels. In UBEM, supervised learning plays a crucial role in predicting future energy consumption in buildings, classifying buildings based on energy efficiency, or identifying anomalies in energy usage. Supervised learning plays a pivotal role in UBEM, especially in the context of predictive modeling. It enables the development of accurate models that forecast future energy consumption in urban buildings. For instance, a supervised learning

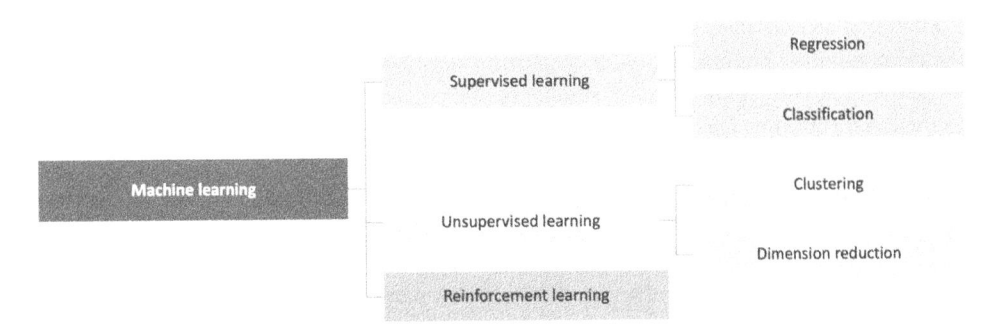

Figure 2.5 Machine Learning categories.

model can take into account historical energy consumption data, building characteristics, and external factors such as weather patterns to predict future energy needs. This capability aids urban planners, architects, and energy managers in designing and retrofitting buildings for optimal energy efficiency. Additionally, classification in supervised learning can help categorize buildings based on energy efficiency, aiding in urban development policies and initiatives focused on sustainability.

The most common supervised models encompassing classification and regression techniques in UBEM include a range of algorithms such as statistical-based ones such as Simple Linear Regression (SLR), Multiple Linear Regression (MLR), Nonlinear (Polynomial) Regression (PR, Conditional Demand Analysis (CDR), Huber M-estimation Regression (HMR), as well as more advanced ML-based algorithms such as Artificial Neural Networks (ANNs), Support Vector Machine (SVM), k-Nearest Neighbor (k-NN), Random Forest (RF) or Random Decision Forest (RDF), and Classification and Regression Tree (CART). Additionally, clustering techniques, such as k-means (KM) clustering and Agglomerative Hierarchical Clustering (AHC) algorithms, have been employed (Abbasabadi and Ashayeri 2019) (Figure 2.6).

Various statistical models that are prevalent in urban energy modeling, including SLR, MLR, Linear Regression with Ordinary Least Squares (OLS), Logistic Regression (LR), and Historical Mean Regression (HMR) are among supervised learning techniques. SLR and MLR are widely used for modeling energy use in urban buildings, offering interpretability and elucidating the relationships between building characteristics and energy consumption (Robinson et al. 2017). MLR has been applied in estimating energy consumption in urban buildings using the New York City Energy Benchmarking dataset (Kontokosta 2012), as well as predicting energy consumption based on aggregated building characteristics at the neighborhood level (Kuusela et al. 2015). Norman et al. employed MLR in a study focusing on the life cycle analysis of energy use in low- and high-density neighborhoods in Toronto (Norman, MacLean, Kennedy 2006).

OLS linear regression, another prevalent method, is known for its computational efficiency, precision, and simplicity (Swan and Ugursal 2009; Kontokosta and Tull 2017; Park et al. 2018; Papadopoulos et al. 2018). Dagnely et al. found both OLS linear regression and SVM to provide acceptable accuracy (Dagnely et al. 2015), and Kontokosta and Tull reported better performance for OLS compared to RF and SVM in a city-scale energy prediction model for New York buildings (Kontokosta and Tull 2017). In a recent study, Cheng et al. compared Polynomial Regression (PR) with ANNs, with PR consistently delivering comparable or superior results (Cheng et al. 2018).

LR is suitable for classification problems, particularly in retrofit prediction (Marasco and Kontokosta 2016). The RDF algorithm is widely used for forecasting monthly and annual energy use in urban buildings (Yu 2018), and Howard et al. employed the HMR for energy use prediction at a ZIP code level (Howard et al. 2012). However, MLR, despite its simplicity and interpretability, has limitations in capturing nonlinear and complex patterns (Leach et al. 2007; Park et al. 2018). MLR coefficients offer insight into how predictors affect the target variable, but they lack the ability to account for nonlinearity and complex real-world patterns (Olden, Joy, and Death 2004).

ANNs, inspired by biological neural systems utilizing interconnected nodes and layers to capture nonlinear patterns (Deng, Fannon, and Eckelman 2018), are employed for classification and regression tasks (Rosenblatt 1958). ANNs include Feedforward Neural Networks (FNN) and Recurrent Neural Networks (RNN). FNN, particularly Multi-Layer Perceptrons (MLP), is the favored choice for energy prediction (Bishop 1995). MLP, featuring one or more hidden layers, offer flexibility in modeling complex data relationships. Extreme Learning

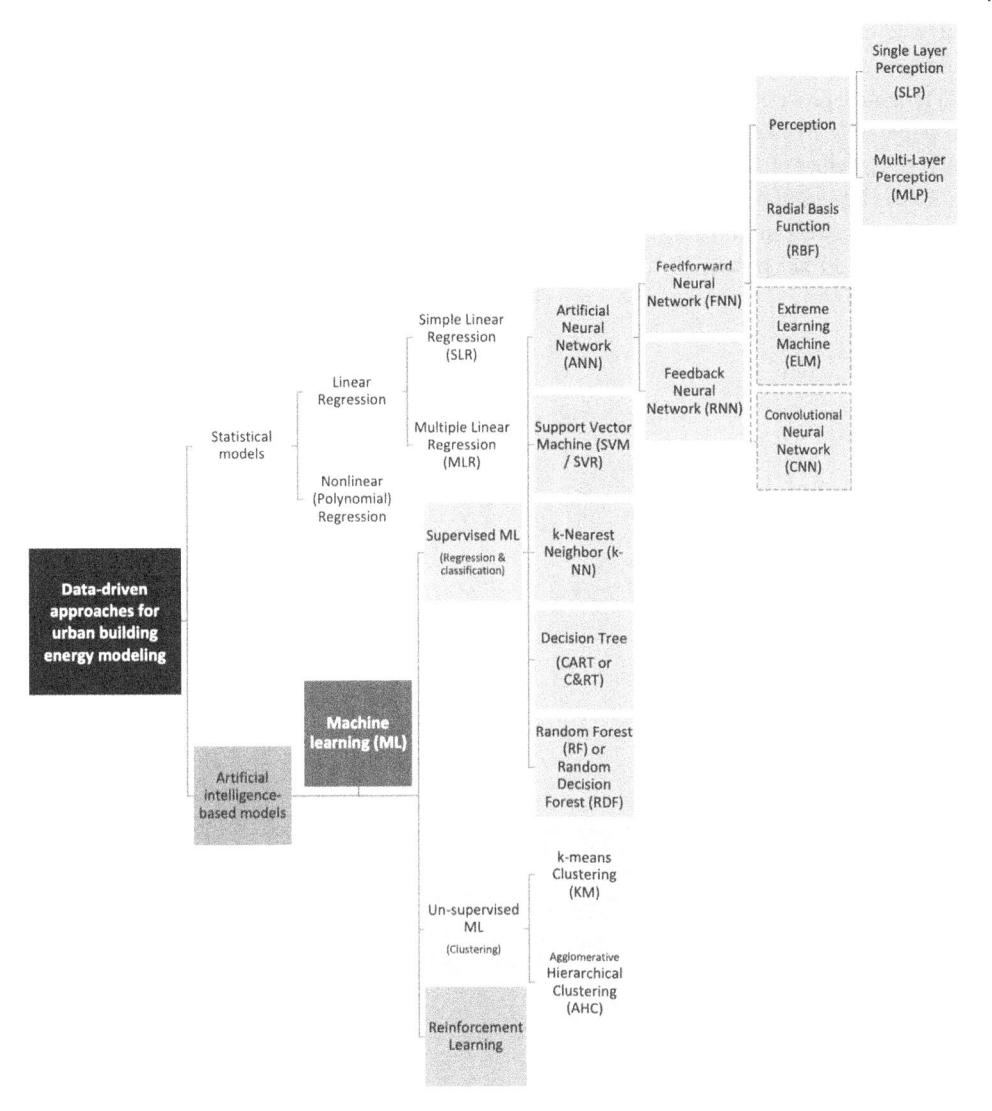

Figure 2.6 The most common data-driven approaches for urban building energy modeling. Source: Abbasabadi and Ashayeri (2019).

Machines (ELM), characterized by randomly assigned biases and weights during training, enable rapid generalization in large-scale urban problems (Huang, Zhu, and Siew 2006; Guorui Feng et al. 2009), although ELM may not guarantee higher prediction accuracy compared to MLPs. ANNs operate through data-driven learning, making predictions based on experience. Sajjadi et al. applied ELM to multistep time-series heat energy prediction, confirming its superiority in accuracy, generalizability, and time efficiency (Sajjadi et al. 2016). Wong et al. utilized MLP–ANNs for operational energy modeling in office buildings (Wong, Wan, and Lam 2010), while Hong et al. used MLP–ANNs for energy benchmarking in educational buildings in the United Kingdom (Hong et al. 2014).

Deep learning is a subset of ML that relies on ANNs, particularly deep neural networks (DNNs) with multiple layers (Figure 2.7). DNNs are formed when ANNs comprise more

42 | *2 Machine Learning in Urban Building Energy Modeling*

than one hidden layer. These networks are capable of processing large, complex datasets, making them particularly well-suited for tasks involving image and speech recognition, natural language processing, and time-series analysis. Convolutional Neural Networks (CNNs) are popular DNNs known for their ability to reduce input data preprocessing by scaling down the number of parameters, meaning not all input variables connect to subsequent layers. CNNs have found applications in solving real-world problems. In UBEM, deep learning is making a significant impact, particularly in areas where data is complex and unstructured. Nutkiewicz et al. proposed a hybrid model, combining CNNs with simulations to

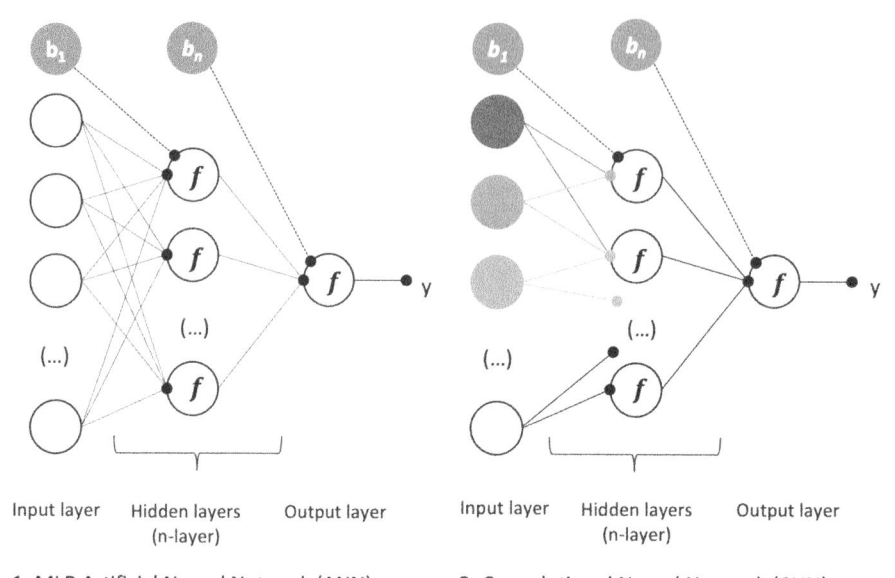

1. MLP Artificial Neural Network (ANN)

2. Convolutional Neural Network (CNN)

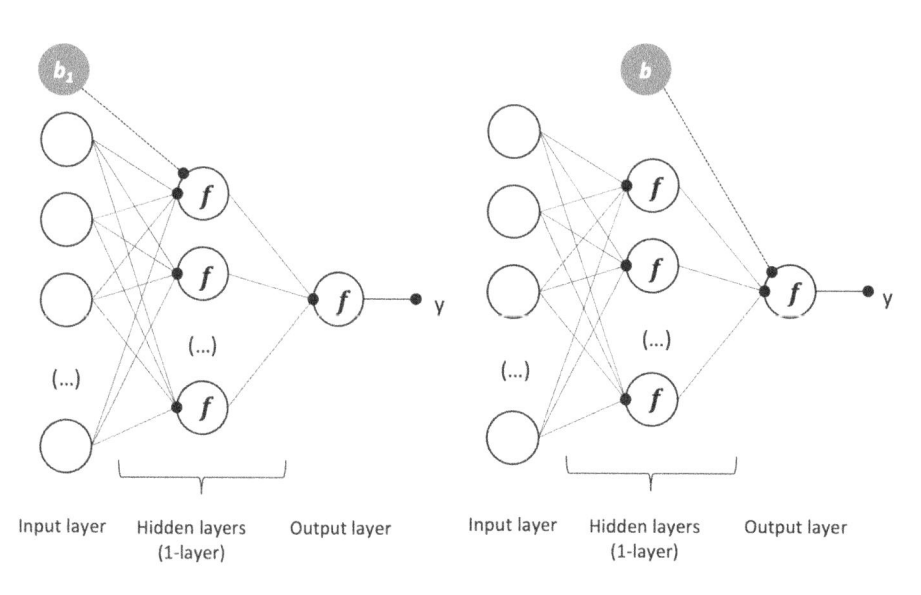

3. Extreme Learning Machine (ELM)

4. Radial Basis Function (RBF)

Figure 2.7 Morphological differences in Four Feedforward Neural Networks (ANN, CNN, ELM, RBF). Source: Abbasabadi and Ashayeri (2019).

incorporate microclimate effects into UEUM (Nutkiewicz, Yang, and Jain 2018; Nutkiewicz, Choi, and Jain 2021). In UBEM, deep learning is also increasingly employed for tasks such as image recognition in energy audits or processing sensor data from IoT devices in smart buildings. CNNs are employed for tasks such as analyzing images for energy audits, while RNNs are used to process time-series data, such as energy consumption records. Rahman et al. utilized RNN models for hourly energy use prediction, demonstrating their superior accuracy compared to regular MLP models at the individual building level (Rahman, Srikumar, and Smith 2018). Deep learning excels in pattern recognition, making it invaluable for understanding and optimizing energy use in urban buildings.

SVM (Cortes and Vapnik 1995) is a versatile ML model used for both nonlinear regression and classification tasks (Ahmad et al. 2014). It operates by defining a hyperplane in an N-dimensional space to classify data points. The ideal hyperplane is the one that maximizes the margin (street) between data classes through an iterative optimization process (see (Figure 2.8). SVM has been applied in predicting urban building operational energy use. Li

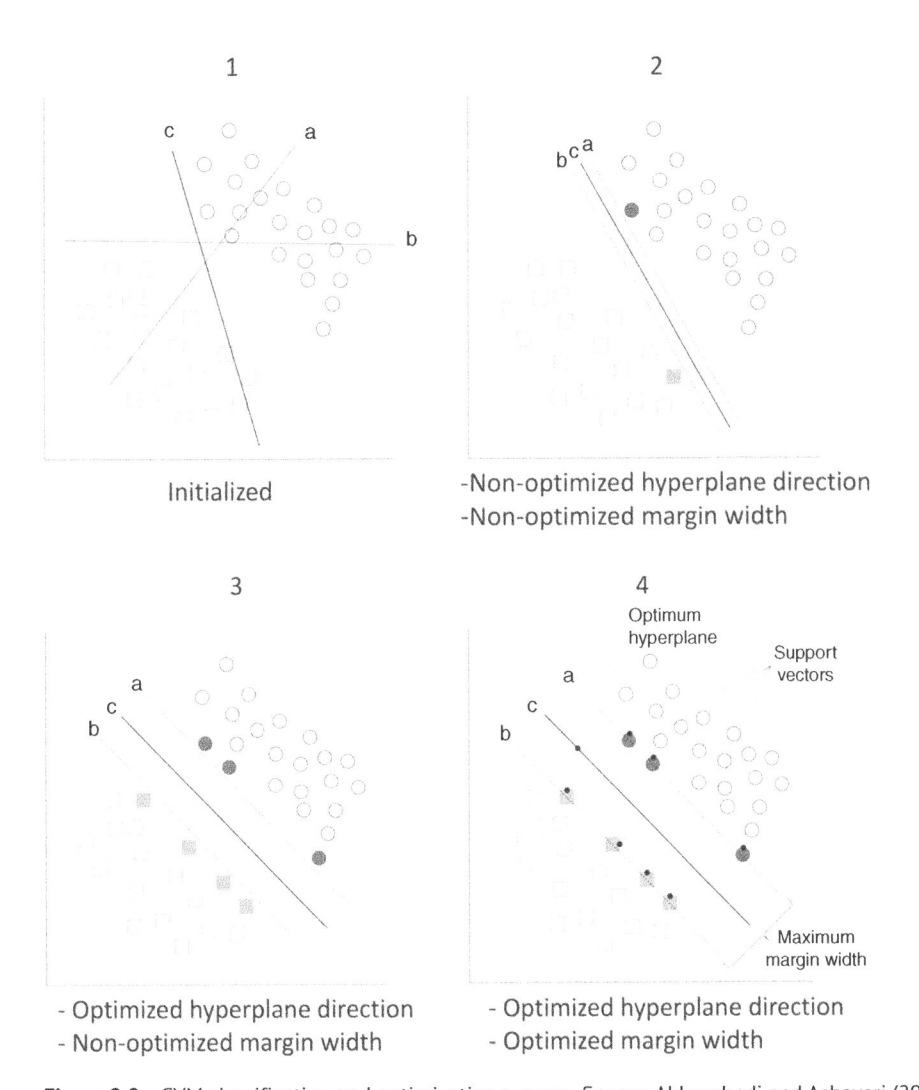

Figure 2.8 SVM classification and optimization process. Source: Abbasabadi and Ashayeri (2019).

et al. developed an enhanced SVM model by combining it with a genetic algorithm optimization and grid-searching to forecast energy use in a smart community (Li et al. 2017). Their results confirmed the accuracy of this hybrid SVM model compared to conventional SVMs. In regression tasks, SVM is referred to as Support Vector Regression (SVR) (Drucker et al. 1997).

Liu and Chen compared SVM and ANNs for energy use prediction, finding that SVM outperformed ANN methods (Liu and Chen 2013). Fernandez et al. tested AR, PR, ANN, and SVM algorithms for energy prediction; however, they found that ANNs and SVM, despite their complex configuration process, did not offer higher accuracy compared to other algorithms (Fernandez, Borges, and Penya 2011). Tso et al. used the CART model to predict electricity demand for various residential building types in Hong Kong, China, based on survey data, and the results favored the CART model over regression and MLP–ANN models (Tso and Yau 2007). Bogomolov et al. developed an energy demand predictive model for the Trentino province, Italy, incorporating user behavior dynamics. They employed a RF model on large-scale, time-series data to forecast daily mean and peak daily electricity consumption, with RFs significantly outperforming conventional baseline methods (Bogomolov et al. 2016).

In one study, a multivariate k-NN regression model was developed to predict electricity demand in the United Kingdom using time-series data, showcasing superior accuracy compared to traditional methods such as MLR (Al-Qahtani and Crone 2013). Another study developed a data-driven framework for UEUM tested in Chicago (Abbasabadi et al. 2019). Six ML algorithms, including MLR, NLR, RF, k-NN, CART, and ANN, were evaluated, with k-NN emerging as significantly more accurate, followed by CART and ANN. In another study, Valgaev et al. applied k-NN to forecast electricity consumption in urban buildings as part of the "Smart City Demo Aspern" project in Vienna, Austria (Valgaev, Kupzog, and Schmeck 2017). The k-NN forecaster demonstrated a notable 7% to 23% accuracy improvement for dormitories and schools, compared to existing Individual Load Profiles (ILPs) models. Housing sector predictions remained consistent (Figures 2.9 and 2.10).

Unsupervised Learning

Unsupervised learning operates with unlabeled data, making it a powerful tool for data exploration and pattern discovery. In this type, the algorithm's primary objective is to uncover hidden structures, clusters, or relationships within the data (Figure 2.11). Common techniques in unsupervised learning include clustering and dimensionality reduction. For example, KM and AHC are employed for clustering without response variables (Fernandez, Borges, and Penya 2011). Unsupervised learning techniques are particularly valuable in UBEM when the objective is to uncover hidden structures or patterns within a vast dataset. One of the key applications is clustering

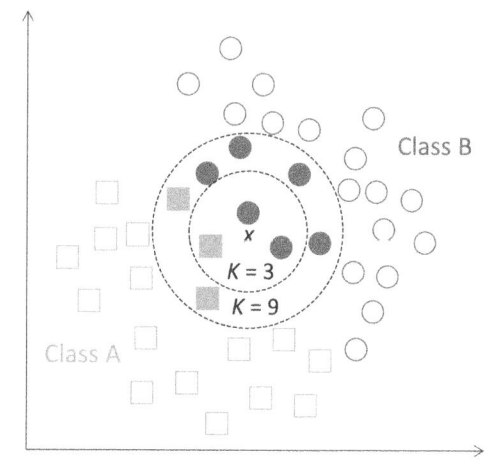

k-NN classification at location x

Figure 2.9 k-NN schematic for two classes with k = 3 and k = 9. Source: Abbasabadi and Ashayeri (2019).

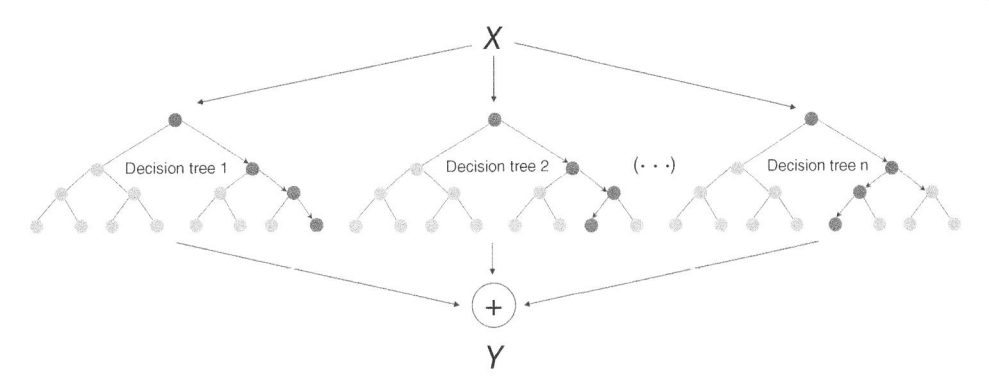

Figure 2.10 RDF schematic with *n* Trees. Source: Abbasabadi and Ashayeri (2019).

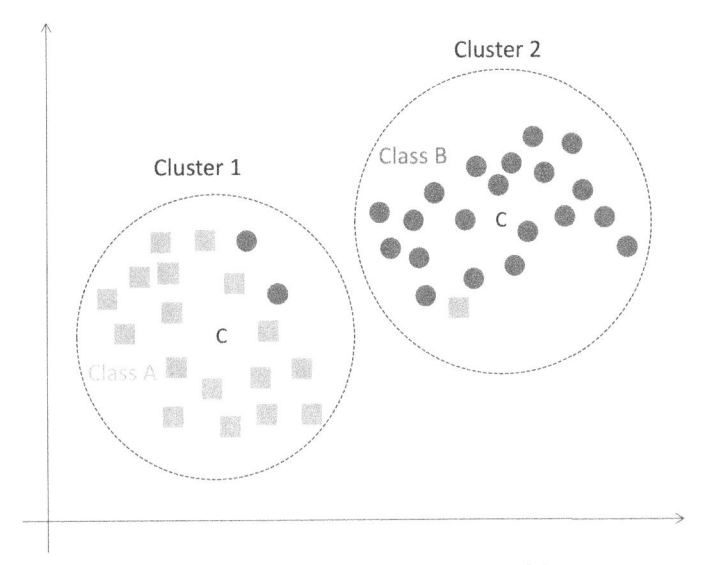

Figure 2.11 *k*-means clustering. Source: Abbasabadi and Ashayeri (2019).

similar buildings based on their energy consumption profiles. By grouping buildings with similar energy patterns, urban planners and retrofit teams can implement targeted energy-saving strategies. Additionally, dimensionality reduction, a technique within unsupervised learning, can help streamline the analysis of large and complex datasets in UBEM. It aids in simplifying the understanding of building energy performance by reducing data complexity and highlighting the most critical features.

Two widely used clustering models, KM (Macqueen, n.d.) and AHC (Johnson 1967), have found applications in UEUM. For example, the KM algorithm was applied to identify building archetypes representing groups of buildings with similar characteristics (Fonseca and Schlueter 2015). Gao et al. utilized KM for urban building energy benchmarking, using aggregated Commercial Buildings Energy Consumption Survey (CBECS) (2008) data conducted by the U.S. Energy Information Administration (EIA) to extract insights into common typologies among national commercial buildings (Gao and Malkawi 2014). AHC, on the other hand, constructs a hierarchical model by merging data into clusters through a bottom–up process, creating larger groups iteratively. Guillaumet et al. integrated the AHC model into an UBEM framework, focusing on generating building archetypes based on electricity consumption data from 883 single and multifamily buildings (Guillaumet et al. 2018). The results highlight that data-driven approaches, especially in data-rich scenarios, can offer more accurate results compared to deterministic methods.

Reinforcement Learning

Reinforcement learning is a fundamental paradigm in ML, alongside supervised and unsupervised learning. Reinforcement learning is a type of ML focused on decision-making and control. It is characterized by an agent that interacts with an environment and learns to make sequences of actions to maximize a cumulative reward (Figure 2.12). Reinforcement learning, though less commonly employed, serves as a valuable approach for acquiring the ability to perform effectively when faced with occasional reward or penalty signals (Fathi et al. 2020). In UBEM, reinforcement learning can be applied to develop adaptive control systems for building energy management. In urban buildings, energy consumption patterns fluctuate throughout the day due to factors such as occupancy and external conditions. Reinforcement learning offers potential for controlling energy consumption in modern intelligent buildings with various smart devices (Fu et al. 2022). Reinforcement learning can be employed to develop control systems that continuously optimize energy use by making decisions on heating, cooling, and lighting based on real-time environmental factors and occupancy patterns, resulting in energy-efficient operations. This dynamic approach not only improves energy efficiency but also reduces operational costs in urban building management.

In the context of future smart grids, where managing unpredictable local energy supply and demand poses significant challenges, precise energy prediction is vital for complex decision-making. A study by Chang et al. (2019) uses reinforcement learning, parametric modeling, and multivariate analysis to identify connections between design parameters and urban performance. This study addresses urban design's performance and relationships with a data-driven approach. The findings offer insights for creating a high-energy-performance campus in terms of both energy demand and supply. In another study by Mocanu et al. (2016), the authors explore two reinforcement learning algorithms to model building energy consumption. They enhance these algorithms with a Deep Belief Network (DBN) to handle continuous states. They tested the methods on a seven-year real database with hourly resolution and reported energy prediction accuracy improvement (91.42% in RMSE) when DBN preprocessing is employed, compared to equivalent methods without DBN. Another study by Vázquez-Canteli

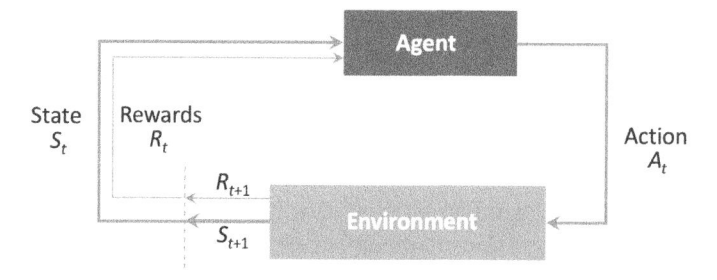

Figure 2.12 Reinforcement Learning.

et al. (2019) introduces an integrated simulation environment that combines CitySim, with TensorFlow, a platform for the implementation of ML algorithms to facilitate research into learning control algorithms for energy management in buildings. Two case studies are presented, demonstrating the potential for energy savings and demand response using this integrated approach. Another research by Pigott et al. (2022) introduces a multiagent reinforcement learning platform for smart grid energy management. It demonstrates how GridLearn can optimize voltage regulation in a network, reducing undervoltages and overvoltages by 34%. The platform balances grid-level goals with building owner comfort and privacy.

In summary, ML is increasingly vital in urban building energy studies. ML applications in UBEM must be tailored to problem nature. The integration of ML-based techniques has the potential to significantly enhance the accuracy of urban energy use predictions. These techniques leverage methods capable of capturing intricate, nonlinear patterns within real-world data, providing decision-makers with invaluable tools for urban energy modeling during both the planning and engineering phases. Effectively harnessing these advanced models, stakeholders can make more informed decisions, optimize resource allocation, and enhance overall energy efficiency within urban environments. However, it's important to acknowledge that there's no one-size-fits-all solution for optimizing ML-based UBEM; accuracy varies depending on problem modeling characteristics. In addition, data-driven models do come with limitations, particularly when confronted with insufficient or incomplete datasets. In such cases, the predictive capabilities of these models may be compromised. Therefore, while these advanced techniques offer substantial benefits, the availability and quality of data remain pivotal factors in realizing their full potential for urban energy modeling and decision-making processes. Addressing data limitations through data collection and preprocessing efforts is essential for ensuring the reliability and effectiveness of these AI-driven models in the context of urban energy management.

Machine Learning-Based Surrogate UBEM

ML-based surrogate modeling refers to the applications of ML techniques to create simplified and computationally efficient models that approximate the behavior of complex physics-based models in UBEM. Meta-models, or surrogate models, efficiently replace costly physics-based simulations in building energy analysis (Yong et al. 2019; Li et al. 2023). They approximate complex input–output relationships, striking a balance between computation and accuracy. These models establish the links between building design, environmental factors, and energy performance, with coefficients derived from statistical analyses of dynamic simulation outcomes. These models find application in uncertainty analysis, model calibration, sensitivity analysis, performance optimization, and predictive control within the building energy field. They are particularly useful when handling extensive simulations. Meta-models expedite these processes by replacing traditional models, aiding in dynamic building performance simulations and control. Optimization studies involve numerous parameters, necessitating extensive simulations. Meta-model-based optimization simplifies this by replacing complex simulations with simpler meta-model functions such as polynomials, reducing computational time while preserving accuracy. Some of the main challenges of current physics-based UBEM include computational intensity, scalability, extensive data requirements, and expertise requirements. ML-based surrogate modeling addresses these challenges.

Physics-based UBEM often involves solving complex mathematical equations and simulations, which can be both computationally expensive and time-consuming. This is a significant challenge, especially when dealing with large urban areas and a multitude of buildings, which often hinder the rapid analysis of numerous urban development scenarios. Surrogate models simplify the complex physical processes in UBEM, making them computationally efficient and much faster to run. This also allows for more efficient analysis of scenario. Surrogate modeling streamlines this process, rendering it significantly faster, more efficient, and cost-effective. This acceleration can be instrumental in guiding urban planners and policymakers in their decision-making processes. Moreover, physics-based models are not easily scalable to address the needs of rapidly growing urban areas and large building portfolios. While surrogate models can be designed to scale easily, making them suitable for use in large urban areas and with extensive building portfolios. They seamlessly adapt to the increasing complexity of urban environments, making them particularly suited for the challenges posed by rapidly expanding cities. In contrast, traditional physics-based models often struggle to accommodate this dynamism. In addition, physics-based UBEM relies on extensive data inputs, which can be challenging to collect and maintain. Surrogate models may require fewer input parameters and less detailed data, which can be advantageous in cases where comprehensive data is limited, making them adaptable to data-scarce contexts without compromising the quality of analyses.

For example, a study by Vazquez-Canteli et al. (2019) employs DNN as surrogate models to accelerate urban energy simulations. It covers 7860 buildings across various U.S. climates, training two DNNs to predict solar gains and thermal losses. These DNNs speed up computations by 2500 times while maintaining high accuracy ($R_2 = 0.85$). The applications include predicting energy demand under climate change and assessing building refurbishment effects. Another study by Thrampoulidis et al. (2021) focuses on creating a surrogate model for efficient building retrofit evaluations using ANNs to strike a balance between accuracy and computation time. This model was tested in Zurich, Switzerland, and compared to advanced building simulation tools. The surrogate model significantly reduces computational time, with retrofit solutions taking only 16.4 μs instead of 3.5 minutes. It maintains high accuracy, approximating retrofit costs and energy system selections, which can accelerate widespread retrofit adoption.

Another study by Li et al. (2023) introduces an ML-based approach for creating more accurate time-series meta-models in building energy analysis. This study by Li et al. (2023) recommends ensemble ML models for hourly energy analysis, including Cubist, gradient boosting machine, and stacking, enhanced by distributed lag models. In another study, Tardioli et al. (2020) presented a methodology for district-scale building energy model calibration using clustering and surrogate techniques. It addresses issues related to data uncertainty, grouping buildings, calibrating energy models, and computational efficiency. The method is validated using a dataset of 2646 buildings in Geneva, Switzerland, with energy consumption and intensity predictions showing accuracy within ±5% at the aggregated scale and within ±20% for approximately 70% of individual buildings.

Another research by Yong et al. (2019) focuses on creating meta-models for predicting building energy loads in diverse climate conditions. These meta-models replace computationally expensive simulations with simpler functions while maintaining accuracy. The meta-models were developed using simulations for various U.S. cities and validated against results from different U.S. and European cities, demonstrating their accuracy. Another study by Jia et al. (2022) explored ML-based meta-models for predicting cooling loads in high-rise residential district cooling in hot and humid climates. Four ML models are evaluated: MLR, SVR, ANN, and eXtreme Gradient Boosting. Sensitivity analysis is used to identify critical independent variables. The study finds that an ANN model with specific parameters outperforms others in predicting monthly energy use intensity for testing cases and requires a minimum of eight independent variables. In another study by Zhang et al. (2022), a data-driven framework is introduced, utilizing ML, optimization, and multi-criteria decision-making for surrogate retrofit. This framework employs ANN for energy performance prediction of retrofit options, optimizing ANN structure and hyperparameters using a genetic algorithm. The approach combines energy consumption with environmental and economic data, identifying Pareto optimal solutions. The framework was tested on residential buildings in British Columbia, Canada.

Traditional calibration methods are time-consuming, and existing automatic calibration techniques are computationally expensive. Another study introduces a cost-effective methodology for auto-calibrating urban building energy models in large building portfolios (Nagpal et al. 2019). This research proposes a data-driven approach using statistical surrogate models, significantly accelerating the calibration process while maintaining accuracy when envelope data is available. Bayesian methods, such as Bayesian neural networks and Gaussian process models, help quantify uncertainty with surrogate energy models, allowing for more accurate predictions. This study by Westermann and Evins (2021) employs Bayesian deep learning to create uncertainty-aware building energy surrogate models. It quantifies and reduces uncertainty in approximating high-fidelity engineering simulations, reducing errors by up to 30%. Two Bayesian models are trained to emulate complex building energy performance simulations with promising results.

Moreover, traditional UBEM is complex and requires domain expertise and specialized knowledge to accurately set up and run the models. This expertise can be a barrier to widespread adoption. Surrogate models are often more user-friendly and require less expertise to set up, operate, and navigate UBEM. Therefore, it democratizes the urban planning and design processes, making these critical activities more accessible to a broader range of professionals. This broader inclusion of expertise can lead to more innovative and sustainable urban solutions. A study by Araujo et al. (2022) addresses the challenges of time-consuming and expertise-intensive UBEM for urban energy performance analysis via an approach integrating Algorithmic Design, UBEM, and ML surrogate models to automate and accelerate simulations. They tested their method in a Lisbon case study, the method outperforms traditional UBEM approaches in terms of speed while maintaining acceptable accuracy.

In summary, ML-based surrogate modeling in UBEM offers a pragmatic solution to make energy modeling more efficient, accessible, and applicable to a broader range of urban scenarios. It allows for evidence-based, streamlined, and faster decision-making, optimization of energy consumption, and more sustainable urban development.

Conclusion

In conclusion, the integration of ML within UBEM represents a promising frontier for enhancing urban energy management and understanding citywide energy performance. The applications of ML techniques in UBEM, including predictive energy consumption modeling and optimization, exemplify the transformative capabilities these technologies bring to the field. This chapter has provided a comprehensive overview of current UBEM methods, highlighting their strengths and limitations while also addressing the potential challenges and opportunities presented by the incorporation of ML. Moreover, we introduced a hybrid UBEM approach that amalgamates data-driven and physics-based simulations, serving as a beacon of innovation to bolster modeling accuracy and mitigate uncertainties in capturing urban energy use. As cities strive to become more sustainable and energy-efficient, the synergy between ML and UBEM will play a pivotal role in advancing urban energy management practices, shaping the cities of the future.

References

Abbasabadi, N. and Ashayeri, M. (2019). Urban Energy Use Modeling Methods and Tools: A Review and an Outlook. *Building and Environment* 161 (August): 106270. https://doi.org/10.1016/j.buildenv.2019.106270.

Abbasabadi, N., Ashayeri, M., Azari, R. et al. (2019). An Integrated Data-Driven Framework for Urban Energy Use Modeling (UEUM). *Applied Energy* 253 (November): 113550. https://doi.org/10.1016/j.apenergy.2019.113550.

Ahmad, A.S., Hassan, M.Y., Abdullah, M.P. et al. (2014). A Review on Applications of ANN and SVM for Building Electrical Energy Consumption Forecasting. *Renewable and Sustainable Energy Reviews* 33 (May): 102–109. https://doi.org/10.1016/J.RSER.2014.01.069.

Al-Qahtani, F.H. and Crone, S.F. (2013). Multivariate K-Nearest Neighbour Regression for Time Series Data – A Novel Algorithm for Forecasting UK Electricity Demand. In: *The 2013 International Joint Conference on Neural Networks (IJCNN)*, 1–8. Dallas, TX, USA: IEEE https://doi.org/10.1109/IJCNN.2013.6706742.

Araujo, G., Santos, L., Leitão, A., and Gomes, R. (2022). *AD-Based Surrogate Models for Simulation and Optimization of Large Urban Areas*POST-CARBON - Proceedings of the 27th CAADRIA Conference, Sydney, 9–15 April 2022 (ed. J. van Ameijde, N. Gardner, K.H. Hyun, et al.), 689–698. https://doi.org/10.52842/conf.caadria.2022.2.689.

Bianco, V., Manca, O., and Nardini, S. (2009). Electricity Consumption Forecasting in Italy Using Linear Regression Models. *Energy* 34 (9): 1413–1421. https://doi.org/10.1016/j.energy.2009.06.034.

Biljecki, F., Stoter, J., Ledoux, H. et al. (2015). Applications of 3D City Models: State of the Art Review. *ISPRS International Journal of Geo-Information* 4 (4): 4. https://doi.org/10.3390/ijgi4042842.

Bishop, C.M. (1995). *Neural Networks for Pattern Recognition.* Oxford, New York: Clarendon Press; Oxford University Press.

Bogomolov, A., Lepri, B., Larcher, R. et al. (2016). Energy Consumption Prediction Using People Dynamics Derived from Cellular Network Data. *EPJ Data Science* 5 (1): https://doi.org/10.1140/epjds/s13688-016-0075-3.

Davila, C.C., Reinhart, C.F., and Bemis, J.L. (2016). Modeling Boston: A Workflow for the Efficient Generation and Maintenance of Urban Building Energy Models from Existing Geospatial Datasets. *Energy* 117 (December): 237–250. https://doi.org/10.1016/J.ENERGY.2016.10.057.

Chang, S., Saha, N., Castro-Lacouture, D., and Yang, P.P.-J. (2019). Multivariate Relationships between Campus Design Parameters and Energy Performance Using Reinforcement Learning and Parametric Modeling. *Applied Energy* 249 (September): 253–264. https://doi.org/10.1016/j.apenergy.2019.04.109.

Chen, Y., Hong, T., and Piette, M.A. (2017). Automatic Generation and Simulation of Urban Building Energy Models Based on City Datasets for City-Scale Building Retrofit Analysis. *Applied Energy* 205 (April): 323–335. https://doi.org/10.1016/j.apenergy.2017.07.128.

Cheng, Xi, Bohdan Khomtchouk, Norman Matloff, and Pete Mohanty. 2018. "Polynomial Regression As an Alternative to Neural Nets," June.

Cortes, C. and Vapnik, V. (1995). Support-Vector Networks. *Machine Learning* 20 (3): 273–297. https://doi.org/10.1007/BF00994018.

Dagnely, P., Ruette, T., Tourwé, T. et al. (2015). Predicting Hourly Energy Consumption. In: *Can Regression Modeling Improve on an Autoregressive Baseline?* 105–122. Cham: Springer https://doi.org/10.1007/978-3-319-27430-0_8.

Davila, C.C. and Reinhart, C. (2011). *Urban Energy Lifecycle: An Analytical Framework to Evaluate the Embodied Energy Use of Urban Developments*. Harvard University, Cambridge, MA 02138, United States Masschusetts Institute of Technology, Cambridge, MA 02139, United States, 1280–1287.

Deng, H., Fannon, D., and Eckelman, M.J. (2018). Predictive Modeling for US Commercial Building Energy Use: A Comparison of Existing Statistical and Machine Learning Algorithms Using CBECS Microdata. *Energy and Buildings* 163: 34–43. https://doi.org/10.1016/j.enbuild.2017.12.031.

Dogan, Timur, and Christoph Reinhart. 2013. "Automated Conversion of Architectural Massing Models into Thermal 'Shoebox' Models."

Drucker, H., Drucker, H., Burges, C.J.C. et al. (1997). Support Vector Regression Machines. *Advances in Neural Information Processing Systems 9* (9): 155–161.

Fathi, S., Srinivasan, R., Fenner, A., and Fathi, S. (2020). Machine Learning Applications in Urban Building Energy Performance Forecasting: A Systematic Review. *Renewable and Sustainable Energy Reviews* 133 (November): 110287. https://doi.org/10.1016/j.rser.2020.110287.

Fernandez, I., Borges, C.E., and Penya, Y.K. (2011). Efficient Building Load Forecasting. *Etfa* 2011: 1–8. https://doi.org/10.1109/ETFA.2011.6059103.

Fonseca, J.A. and Schlueter, A. (2015). Integrated Model for Characterization of Spatiotemporal Building Energy Consumption Patterns in Neighborhoods and City Districts. *Applied Energy* 142 (March): 247–265. https://doi.org/10.1016/j.apenergy.2014.12.068.

Fu, Q., Han, Z., Chen, J. et al. (2022). Applications of Reinforcement Learning for Building Energy Efficiency Control: A Review. *Journal of Building Engineering* 50 (June): 104165. https://doi.org/10.1016/j.jobe.2022.104165.

Gao, X. and Malkawi, A. (2014). A New Methodology for Building Energy Performance Benchmarking: An Approach Based on Intelligent Clustering Algorithm. *Energy and Buildings* 84 (December): 607–616. https://doi.org/10.1016/j.enbuild.2014.08.030.

Guillaumet, M.P., Borges, P., Rosas-Casals, M., and Travesset-Baro, O. (2018). Building Archetypes in Urban Energy Models. A Comparative Case Study of Deterministic and Statistical Methods in Andorra. In: *Conference: USIM 2018 - Urban Energy Simulation, at the University of Strathclyde Technology and Innovation Centre, 99 George St, Glasgow G1 1RD*, 10. https://www.researchgate.net/publication/329529033.

Feng, G., Huang, G.-B., Lin, Q., and Gay, R. (2009). Error Minimized Extreme Learning Machine With Growth of Hidden Nodes and Incremental Learning. *IEEE Transactions on Neural Networks* 20 (8): 1352–1357. https://doi.org/10.1109/TNN.2009.2024147.

Happle, G., Fonseca, J.A., and Schlueter, A. (2018). A Review on Occupant Behavior in Urban Building Energy Models. *Energy and Buildings* 174 (September): 276–292. https://doi.org/10.1016/J.ENBUILD.2018.06.030.

Heidarinejad, M., Mattise, N., Dahlhausen, M. et al. (2017). Demonstration of Suggest Su. *Energy and Buildings* 156 (December): 17–28. https://doi.org/10.1016/J.ENBUILD.2017.08.086.

Hong, S.-M., Paterson, G., Mumovic, D., and Steadman, P. (2014). Improved Benchmarking Comparability for Energy Consumption in Schools. *Building Research & Information* 42 (1): 47–61. https://doi.org/10.1080/09613218.2013.814746.

Howard, B., Parshall, L., Thompson, J. et al. (2012). Spatial Distribution of Urban Building Energy Consumption by End Use. *Energy and Buildings* 45: 141–151. https://doi.org/10.1016/j.enbuild.2011.10.061.

Hsu, D. (2015). Identifying Key Variables and Interactions in Statistical Models of Building Energy Consumption Using Regularization. *Energy* 83 (April): 144–155. https://doi.org/10.1016/J.ENERGY.2015.02.008.

Huang, G.-B., Zhu, Q.-Y., and Siew, C.-K. (2006). Extreme Learning Machine: Theory and Applications. *Neurocomputing* 70 (1–3): 489–501. https://doi.org/10.1016/j.neucom.2005.12.126.

IPCC (2014). *Climate Change 2014: Synthesis Report. Contribution of Working Groups I, II and III to the Fifth Assessment Report of the Intergovernmental Panel on Climate Change*. Geneva, Switzerland: *IPCC* https://doi.org/10.1017/CBO9781107415324.

Jia, B., Hou, D., Kamal, A. et al. (2022). Developing Machine-Learning Meta-Models for High-Rise Residential District Cooling in Hot and Humid Climate. *Journal of Building Performance Simulation* 15 (4): 553–573. https://doi.org/10.1080/19401493.2021.2001573.

Johnson, S.C. (1967). Hierarchical Clustering Schemes. *Psychometrika* 32 (3): 241–254. https://doi.org/10.1007/BF02289588.

Norman, J., MacLean, M. ASCE, H.L., and Kennedy, C.A. (2006). Comparing High and Low Residential Density: Life-Cycle Analysis of Energy Use and Greenhouse Gas Emissions. *Journal of Urban Planning and Development* 2006 (March): 10–21. https://doi.org/10.1061/(ASCE)0733-9488(2006)132.

Kavgic, M., Mavrogianni, A., Mumovic, D. et al. (2010). A Review of Bottom-up Building Stock Models for Energy Consumption in the Residential Sector. *Building and Environment* 45 (7): 1683–1697. https://doi.org/10.1016/J.BUILDENV.2010.01.021.

Keirstead, J., Jennings, M., and Sivakumar, A. (2012). A Review of Urban Energy System Models: Approaches, Challenges and Opportunities. *Renewable and Sustainable Energy Reviews* 16 (6): 3847–3866. https://doi.org/10.1016/j.rser.2012.02.047.

Kontokosta, C.E. (2012). Predicting building energy efficiency using New York City benchmarking data. In: *Proceedings of the 2012 ACEEE Summer Study on Energy Efficiency in Buildings, Washington, DC, American Council for an Energy-Efficient Economy*.

Kontokosta, C., Bonczak, B., and Duer-Balkind, M. (2016). DataIQ–a machine learning approach to anomaly detection for energy performance data quality and reliability. In: *Proceedings of the ACEEE*.

Kontokosta, C.E. and Tull, C. (2017). A Data-Driven Predictive Model of City-Scale Energy Use in Buildings. *Applied Energy* 197: 303–317. https://doi.org/10.1016/j.apenergy.2017.04.005.

Kuusela, P., Norros, I., Weiss, R., and Sorasalmi, T. (2015). Practical Lognormal Framework for Household Energy Consumption Modeling. *Energy and Buildings* 108 (December): 223–235. https://doi.org/10.1016/J.ENBUILD.2015.09.008.

Leach, L.F., Henson, R.K., Holmes Finch, W. et al. (2007). Multiple Linear Regression Viewpoints. *Multiple Linear Regression Viewpoints* 33 (1): http://www.glmj.org/archives/MLRV_2007_33_1.pdf#page=4.

Li, G., Tian, W., Zhang, H., and Fu, X. (2023). A Novel Method of Creating Machine Learning-Based Time Series Meta-Models for Building Energy Analysis. *Energy and Buildings* 281 (February): 112752. https://doi.org/10.1016/j.enbuild.2022.112752.

Li, Q., Quan, S.J., Augenbroe, G. et al. (2015). Building Energy Modelling at Urban Scale: Integration of Reduced Order Energy Model With Geographical Information. In: *14th Conference of International Building Performance Simulation Association*, 190–199. Hyderabad, India: http://www.ibpsa.org/proceedings/BS2015/p2706.pdf.

Li, Y., Wen, Z., Cao, Y. et al. (2017). A Combined Forecasting Approach with Model Self-Adjustment for Renewable Generations and Energy Loads in Smart Community. *Energy* 129 (June): 216–227. https://doi.org/10.1016/j.energy.2017.04.032.

Lin, B. and Liu, H. (2015). China's Building Energy Efficiency and Urbanization. *Energy and Buildings* 86 (January): 356–365. https://doi.org/10.1016/j.enbuild.2014.09.069.

Liu, D. and Chen, Q. (2013). Prediction of Building Lighting Energy Consumption Based on Support Vector Regression. In: *2013 9th Asian Control Conference (ASCC)*, 1–5. IEEE https://doi.org/10.1109/ASCC.2013.6606376.

Macqueen, J. (n.d.). *Some Methods For Classification and Analysis Of Multivariate Observations, Multivariate Observations*, vol. 17.

Mahesh, Batta. 2019. *Machine Learning Algorithms - A Review*. https://doi.org/10.21275/ART20203995.

Marasco, D.E. and Kontokosta, C.E. (2016). Applications of Machine Learning Methods to Identifying and Predicting Building Retrofit Opportunities. *Energy and Buildings* 128: 431–441. https://doi.org/10.1016/j.enbuild.2016.06.092.

Mastrucci, A., Baume, O., Stazi, F. et al. (2014). A GIS-Based Approach To Estimate Energy Savings and Indoor Thermal Comfort For Urban Housing Stock Retrofitting. In: *Fifth German-Austrian IBPSA Conference (BauSIM 2014), Aachen, Germany*, 22–24.

Mocanu, E., Nguyen, P.H., Kling, W.L., and Gibescu, M. (2016). Unsupervised Energy Prediction in a Smart Grid Context Using Reinforcement Cross-Building Transfer Learning. *Energy and Buildings* 116 (March): 646–655. https://doi.org/10.1016/j.enbuild.2016.01.030.

Montáns, F.J., Chinesta, F., Gómez-Bombarelli, R., and Nathan Kutz, J. (2019). Data-Driven Modeling and Learning in Science and Engineering. *Comptes Rendus Mécanique* 347 (11): 845–855. https://doi.org/10.1016/j.crme.2019.11.009.

Mostafavi, N., Farzinmoghadam, M., and Hoque, S. (2017). Urban Residential Energy Consumption Modeling in the Integrated Urban Metabolism Analysis Tool (IUMAT). *Building and Environment* 114 (March): 429–444. https://doi.org/10.1016/J.BUILDENV.2016.12.035.

Nagpal, S., Mueller, C., Aijazi, A., and Reinhart, C.F. (2019). A Methodology for Auto-Calibrating Urban Building Energy Models Using Surrogate Modeling Techniques. *Journal of Building Performance Simulation* 12 (1): 1–16. https://doi.org/10.1080/19401493.2018.1457722.

Nutkiewicz, A., Choi, B., and Jain, R.K. (2021). Exploring the Influence of Urban Context on Building Energy Retrofit Performance: A Hybrid Simulation and Data-Driven Approach. *Advances in Applied Energy* 3 (August): 100038. https://doi.org/10.1016/j.adapen.2021.100038.

Nutkiewicz, A., Yang, Z., and Jain, R.K. (2018). Data-Driven Urban Energy Simulation (DUE-S): A Framework for Integrating Engineering Simulation and Machine Learning Methods in a Multi-Scale Urban Energy Modeling Workflow. *Applied Energy* 225 (January): 1176–1189. https://doi.org/10.1016/j.apenergy.2018.05.023.

Olden, J.D., Joy, M.K., and Death, R.G. (2004). An Accurate Comparison of Methods for Quantifying Variable Importance in Artificial Neural Networks Using Simulated Data. *Ecological Modelling* 178 (3–4): 389–397. https://doi.org/10.1016/j.ecolmodel.2004.03.013.

Papadopoulos, S., Azar, E., Woon, W.-L., and Kontokosta, C.E. (2018). Evaluation of Tree-Based Ensemble Learning Algorithms for Building Energy Performance Estimation. *Journal of Building Performance Simulation* 11 (3): 322–332. https://doi.org/10.1080/19401493.2017.1354919.

Park, S.K., Moon, H.J., Min, K.C. et al. (2018). Application of a Multiple Linear Regression and an Artificial Neural Network Model for the Heating Performance Analysis and Hourly Prediction of a Large-Scale Ground Source Heat Pump System. *Energy and Buildings* 165: 206–215. https://doi.org/10.1016/j.enbuild.2018.01.029.

Paula Guillaumet, M., Rosas-Casals, M., and Travesset-Baro, O. (2018). Building Archetypes in Urban Energy Models. A Comparative Case Study of Deterministic and Statistical Methods in Andorra. In: *Conference: USIM 2018 - Urban Energy Simulation, at the University of Strathclyde Technology and Innovation Centre, 99 George St, Glasgow G1 1RD*.

Pigott, A., Crozier, C., Baker, K., and Nagy, Z. (2022). GridLearn: Multiagent Reinforcement Learning for Grid-Aware Building Energy Management. *Electric Power Systems Research* 213 (December): 108521. https://doi.org/10.1016/j.epsr.2022.108521.

Prataviera, E., Vivian, J., Lombardo, G., and Zarrella, A. (2022). Evaluation of the Impact of Input Uncertainty on Urban Building Energy Simulations Using Uncertainty and Sensitivity Analysis. *Applied Energy* 311 (April): 118691. https://doi.org/10.1016/j.apenergy.2022.118691.

Rahman, A., Srikumar, V., and Smith, A.D. (2018). Predicting Electricity Consumption for Commercial and Residential Buildings Using Deep Recurrent Neural Networks. *Applied Energy* 212 (February): 372–385. https://doi.org/10.1016/j.apenergy.2017.12.051.

Reinhart, C.F. and Davila, C.C. (2016). Urban Building Energy Modeling – A Review of a Nascent Field. *Building and Environment* 97 (February): 196–202. https://doi.org/10.1016/J.BUILDENV.2015.12.001.

Robinson, C., Dilkina, B., Zhang, W. et al. (2017). Machine Learning Approaches for Estimating Commercial Building Energy Consumption. *Applied Energy* 208 (May): 889–904. https://doi.org/10.1016/j.apenergy.2017.09.060.

Rosenblatt, F. (1958). The Perceptron: A Probabilistic Model for Information Storage and Organization in the Brain. *Psychological Review* 65 (6): 386–408. https://doi.org/10.1037/h0042519.

Sajjadi, S., Shamshirband, S., Alizamir, M. et al. (2016). Extreme Learning Machine for Prediction of Heat Load in District Heating Systems. *Energy and Buildings* 122 (June): 222–227. https://doi.org/10.1016/j.enbuild.2016.04.021.

Schiefelbein, J., Rudnick, J., Scholl, A. et al. (2019). Automated Urban Energy System Modeling and Thermal Building Simulation Based on OpenStreetMap Data Sets. *Building and Environment* 149 (February): 630–639. https://doi.org/10.1016/j.buildenv.2018.12.025.

Shamsi, M.H., O'Grady, W., Ali, U., and O'Donnell, J. (2017). A Generalization Approach for Reduced Order Modelling of Commercial Buildings. *Energy Procedia* 122 (September): 901–906. https://doi.org/10.1016/J.EGYPRO.2017.07.401.

Shorrock, L.D. and Dunster, J.E. (1997). The Physically-Based Model BREHOMES and Its Use in Deriving Scenarios for the Energy Use and Carbon Dioxide Emissions of the UK Housing Stock. *Energy Policy* 25 (12): 1027–1037. https://doi.org/10.1016/S0301-4215(97)00130-4.

Silva, M.C., Horta, I.M., Leal, V., and Oliveira, V. (2017). A Spatially-Explicit Methodological Framework Based on Neural Networks to Assess the Effect of Urban Form on Energy Demand. *Applied Energy* 202: 386–398. https://doi.org/10.1016/j.apenergy.2017.05.113.

Sohn, M.D. and Dunn, L.N. (2019). Exploratory Analysis of Energy Use Across Building Types and Geographic Regions in the United States. *Frontiers in Built Environment* 5 (September): 105. https://doi.org/10.3389/fbuil.2019.00105.

Sola, A., Corchero, C., Salom, J., and Sanmarti, M. (2018). Simulation Tools to Build Urban-Scale Energy Models: A Review. *Energies* 11 (12): 3269–3269. https://doi.org/10.3390/en11123269.

Sun, Y., Heo, Y., Tan, M. et al. (2014). Uncertainty Quantification of Microclimate Variables in Building Energy Models. *Journal of Building Performance Simulation* 7 (1): 17–32. https://doi.org/10.1080/19401493.2012.757368.

Swan, L.G. and Ismet Ugursal, V. (2009). Modeling of End-Use Energy Consumption in the Residential Sector: A Review of Modeling Techniques. *Renewable and Sustainable Energy Reviews* 13 (8): 1819–1835. https://doi.org/10.1016/j.rser.2008.09.033.

Tardioli, G., Narayan, A., Kerrigan, R. et al. (2020). A Methodology for Calibration of Building Energy Models at District Scale Using Clustering and Surrogate Techniques. *Energy and Buildings* 226 (November): 110309. https://doi.org/10.1016/j.enbuild.2020.110309.

Thrampoulidis, E., Mavromatidis, G., Lucchi, A., and Orehounig, K. (2021). A Machine Learning-Based Surrogate Model to Approximate Optimal Building Retrofit Solutions. *Applied Energy* 281 (January): 116024. https://doi.org/10.1016/j.apenergy.2020.116024.

Tso, G.K.F. and Yau, K.K.W. (2007). Predicting Electricity Energy Consumption: A Comparison of Regression Analysis, Decision Tree and Neural Networks. *Energy* 32 (9): 1761–1768. https://doi.org/10.1016/j.energy.2006.11.010.

Valgaev, O., Kupzog, F., and Schmeck, H. (2017). Building Power Demand Forecasting Using K-Nearest Neighbours Model – Practical Application in Smart City Demo Aspern Project. *CIRED - Open Access Proceedings Journal* 2017 (1): 1601–1604. https://doi.org/10.1049/oap-cired.2017.0419.

Vazquez-Canteli, J., Demir, A.D., Brown, J., and Nagy, Z. (2019). Deep Neural Networks as Surrogate Models for Urban Energy Simulations. *Journal of Physics: Conference Series* 1343 (1): 012002. https://doi.org/10.1088/1742-6596/1343/1/012002.

Vázquez-Canteli, J.R., Ulyanin, S., Kämpf, J., and Nagy, Z. (2019). Fusing TensorFlow with Building Energy Simulation for Intelligent Energy Management in Smart Cities. *Sustainable Cities and Society* 45 (February): 243–257. https://doi.org/10.1016/j.scs.2018.11.021.

Westermann, P. and Evins, R. (2021). Using Bayesian Deep Learning Approaches for Uncertainty-Aware Building Energy Surrogate Models. *Energy and AI* 3 (March): 100039. https://doi.org/10.1016/j.egyai.2020.100039.

Wong, S.L., Wan, K.K.W., and Lam, T.N.T. (2010). Artificial Neural Networks for Energy Analysis of Office Buildings with Daylighting. *Applied Energy* 87 (2): 551–557. https://doi.org/10.1016/j.apenergy.2009.06.028.

Yong, S.-G., Kim, J., Cho, J., and Koo, J. (2019). Meta-Models for Building Energy Loads at an Arbitrary Location. *Journal of Building Engineering* 25 (September): 100823. https://doi.org/10.1016/j.jobe.2019.100823.

Yu, D. (2018). A Two-Step Approach to Forecasting City-Wide Building Energy Demand. *Energy and Buildings* 160: 1–9. https://doi.org/10.1016/j.enbuild.2017.11.063.

Zhang, H., Feng, H., Hewage, K., and Arashpour, M. (2022). Artificial Neural Network for Predicting Building Energy Performance: A Surrogate Energy Retrofits Decision Support Framework. *Buildings* 12 (6): 829. https://doi.org/10.3390/buildings12060829.

3

A Hybrid Physics-Based Machine Learning Approach for Integrated Energy and Exposure Modeling

Mehdi Ashayeri[1] and Narjes Abbasabadi[2]

[1] *School of Architecture, College of Arts and Media, Southern Illinois University Carbondale, Carbondale, IL, USA*
[2] *Department of Architecture, School of Architecture, College of Built Environments, University of Washington, Seattle, WA, USA*

Introduction

According to the National Human Activity Pattern Survey (NHAPS), in the United States, people spend about 87% of their time indoors (Klepeis et al. 2001). Indoor spaces are required to ensure health and comfort for the occupants, ensuring sustainable built-environment goals. Heating, ventilating, and air conditioning (HVAC) systems are used to provide thermally comfortable conditions and maintain "better" indoor air quality (IAQ) for occupant health (Dutton et al. 2013). According to the U.S. Environmental Protection Agency (EPA), IAQ "refers to the air quality within and around buildings and structures, especially as it relates to the health and comfort of building occupants" (US EPA 2014). The HVAC systems, however, contribute to 39% of the overall building energy consumption (Annual Energy Review 2011 2012); and cooling and ventilation systems account for 31% of the end-use energy in the U.S. commercial building stock (Use of Energy Explained-Energy Use in Commercial Buildings 2018). Natural ventilation (NV), as a passive strategy, which often is used to reduce cooling and ventilation energy loads for office buildings, can maintain occupants' health and productivity by bringing in the ambient fresh air. The performance of an NV-operated building, however, highly depends on the building context. The lack of proven approaches to understanding the impacts of the context in the NV-design process (Emmerich and Axley 2001; Ashayeri and Abbasabadi 2022) prohibits making a proper decision at the early stage design.

For example, exposure to ambient particulate pollution equal to or less than 2.5 μm in aerodynamic diameter (PM2.5) plays a major role in adverse human health risks (WHO | Air Pollution 2019; Cohen et al. 2017) . Further, the direct correlations between long-term exposure to PM2.5 concentrations and mortality rates from airborne viruses such as SARS-CoV2 are evident (Wu et al. 2020; Chakrabarty et al. 2021; Mendy et al. 2021). Therefore, the magnitude of PM2.5 concentrations within and around buildings can be considered an indicator for assessing the healthiness of built environments, particularly in the design of naturally ventilated buildings. However, the lack of high-granular intraurban environmental data, both spatially and temporarily, prohibits evaluation of the impacts of PM2.5 concentrations in the proper design of buildings, and the available workflows are computationally too extensive.

Artificial Intelligence in Performance-Driven Design: Theories, Methods, and Tools, First Edition.
Edited by Narjes Abbasabadi and Mehdi Ashayeri.
©2024 John Wiley & Sons Inc. Published 2024 by John Wiley & Sons Inc.

Improper design of naturally ventilated systems causes pervasive occupants' exposure to PM2.5 pollution, contributing to certain chronic diseases (Suh et al. 2000) (e.g. respiratory-cardiovascular (Weber et al. 2016), and kidney (Bowe et al. 2018) diseases) particularly when polluted outdoor air inhaled. In addition, the impacts become escalated in buildings located in dense urban areas (Tong et al. 2016a,b) and in urban major roadway and highway environments (Tong et al. 2012), where the PM2.5 concentrations are usually above the standard levels. Indeed, concentrations of outdoor-origin pollutants indoors are unavoidable in NV-operated buildings because no filters are installed at openings (Ben-David and Waring 2016). In addition, these buildings are often blamed for their inconsistent performance due to weather variations, such as inconsistent wind speed and direction (Yang and Zhao 2012; Rong et al. 2015), and seasonal and severe weather conditions (Shi et al. 2018). Hence, the building's immediate context can act as a pivotal determinant for designing healthy and energy-efficient buildings that need to be well-investigated throughout the early stage design. Recent studies illustrate significant discrepancies in the energy-saving potentials (ESP) for evaluation of NV-operated buildings when outdoor pollution is taken into account (e.g. Tong et al. 2016b); however, the current studies have relied only on general weather data (e.g. wind speed) consistent for the entire city. The limitation primarily stems from lack of an effective physics-based approach to portray local environmental profiles at high-granular spatial and temporal intervals.

As data is becoming more accessible along with advances in big data initiatives and evolution in computational modeling approaches such as machine learning (ML) techniques, a data-driven approach (Aelenei et al. 2016; Bibri 2021) can be developed to fill in some of those gaps. These techniques have the potential to be applied for obtaining a faster and deeper understanding of urban context dynamics for designing energy-efficient and healthy built environments (Abbasabadi and Ashayeri 2019; Luitjohan et al. 2022). For example, a study by Ashayeri et al. (2021) demonstrates the high level of correlations between urban mobility patterns and dynamics of local PM2.5 concentrations. Yet, limited studies have applied urban big data and ML frameworks to conventional physics-based design decision-support workflows, particularly for context-sensitive, healthy, and energy-efficient design objectives. This can be achieved if urban explanatory factors are properly identified and effectively connected to the current building assessment workflows (Abbasabadi et al. 2019).

According to the status quo of ESP studies for NV systems, Computational Fluid Dynamics (CFD) is the most reliable approach for localizing airflow behaviors around buildings (Ai and Mak 2018; Shirzadi et al. 2018). Existing studies on CFD simulations in the early design stages are usually performed for very limited time intervals due to high computational demands in executing time-dependent (transient) simulations. Most recently, the data-driven approach, particularly ML techniques, such as artificial neural networks (ANNs), are coupled with CFDs to enhance the performance of transient simulations through predictive models for both indoor (Song et al. 2013; Zhou and Ooka 2020; Gheziel et al. 2021) and outdoor (Calautit et al. 2015; Liu et al. 2019) airflow and heat transfer analysis. For example, a study by Yi et al. (2012) developed a method to improve the performance of transient CFD analysis for local airflow in designing building geometry through coupling it with ANNs. Another study by Wang and Malkawi (2014) coupled ANNs with CFD to predict yearlong airflow around a building for hourly time intervals and reported substantial performance improvements (400×). The coupled CFD–ML approach, however, has not been developed for predicting airflow and air pollution concentration together for a comprehensive ESP evaluation.

On the other hand, the U.S. National Institute of Standards and Technology (NIST) has introduced a platform allowing for bridging the CFD, heat transfer, and mass balance physics-based co-simulation for airflow, operational energy, and IAQ analyses, respectively. In doing so, through coupling CFD0, CONTAM, and EnergyPlus engines, such integrated analyses can take place. However, EnergyPlus software can solely simulate energy and IAQ (e.g. Ben-David et al. 2017), it cannot incorporate wind direction in the simulation. CONTAM, on the other hand, brings both wind speed and direction into the simulation workflow, while it cannot solve heat transfer equations (Ng et al. 2015). To take advantage of the two, CONTAM and EnergyPlus are coupled together through the FMI platform (Dols and Polidoro 2015; Alonso et al. 2019). FMI stands for Functional Mock-up Interface, which is a standard platform that enables model exchange and co-simulation of dynamic models between different simulation tools. It provides a standardized interface for exchanging models and data between various software tools that are used in the development of complex cyber-physical systems. Despite the integration of three distinct simulation engines, the simulation platform suffers from two critical issues that warrant critical attention. First, the platform's computational performance is suboptimal due to the need for executing the model for each hourly interval throughout the entire simulation period. Second, while the platform is suitable for general physics-based energy-IAQ simulation, it lacks efficacy in exploring the trade-offs between energy reduction and exposure to pollution. As a result, evaluating and optimizing these trade-offs remain a challenging and inefficient task. Consequently, there is a pressing need to optimize the simulation platform to improve its computational performance and enable a more effective evaluation of the trade-offs between energy reduction and exposure to pollution.

This study addresses the aforementioned limitations by proposing a novel hybrid methodology that combines physics-based and data-driven approaches. The existing NIST co-simulation workflow has been augmented to incorporate urban morphological and local mobility patterns, thereby predicting ESPs while reducing the computational load associated with traditional physics-based methods. The multidomain approach is designed to reveal synergies between cooling energy and related health risks, allowing for more informed decision-making. The proposed framework integrates three physics-based simulation approaches (CFD, energy, and IAQ) with multivariate time series ANNs. This enables the model to learn from both simulated and real-world contextual data obtained from city and Internet of Things (IoT) data portals, resulting in more reliable performance simulation. The open-source RStudio software is used for data-driven simulations, facilitating more efficient and sustainable design of buildings operated by NV. The framework's outcomes are expected to benefit architects and designers in the early stages of building design by facilitating the discovery of trade-offs between occupant health and energy goals. By providing a more comprehensive understanding of the impact of urban morphological contexts and mobility patterns on ESPs, the proposed framework enables the selection of the most effective design strategies for NV buildings.

Materials and Methods

Data, Data Sources, and Dataset Processing

Building Surrounding Context
The present study focuses on the Federal Plaza located in Downtown Chicago (Loop). This site was chosen due to its unique urban characteristics, which include various categories of covariates that significantly impact airflow and air quality dynamics within built environments. The objective of this research is to predict the wind pressure coefficient (Cp) and

Table 3.1 Urban factors used for predicting IAQ-ESP using multivariate ANN algorithm.

Data category	Factor (X-variable)	Abbreviation	Unit
Meteorological (TMY3)	Wind speed	Ws	m s^{-1}
	Wind direction	Wd	–
	Dry bulb temperature	Td	°C
	Wet bulb temperature	Tw	°C
	Relative humidity	RH	–
	Precipitation (Rain)	Pr	mm
	Enthalpy at max. Td	En	J kg^{-1}
	Solar model indicator	Si	–
	Clearness	C_l	–
Particulate pollution	PM2.5 concentrations	PM2.5	μg m^{-3}
Traffic profile	Sum of vehicle and bus counts	Trfc	–
Daytime/calendar	Hour-of-day	Hour	–
	Weekdays/weekends	Week	–

contaminant coefficient (Cc) for each of the building openings at the study site. To achieve this goal, a comprehensive dataset was created that comprises hourly data for four distinct categories of factors: meteorological parameters, PM2.5 concentrations, traffic profiles, and daytime/calendar properties (see Table 3.1). These data were utilized to develop a predictive model for Cp and Cc, which enables us to better understand the air quality and ventilation dynamics of the Federal Plaza building.

Hourly meteorological dataset consists of several key parameters, including wind speed, wind direction, dry bulb temperature, wet bulb temperature, relative humidity, precipitation (rain), enthalpy at maximum dry bulb temperature, solar model indicator, and cleanness. This meteorological data was obtained from the Typical Meteorological Year 3 (TMY3) database for O'Hare International Airport in Chicago, IL (Wilcox and Marion 2008).

Hourly PM2.5 concentrations were obtained from the PurpleAir database, which is a network of low-cost air pollution monitoring sensors that record local PM2.5 concentrations worldwide on a 2-minute interval for both indoor and outdoor settings. In this study, PM2.5 concentrations were selected as a representative of airborne particulate pollution in the urban context. This choice is due to PM2.5's potential contribution to the spread of SARS-CoV2 viruses within built environments, unlike gaseous pollutants such as nitrogen dioxide and ozone. The authors of this article downloaded the PM2.5 data directly from the PurpleAir database and obtained an hourly time-series dataset from the closest sensor to the study site, which is called "1138 PLYMOUTH," located in the Chicago Loop area. The sensor's location is at latitude 41.869°N and longitude 87.628°W, with a height of approximately 7 m. The literature confirms a high Pearson correlation ($R > 0.99$) between NIST-certified Urban PM and PurpleAir sensors for the collected data (Tryner et al. 2020). The reliability of these low-cost monitoring sensors has been supported by prior research (Ardon-Dryer et al. 2019).

Mobility patterns. In this study, we utilized *hourly traffic profiles* as a representation of mobility patterns during the month of May 2019. These profiles were obtained from the official data portal of the city of Chicago (Chicago Traffic Tracker - Historical Congestion

Estimates by Region - 2018-Current | City of Chicago | Data Portal 2021), which collects real-time traffic congestion data from all urban districts and consolidates them into a historical dataset with a 5-min time interval. Specifically, we used the vehicle count factor to represent the magnitude of car congestion within the district, and we selected Region 13, which encompasses traffic data for the Loop area.

Daytime/calendar characteristic. Additionally, we included daytime and calendar characteristics as discrete factors in our dataset. These factors were extracted from the U.S. federal and local time-zone (Central Time) calendar.

Building

In this research, we used the reference buildings dataset provided by the U.S. DOE to examine the proposed ESP-IAQ framework. The reference models, as nationally representative models, convey about 60% of the commercial building's characteristics in the U.S. These models have been developed by DOE for improving energy efficiency in the building sector by providing a platform for research in advanced control, design optimization, energy code development, lighting, daylighting, ventilation, and IAQ (Deru et al. 2011). In this study, the available large-size office building model (Commercial Reference Buildings | Department of Energy 2010) from Chicago, IL, was selected for analysis. The building is characterized as a 12-story office with a 46,320 m^2 footprint (Figure 3.1). The new construction vintage was used following the input allocations based on the ANSI/ASHRAE/IESNA Standard 90.1–2009 (American Society of Heating 2009). In this research, we assumed all windows are operable. Each floor of the building was also assumed to be a single zone. Table 3.2 lists summary of the geometry and major characteristics for the tested building.

Methodology

In this study, a combination of physics-based and data-driven methods was utilized, along with the acquisition and implementation of artificial intelligence techniques, to perform a series of simulations aimed at predicting outdoor-sourced IAQ and ESPs in buildings. The data required for developing predictive models were collected from smart city infrastructures. A flowchart of the proposed framework is presented in Figure 3.2, which outlines the three major steps required to perform an integrated analysis for outdoor-sourced IAQ and

Figure 3.1 Aerial view of DOE's large-size office building. This model is visualized in Rhino Grasshopper, using Ladybug and Honeybee plug-ins. Source: Prototype Building Models (2019).

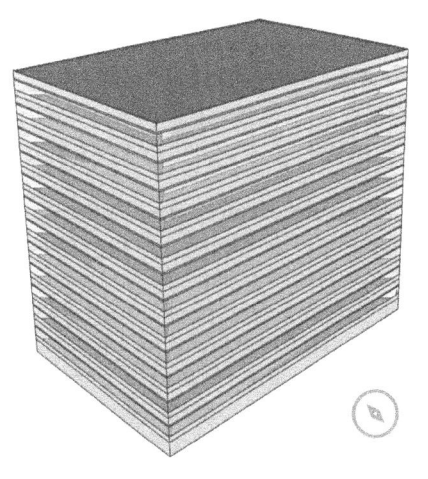

Table 3.2 List of building characteristics for DOE's large-size office prototype for new vintage, Chicago, IL.

Item	Value
Building typology	Large-size office
Number of floors	12 + basement
Total gross area (m^2)	46,320
Floor dimension (m)	73.107 × 48.738
Aspect ration	1.5
Floor-to-ceiling height (m)	2.74
Floor-to-floor height (m)	3.96
Window wall ratio	38% (all sides)
Window type	Operable (all windows)
Exterior wall	Steel framed
Number of zones per floor	5
Space conditioning type	Nonresidential
Energy sources	Gas, electricity
U-value (exterior walls)	0.477
U-value (windows)	3.24
SHGH windows	0.39
Heating system	Gas boiler
Cooling system	AHU
Infiltration (ACH)	0.10
Thermal efficiency (%)	80
Temperature setpoint (°C)	60

Source: Prototype Building Models (2019).

ESP for the test building. The detailed processes for each step are provided in the corresponding subsections. The study was conducted in May 2019, using an hourly time-series analysis. In a previous research, Chen et al. 2018 conducted a historical data analysis for NV suitable hours across multiple cities in the U.S. and reported that May, August, and September are the three thermally suitable months for NV operation in Chicago, with May being the most suitable month, accounting for approximately 33% of the mean annual NV suitable hours, which are reported to be around 11.30%.

Step (a): Localize Airflow on Air Paths

In the first step of the proposed framework, airflow is localized on air paths using a coupled approach of two open-source software, CFD0 Editor 3.4 and ×3.4. This process involves generating infiltration rates for each flow path, such as cracks and openings, across building enclosures. CFD0 Editor incorporates CFD equations that have been developed and validated by the NIST [51]. On the other hand, CONTAM is a multizone IAQ simulation software that calculates various parameters, including airflow rates, contaminant transport, concentrations, as well as personal exposures in buildings [41]. Airflows consist of infiltration, exfiltration, and

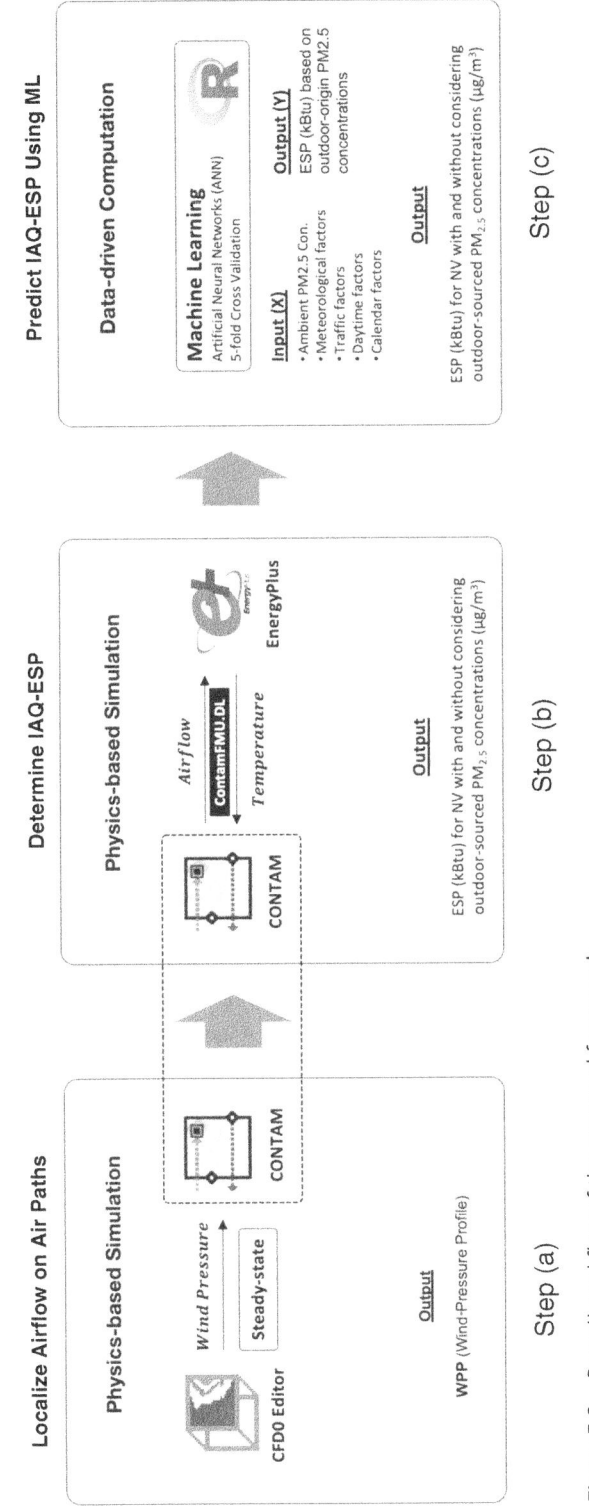

Figure 3.2 Overall workflow of the proposed framework.

air movement between zones, which can be driven by natural or mechanical forces [52]. The multizone airflow model is utilized in this study due to its ability to interact dynamically with HVAC systems and real-time weather and airflows in a quick manner [52]. However, the homogeneous assumption of airflow patterns within zones in CONTAM is inappropriate for air distribution and turbulence analysis [53] for NV [54]. Hence, the CFD0 software was enhanced to be coupled with CONTAM by NIST [55] to solve conservation equations, such as using Reynolds-averaged Navier-Stokes (RANS) double equations for airflow and contaminant transmission [49]. This coupled simulation approach has been validated by previous studies for both airflow and contaminant transport analysis [57].

In this study, we used the k–ε turbulence model and wall functions for solving the RANS equations. The power-law as the interpolation scheme is also chosen for this work as it has shown more reliable results in flow simulations [32]. It should be noted that the RANS method for CFD analysis is both timely and computationally expensive; however, this method is considered the fastest CFD model among others, such as Large Eddy Simulations (LES) or Direct Numerical Simulation (DNS) (Wang and Chen 2007). The major discrepancy between these turbulence models is seen where strong turbulence around buildings accrues due to the time-averaging flow simulations instead of time-dependent calculations (Wang et al. 2010).

We applied a steady-state CFD simulation approach to localize airflow rate upon each air path through the wind pressure and contaminant (WPC) profile conversion to be read by CONTAM during energy-IAQ simulation in Step (b). Steps (a) and (b) aimed to simulate about 25% of hourly intervals for May 2019 (the first week in May) with a physics-based engineering simulation approach, and the remaining ~75% of scenarios to be predicted using a multivariate ANN approach, which is described in Step (c). Figure 3.3 illustrates the diagram of the co-simulation process in Figure 3.2 (Step (a) and Step (b)) in detail for the physics-based simulation. For modeling the building and contextual geometries in the CFD environment, three layers of surrounding buildings from the real city grid were modeled to reduce uncertainties in capturing more realistic WPC on each of the air paths (Figure 3.4). Research by Tong, Chen, and Malkawi (2016) suggests such a CFD modeling approach for outdoor airflow studies to lower the uncertainty in an urban context. Figure 3.4b shows the layers of neighboring buildings around the target office building, which comprise 98 existing buildings surrounding the Plaza (the blue, yellow, and green structures). We coupled the two software tools using CFD0–CONTAM approach, by which geometry and contextual information are defined in CFD0 Editor by the user; CFD0 provides boundary conditions to solve turbulence equations, then passes the WPCs per air path to CONTAM for outdoor-driven indoor investigations. CFD0 iterates the simulation until the expected criteria are met for convergence. The context geometries were modeled in computer-aided design (CAD) environment in Rhino environment, where the context is bound to 566 m × 497 m ($L \times W$) (Figure 3.4a), then the CFD boundary for the context extended to larger boundaries using criteria obtained from Tong, Chen, and Malkawi (2016): the lateral (side) boundary extended by $5H$ (H = the height of the tallest building) from the outer side of the context, led to a width of 1054 m; the leeward and windward sides of the context extended by $15H$ and $5H$, respectively, creating 1473 m of length; and the height extended by $5H$ let to a boundary with a $6H$ height, creating 293 m of height, where H is the height of the target building.

Thus, with a 1:10 scale for the wind tunnel, the 3D boundary in the CFD environment is defined as $105.4\,dm \times 147.3\,dm \times 29.3\,dm$ ($L \times W \times H$). We discretized this boundary into 1.8–2 million finite volumes (cells) depending on the modeling scenarios. In this study, we set 0.001 and 1000 for convergence criteria and maximum iterations, respectively. To

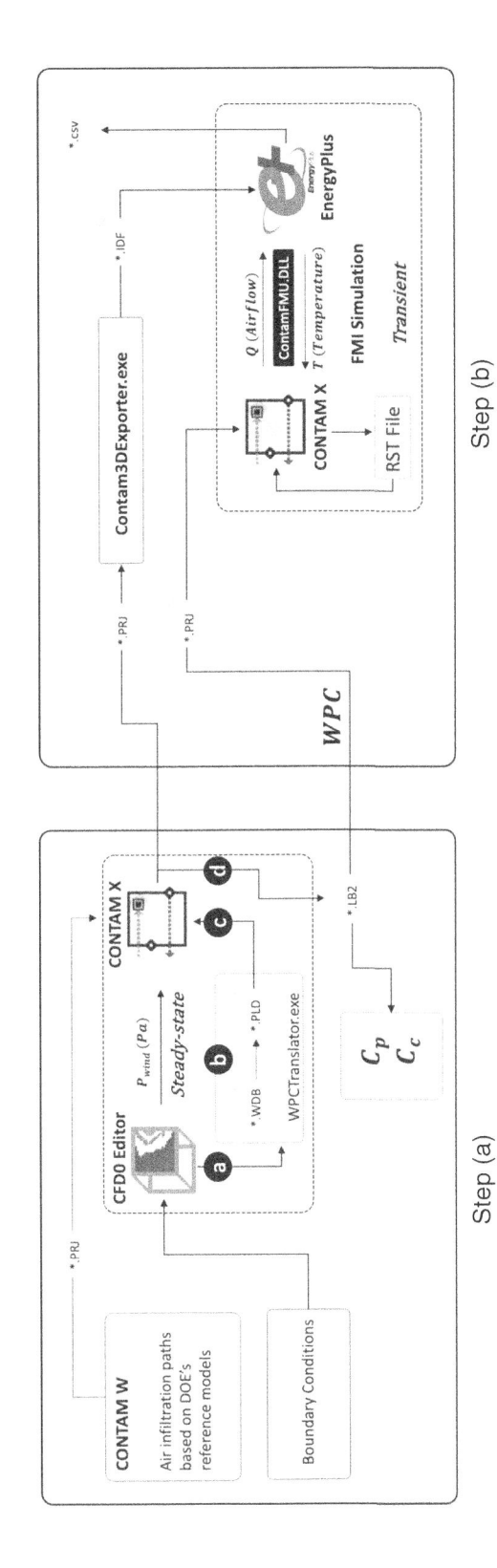

Figure 3.3 Detailed workflow in step (a) and step (b) for coupling CFD0 Editor–CONTAM and CONTAM–EnergyPlus software, respectively, along with input/output file types. WPC stands for Wind Pressure and Contaminant profiles.

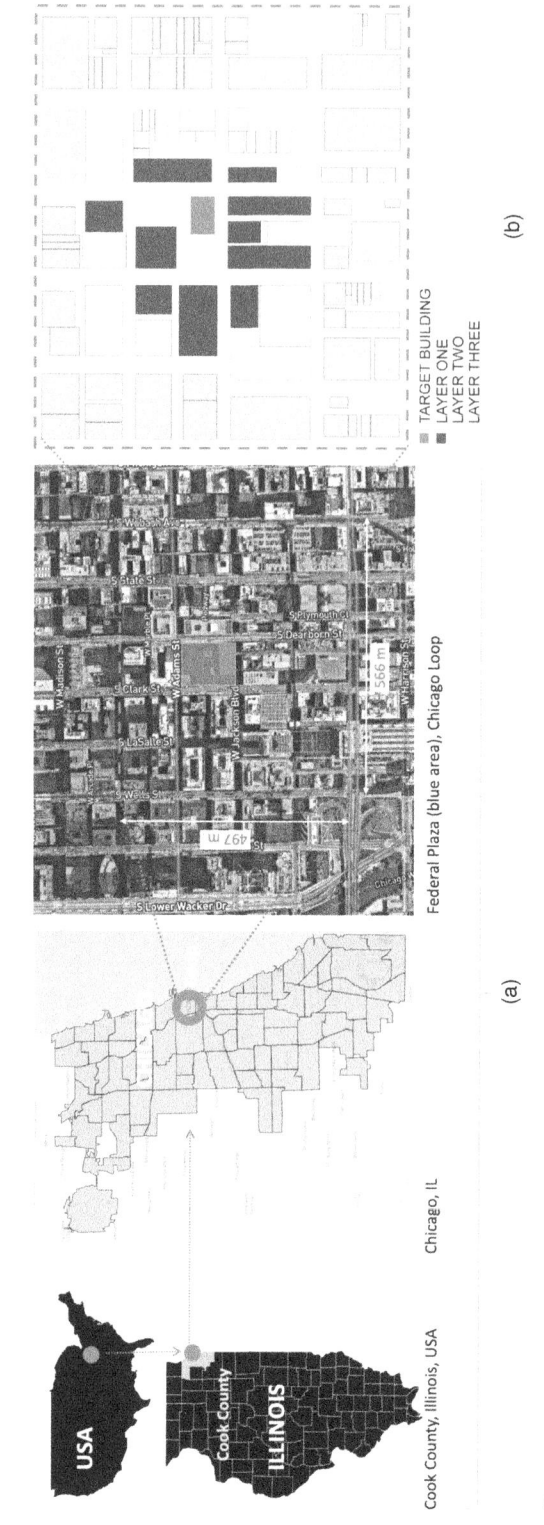

Cook County, Illinois, USA   Chicago, IL   Federal Plaza (blue area), Chicago Loop

(a)

TARGET BUILDING
LAYER ONE
LAYER TWO
LAYER THREE

(b)

Figure 3.4 (a) Location of target building in the urban context, Federal Plaza, Chicago Loop (Source: OpenStreetMap, 2021), (b) modeled building in CFD0 Editor environment with three layers of surrounding buildings.

Table 3.3 Local wind speed profile coefficients.

Type of terrain	α-Exponent	δ* (m)
Flat, open country	0.14	270
Rough, wooded country	0.22	370
Towns and cities	0.33	460
Ocean	0.1	210
Urban, industrial, forest	0.22	370

* Boundary layer thickness.
Source: Adapted from ASHRAE 2009.

calculate WPC, a series of input parameters were provided for CFD0 Editor, using the ASHRAE Handbook; Fundamental-2009 (American Society of Heating 2009). First, we extrapolated the local wind velocity based on building height relative to the meteorological station height, which is usually 10 m provided in TMY3 files, using Equation 3.1 from the handbook:

$$V_z = V_{met} \left(\frac{\delta_{met}}{z_{met}}\right) \alpha_{met} \left(\frac{z}{\delta}\right)^\alpha \tag{3.1}$$

where V_z is the local wind velocity at an altitude of Z in m/s, V_{met} is the velocity measured at an anemometer height of Z in m/s, δ_{met} is the wind speed profile boundary layer thickness at the meteorological station in meters, m, α_{met} is the wind speed profile exponent at the meteorological station in m/s, Z is the height of building eaves above ground in meters, m, which is assumed to be 10 m in this work, δ is the wind speed profile boundary layer thickness at the site in meters, m, and α is the wind-speed profile exponent at the building site. The wind-speed profile coefficients α, α_{met}, δ, and δ_{met} are the parameters that become affected by the surrounding terrain. Table 3.3 lists the power-law exponent as well as the boundary layer thickness of different terrains.

The reference meteorological station in this research was determined as an inner-city station. Therefore, the α-exponent and boundary layer thickness were set to 0.33 and 460 m, respectively (Table 3.3). The V_{met} values were also extracted from the TMY3 dataset. For introducing local wind-direction characteristics into the model, the relative wind direction (θ) was set to 0° at the North, then 15° equal increments of relative directions were defined for modeling a wind-driven site condition in the CFD environment. These procedures enable the WPC to be calculated for each opening and across the height of the building for each time interval.

Step (b): Determine IAQ-ESP

After providing local ambient airflow and air pollution around the building for the entire hourly scenarios, this information was then used as input for integrated IAQ and ESP analysis. Coupled CONTAM and EnergyPlus software is an effective approach for conducting such investigations. In this study, the co-simulation is implemented based on CONTAM–EnergyPlus approach. For coupling, the already simulated data in the previous step that are already kept in the CONTAM's .prj file is passed to EnergyPlus for adding energy analysis into the workflow. Since EnergyPlus only reads .idf files, CONTAM3DExport tool is used for generating *.idf* files out of the *.prj* file. In this conversion, building geometry, airflow paths, location of windows, infiltration rates, ducts, and control systems created in CONTAM are shared with EnergyPlus. It should be noted that the FMI file provides a platform for exchanging data between the two, using ContamFMU.DLL file. Through this, the hourly outdoor-sourced PM2.5 concentrations and ESP (for cooling and ventilation) are calculated in a transient simulation. In this process, CONTAM calculates inter-zonal airflows (Q) and passes it to EnergyPlus; then, EnergyPlus calculates surface temperatures (T) and returns them to the CONTAM. This process is automatically iterated until the two parameters become converged. More detailed processing for the coupled simulations can be found in the CONTAM User Guide, Chapter 6 (Dols and Polidoro 2020), and research conducted by Dols et al. (2016).

To capture the ESP, the HVAC control system was scheduled in a way that the cooling and ventilation systems are turned off when the indoor thermal conditions are satisfied. In doing so, the heating and cooling temperature set-points were set to 21.1 °C and 23.9 °C, respectively. The HVAC operation schedule was defined as 6:00 am to 10:00 pm from Monday to Friday (weekdays), 6:00 am to 6:00 pm on Saturdays, turned off otherwise, and all turned off on Sundays. This schedule is captured from the NIST's large-scale office model dataset (Ng et al. 2019).

The minimum and maximum supply air temperatures were set to 12.8 °C and 40 °C, respectively. In addition, the air exchange rate was set to 8.3 L/s-person according to Standard 90.1–2010 (62.1–2013). This research also assumed that the baseline model that is operated by mechanical systems provides "better" IAQ for occupants as it uses filters in the intake air paths. In this research, we set maximum hourly PM2.5 concentrations at $12\,\mu g\,m^{-3}$ and $35\,\mu g\,m^{-3}$ for annual and 24-hour averaged values for both outdoors and indoors to maintain "Good" air quality using EPA's latest thresholds (Environmental Protection Agency (EPA) 2020). For capturing the differences between ESP for two scenarios: with and without incorporating ambient PM2.5 concentrations, the coupled simulation was implemented separately by adding and removing PM2.5 in the model. Figures 3.2b and 3.3 illustrate the workflow of coupled CONTAM and EnergyPlus for co-simulating IAQ and ESP for the studied building.

Step (c): Predict IAQ-ESP Using Machine Learning

This step, which is based upon a data-driven approach, applies ML techniques to train the one-week simulated data, in order to predict the remaining intervals (three weeks) in May. Thus, a multivariate ANN model was developed that used various urban characteristics as X as explanatory (X) variables (Table 3.2) to forecast the response variables (ESP-1 and ESP-2) that are captured from the physics-based simulations for the remaining 75% of time intervals. Urban characteristics were obtained from the city data portal, DOE, and the smart city network of sensors. We picked the ANN algorithm over other ML algorithms due to its non-linear explorations' capacity. A fivefold cross-validation approach was applied for the ANN model to avoid biased results. We used a multi-layer perception (MLP) approach for developing the ANN model that structured a single hidden layer and optimized it by the Broyden–Fletcher–Goldfarb–Shanno (BFGS) algorithm (Venables and Ripley 2002). The BFGS algorithm is a method for solving optimization problems, such as finding the minimum or maximum of a function. It is an iterative algorithm that uses gradients of the function to search for the optimal solution. The BFGS algorithm belongs to the family of quasi-Newton methods, which use approximations of the second derivative of the function to update the search direction at each iteration. The BFGS algorithm is widely used in ML and numerical optimization due to its efficiency and good convergence properties. More information on the MLP-based ANN model can be found in a review article by Abbasabadi and Ashayeri (2019). Moreover, in this research, we used an ensemble approach in the ANN training process to lower the predictive model's uncertainties.

To perform ANN computations, RStudio software was used. RStudio is a free computation tool based on the R programming language. In this research, we used 70% of simulated data from step (a) for training and 30% for the test. For dividing the datasets into train and test sets, we used random sub-sampling approach to avoid biased results. Step (c) in Figure 3.2 illustrates the materials for executing this step. Figure 3.5 illustrates the architecture of the ANN model in this research, which comprises input data, a single hidden layer, and outputs.

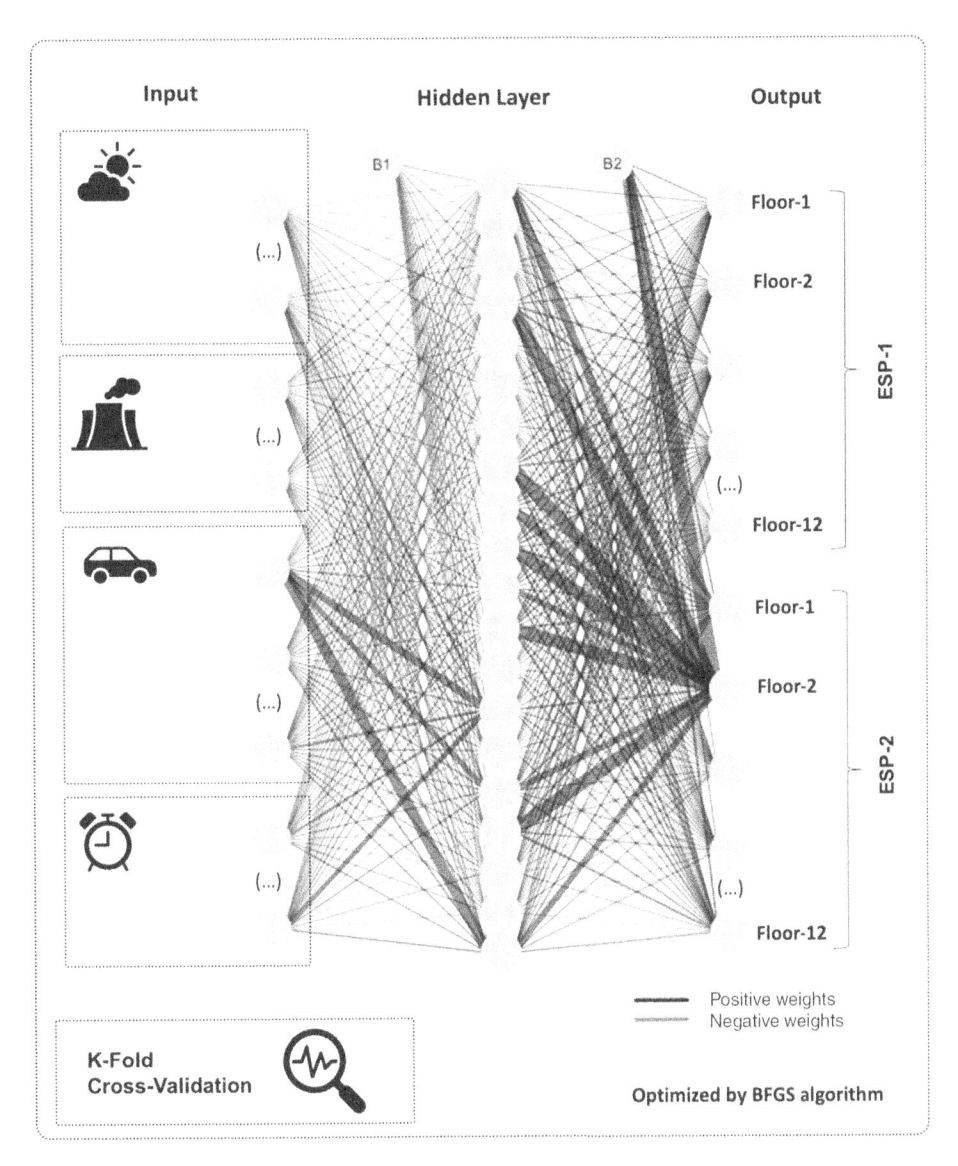

Figure 3.5 Schematic diagram of the MLP–ANN predictive model comprises input data, a hidden layer, and outputs. Inputs include weather, traffic, PM2.5 concentrations, and daytime/calendar set of variables.

In this study, we used the coefficient of determination or *R*-squared (R^2) (Ashayeri et al. 2021) in order to evaluate the performance of the predictive ANN model (Equation 3.2):

$$R^2 = 1 - \frac{\sum_{i=1}^{k}\left(y_{\text{pred},i} - y_{\text{act},i}\right)^2}{\sum_{i=1}^{k}\left(y_{\text{act},i} - \bar{y}_{\text{act}}\right)^2} \tag{3.2}$$

where $y_{\text{act},i}$ and $y_{\text{pred},i}$ denote the actual and predicted ESP for the *i*th observation, $\bar{y}_{\text{act}}$ denotes the mean ESP, and *k* represents the total number of observations. *R*-squared is a statistical measure that indicates the explanatory power of a statistical model by independent variables to predict a dependent variable. It ranges values between 0 and 1, with the higher values representing the higher accuracy of the model. *R*-squared is used in many studies for evaluating performance of predictive models (e.g. Moore et al. 2007; Abbasabadi et al. 2019).

We also used the variance inflation factor (VIF) to test the multicollinearity of the dataset before introducing them in the ANN model. It should be noted that the collinear factors cause biased results. We kept VIF lesser or equal to 5 (VIF ≤ 5) (Masiol et al. 2018) as the collinearity criteria to exclude collinear variables from the dataset prior to subsampling datasets. The VIF value is calculated using Equation 3.3 (Ashayeri et al. 2021):

$$\text{VIF}_i = 1 - \frac{1}{1 - R_i^2} \tag{3.3}$$

where R_i^2 denotes the coefficient of determination per input variable.

Results

Physics-Based Simulation

In step (a) of the framework, we coupled CFD0 Editor with CONTAM software to provide context-sensitive airflow profiles for estimating IAQ. The CFD simulation converged after 436 iterations, using a computer system with an Intel Core I-9 and 64 GB of DDR-4 RAM Memory. Figure 3.6 depicts a heatmap of the airflow regime across buildings and upon building facades. In step (b), the coupled IAQ and ESP analysis was performed. Table 3.4 lists percentages of ESPs of the building during May against building height for two scenarios: without (ESP-1) and with (ESP-2) incorporating outdoor PM2.5 concentrations in the workflow, respectively. According to the results, the average ESP-2 for the entire building is 52% lower than ESP-1 (35.78% vs. 22.71%), indicating the uncertainties in NV applications where outdoor air quality and flow patterns are overlooked in the early design stage. The results of ESP-2 analysis indicate that lower floors have less capacity for NVs compared with the upper floors, which may be associated with a higher level of PM2.5 concentrations at street level, which is confirmed via empirical studies conducted by Azimi et al. (2018) and Jung et al. (2011) in Chicago and New York City, respectively. They reported that by increasing urban building elevation, the concentrations of PM2.5 are decreased.

Data-Driven Computation (Prediction)

This research used MLP–ANN algorithm to predict ESPs based on the integrated airflow and PM2.5 variations for each building floor. Table 3.5 lists R^2 values of the predictive models across floors for the two scenarios: ESP-1 and ESP-2, respectively. The results indicate that

Results | 71

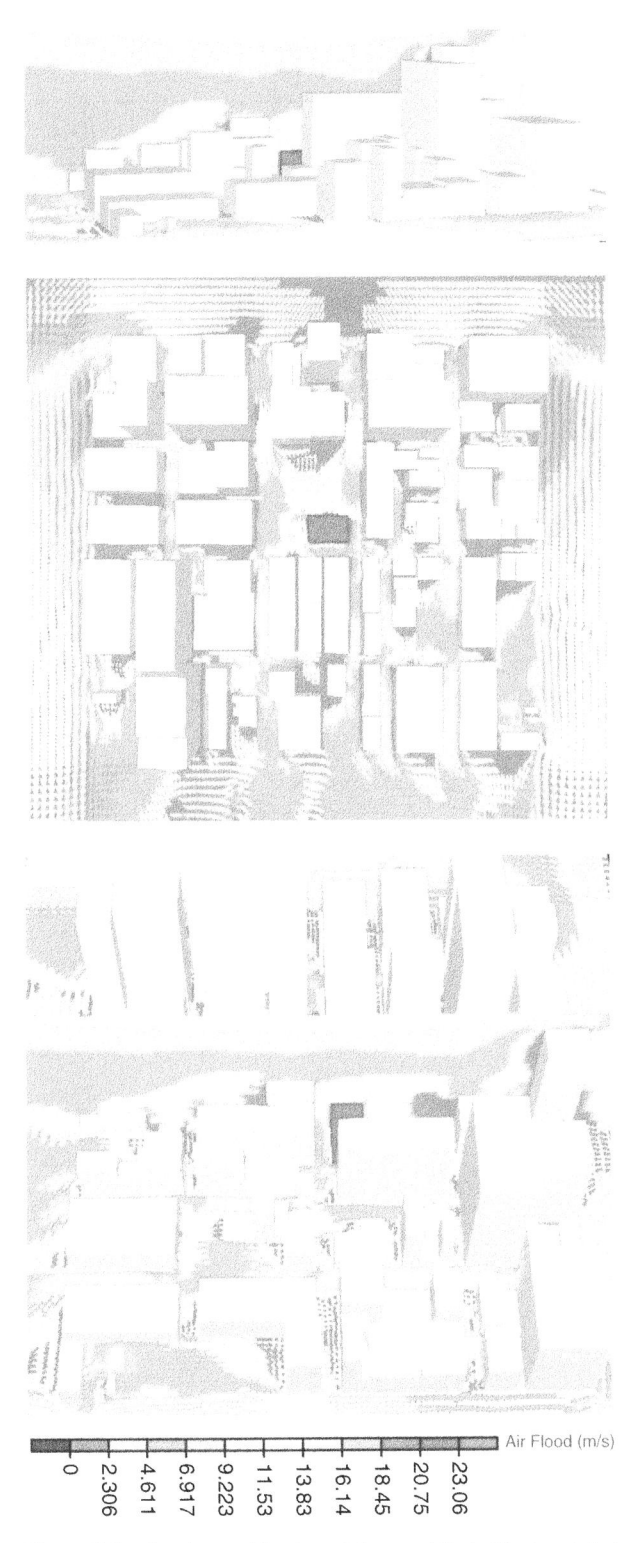

Figure 3.6 Southeast–Northwest, top, and East–West aerial views of wind tunnel analysis performed in CFD0 Editor under North wind speed (Flood). The image is cut to illustrate the focus area in CFD environment.

Table 3.4 % ESPs for the office building in Chicago, IL, during May for two scenarios (ESP-1 and ESP-2).

Floor #	ESP-1* (%)	ESP-2** (%)
1	28.99	18.46
2	30.55	19.15
3	30.94	19.59
4	31.46	20.22
5	32.89	20.92
6	33.54	21.43
7	35.49	22.76
8	36.92	23.66
9	38.22	23.68
10	40.43	25.87
11	43.55	27.14
12	46.41	29.67
Average	**35.78**	**22.71**

* Without ambient PM2.5 concentrations.
** With ambient PM2.5 concentrations.

Table 3.5 R^2 for predicted ESPs for May.

Floor #	R^2 (ESP-1)	R^2 (ESP-2)
1	0.97	0.96
2	0.96	0.94
3	0.96	0.93
4	0.95	0.92
5	0.96	0.91
6	0.95	0.92
7	0.95	0.88
8	0.94	0.89
9	0.95	0.84
10	0.94	0.82
11	0.94	0.81
12	0.93	0.79
Average	**0.95**	**0.88**

the ANN model can predict ESP-1, which includes no PM2.5 data in the model, with a higher level of accuracy, showing reduction in R^2 accuracy by increasing building height. Since, in this study, we used an ensemble ANN model averaging 100 individual ANNs, the hyperparameters such as the number of neurons in the hidden layer varied for each of the individual

Table 3.6 Properties of ANN models and the list of given hyperparameters with the range of values of each for the best model per ESP approach.

ESP-1		ESP-2	
Best A	Best B	Best A	Best B
10	0.05	11	0.05

X: Number of explanatory variables (inputs): 11
(After VIF analysis and dimensionality reduction)
Y: Number of dependent variables (outputs): 24
(ESP-1 and ESP-2 per floor)
A: Range of the number of neurons in hidden layer:
[2, |2/3 * number of X Variables|, seq = 1]
B: Decay: {0.05, 0.5. 0.1}

model. We set the hyperparameters by giving minimum and maximum values for each parameter, and the obtained R^2 was then based on the average of 100 models with different ANN structures. It should be noted that the selected algorithm from the R library automatically handles such an automation strategy for optimizing the models. Table 3.6 lists the range of hyperparameters defined for structuring ensemble ANN models and the hyperparameters for the best model per ESP approach.

The execution for physics-based co-simulation (CFD0–CONTAM and CONTAM–EnergyPlus) for capturing percentages of ESPs, elapsed 1:16′:8″ per time step (hour-of-day). This is the average of 144 simulations implemented for one week (May 1st to 7th). The total time expenditure for this set of simulations for the week took about 08 hours, 43 minutes, and 12 seconds. The ANN algorithm predicted ESP for both scenarios (ESP-1 and ESP-2) with 95% ($R^2 = 0.95$) and 85% ($R^2 = 0.85$) of the variance for the two scenarios, respectively. The prediction only took 08 hours, 43 minutes, and 12 seconds (for average of the two scenarios). This indicates the efficiency that ANNs provide for estimating ESPs for urban buildings operated by NV systems in dense urban contexts.

Discussion

In this research, we applied CFD0–CONTAM as a robust approach to localize ambient airflow profiles for each of the building openings. This approach has already been tested and validated in previous studies. However, to date, limited work has been developed applying such a method, or existing studies have not simulated clusters of neighboring buildings to localize workflow regimes.

We also developed a CONTAM–EnergyPlus model to calculate both ESPs and outdoor-driven PM2.5 concentrations indoors for the studied building more accurately. Similarly, this coupling method has been investigated in limited studies in the literature, despite its unique co-simulation power. The current research adopted the existing physics-based workflow by bringing big data and ANN framework to it to enable more accurate and efficient results. A review by Wei et al. (2019) confirms the power of ANNs for predicting IAQ in terms of

PM2.5 concentrations indoors. Another recent study by Lagesse et al. (2020) confirms such capacity for the large-size prototype office buildings. The current research predicted combined airflow, IAQ, and ESP analysis for a coupled approach, which has not been tested in the literature.

Comparing the obtained ESPs, results suggest that the predictive model accuracy is 7% higher for ESP-1 compared with ESP-2. This can be because of the uncertainties PM2.5 concentrations bring into the model. This stems from a higher level of complexities involved in intraurban PM2.5 dynamics in non-heating seasons (Ashayeri et al. 2021). The results also illustrate a reduction in predictive model accuracy withy increasing building height for the second scenario (ESP-2), demonstrating that collected PM2.5 data that have occurred at the street level provides higher predictive power at lower levels than at the upper levels in predicting ESP-2 for the NV strategies. Furthermore, predicting ESPs by ANNs provided an opportunity to improve modeling performance by lowering computational loads, leading to the investigation of a wide time horizon for such analysis. The prediction took 30 minutes and 46 seconds for both scenarios combined, for 24/31 of time steps, while the physics-based simulations took nearly 109 hours for 7/31 of scenarios (~202 times faster). This is supported by a study referenced by Wang and Malkawi (2014), which indicates that the computational power of ANNs is 400 times greater than traditional methods for predicting CFD-based airflow analysis during the early stages of building design.

Limitations involved in this research come from data, physics-based simulation, and data-driven computations (prediction). In addition, in this study, we used PM2.5 as the only air pollution indicator; other pollutants such as nitrogen dioxide (NO_2), sulfur dioxide (SO_2), and ozone (O_3), among others, were not tested. The physics-based simulations only utilized the RANS equations for solving turbulence equations, while the LES approach can provide more accurate results. It should be noted that CFD0 Editor cannot handle LES and DNS types of CFD modeling approaches. Other open-source software is required to test these methods for the framework; however, they cannot be effectively coupled with CONTAM. For the predictions, we applied ANNs for this framework. This framework was only tested for May 2019 (744 time steps). Using a longer time horizon for generalizing ESPs can depict the annual ESPs for the building.

Conclusion

This chapter presents a novel framework that combines physics-based simulations and ML to estimate building ESPs while maintaining occupant health. By localizing ambient airflow and particulate pollution concentrations, the framework provides insight into the trade-offs between health burden and energy reduction loads, making it possible for designers to effectively estimate ESPs in the early stages of design. The incorporation of local ambient air quality profiles in the framework allows for a comprehensive estimation of ESPs for naturally ventilated office buildings in an urban context. The study found that significant uncertainties arise due to outdoor air dynamics in designing a naturally ventilated building, and the energy-saving benefits of the NV system can put human health at risk if the building context is not well understood.

The findings further demonstrate the importance of integrated physics-based and data-driven approaches in the evaluation of building performance at the early stages of design. In terms of modeling performance, the study revealed that employing the ANN algorithm notably reduced the simulation time, especially for CFD simulations which are inherently time intensive. The study suggests that ML, in general, and ANNs, in particular, are essential tools in building performance evaluation, allowing for significant time savings in simulation processes. Overall, the proposed framework aids architects, engineers, policymakers, and public health authorities in assessing the interplay between occupant health and urban building energy conservation objectives during early stage decision-making. This leads to holistic solutions that prioritize human health while also addressing the impacts of climate change. The study opens up new avenues for future research to advance the understanding of the interplay between building performance, occupant health, and urban environments for future sustainable cities.

Acknowledgment

We would like to acknowledge the financial support for this research; MA received start-up grants from Southern Illinois University Carbondale (SIUC), and NA received start-up grants from the College of Built Environments at the University of Washington in Seattle.

References

Abbasabadi, N. and Ashayeri, M. (2019). Urban Energy Use Modeling Methods and Tools: A Review and an Outlook. *Building and Environment* 161 (August): 106270. https://doi.org/10.1016/j.buildenv.2019.106270.

Abbasabadi, N., Ashayeri, M., Azari, R. et al. (2019). An Integrated Data-Driven Framework for Urban Energy Use Modeling (UEUM). *Applied Energy* 253 (November): 113550. https://doi.org/10.1016/j.apenergy.2019.113550.

Aelenei, L., Ferreira, A., Monteiro, C.S. et al. (2016). Smart City: A Systematic Approach towards a Sustainable Urban Transformation. *Energy Procedia* 91 (June): 970–979. https://doi.org/10.1016/j.egypro.2016.06.264.

Ai, Z.T. and Mak, C.M. (2018). Wind-Induced Single-Sided Natural Ventilation in Buildings Near a Long Street Canyon: CFD Evaluation of Street Configuration and Envelope Design. *Journal of Wind Engineering and Industrial Aerodynamics* 172 (January): 96–106. https://doi.org/10.1016/j.jweia.2017.10.024.

Alonso, M.J., Stuart Dols, W., and Mathisen, H.M. (2019). *Using Co-Simulation between EnergyPlus and CONTAM to Develop IAQ and Energy-Centric Demand-Controlled Ventilation Systems*, 11.

American Society of Heating, Refrigerating and Air-Conditioning Engineers (2009). *2009 ASHRAE Handbook: Fundamentals (I-P and SI Ed.)*. Atlanta, GA: American Society of Heating, Refrigerating, and Air-Conditioning Engineers.

"Annual Energy Review 2011." 2012. 0384. Washington, DC 20585: U.S. Department of Energy. https://www.eia.gov/totalenergy/data/annual/pdf/aer.pdf.

Ardon-Dryer, Karin, Yuval Dryer, Jake N. Williams, and Nastaran Moghimi. 2019. Measurements of PM2.5 with PurpleAir under Atmospheric Conditions. Preprint. *Aerosols/In Situ Measurement/Instruments and Platforms*. https://doi.org/10.5194/amt-2019-396.

Ashayeri, M. and Abbasabadi, N. (2022). A Framework for Integrated Energy and Exposure to Ambient Pollution (IEnEx) Assessment toward Low-Carbon, Healthy, and Equitable Cities. *Sustainable Cities and Society* 78 (March): 103647. https://doi.org/10.1016/j.scs.2021.103647.

Ashayeri, M., Abbasabadi, N., Heidarinejad, M., and Stephens, B. (2021). Predicting Intraurban PM2.5 Concentrations Using Enhanced Machine Learning Approaches and Incorporating Human Activity Patterns. *Environmental Research* 196 (May): 110423. https://doi.org/10.1016/j.envres.2020.110423.

Azimi, P., Zhao, H., Fazli, T. et al. (2018). Pilot Study of the Vertical Variations in Outdoor Pollutant Concentrations and Environmental Conditions along the Height of a Tall Building. *Building and Environment* 138 (June): 124–134. https://doi.org/10.1016/j.buildenv.2018.04.031.

Ben-David, T. and Waring, M.S. (2016). Impact of Natural versus Mechanical Ventilation on Simulated Indoor Air Quality and Energy Consumption in Offices in Fourteen U.S. Cities. *Building and Environment* 104: 320–336. https://doi.org/10.1016/j.buildenv.2016.05.007.

Ben-David, T., Rackes, A., and Waring, M.S. (2017). Alternative Ventilation Strategies in U.S. Offices: Saving Energy While Enhancing Work Performance, Reducing Absenteeism, and Considering Outdoor Pollutant Exposure Tradeoffs. *Building and Environment* 116 (May): 140–157. https://doi.org/10.1016/j.buildenv.2017.02.004.

Bibri, S.E. (2021). Data-Driven Smart Sustainable Cities of the Future: An Evidence Synthesis Approach to a Comprehensive State-of-the-Art Literature Review. *Sustainable Futures* 3: 100047. https://doi.org/10.1016/j.sftr.2021.100047.

Bowe, B., Xie, Y., Li, T. et al. (2018). Particulate Matter Air Pollution and the Risk of Incident CKD and Progression to ESRD. *Journal of the American Society of Nephrology* 29 (1): 218–230. https://doi.org/10.1681/ASN.2017030253.

Calautit, J., O'Connor, D., Sofotasiou, P., and Hughes, B. (2015). CFD Simulation and Optimisation of a Low Energy Ventilation and Cooling System. *Computation* 3 (2): 128–149. https://doi.org/10.3390/computation3020128.

Chakrabarty, R.K., Beeler, P., Liu, P. et al. (2021). Ambient PM2.5 Exposure and Rapid Spread of COVID-19 in the United States. *Science of The Total Environment* 760 (March): 143391. https://doi.org/10.1016/j.scitotenv.2020.143391.

Chen, J., Augenbroe, G., and Song, X. (2018). Evaluating the Potential of Hybrid Ventilation for Small to Medium Sized Office Buildings with Different Intelligent Controls and Uncertainties in US Climates. *Energy and Buildings* 158 (January): 1648–1661. https://doi.org/10.1016/j.enbuild.2017.12.004.

Chicago Traffic Tracker (2021). *Historical Congestion Estimates by Region - 2018-Current*. City of Chicago: Data Portal https://data.cityofchicago.org/Transportation/Chicago-Traffic-Tracker-Historical-Congestion-Esti/kf7e-cur8.

Cohen, A.J., Brauer, M., Richard Burnett, H. et al. (2017). Estimates and 25-year trends of the global burden of disease attributable to ambient air pollution: an analysis of data from the global burden of diseases study 2015. *The Lancet* 389 (10082): 1907–1918. https://doi.org/10.1016/S0140-6736(17)30505-6.

"Commercial Reference Buildings | Department of Energy." 2010. 27, 2010. https://www.energy.gov/eere/buildings/commercial-reference-buildings.

Deru, Michael, Kristin Field, Daniel Studer, Kyle Benne, Brent Griffith, Paul Torcellini, Bing Liu, et al. 2011. "U.S. Department of Energy Commercial Reference Building Models of the National Building Stock." NREL/TP-5500-46861, 1009264. https://doi.org/10.2172/1009264.

Dols, W.S. and Polidoro, B.J. (2015). *CONTAM User Guide and Program Documentation Version 3.2*." NIST TN 1887. National Institute of Standards and Technology https://doi.org/10.6028/NIST.TN.1887.

References

Dols, W.S. and Polidoro, B.J. (2020). *CONTAM User Guide and Program Documentation Version 3.4*. National Institute of Standards and Technology https://doi.org/10.6028/NIST.TN.1887r1.

Dols, W.S., Emmerich, S.J., and Polidoro, B.J. (2016). Coupling the Multizone Airflow and Contaminant Transport Software CONTAM with EnergyPlus Using Co-Simulation. *Building Simulation* 9 (4): 469–479. https://doi.org/10.1007/s12273-016-0279-2.

Dutton, S.M., Banks, D., Brunswick, S.L., and Fisk, W.J. (2013). Health and Economic Implications of Natural Ventilation in California Offices. *Building and Environment* 67 (September): 34–45. https://doi.org/10.1016/j.buildenv.2013.05.002.

Emmerich, S.J. and Axley, J.W. (2001). *Natural Ventilation Review and Plan for Design and Analysis Tools*." NIST IR 6781. Gaithersburg, MD: National Institute of Standards and Technology https://doi.org/10.6028/NIST.IR.6781.

Environmental Protection Agency (EPA) (2020). *Review of the National Ambient Air Quality Standards for Particulate Matter. 40 CFR Part 50*, vol. Vol. 85. https://www.govinfo.gov/content/pkg/FR-2020-12-18/pdf/2020-27125.pdf.

Gheziel, A., Hanini, S., and Mohamedi, B. (2021). Artificial neural network (ANN) for prediction indoor airborne particle concentration. *International Journal of Ventilation* February: 1–14. https://doi.org/10.1080/14733315.2021.1876408.

Jung, K.H., Bernabé, K., Moors, K. et al. (2011). Effects of Floor Level and Building Type on Residential Levels of Outdoor and Indoor Polycyclic Aromatic Hydrocarbons, Black Carbon, and Particulate Matter in New York City. *Atmosphere* 2 (2): 96–109. https://doi.org/10.3390/atmos2020096.

Klepeis, N.E., Nelson, W.C., Ott, W.R. et al. (2001). The National Human Activity Pattern Survey (NHAPS): A Resource for Assessing Exposure to Environmental Pollutants. *Journal of Exposure Science & Environmental Epidemiology* 11 (3): 231–252. https://doi.org/10.1038/sj.jea.7500165.

Lagesse, B., Wang, S., Larson, T.V., and Kim, A.A. (2020). Predicting $PM_{2.5}$ in Well-Mixed Indoor Air for a Large Office Building Using Regression and Artificial Neural Network Models. *Environmental Science & Technology* 54 (23): 15320–15328. https://doi.org/10.1021/acs.est.0c02549.

Liu, J., Heidarinejad, M., Nikkho, S.K. et al. (2019). Quantifying Impacts of Urban Microclimate on a Building Energy consumption—a case study. *Sustainability* 11 (18): 4921. https://doi.org/10.3390/su11184921.

Luitjohan, S., Ashayeri, M., and Abbasabadi, N. (2022). An Optimization Framework and Tool for Context-Sensitive Solar-Driven Design Using Cellular Automata (SDCA). In: *2022 Annual Modeling and Simulation Conference (ANNSIM)*, 593–604. San Diego, CA, USA: IEEE https://doi.org/10.23919/ANNSIM55834.2022.9859496.

Masiol, M., Zíková, N., Chalupa, D.C. et al. (2018). Hourly Land-Use Regression Models Based on Low-Cost PM Monitor Data. *Environmental Research* 167 (November): 7–14. https://doi.org/10.1016/j.envres.2018.06.052.

Mendy, A., Xiao, W., Keller, J.L. et al. (2021). Long-term Exposure to Fine Particulate Matter and Hospitalization in COVID-19 Patients. *Respiratory Medicine* 178 (March): 106313. https://doi.org/10.1016/j.rmed.2021.106313.

Moore, D.K., Jerrett, M., Mack, W.J., and Künzli, N. (2007). A Land Use Regression Model for Predicting Ambient Fine Particulate Matter across Los Angeles, CA. *Journal of Environmental Monitoring* 9 (3): 246–252. https://doi.org/10.1039/B615795E.

Ng, L.C., Persily, A.K., and Emmerich, S.J. (2015). IAQ and energy impacts of ventilation strategies and building envelope airtightness in a big box retail building. *Building and Environment* 92 (October): 627–634. https://doi.org/10.1016/j.buildenv.2015.05.038.

Ng, L.C., Musser, A., Persily, A.K., and Emmerich, S.J. (2019). Airflow and Indoor Air Quality Models of DOE Prototype Commercial Buildings. In: *NIST TN 2072*. Gaithersburg, MD: National Institute of Standards and Technology https://doi.org/10.6028/NIST.TN.2072.

Prototype Building Models (2019). Governmental. *Building Energy Codes Program (blog)*. 2019: https://www.energycodes.gov/prototype-building-models.

Rong, L., Liu, D., Pedersen, E.F., and Zhang, G. (2015). The Effect of Wind Speed and Direction and Surrounding Maize on Hybrid Ventilation in a Dairy Cow Building in Denmark. *Energy and Buildings* 86 (January): 25–34. https://doi.org/10.1016/j.enbuild.2014.10.016.

Shi, Z., Qian, H., Zheng, X. et al. (2018). Seasonal Variation of Window Opening Behaviors in Two Naturally Ventilated Hospital Wards. *Building and Environment* 130 (February): 85–93. https://doi.org/10.1016/j.buildenv.2017.12.019.

Shirzadi, M., Naghashzadegan, M., and Mirzaei, P.A. (2018). Improving the CFD Modelling of Cross-Ventilation in Highly-Packed Urban Areas. *Sustainable Cities and Society* 37 (February): 451–465. https://doi.org/10.1016/j.scs.2017.11.020.

Song, Z., Murray, B.T., and Sammakia, B. (2013). Airflow and Temperature Distribution Optimization in Data Centers Using Artificial Neural Networks. *International Journal of Heat and Mass Transfer* 64 (September): 80–90. https://doi.org/10.1016/j.ijheatmasstransfer.2013.04.017.

Suh, H.H., Bahadori, T., Vallarino, J., and Spengler, J.D. (2000). Criteria Air Pollutants and Toxic Air Pollutants. *Environmental Health Perspectives* 108: 9.

Tong, Z., Wang, Y.J., Patel, M. et al. (2012). Modeling Spatial Variations of Black Carbon Particles in an Urban Highway-Building Environment. *Environmental Science & Technology* 46 (1): 312–319. https://doi.org/10.1021/es201938v.

Tong, Z., Chen, Y., and Malkawi, A. (2016). Defining the Influence Region in Neighborhood-Scale CFD Simulations for Natural Ventilation Design. *Applied Energy* 182 (November): 625–633. https://doi.org/10.1016/j.apenergy.2016.08.098.

Tong, Z., Chen, Y., Malkawi, A. et al. (2016a). Quantifying the Impact of Traffic-Related Air Pollution on the Indoor Air Quality of a Naturally Ventilated Building. *Environment International* 89–90 (April): 138–146. https://doi.org/10.1016/j.envint.2016.01.016.

Tong, Z., Chen, Y., Malkawi, A. et al. (2016b). Energy Saving Potential of Natural Ventilation in China: The Impact of Ambient Air Pollution. *Applied Energy* 179 (October): 660–668. https://doi.org/10.1016/j.apenergy.2016.07.019.

Tryner, J., L'Orange, C., Mehaffy, J. et al. (2020). Laboratory Evaluation of Low-Cost PurpleAir PM Monitors and in-Field Correction Using Co-Located Portable Filter Samplers. *Atmospheric Environment* 220 (January): 117067. https://doi.org/10.1016/j.atmosenv.2019.117067.

US EPA, OAR (2014). Introduction to Indoor Air Quality. In: *Collections and Lists*, vol. 14, 2014. US EPA https://www.epa.gov/indoor-air-quality-iaq/introduction-indoor-air-quality.

"Use of Energy Explained-Energy Use in Commercial Buildings." 2018. Use of Energy Explained Energy Use in Commercial Buildings.

Venables, W.N. and Ripley, B.D. (2002). *Modern Applied Statistics with S*, Fourthe. New York: Springer.

Wang, L. and Chen, Q. (2007). Theoretical and Numerical Studies of Coupling Multizone and CFD Models for Building Air Distribution Simulations. *Indoor Air* 17 (5): 348–361. https://doi.org/10.1111/j.1600-0668.2007.00481.x.

Wang, Y. and Malkawi, A. (2014). Annual Hourly CFD Simulation: New Approach—An Efficient Scheduling Algorithm for Fast Iteration Convergence. *Building Simulation* 7 (4): 401–415. https://doi.org/10.1007/s12273-013-0156-1.

Wang, L.L., Stuart Dols, W., and Chen, Q. (2010). Using CFD Capabilities of CONTAM 3.0 for Simulating Airflow and Contaminant Transport in and Around Buildings. *HVAC&R Research* 16 (6): 749–763. https://doi.org/10.1080/10789669.2010.10390932.

Weber, S.A., Insaf, T.Z., Hall, E.S. et al. (2016). Assessing the Impact of Fine Particulate Matter (PM 2.5) on Respiratory-Cardiovascular Chronic Diseases in the New York City Metropolitan Area Using Hierarchical Bayesian Model Estimates. *Environmental Research* 151 (November): 399–409. https://doi.org/10.1016/j.envres.2016.07.012.

Wei, W., Ramalho, O., Malingre, L. et al. (2019). Machine Learning and Statistical Models for Predicting Indoor Air Quality. *Indoor Air* 29 (5): 704–726. https://doi.org/10.1111/ina.12580.

"WHO | Air Pollution." 2019 WHO. Accessed February 2, 2019. http://www.who.int/airpollution/en/.

Wilcox, S. and Marion, W. (2008). *Users Manual for TMY3 Data Sets*." Technical Report NREL/TP-581-43156. 1617. Cole Boulevard, Golden, Colorado 80401-3393: National Renewable Energy Laboratory www.nrel.gov.

Wu, X., Nethery, R.C., Sabath, M.B. et al. (2020). Air Pollution and COVID-19 Mortality in the United States: Strengths and Limitations of an Ecological Regression Analysis. *Science Advances* 6 (45): eabd4049. https://doi.org/10.1126/sciadv.abd4049.

Yang, Y. and Zhao, Y. (2012). Prevailing Wind Direction Forecasting for Natural Ventilation Djustment in Greenhouses Based on LE-SVM. *Energy Procedia* 16: 252–258. https://doi.org/10.1016/j.egypro.2012.01.042.

Yi, Y.K. and Ali, M.M. (2012). Site-Specific Optimal Energy Form Generation Based on Hierarchical Geometry Relation. *Automation in Construction* 26 (October): 77–91. https://doi.org/10.1016/j.autcon.2012.05.004.

Zhou, Q. and Ooka, R. (2020). Comparison of Different Deep Neural Network Architectures for Isothermal Indoor Airflow Prediction. *Building Simulation* 13 (6): 1409–1423. https://doi.org/10.1007/s12273-020-0664-8.

4

An Integrative Deep Performance Framework for Daylight Prediction in Early Design Ideation

Shermeen Yousif and Daniel Bolojan

School of Architecture, Florida Atlantic University, Fort Lauderdale, FL, USA

Introduction

By 2050, the global population will expand by 2.1 billion, posing new challenges for housing and infrastructure provision and requiring us to rethink current design and construction methods (UN-Environment-Programme 2022). It is also anticipated that the equivalent of New York City will need to be built every 34 days for the next 40 years (Architecture-2030 2018) to accommodate such population growth. Intertwined with overpopulation are climate change challenges and increasing resource consumption. In the US, buildings consume approximately 40% of our total energy and contribute approximately 40% of the annual Greenhouse Gas emissions (DoE 2015). Effective energy performance evaluation and optimization are required to achieve building design resilience and adaptation to growing environmental challenges (Attia and De Herde 2011). To achieve energy efficiency across all building designs, real-time performance feedback needs to be integrated into performance-driven frameworks and be made accessible to a broad audience of building designers and engineers.

In recent years, there has been a shift toward developing real-time and predictive methods for building performance, moving away from traditional simulation methods. Machine learning (ML) algorithms have proven to be a promising tool in this area by learning patterns and relationships in data that can be used to make accurate predictions in real time. These methods are being utilized to predict daylight performance, energy consumption, and other environmental criteria at various scales, including individual building and city scales, thereby informing energy efficiency-related decisions. The potential benefits of real-time and predictive methods for building energy consumption are substantial, making their development an important area of research and innovation.

The growing ecological concerns have emphasized the need for performance evaluation in the building design process. Building Performance Simulation (BPS) is the established technique for accurately predicting the environmental performance of a building design (Yigit and Ozorhon 2018). Unfortunately, many designers lack the necessary expertise to use BPS effectively; therefore, the adoption of BPS to achieve superior building design performance faces significant challenges. Performance-Driven Generative Design Systems (PDGDSs)

Artificial Intelligence in Performance-Driven Design: Theories, Methods, and Tools, First Edition.
Edited by Narjes Abbasabadi and Mehdi Ashayeri.
©2024 John Wiley & Sons Inc. Published 2024 by John Wiley & Sons Inc.

incorporate BPS into generative parametric systems and have been shown to improve environmental efficiency in building design. Achieving optimal environmental performance, including increased energy efficiency and reduced carbon footprint, adds complexity to generative design systems, especially when thousands of design options are generated during the process. However, these systems still present significant challenges to nonexpert designers and engineers, including the need for a deep understanding of simulation procedures and optimization techniques.

The widespread use of BPS in the generative design process is hindered by its technically complex nature and the requirement for a deep understanding of building physics (Touloupaki and Theodosiou 2017), which presents the initial challenge. (i) BPS involves a dynamic process that utilizes multidisciplinary methods, making it challenging to accurately model environmental performance. The complexity of BPS is attributed to the interrelated variables required for environmental simulation (Nguyen, Reiter, and Rigo 2014). The second challenge (ii) is the seamless integration of BPS into the design framework to increase efficiency, which is problematic due to inadequate designer–system interaction and user interface. Despite attempts to develop methods that integrate performance simulation into generative protocols, such efforts are still computationally expensive and time-consuming (Farzaneh, Monfet, and Forgues 2019). Daylight simulation is particularly time-consuming and computationally expensive due to ray tracing and requires an extended time for annual studies. The third challenge (iii) is the computational expense of BPS methods, especially in generative parametric systems where thousands of design options emerge, making it challenging to establish the framework for the iterative simulation process. To address these challenges, designers could benefit from an automatic, real-time building performance evaluation for each design option generated in the design space. While environmental modeling research developments are typically intended after major design decisions have been made in the design development phase, there is a need to incorporate such performance simulation (i.e. daylight simulation) earlier in the conceptual design phase (Hemsath 2013). This shift in practice would allow designers to make informed design decisions regarding morphology and design alteration early in the design process; before major design decisions are finalized, the cost of design changes becomes costly in design development phases (MacLeamy 2004). In particular, daylight performance is a "form giver" (Reinhart 2019; Weber 2020) and designers must be aware of their design's daylight performance to make informed decisions regarding morphology and design alterations early in the design process.

The advent of Deep Learning (DL) models has facilitated the transition to the second generation of generative systems in design, as DL models can analyze, learn, and synthesize data (Goodfellow et al. 2014; Goodfellow, Bengio, and Courville 2016). Furthermore, Surrogate Models (SM) which are prediction models, are capable of accurately approximating the output of the simulation, substituting the original simulation model (Kim and Boukouvala 2020). SM can offer high-fidelity prediction of environmental parameters of designs and assist designers in making successful decisions. DL-based SM represent a promising solution for predicting environmental performance criteria and addressing the challenge of integrating performance evaluation in early design phases. These models closely emulate the behavior of BPS models while being less computationally expensive. Surrogate modeling involves developing an approximation of the input–output data obtained by the simulation, and DL models, which have multiple processing layers, can learn representations of data at different levels of abstraction. Therefore, Generative Adversarial Networks (GAN) can be utilized for surrogate modeling by allowing machines to learn structures and semantics by extracting features from input datasets (Goodfellow et al. 2014). However, developing an accurate, user-friendly, real-time SM for predicting daylight performance in building design remains a challenge and requires further investigation.

The research project aims to develop SM that can automate the retrieval of environmental daylight performance data in expanded design spaces (i.e. generative systems) and iterative parametric analyses. The focus here is on a recently developed method for predicting daylight performance to achieve higher efficiency in building design. The method, called Deep-Performance (DP) method, is designed to be accessible to a larger audience of designers, and it incorporates discrete technologies of DL, computational/parametric modeling, and daylight simulation. This study is part of a broader research project that aims at developing SM to automate multiple environmental aspects. The use of prediction-based methods instead of simulation-based methods overcomes the issue of domain expertise and computational requirements. The proposed fully functioning high-fidelity predictive model, enables accurate daylight prediction and real-time feedback, supporting informed design decision-making.

To develop the DP, we employed a supervised DL model, Pix2Pix (Isola et al. 2017), to offer designers a high-fidelity prediction of daylight performance for each design option. This automated prediction of daylight performance for design options liberates designers from the simulation task and enables their creative exploration. The proposed method involves a three-stage process, including data acquisition, SM training, as well as assessment and validation. This was conducted through prototype development and multiple test-case applications.

The development of the DP prototype followed a two-phase process. In Phase 1, the SM was trained on simple single-space floor plan designs without interior walls to evaluate the initial prototype. In Phase 2, we further refined our method by enhancing the SM and conducting additional experiments with more complex spatial configurations, including floor plans with interior walls and multi-room layouts. The improved model yielded promising results in terms of the accurate prediction of daylight performance. These two phases demonstrate how the DP method can be implemented in multiple design phases, such as the conceptual and schematic design stages. In the initial stages of design, the use of mass models allows for the rapid retrieval of daylight predictions to evaluate volumetric designs. As partitions are introduced in later design phases of the floor plan design, the daylight prediction is further refined and updated using our second trained models. For each daylight metric (i.e. spatial daylight autonomy [sDA] and useful daylight illuminance [UDLI]), we trained a separate model, leading to five trained models for each phase. Our methodology is considered an integrative design tool that serves to enhance the design process rather than being relegated to a separate evaluation phase. The primary aim of this approach is to enable designers to gain a comprehensive understanding of the interdependence between morphology/geometry and daylight.

Background

As per existing literature, the most significant and immediate effect of artificial intelligence (AI) is predicted to occur in performance-based fields, such as architectural and urban design (Leach 2022). The growing significance of data-driven methodologies and performance-informed design in architecture-engineering-construction (AEC) field has resulted in a steep surge in research on "performative AI" in architecture, as reflected in the available literature. The use of DL models in architectural research and practice is relatively new, dating back to only six years (Leach 2018). Prior to this, expert systems have been extensively used by architectural practitioners and researchers to generate design possibilities, optimize solutions, and streamline fabrication processes. The latest technologies, such as DL networks, allow designers to obtain critical information about a building's performance, enabling better-informed decision-making. The aim is to facilitate human–machine collaboration and augment human decision-making, rather than replacing it with autonomous AI systems, as suggested by Garry Kasparov (Kasparov 2017). Although ML was initially introduced in engineering to speed up complex simulations, such as computational fluid dynamics (CFD) simulations (Wilkinson and Hanna 2014), it has also found application in architectural design research. For example, Synthesize Fast CFD by ML (Zaghloul 2017) developed an ML-based computational design tool that can predict real-time airflow fields, enabling early exploration of multiple design options. However, the application of DL models to create performative systems remains limited.

In the realm of automating BPSs, prior research has relied heavily on the use of ML algorithms. Examples of this include support vector machines (SVM), which have been used to predict energy consumption in energy modeling (Lee, Jung, and Lee 2019). In addition, ML has found applications in other areas of building performance research, such as CFD. For instance, the Austrian Institute of Technology's Wind-flow Prediction through ML project employed ML approaches to predict wind-flow patterns (Galanos, Chronis, and Vesely 2019).

However, according to Ngarambe et al. (2023), the use of ML techniques in daylighting studies is still relatively recent, despite their potential in this area. Previous studies have only evaluated the effectiveness of a handful of algorithms in daylight-related research (Ahmad et al. 2017; Lorenz et al. 2018; Waheeb et al. 2019), and these daylight prediction studies are not yet directly applicable as design tools for generative systems. In the past, artificial neural networks (ANNs) have been employed to predict illuminance in office buildings (Kazanasmaz, Günaydin, and Binol 2009). In a recent study, shape classification was achieved using Neural Networks, and Auxiliary Classifier GAN (AC-GAN) was used to generate light and shadow patterns of windows and walls based on daylight performance (Shaghaghian and Yan 2019).

Notwithstanding the advancement in performative AI, the methodologies pertaining to daylight-related approaches are still undergoing experimentation and have not been verified as validated techniques for real-time daylight performance prediction in generative systems. It is this inadequacy that has motivated the current undertaking. The following paragraphs provide an overview of the key methods and concepts that are required when applying DL models for prediction-based performance simulation evaluation.

Daylight Simulation

To achieve sustainability, maximizing passive strategies such as daylight design becomes crucial. Creating well daylight architectural spaces should be an objective to counteract the waste of artificial lighting and poor illumination (Lam, 1977). Simulation of daylighting performance is highly related to the recent escalating focus on energy efficiency and environmentally conscious building design (Elghazi et al. 2014). In such a performance-based design approach, it is essential to identify environmental factors that impact the building design in the early design phases (Roudsari and Pak 2013). Successful daylight is targeted in the generative process of this study, where each emerging design option is analyzed against 5 daylight metrics, as explained in the test-case application section.

Deep Learning Models

GANs are models pitted against adversaries, like in a minimax game. In such models, a neural network called Discriminator (D) works against another neural network called Generator (G), as an opponent. In analogy to counterfeiters, the generator is attempting to produce fake currency to deceive the discriminator, while the latter works as a detective who attempts to detect the real from the "fake" or synthesized currency. Both G and D networks learn better in the training process in a competitive manner, improving their performances simultaneously (Goodfellow et al. 2014). A subclass of GANs is the conditional or "supervised" models such as Pix2Pix. In this image-to-image translation model, synthesizing images is based on labeling or pairing corresponding datasets, where reconstructing and producing images occur based on their labels of one image of the pair (Isola et al. 2017). We have adopted the Pix2Pix model and further improved it, formulating a revised strategy to be applied in building designs and their corresponding datasets.

DL-Based Surrogate Modeling

DL-based surrogate modeling is a research methodology that involves the use of neural networks to construct an approximate representation of a complex system. SM are often developed to provide fast approximations of more expensive models in order to reduce the computational burden (Qian et al. 2005). SM are prediction/statistical models that aim at accurately approximating the output of simulation models, substituting the original simulation model. The model is trained on data generated via selecting key simulation outputs representative of the design parameters' space (Kim and Boukouvala 2020). Full simulation is conducted at each important simulation point, in order to calculate the corresponding simulation result. A statistical model is built based on pairs of design parameters as input and their corresponding simulation output. SM have been extensively utilized in science and engineering optimization problems. To obtain a SM, the process involves dataset acquisition, training the prediction model, and measuring prediction accuracy compared to simulation data (Sobester, Forrester, and Keane 2008). SM can offer compact and instantaneous performance information (instead of simulation).

Verification Methods

To verify and validate the accuracy of the DL prediction results, we implemented two quantified metrics: the Structural Similarity Index Model (SSIM) of Wang et al. (2004), and Perceptual Similarity (PS), which are networks developed by Zhang et al. (2018). SSIM is a method for image quality assessment that involves extracting structural information and measuring the degradation of the structural data for the images under analysis. It is a newly developed method beyond the more traditional techniques that measure the visibility of errors or differences between two images (Wang et al. 2004). PS is another approach developed to evaluate the effectiveness of DL-produced images in a similar way humans perform perceptual judgments. According to the PS developers, verification and assessment, the method outperforms previous metrics (Zhang et al. 2018).

Research Methods

The research project aims to develop a novel DP framework for providing real-time feedback on daylight performance evaluation. The framework is composed of two primary components, each with distinct functionality. The front-end component facilitates user interaction with the framework through a user-friendly interface, while the back-end component is responsible for generating predictions. For system users (designers), in the application phase, the system becomes a two-process workflow that consists of a generative process (with floor plan design options) and an automatic daylight performance prediction offered by our trained model.

To develop the back-end component of the framework, the research addressed three main tasks. The first task involved developing a generative/parametric system that was coupled with daylight performance simulations to produce training samples for training the DL models. The second task was focused on experimenting, prototyping, and testing the DP method along with its associated processes and tools. Finally, the third task was dedicated to developing methods and tools for validating and evaluating the effectiveness of the framework.

To develop the first task, an incremental approach was followed. In the preliminary phase, a generative/parametric system was developed to generate simple floor plan layouts (single space) to produce daylight simulations and training samples for the SM. In the subsequent phase, the complexity of the generative model was increased by integrating interior partitions into the floor plan layouts (multiple spaces), and training samples were generated which were then used to further train the SM.

To develop the SM, a protocol of three tasks was followed, including (1) dataset acquisition was pursued using a parametric system with daylight simulation integrated, (2) the DL-based model was trained for prediction of daylight performance, and (3) assessment and validation studies were conducted, comparing prediction with actual simulations.

Data Acquisition

To develop the method, a SM training was necessary, which required data acquisition. The data acquisition process involved two phases of synthetic floor plan design creation (floor plans range between 50 and 200 square meters) using a generative parametric system paired with daylight simulation (Figure 4.1). The first phase focused on generating simple open floor plans without partitions. The second phase involved more complex floor plan designs with multi-room and partitions. In both phases, the synthetic designs were paired with daylight simulations to analyze their performance. In both phases, dataset processing, and augmentation were then employed to prepare the data for the SM training.

In both phases, conducting the experiment involved employing a (i) generative system to generate between 2000 and 3000 unique floor plan designs, which were used as input to generate five distinct metrics related to annual daylight performance. These metrics include spatial sDA, Direct Light Access (DLA), and UDLI ranges of UDLI0-100, UDLI100-2000, and UDLI2000, and more. The floor plans were annotated and labeled into three main classes, including the floor area (gray), wall (black), and window (yellow) classes. (ii) To improve the DL model's performance, data augmentation was performed before training. Data quality and quantity, along with the neural network model's architecture, are critical factors affecting performance. To

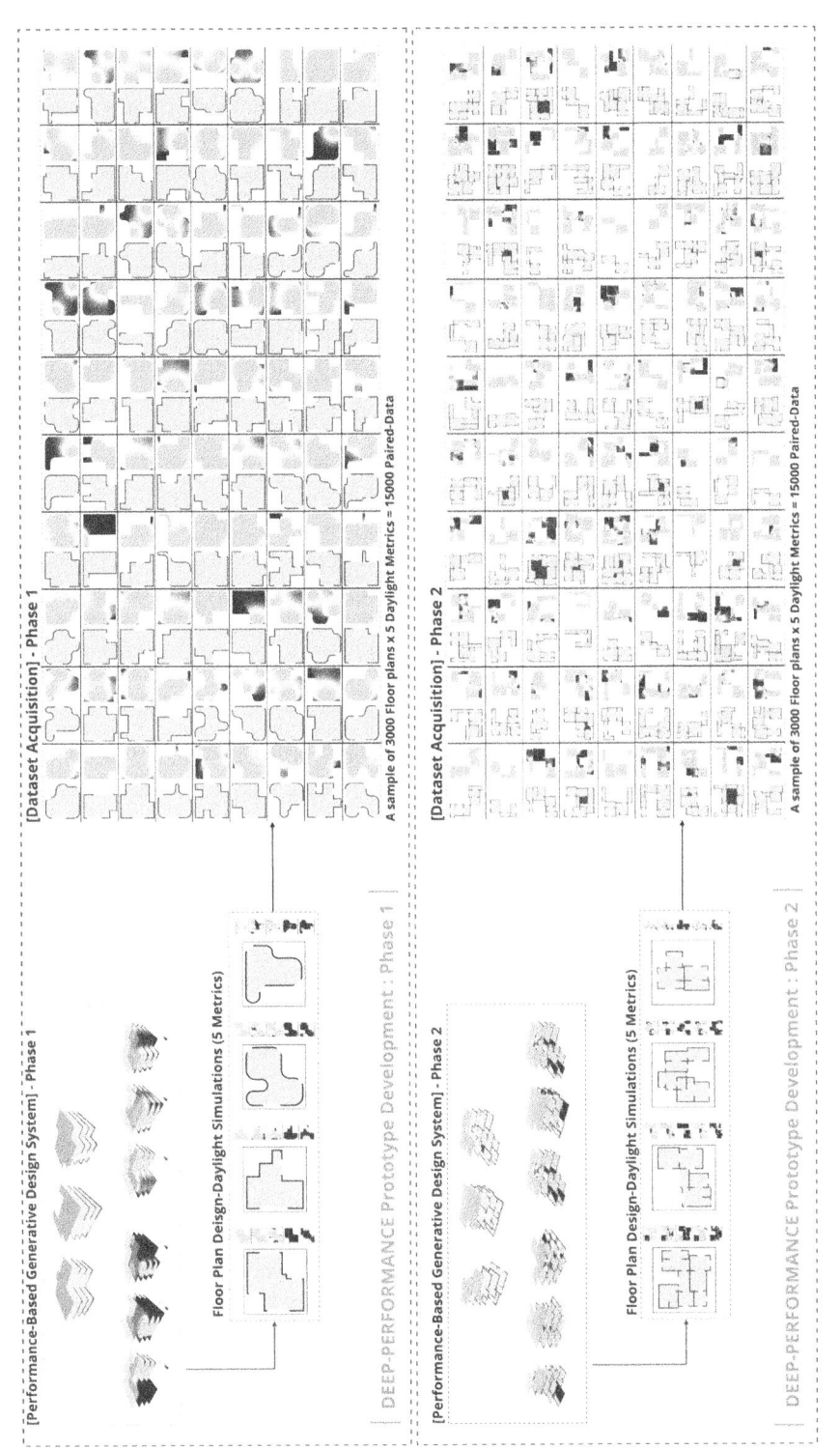

Figure 4.1 The datasets employed to train the surrogate model for both Phases 1 and 2 are generated from a parametric system, which integrates a daylight simulation of five key metrics.

analyze the dataset's topology, a U-Map algorithm was used to visualize the feature manifold dimensionality. Domain-specific augmentation techniques were applied to create new data points, resulting in a more diverse and improved dataset distribution. The initial dataset had limited variation, but the augmented dataset showed significant improvement (see Figure 4.2). The resulting paired dataset was augmented to 6000 (Phase 1) and 5400 (Phase 2) paired images representing floor plans and their corresponding daylight simulations.

Model Training

For the two phases, five distinct models for each daylight metric (sDA, DLA, UDLI 0-100, UDLI 100-2000, and UDLI 2000) were trained in a sequential accumulative fashion, progressively. The first set of models was trained with datasets from Phase 1 of simple single-room floor plans, and in the subsequent phase, the models were further trained with datasets from Phase 2, of complex multi-room floor plans. We used a modified Pix2Pix architecture for training, with changes made to the network's filters to create feature maps summarizing the input data features.

During Phase 1 testing, only synthetic testing samples were used. However, in Phase 2, the network was tested with both synthetic and real floor plan samples, specifically from "CubiCasa" (Kalervo et al. 2019), to evaluate its generalizability. The trained model achieved an average prediction accuracy of 89% when presented with new samples of real CubiCasa floor plans.

Results and Validation

During the inference phase, when provided with a floor plan as input, the model demonstrates the ability to generate highly precise daylight meshes for the five metrics (sDA, DLA, UDLI 0-100, UDLI 100-2000, and UDLI 2000). During the assessment and validation phase, the SM was evaluated for its ability to accurately predict daylight simulation in response to newly introduced floor plan designs, compared to the actual simulation data. Therefore, the results of the SM training were assessed following three methods: (1) SSIM, (2) PS index (Figure 4.3), and (3) our computational method calculated test points' daylight availability reading a specific threshold, similar to the simulation method (Honeybee®)'s way of calculation (Figure 4.4). Fifty samples of floor plans were used as an input to test and validate the abovementioned evaluation methods, comparing the results of the Honeybee® simulations with the results of the DP prediction.

For the SSIM method, in Phase 1, comparing the daylight prediction results (UDLI over 2000) to the simulation results, the predictions showed an average similarity value of 0.94, with an overall similarity value range of 0.84–0.96. In Phase 2, the similarity ranged between 0.91 and 0.99. In the two phases, a set of eight floor plans was used for this validation process. It is important to add that in Phase 1 additional assessment was conducted using 25 floor plans to evaluate the prediction against the simulation results, while in Phase 2, in addition to the 8 floor plans, the CubiCasa were used for additional assessment. This was applied to both the SSIM and PS metrics.

In using the PS measure, Phase 1 showed a high similarity with the lowest value was 0.89 and the highest value of 0.98. For the second phase, the lowest value of PS retrieved was 0.93 and the highest value was 0.97. In both phases, assessments were performed using the UDLI over 2000 metrics. Also, in both phases, a set of eight floor plans was used.

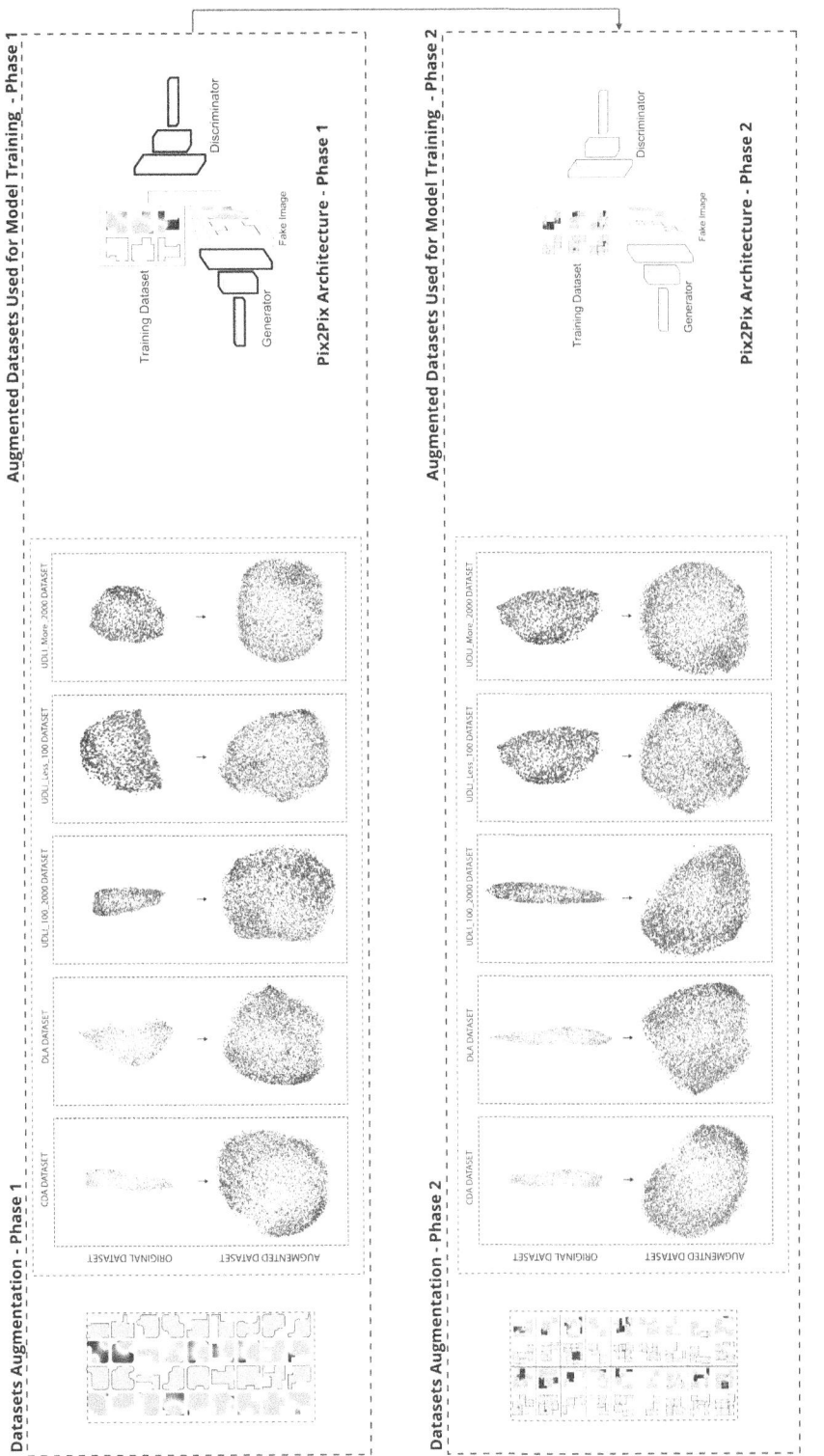

Figure 4.2 Topological data analysis was employed, and dataset augmentation was pursued and represented through the U-Map algorithm. For each of the two phases, the original dataset distribution is depicted in the top row and the augmented dataset distribution is illustrated in the bottom row.

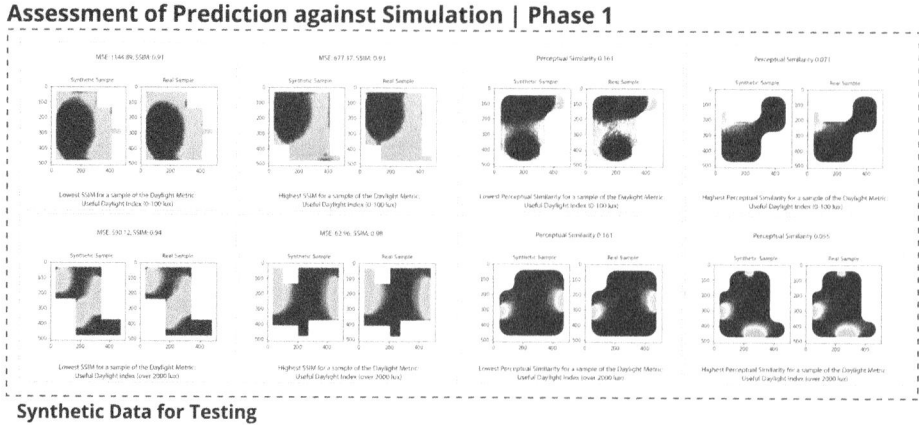

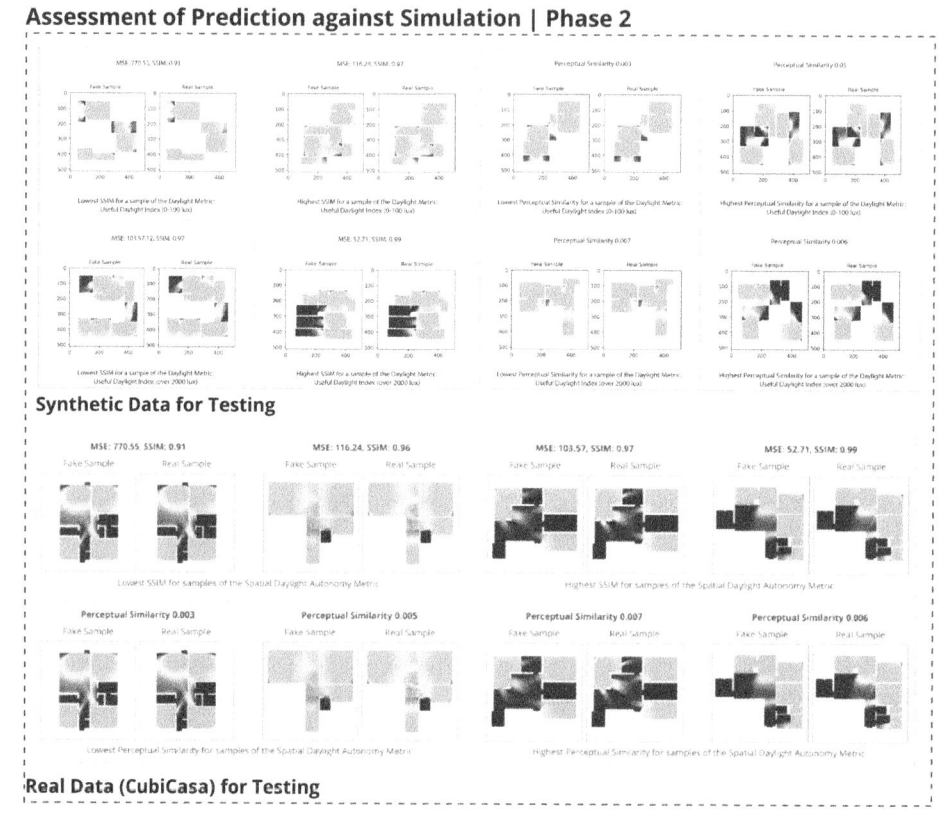

Figure 4.3 For each of Phases 1 and 2, prediction data were assessed in synthetic-real pairs; assessment was conducted using SSIM and PS measures. In Phase 2, additional assessment was pursued using real data (CubiCasa).

Discussions of Results

The performance of daylight in buildings has a significant influence on the building form (Reinhart 2019). This implies that daylight plays a vital role in shaping the design of buildings. Specifically, compact building forms tend to have limited opportunities for daylighting due to

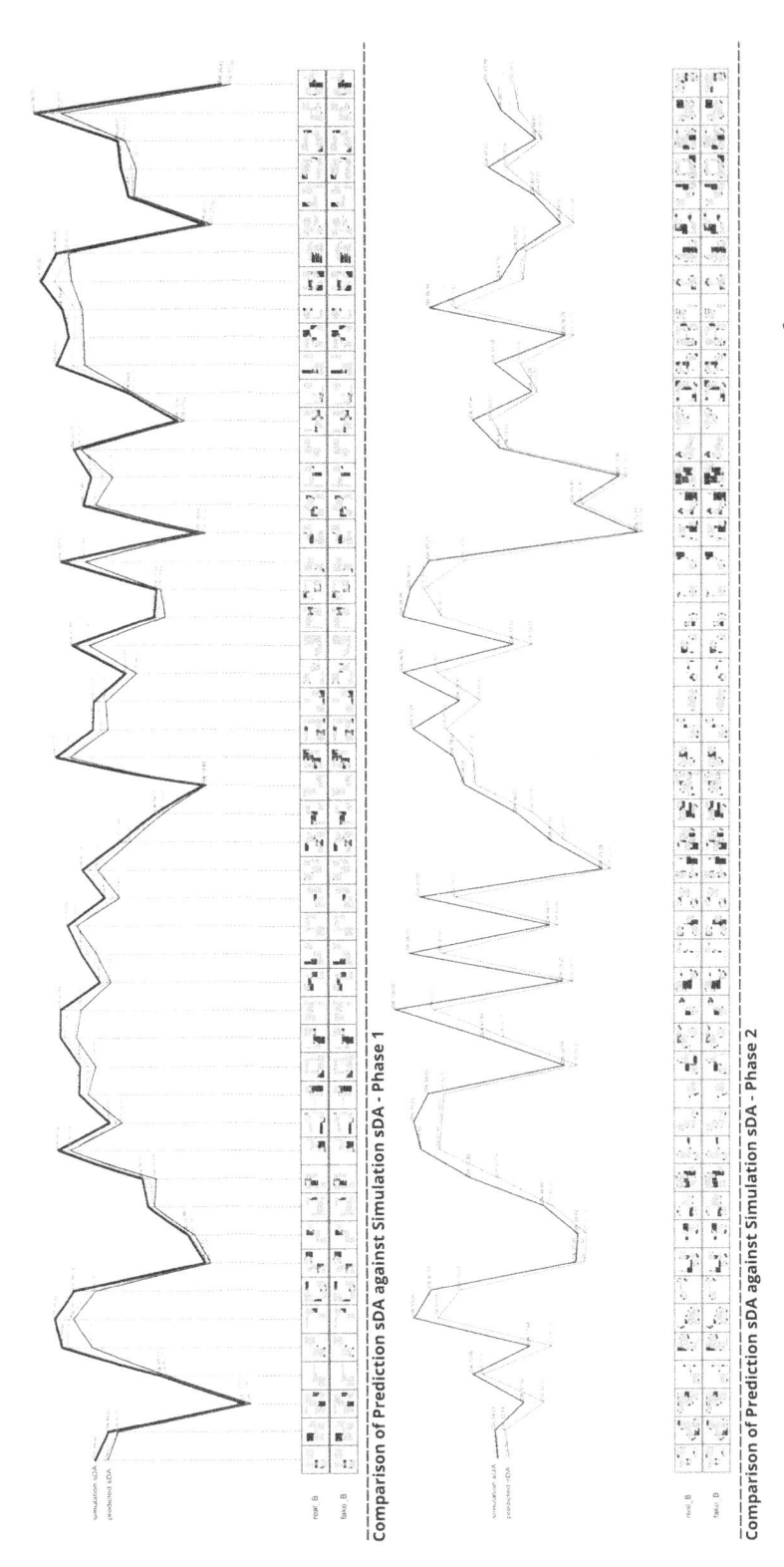

Comparison of Prediction sDA against Simulation sDA - Phase 1

Comparison of Prediction sDA against Simulation sDA - Phase 2

Figure 4.4 Comparison between the results of daylight prediction and the results of daylight simulation using the Honeybee® calculation method for daylight meshes in both phases 1 and 2.

the relatively smaller surface area, while extended building forms are more conducive to daylighting due to their larger surface-to-volume ratio, which allows for greater window surface area. Therefore, designers must possess a thorough understanding of the daylight performance of each design to enable informed decision-making regarding morphology and design modifications in the early stages of the design process, as noted by Caldas, Luisa, and da Oliveira Gama Caldas (2001).

In the realm of architectural design, early integration of daylight analysis is deemed an essential element that ensures optimal performance of buildings. The rationale behind this assertion stems from the significant impact of daylighting on several design decisions such as building shape, orientation, placement and sizing of windows, and selection of building materials. The integration of daylight analysis in the early design phase facilitates the identification of areas that exhibit suboptimal illumination performance, allowing designers to explore and employ alternative solutions that refine their design concepts and improve building efficiency.

By using daylight analysis in the early stages of design, designers can uncover crucial information such as whether a particular building form or window placement is hindering daylight penetration into the building. This, in turn, helps the designer to fine-tune the building morphology or window placement, enhancing daylighting performance. Furthermore, early stage daylight analysis also presents opportunities for creative design solutions that leverage natural illumination, such as the use of light wells or skylights. Ultimately, the early integration of daylight analysis in the design process enables designers to make more informed design decisions that enhance the quality of the building, aligned with the client's expectations, and promote environmental sustainability.

The SM demonstrated high accuracy in daylighting predictions, which facilitates the model's integration into design generation, enabling designers to automatically retrieve design performance evaluation. The method makes a significant contribution to the development of efficient and resilient building design through the adoption of prediction-based methods in lieu of simulation-based techniques. This approach seeks to address the challenges posed by domain expertise and computational complexity, and ultimately facilitate the design process. By adopting prediction-based methods, the method seeks to streamline the design process and make it more accessible to designers with limited environmental simulation expertise, with the aim of facilitating performance-driven design. By automating performative aspects, design decision-making is accelerated and improved, resulting in a faster feedback loop between design decisions and environmental evaluation. The proposed method is 600 times faster and provides a comparable accuracy of 90% when compared to HoneyBee® and Diva®. Designers can retrieve daylight simulation results in less than 0.3 seconds for each prediction, and a pre-trained model is available for instant feedback on daylight performance, making this an efficient and accurate solution for daylight simulation in the design process. Potential limitations could include the model's generalizability to more intricate architectural layouts, and future work involves increasing the diversity and complexity of the architectural floor plan layouts, including multiple rooms, scale, program, and zoning. The model should be further trained and tested.

The method aims to establish the integration of the developed DP as a design tool in a manner that is fully integrative with the design process. This integration is expected to provide the designer with the ability to initiate the diagramming process and, during the ideation phase, commence the drawing of a building's outline, while concurrently obtaining real-time feedback on daylight prediction. This feedback mechanism affords the designer an opportunity to respond with a new design iteration that forms the basis of an iterative process. Ultimately, this iterative process culminates in a constant feedback loop between the SM and the design changes, thereby facilitating a more comprehensive and responsive design approach (Figure 4.5).

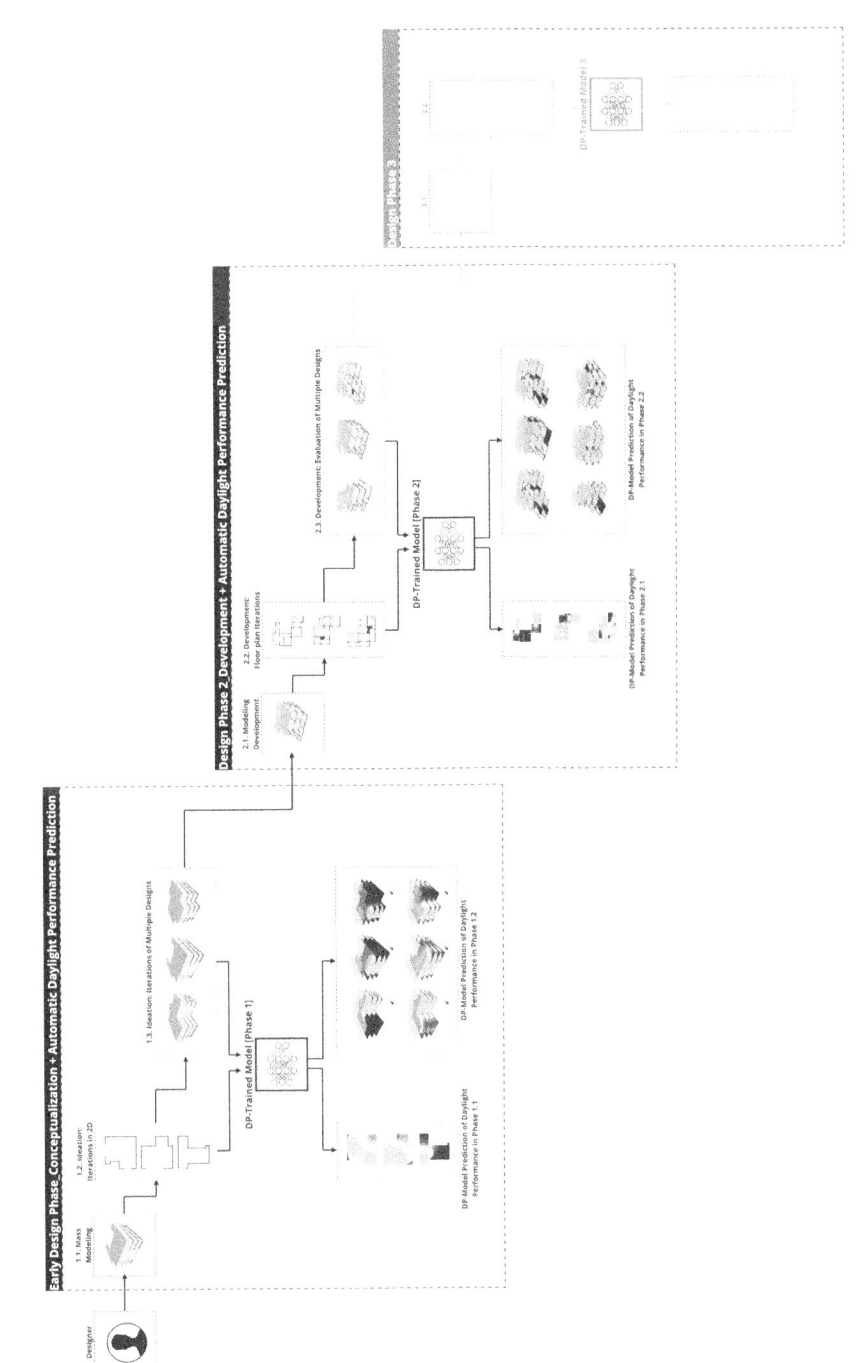

Figure 4.5 A workflow with multiple design phases and DP prediction model used at each phase.

Conclusions

The present study highlights the efficacy of employing DL techniques to establish SM for accurate and efficient daylight simulation in the architectural design process. Such an approach streamlines the design process and enhances accessibility for designers who may not possess environmental simulation expertise. The utilization of the DL-based surrogate modeling approach proposed here has the potential to democratize performance evaluation, making it more widely accessible to non-experts, particularly during the initial phases of the design process. With respect to daylight simulations, this approach represents a paradigm shift in thinking, as the traditional technical view of daylight is replaced by a more nuanced perspective, which acknowledges the significant hurdles that designers face when trying to manage the complexities of environmental simulation. By removing these barriers, the proposed method enables designers to more effectively integrate daylight prediction into early design processes, leading to a more efficient and comprehensive approach to building design. By automating performative aspects of the design process, the proposed method expedites decision-making and facilitates faster feedback loops between design decisions and environmental evaluations.

The study's overarching goal is to enable sustainable and cost-effective building design utilizing data-driven methods. The proposed daylight prediction tool's integration aims to provide designers with the ability to receive real-time feedback during the ideation phase, allowing for iterative design processes. This approach enhances the designer's responsiveness and provides a more comprehensive and iterative design approach, culminating in a constant feedback loop between the SM and design changes.

Future research directions include developing additional labeling techniques for more complex architectural layouts to achieve an accurate simulation for multiple-program activities. Additionally, the integration of window heights and shading devices into floor plan labels and the exploration of more fluid, angled, and more irregular floor plans could further improve the generalizability of the model. To enhance navigation through thousands of design options, the framework will be improved to achieve an articulated and searchable design space. The development of additional AI models will help sort out successful design alternatives with higher environmental performance. The formulation of a designer-friendly interface will be assessed in empirical studies, and a cloud-based interface integrating this method will be targeted to achieve computation efficiency.

References

Ahmad, Muhammad, Jean-Laurent Hippolyte, Monjur Mourshed, and Yacine Rezgui. 2017. Random Forests and Artificial Neural Network for Predicting Daylight Illuminance and Energy Consumption.

Architecture-2030. 2018. Why the Building Sector? https://architecture2030.org/buildings_problem_why/.

Attia, S. and De Herde, A. (2011). Early Design Simulation Tools for Net Zero Energy Buildings: A Comparison of Ten Tools. In: *Conference Proceedings of 12th International Building Performance Simulation Association, 2011*.

Caldas, L.G., Luisa, M., and da Oliveira Gama Caldas (2001). *An Evolution-Based Generative Design System: Using Adaptation to Shape Architectural Form*. Massachusetts Institute of Technology.

DoE. 2015. Chapter 5: Increasing Efficiency of Building Systems and Technologies. https://www.energy.gov/sites/prod/files/2017/03/f34/qtr-2015-chapter5.pdf

Elghazi, Y., Wagdy, A., Mohamed, S., and Hassan, A. (2014). *Daylighting Driven Design: Optimizing Kaleidocycle Facade for Hot Arid Climate.* Aachen: Fifth German-Austrian IBPSA Conference, RWTH Aachen University.

Farzaneh, A., Monfet, D., and Forgues, D. (2019). Review of using Building Information Modeling for building energy modeling during the design process. *Journal of Building Engineering* 23: 127–135.

Galanos, T., Chronis, A., and Vesely, O. (2019). Wind flow prediction through machine learning. *AIT* http://cities.ait.ac.at/site/index.php/2019/05/29/wind-flow-prediction-through-machine-learning/.

Goodfellow, I., Pouget-Abadie, J., Mirza, M. et al. (2014). Generative adversarial nets. *Advances in Neural Information Processing Systems* 27.

Goodfellow, I., Bengio, Y., and Courville, A. (2016). *Deep Learning.* MIT Press.

Hemsath, T.L. (2013). Conceptual Energy Modeling for Architecture, Planning and Design: Impact of Using Building Performance Simulation in Early Design Stages. In: *13th Conference of International Building Performance Simulation Association.*

Isola, P., Zhu, J.-Y., Zhou, T., and Efros, A.A. (2017). Image-to-Image Translation with Conditional Adversarial Networks. In: *Proceedings of the IEEE Conference on Computer Vision and Pattern Recognition.*

Kalervo, A., Ylioinas, J., Häikiö, M. et al. (2019). Cubicasa5k: A Dataset and an Improved Multi-task Model for Floorplan Image Analysis. In: *Image Analysis: 21st Scandinavian Conference, SCIA 2019, Norrköping, Sweden, June 11–13, 2019, Proceedings,* 21.

Kasparov, G. (2017). *Deep Thinking: Where Machine Intelligence Ends and Human Creativity Begins.* Hachette UK.

Kazanasmaz, T., Günaydin, M., and Binol, S. (2009). Artificial Neural Networks to Predict Daylight Illuminance in Office Buildings. *Building and Environment* 44 (8): 1751–1757.

Kim, S.H. and Boukouvala, F. (2020). Surrogate-Based Optimization for Mixed-Integer Nonlinear Problems. *Computers & Chemical Engineering* 140: 106847.

Lam, W. (1977). *Perception and Lighting as Formgivers for Architecture.* McGraw-Hill.

Leach, N. (2018). Design in the Age of Artificial Intelligence. *Landscape Architecture Frontiers* 6 (2): 8–20.

Leach, N. (2022). *Architecture in the Age of Artificial Intelligence: An introduction to AI for Architects.* Bloomsbury Publishing.

Lee, S., Jung, S., and Lee, J. (2019). Prediction Model Based on an Artificial Neural Network for User-Based Building Energy Consumption in South Korea. *Energies* 12 (4): 608.

Lorenz, Clara-Larissa, Michael Packianather, Achim Spaeth, and Clarice Bleil De Souza. 2018. *Artificial Neural Network-Based Modelling for Daylight Evaluations.*

MacLeamy, P. 2004. "MacLeamy curve." Collaboration, Integrated Information, and the Project Lifecycle in Building Design and Construction and Operation (WP-1202).

Ngarambe, Jack, Patrick Nzivugira Duhirwe, Tran Van Quang, Jean d'Amour Nzarigema, and Geun Young Yun. 2023. "Coupling Convolutional Neural Networks With Gated Recurrent Units to Model Illuminance Distribution From Light Pipe Systems." *Building and Environment* 110276. https://doi.org/10.1016/j.buildenv.2023.110276. https://www.sciencedirect.com/science/article/pii/S0360132323003037.

Nguyen, A.-T., Reiter, S., and Rigo, P. (2014). A Review on Simulation-Based Optimization Methods Applied to Building Performance Analysis. *Applied Energy* 113: 1043–1058.

Qian, Z., Seepersad, C.C., Roshan Joseph, V. et al. (2005). Building Surrogate Models Based on Detailed and Approximate Simulations. *Journal of Mechanical Design* 128 (4): 668–677. https://doi.org/10.1115/1.2179459.

Reinhart, C. (2019). Daylight performance predictions. In: *Building Performance Simulation for Design and Operation*, 221–269. Routledge.

Roudsari, Mostapha Sadeghipour, and Michelle Pak. 2013. "Ladybug: A Parametric Environmental Plugin for Grasshopper to Help Designers Create an Environmentally-Conscious Design".

Shaghaghian, Z. and Yan, W. (2019). Application of Deep Learning in Generating Desired Design Options: Experiments Using Synthetic Training Dataset. *arXiv* preprint arXiv:2001.05849.

Sobester, A., Forrester, A., and Keane, A. (2008). *Engineering Design via Surrogate Modelling: a Practical Guide*. John Wiley & Sons.

Touloupaki, E. and Theodosiou, T. (2017). Energy Performance Optimization as a Generative Design Tool for Nearly Zero Energy Buildings. *Procedia Engineering* 180: 1178–1185.

UN-Environment-Programme. 2022. *2021 Global Status Report for Buildings and Construction. Towards a Zero-Emissions, Efficient and Resilient Buildings and Construction Sector*.

Waheeb, W., Ghazali, R., Ismail, L.H., and Kadir, A.A. (2019). Modelling and Forecasting Indoor Illumination Time Series Data from Light Pipe System. In: *Recent Trends in Data Science and Soft Computing: Proceedings of the 3rd International Conference of Reliable Information and Communication Technology (IRICT 2018)*.

Wang, Z., Bovik, A.C., Sheikh, H.R., and Simoncelli, E.P. (2004). Image Quality Assessment: From Error Visibility to Structural Similarity. *IEEE Transactions on Image Processing* 13 (4): 600–612.

Weber, R.E. (2020). *Geometries of light*. Massachusetts Institute of Technology.

Wilkinson, S. and Hanna, S. (2014). Approximating Computational Fluid Dynamics for Generative Tall Building Design. *International Journal of Architectural Computing* 12 (2): 155–177.

Yigit, S. and Ozorhon, B. (2018). A Simulation-Based Optimization Method for Designing Energy Efficient Buildings. *Energy and Buildings* 178: 216–227.

Zaghloul, M. (2017). *Machine-Learning Aided Architectural Design-Synthesize Fast CFD by Machine-Learning*. Zurich: ETH.

Zhang, R., Isola, P., Efros, A.A. et al. (2018). The Unreasonable Effectiveness of Deep Features as a Perceptual Metric. *Proceedings of the IEEE Conference on Computer Vision and Pattern Recognition*.

5

Artificial Intelligence in Building Enclosure Performance Optimization: Frameworks, Methods, and Tools

Farshad Kheiri

School of Architecture, Southern Illinois University Carbondale, Carbondale, IL, USA

Building Envelope and Performance

A building envelope refers to the parts of a building that act as barriers between the interior and exterior environments. Building envelope components can include external walls, windows, skylights, doors, and floors. The configurations and the properties of a building envelope play a crucial role in multiple aspects, including the environmental performance of a building, as well as other criteria, such as esthetics.

One of the primary considerations of a building envelope is its environmental impact. The main aspects of the environmental performance of a building influenced by envelope design include thermal comfort, energy efficiency, daylighting, visual connection to the outdoors, acoustics, indoor air quality, and in general, the life cycle impact of the design. Figure 5.1 illustrates building attributes that impact building environmental performance. The design of a building envelope requires the *analysis* of the conditions and the formulation of the design problem, the design *synthesis* through generating solutions, and the *evaluation* of design alternatives. Building envelope attributes in these alternatives range from the geometrical features and configurations to the material properties. Incorporating sustainable criteria in buildings requires a comprehensive approach, which entails considering different attributes of the building envelope design.

The design of a building envelope is a unique problem that addresses the specific needs of the building in its context. Additionally, the design of a building envelope requires careful trade-offs, as a better performance in one criterion may require compromise in some other criteria. Therefore, the goal of the design team is to find a solution that successfully addresses the unique needs of a certain building envelope design and wholistically addresses the environmental and other criteria.

Artificial Intelligence and Building Envelope Overview

The analysis, synthesis, and evaluation phases of a building envelope design process have been traditionally handled by the design team. However, the multifaceted nature of a

Artificial Intelligence in Performance-Driven Design: Theories, Methods, and Tools, First Edition.
Edited by Narjes Abbasabadi and Mehdi Ashayeri.
©2024 John Wiley & Sons Inc. Published 2024 by John Wiley & Sons Inc.

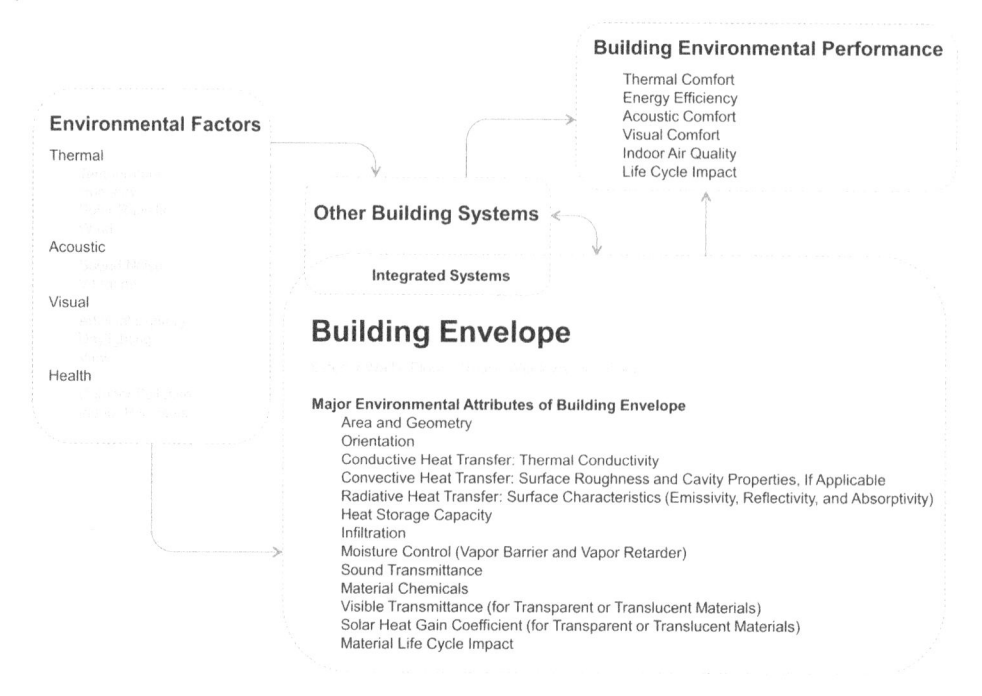

Figure 5.1 Building envelope attributes in relation to environmental factors.

building envelope design, commonly comprised of conflicting requirements, makes it challenging to easily reach optimal design solutions. Artificial intelligence (AI) is an effective way of performing these tasks. The complexity of the design problem, on the one hand, and the more readily available computational power today combined with the advent of necessary tools has made the use of machines a suitable choice in building envelope design. Although currently, the traditional approach is the dominant approach in the different phases of a building envelope design, the use of AI in the design process is growing fast, where the automated process of the building envelope design can help more effectively search through possible design alternatives, synthesize design solutions, and evaluate multiple alternatives with little or no intervention of the human. There are different AI techniques used in building envelope design and evaluation. The following sections discuss major optimization methods and machine learning methodologies that have been extensively used in designing and evaluating building envelope performance.

Optimization Routes and Building Envelope

Optimization means finding the best solution(s) among different feasible alternatives, where feasible solutions mean those that satisfy all the constraints. A building envelope design is an optimization problem where the objective is to find the best design alternative–or, more practically, a near-optimal solution–with regard to specific criteria prioritized for the project and typically documented in the owner's project requirements. There are numerous optimization methods. In general, optimization methods integrated with building modeling tools such as Rhino-Grasshopper (McNeel 2010) and Revit Generative Design (Revit 2021), along with generative design dashboard tools, such as NBBJ (Duong 2022), Generative Design Tool for Modular Buildings (Cheng et al. 2020), has been used to automate part of the design and evaluation processes.

This section provides an overview of the framework and considerations for the widely used methods in building envelope design and analysis.

Optimization Frameworks

Optimization requires problem formulation. In this first step, variables and the ranges in which these parameters can vary should be defined. There are also constraints and fixed parameters that are required in the design but are defined as fixed parameters. Additionally, the objectives of the design will be defined, which will derive the search process. A correct formulation of the problem will impact the final solutions significantly. Following the formulation of the problem, an evaluation mechanism should be defined to enable quantifying the performance of any given alternative that satisfies the problem formation criteria. In building performance, this phase typically requires the integration of simulations or calculation procedures in the optimization. Finally, there needs to be a search mechanism that probes among possible options to find the optimal or near-optimal solution. The general flowchart of the computational optimization is shown in Figure 5.2.

Optimization Methods

Optimization methods can vary based on the search methodologies. In general terms, Goldberg (1989) classified optimization methods into three classes: enumerative or exhaustive methods, calculus methods, and stochastic methods. In a building envelope design, analysis of all possible alternatives in the search space as in exhaustive methods is typically impossible. Also, the application of calculus methods is generally limited to problems with explicit expressions and those that permit derivatives. The significantly large search space of a building envelope design, typically comprising both continuous and discrete variables, has made stochastic optimization methods a suitable option for these problems. Bio-inspired or other stochastic optimization methods intelligently direct the search process into certain areas of the search space to which the optimization method has statistically converged. The selection of the appropriate optimization routine depends on the nature of the problem and the features of the optimization method.

While metaheuristic algorithms have been shown to be effective in building envelope design, there are limitations associated with each method that hinder the search performance. In general, besides the search performance of an algorithm, one would expect consistency and robustness in the algorithm as well. However, given the randomness in the algorithms and the complexities of building envelope design, there may be cases that the algorithm prematurely converges to a local optimum. Common methods to overcome this issue are providing mechanisms that encourage diversifying the search process in the algorithm and utilizing hybrid search algorithms. An example of diversification in the algorithm is the crowd distance computation in Nondominated Sorting Genetic Algorithm II (NSGA-II), and a classic case of hybridization is the combination of a metaheuristic algorithm with a mathematical optimization technique such as hill climbing. However, modification to algorithms

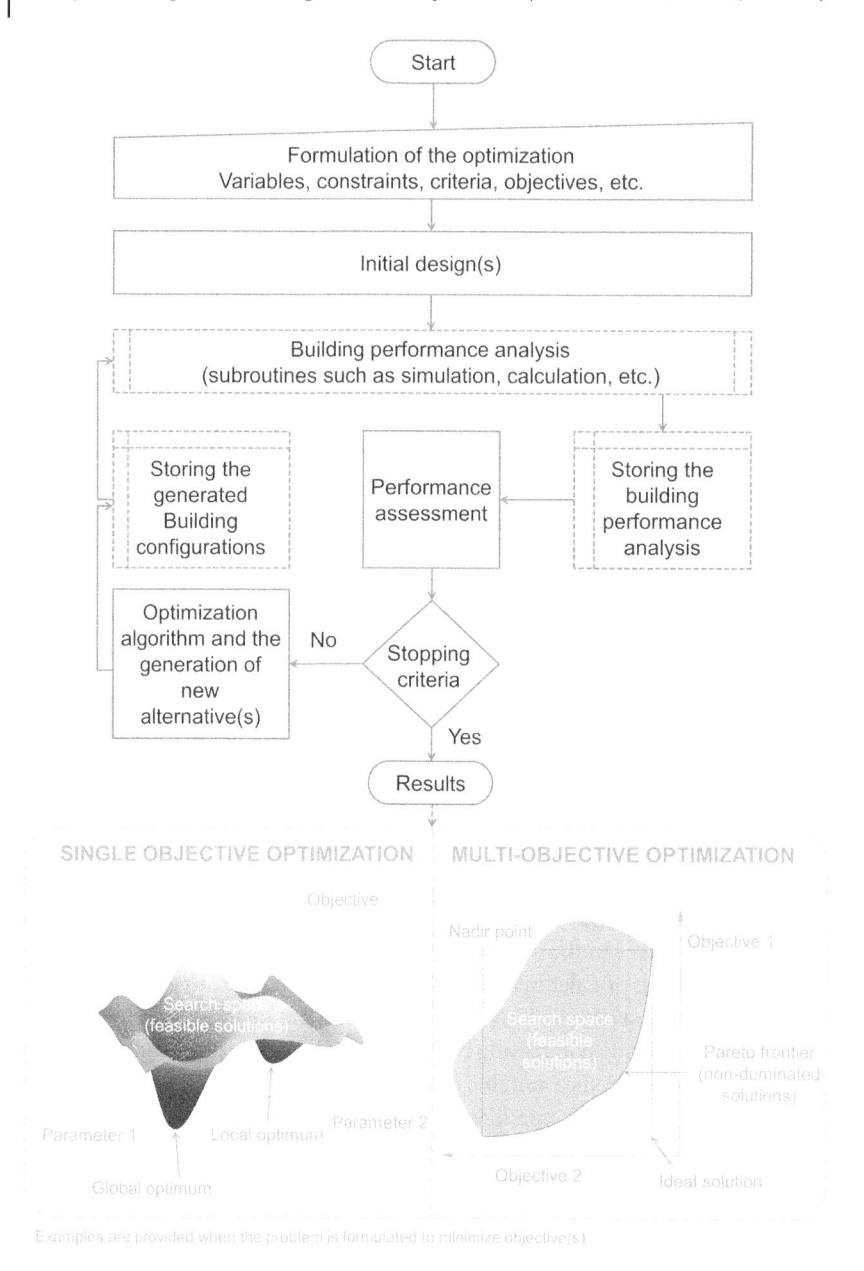

Figure 5.2 General flowchart of the computational optimization.

or hybridization should be carefully selected to avoid both trapping in the local optimum and search failures. An example of a case where simple hill-climbing fails to find the optimal solution is shown in the optimization of the shading for daylighting in Figure 5.3, where the initial case is shown with the black dot. The simple hill-climbing with a one-at-a-time change of parameters will skip the one-step diagonal path that leads to the global optimum. Further improvements by using proper randomization for this case are discussed in Kheiri (2021).

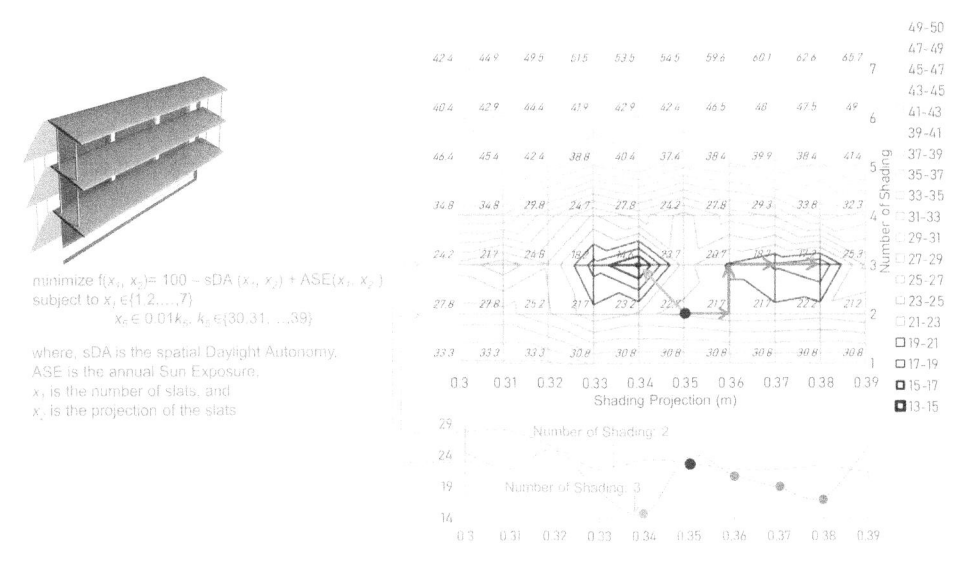

Figure 5.3 Hill-climbing approach in a daylighting optimization.

Machine Learning and Building Envelope

Different machine learning techniques have been utilized in building envelope design and evaluation. In general, machine learning methods include supervised learning, which uses a set of labeled data training and unsupervised learning, which does not require labeled data for training, and classifies the inputs into different groups, or semi-supervised learning, where models are trained partially using the labeled data and the model progressively continues to generate labeled data, which will be then used for the training, and reinforced learning, which is based on rewarding desired outputs and punishing undesired ones without requiring a training dataset. This section provides an overview of the commonly used machine learning methods in building performance based on the structure of the methods.

Artificial Neural Network

Artificial Neural Network (ANN) is a biologically inspired computational model that can be used to estimate a numerical value or classify inputs into one of the defined classes. In the brain, a neuron receives, processes, and passes the signals using axons, synapses, and dendrites. If a neuron is activated by the processed electrical pulses, it will stimulate other neighboring neurons in the interconnected network of neurons. As described by Krogh (2008), the computational model based on neurons was initiated in 1943, when McCulloch and Pitts modeled a neuron that could be activated based on the total weighted input. Later, computational models to classify linearly separable data were proposed (Minsky and Papert 1969), followed by an error back-propagation method for more complex nonlinear problems (Rumelhart, Hinton, and Williams 1986). Since the initial formulations of the ANN, there have been numerous advancements in the architecture of ANNs that have extended their use in different fields.

A deep learning network is a multilayer neural network model that unravels intricate structures within large datasets through a backpropagation algorithm (LeCun, Bengio, and Hinton 2015). They are structured to create interconnected layers of neurons where mathematical operations will pass activation values. In general, an ANN typically consists of several neurons as inputs, a number of hidden layers, and one or more outputs. All the neurons in each layer are connected to every single neuron in the following layer. These connections, in fact, indicate that the values in a given neuron will be multiplied by a weight assigned to the connection of the neuron and a given neuron in the following layer. Each neuron will be activated more or less depending on the features in the inputs to result in an appropriate output. In fact, the activation value for each neuron will determine how significantly the value in a certain neuron will impact the final outputs. Consequently, there will be a weighted sum of the values in the preceding layer based on the weights corresponding to each connection. Additionally, a bias term shifts the weighted sum value as desired to manipulate the activation of a neuron as desired for optimal outputs. The bias helps a neuron to activate only when it should be activated. Since the process deals with real numbers, the weighted average values and the bias may result in any number. Consequently, functions will be used to normalize the values to a number between zero to one to facilitate encoding activation operations. Common activation functions in ANN include the sigmoid function and Rectified Linear Unit (ReLU) function. Similar operations are applied to all the different layers connecting the neurons.

For a given structure of an ANN, the weights and values for any connection between any two given neurons and the bias value of the neuron mainly determine an ANN model to accurately predict output values. An ANN, therefore, should first be trained, where it recursively updates the weights and biases to achieve optimal results. Through the training process, an ANN will learn how to set the weights and biases that, for a given set of inputs, the operations in the network will result in values close to the actual corresponding outputs. Therefore, the ANN learning process first requires a dataset with known inputs and outputs, which is referred to as the labeled dataset. The labeled dataset consists of several inputs and one or more outputs. A training dataset should be large enough to ensure that the ANN model is able to learn from the dataset. Second, there needs to be a cost function that quantifies the outputs' accuracy. A typical cost function is the Mean Squared Error (MSE), where the average of the squared differences between every single output of the ANN and the actual output determines how accurately the ANN predicts the output. Third, the model needs a mechanism to adjust the weights and biases to improve accuracy. An ANN typically starts with a random set of numbers for these values that may be far from optimal values. A commonly preferred method to adjust the weights is called backpropagation, where using gradient descent, weights and biases that will most impact the outputs will be tuned to result in a more accurate model. As the name of the backpropagation indicates, the process starts from the cost function and finds its way toward the weights and biases of the precedent layers. It is worthwhile mentioning that while the objective is to reduce the MSE, which is calculated for all the inputs in the whole training dataset, in practice, gradient descent is used for a random subset of the dataset; hence, the name stochastic gradient descent. Eventually, using these three main components, an ANN will be trained, typically in multiple cycles, called epochs, using the whole training dataset to fine-tune the weights and biases.

During the training of an ANN, besides the training dataset, there is a validation dataset for which the accuracy of the model will be calculated. The validation dataset is a similar dataset to the training dataset, typically comprising 10 to 20% of the total labeled data, which has never been used as the training dataset and is continuously used in each epoch to unbiasedly evaluate the accuracy of the model by using a data that the model is not trained for. A high accuracy in a testing dataset and a low accuracy in the validation dataset means that the data has *memorized* the data in the dataset and cannot perform as well when used for a new similar dataset. A similar less accurate performance of the model as in the validation data is then expected when the ANN is eventually used for test data, which is the data we have typically trained the ANN for and do not know the outputs. This common issue is called overfitting, where the model is too complex and is incentivized for being tuned for the noise in the data rather than generalizing the data. On the other hand, a model with a less complex structure than required for a dataset will result in low accuracies in both the testing and the validation datasets, and most probably for the testing data. This is called underfitting, where either more number of inputs, layers, neurons, or other structures and activation functions are needed to generalize a dataset.

The cost function values of the validation dataset allow for tuning the hyperparameters, the variables that determine the network structure. Adding more data is an approach to reduce the risk of overfitting. By providing a larger training dataset, the probability of introducing more diverse variations possible in any given arbitrary data that the ANN will be tested for is increased. Hence, the model would be adjusted to generalize the features of the dataset more robustly. Additionally, strategically modifying the data to remove possible features that, although presented in the dataset, should not be considered as a feature would help the model better generalize the data. A clear example is where the input is an image and the images with all the objects oriented in a certain way. An ANN would falsely capture this consistent inadvertent feature in the data. Synthetic data, however, can avoid such overfitting. On the other hand, when a model is underfitting, additional inputs, layers, and neurons can create a platform to generalize the features in the dataset more accurately.

Among the applications of ANN is its use in building energy performance and envelope design. A trained ANN can be used to interpolate the effect of new design solutions. Actual data (Buratti et al. 2014) or simulated data (Saryazdi et al. 2022) representing building performance can be used to train the network. Consequently, ANN has been used as a surrogate model in building performance optimization problems. Additionally, a trained ANN can be used to interpolate the effect of new design solutions. Figure 5.4 shows the generic architecture of ANN and the example of input and outputs for the design and performance analysis of the building envelope.

Moon, Lee, and Kim (2014) developed ANN-based temperature control for predictive and adaptive thermal control to maintain optimal thermal comfort using integrated heating system control and envelope opening. In another study, Urresti, Campos-Celador, and Sala (2019) used dynamic neural networks, which include time-dependent behavior, to simulate the behavior of a phase change material layer of a building envelope, usually under varying conditions. ANN has also been used to predict the daylighting performance of a building and its impact on the cooling, heating, electric lighting, and total building electricity use (Wong, Wan, and Lam 2010). The model's inputs included several weather and building envelope parameters and a parameter that differentiated weekdays, Saturdays, and Sundays. Additionally, ANN coupled with building energy simulation has been used as a surrogate model for daylighting analysis to predict the lighting consumption of a typical office with a vacuum photovoltaic glazing system (Qiu et al. 2020). Also, Han et al. (2020) have used

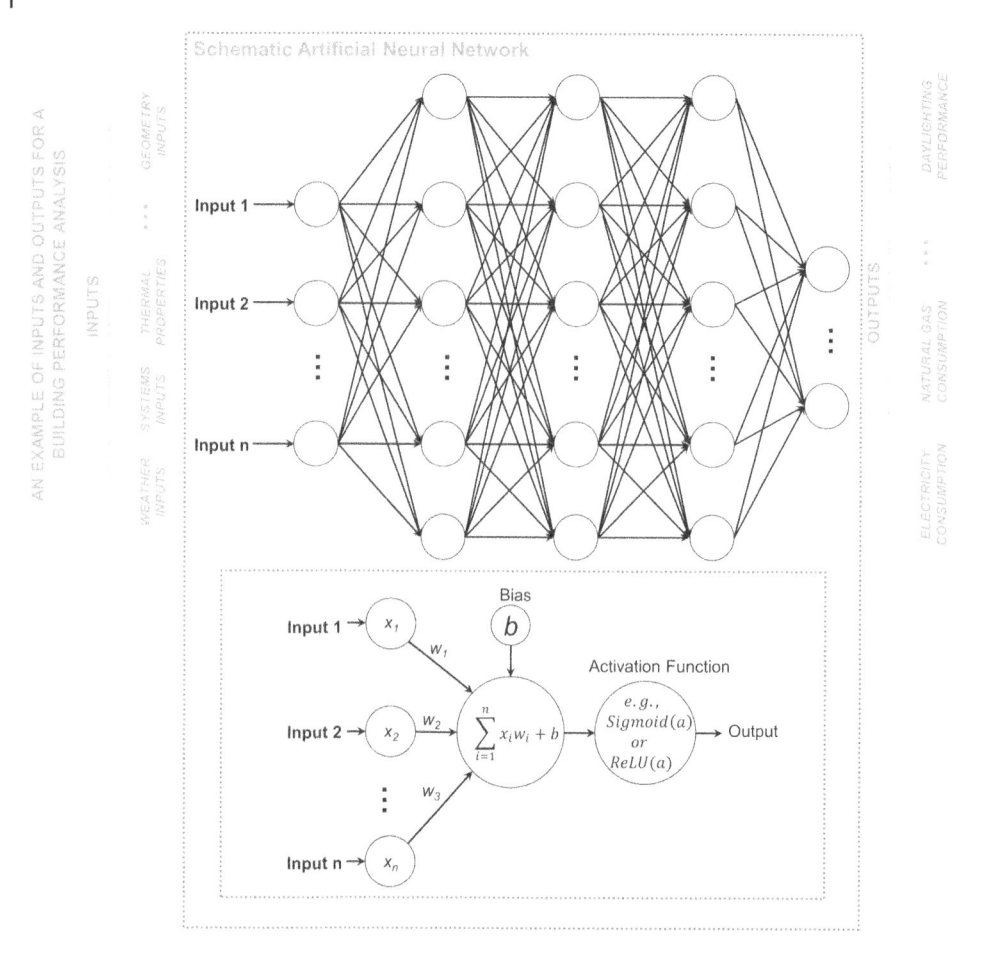

Figure 5.4 The architecture of the ANN.

Radial Basis Function (RBF) ANN with affinity propagation to predict building energy performance. RBF consists of an input, a hidden, and an output layer where each of the neurons in the hidden layer will use the RBF, for example, a Gaussian function, as the transfer function. Also, affinity propagation, developed by Frey and Dueck (2007), is a clustering algorithm that does not require the number of clusters to be determined before the execution of the algorithm.

ANN has also been coupled with optimization methods in building envelope problems. Gossard, Lartigue, and Thellier (2013) have used ANN coupled with the genetic algorithm NSGA-II to optimize the thermal conductivity and volumetric specific heat of the external walls for optimal annual energy consumption and the summer comfort degree. Additionally, researchers have proposed a neural-network-based system identification technique to determine the z-transfer function of a building envelope (Chen and Chen 2000), which is a transfer function that describes how the output signal responds to an arbitrary input signal by converting a discrete-time signal into a complex frequency-domain representation and bypasses the underlying calculations.

Convolutional Neural Network

Convolutional Neural Network (CNN) is a class of ANNs comprising one or more convolutional layers. Although CNNs are most widely used in image analysis, they can also be used for other analyses, such as classification. The architecture of CNN allows the network to detect patterns.

The convolution in these layers mainly differentiates CNN from other multilayer perceptron networks. Each convolutional layer is considered a filter that detects specific patterns. These patterns in an image are more basic filters, such as edges and corners, in the initial convolutional layers. As we go deeper into the convolutional layers, the output of more primitive filters will combine to detect more sophisticated patterns, such as those that combine the shapes, edges, and patterns of a specific part of the image, or large objects in deeper layers. A filter, also called kernel or feature detector, can be an $n \times m$ matrix of numbers that will be slid on every $n \times m$ block in the image. The dot product of the filter with each $n \times m$ block in the image is a new representation of the image that will be the output of the perceptron.

A deep neural network that applies a linear convolution to the output of the previous layer and then applies a nonlinear activation function ReLU was proposed to generate annual luminance maps of indoor space from a subset of point-in-time High-Dynamic-Range (HDR) images (Liu, Colburn, and Inanici 2020). The results of this study showed that only by rendering 5% of annual luminance maps, the proposed model could predict the rest with comparable accuracy with high-quality point-in-time renderings generated by Radiance software. In another study, U-Net, a CNN developed by Ronneberger, Fischer, and Brox (2015) that consists of a contracting path and a symmetric expanding path, was used to predict the annual luminance maps using only a limited number of rendered HDR images (Qorbani et al. 2022). Results showed that the model could robustly predict HDR images from other viewpoints in the space with fewer rendered images and less training required. Finally, Bayomi et al. (2022) used You Only Look Once (YOLO), which is an algorithm that uses CNN to provide real-time object detection in an image to detect building envelope components that can be applied to building energy performance analysis and assessment of thermal irregularities. A sparse CNN, SpaRSE-BIM, was proposed for the classification of Industry Foundation Classes (IFC)-based geometry and semantic enrichment of BIM models (Emunds et al. 2022).

Recurrent Neural Network

Recurrent Neural Networks (RNNs) are a type of neural network that is designed to learn sequential or time-varying patterns. Besides weights, biases, layers, and activation functions, RNN has feedback loops, which makes it possible to use sequential input values to make predictions. In RNN, the internal state, which depends on the inputs and the old internal states, captures the notion of memory.

RNN is used to generate synthetic localized weather data, which is the basis for performance analysis in a location (Han et al. 2021). The model was shown to more accurately represent local conditions compared to standard weather files. RNN is applied to targeted retrofit analysis through the prediction of building envelope thermal properties (Baasch and Evins 2019). In another study, RNN has been used to identify cost-optimal building retrofit (Deb, Dai, and Schlueter 2021). RNNs have been used in sequential problems with temporal dependencies. A sequence-to-sequence (seq2seq) model using Long Short-Term Memory (LSTM) cells in RNN algorithms was used to predict building energy demand (Kim, Kim, and Song 2021). Bayesian RNN was used to model the uncertainty of weather elements for robust solar energy generation of a building (Wang, Mae, and Taniguchi 2022). RNN has also been used in the analysis of ventilation performance in a residential building measured (Kim et al. 2022).

Generative Adversarial Networks

Generative Adversarial Networks (GANs) are unsupervised deep learning algorithms that generate samples from the estimated probability distribution of a dataset (Goodfellow et al. 2014). In order to do this, GAN trains a generative model that captures the data distribution and a discriminative model that estimates the probability that a sample came from the training data or not. The discriminative model is trained, typically by backpropagation, to identify the features in the real dataset. The generative model, on the other hand, generates fake datasets and will be trained to trick the discriminative model. Based on the prediction of the discriminative model, either of these models will be trained. The competition between these models, which leads to the name adversarial, results in a model that is trained to identify real data, and a model that generates samples that closely resemble the features of the real data. Therefore, GAN can be used to reveal an unknown probability distribution of a given data and has been shown to effectively generate samples, especially when using images.

GAN has been utilized in the context of building performance in different scales, from entire cities to neighborhoods and buildings, either as an alternative method for the other methods or as a new method for previously overlooked problems (Wu, Stouffs, and Biljecki 2022). Lu et al. (2022) have used the integrated GAN and genetic algorithm as a design framework for building environmental performance optimization for daylight autonomy and thermal autonomy. The case study building for the experiment is a façade model based on Mikimoto Ginza 2 in Japan, designed by architect Toyo Ito. The façade of the building is parametrized using Voronoi Tessellation, which is a subdivision of the space into a number of cells segmenting an area based on their proximity to a given number of points. The points that determine the partitioning were parametrically modeled that during the optimization process would change the façade geometrical configurations, which would, in turn, result in a different daylight autonomy and thermal autonomy. The pix2pixHD (Wang et al. 2018), a Pytorch implementation of a deep learning-based method for high-resolution photorealistic image-to-image translation, was used for mapping the training input façade images and output simulation visualization images. An extension of the GAN was used to bypass the time-consuming and computationally expensive building performance simulation and instead estimate building performance from images of the building façade. The façade is finally optimized for the objectives using Galapagos (Rutten 2013), a native genetic algorithm in Rhino-Grasshopper (McNeel 2010). Similarly, in an environmental performance-driven urban design study, GAN was used as a surrogate model integrated with a multi-objective genetic algorithm to accelerate the environmental performance-driven design (Huang et al. 2022).

Additionally, Chokwitthaya et al. (2020) presented a computational framework for context-aware design-specific data and the existing building performance models. In this model, the performance target based on the building goals and objectives trained the discriminator model of the GAN and an existing building model, and context-aware design-specific data from immersive virtual environments were used to train the generator model. The GAN-based framework was used in the performance prediction. The results of this study applied in a single-occupancy office space with 30 participants in an experiment on the simulation of artificial lighting confirmed the framework's efficacy.

Ensemble Learning

Ensemble learning is an approach in machine learning that combines the insights obtained from multiple models for improved robustness and predictive performance. Ensemble learning techniques can be broadly categorized into two main types: homogeneous and heterogeneous ensemble methods. In homogeneous ensemble methods, multiple instances of the same type of base model are combined to create a stronger model. Some commonly used homogeneous ensemble methods are bagging and bootstrapping. In bagging, multiple instances of the same base model are trained on different subsets of the training data. For example, Random Forest is an ensemble learning that combines multiple decision trees to provide a more generalized model. Boosting, as in boosting algorithms such as AdaBoost, Gradient Boosting, and XGBoost, utilizes a sequential iterative approach where a series of weak base models are combined to create a strong model. Heterogeneous ensemble methods, on the other hand, use different learning algorithms to achieve ensemble diversity. Examples include the ensemble of classifiers such as decision trees, support vector machines, or regressors such as linear regression, decision trees, and k-nearest neighbors. Additionally, stacking is an ensemble method where a meta-model will predict based on the outputs of multiple instances of the same base model, in the homogeneous approach, and different models, in the heterogeneous approach, that are trained on the same training data.

Ensemble learning has been used in research related to the performance of the built environment on different scales. On an urban scale, researchers have proposed a framework for integrated energy and exposure to ambient pollution (iEnEx) assessment (Ashayeri and Abbasabadi 2022). The proposed multistep workflow consists of spatiotemporal land use regression with gradient boosting machine along with human behavioral patterns and urban big data from smart city platforms. The deployment of the proposed method in Chicago, as the case study, showed improved explanatory capacities and increased effectiveness when using the integrated urban energy and human health systems. Ensemble learning can be used in building envelope design and its performance assessment to overcome the limitations of individual models by combining multiple models. For example, the day-ahead and hour-ahead prediction models were developed and periodically updated considering the dynamic feature of a selected residential occupancy pattern using an ensemble learning framework that consists of four algorithms, random forests, multilayer perceptron neural network, support vector machine, and extreme gradient boosting (Bampoulas et al. 2022). In a study, ensemble learning was used for the thermal performance prediction of the phase change material integrated roof using random forest regression, extra trees regression, gradient boosting regression, extreme gradient boosting regression, and CatBoost regression (Bhamare et al. 2021). Results indicate that gradient boosting regression is the best-performing model compared to the other selected machine learning models. Random forest algorithm was also used to predict the impact of building design and construction characteristics on energy consumption, showing that factors such as wall thickness, orientation, and thermal mass, which affect energy efficiency and indoor thermal comfort (Hussien et al. 2023). Additionally, a hybrid ensemble learning framework using extreme gradient boosting for predicting zero-energy probability and the Bayesian optimization adopted to identify the optimal hyperparameters was proposed for analyzing and predicting zero-energy potential in the real-time matching of photovoltaic direct-driven air conditioner systems (Lu et al. 2023). Other examples of ensemble learning include the use of CNN and gated recurrent units to model illuminance distribution from light pipe systems (Ngarambe et al. 2023) and predictive models for daylight performance of general floorplans based on CNN and GAN (He et al. 2021).

Discussions on Practical Implications

There are different instances where AI is used in building design. Zaha Hadid Architects (ZHA), for example, have used text-to-image platforms, such as DALL.E 2 (OpenAI 2023), Midjourney (Midjourney Inc. 2022), and Stable Diffusion (Rombach et al. 2022), that generate images based on a provided descriptive language. Dongdaemun Design Plaza is an example of images generated using DALL.E in the design process (Barker 2023). Other designers, such as Vojtek Morsztyn, have also utilized these tools in the design process. Other image-to-image AI-based platforms have also been used in building design (Kuchukov 2021). Additionally, various machine learning and optimization routines discussed in this chapter have been used to analyze building envelope design performance. Altogether, these methods have expanded and facilitated design ideas.

While these technologies, and in general, AI have been successfully used for design inspiration, they may not have necessarily been used in adapting the general concepts to the desired detailed documentation. A substantial portion of a high-performance design is fine-tuning a model to create a fully functional design that meets the codes and project requirements. However, one of the main challenges in the current phase of most of these tools is the lack of domain-specific knowledge. Similar to generative tools, machine learning methods used to evaluate the building envelope have the same deficiencies. For instance, while neural networks are powerful tools for high-building performance envelope design and evaluation, they lack domain-specific knowledge. Building envelope design requires considering various architectural, structural, and environmental factors, which may not be explicitly captured in the training data and makes the integration of expert knowledge into neural network models challenging. Neural networks are considered black-box models, which lack interpretability. The deficiency in the interpretation makes it challenging to gain insights into the underlying design principles and limits the model's value in providing accountable recommendations. This is more pronounced when dealing with complex building performance design problems.

Additionally, training neural networks requires a large, labeled dataset. However, obtaining high-quality labeled data can be challenging in building performance design. The actual building performance data are available from a pool of existing buildings with configurations that may substantially differ from the design case. On the other hand, using simulations to populate data can be computationally expensive with a laborious input preparation process. Furthermore, inaccuracies and uncertainties in simulated data could bias the network training.

Another concern is determining the balance between accuracy and robustness. A neural network can overfit by becoming too specialized to the training data and failing to generalize to new data. On the other hand, a network with insufficient architecture can result in inaccurate predictions. Also, neural networks are susceptible to biases present in the training data.

Consequently, several factors should be considered to improve the performance of machine learning techniques in the design and analysis of a building envelope. These considerations range from large-scale efforts in data collection and availability of the data in municipal or national portfolios to more detailed considerations related to machine learning techniques. A carefully prepared dataset that avoids inherited biases is necessary to tune the model based on the complexity of the model. The data should be statistically analyzed and carefully synthesized, if needed, to ensure there are no misleading patterns in the data that the network can capture as a feature. Another critical factor is the source of the data itself. Building performance data such as the Building Data Genome 2 (BDG2) Dataset (Miller et al. 2020) can serve as valuable actual data to train models, which mainly rely on large-scale national or regional research projects. On the other hand, advancements in the automation of building performance modeling are another aspect that facilitates the process. These advancements include both the flexibility and ease of use of individual programs as well as the improvements in the interoperability of different specialized programs when the objective accounts for different metrics. Furthermore, a well-structured architecture of the network is an indispensable factor. Determining the architecture of the network, based on the complexity of the problem, is essential to provide the desired robustness and accuracy. Additionally, hybrid methodologies, such as gray box models that include both physics-based specialized knowledge and black-box models, can be more helpful in reducing uncertainties and verifying the results. Finally, stepwise models can simplify the design and evaluation process. It is challenging to include all requirements, such as the continuity and integrity of the structural components and other technical aspects of the design, encoded in a single model. However, sequential subroutines focusing on specific parts of the design and evaluation process can break the design process down into manageable pieces where experts can verify the outcome of each step.

Summary and Conclusion

Machine learning and optimization methods have been increasingly integrated into building envelope design and performance assessment. While it has been decades since the concepts of many of these methods were developed, advancements in methods tuned and programmed for architectural design on the one hand and more accessible computational power and cloud-based simulation platforms, on the other hand, have facilitated the integration of these methods in building envelope design during the past decade.

While there are numerous methods and tools developed, there are barriers to the effective implementation of machine learning and optimizations in building envelope design and performance evaluation. Future research is needed to study the performance targets and uncertainties associated with using these techniques in performance-driven design and analysis and to better understand and control the reliability of the framework. Additionally, more efficient workflows can help users more purposefully utilize these techniques in the design and evaluation process. Moreover, there are limitations in the interoperability between different applications. In many cases, users must undergo a time-consuming remodeling process in order to be able to use certain interfaces. Lastly, many workflows require specific technical aspects with limited user manuals. Consequently, a holistic inclusion of the related knowledge in the education of the architectures and closely related fields is required to ensure the effective adoption of these techniques in the design and evaluation phases in the industry.

References

Ashayeri, M. and Abbasabadi, N. (2022). A Framework for Integrated Energy and Exposure to Ambient Pollution (IEnEx) Assessment Toward Low-Carbon, Healthy, and Equitable Cities. *Sustainable Cities and Society* https://doi.org/10.1016/j.scs.2021.103647.

Baasch, G.M. and Evins, R. (2019). Targeting Buildings for Energy Retrofit Using Recurrent Neural Networks with Multivariate Time Series. In: *33rd Conference on Neural Information Processing Systems*.

Bampoulas, A., Pallonetto, F., Mangina, E., and Finn, D.P. (2022). An Ensemble Learning-Based Framework for Assessing the Energy Flexibility of Residential Buildings with Multicomponent Energy Systems. *Applied Energy* https://doi.org/10.1016/j.apenergy.2022.118947.

Barker, N. (2023). ZHA Developing "Most" Projects Using AI-Generated Images Says Patrik Schumacher. *Dezeen* https://www.dezeen.com/2023/04/26/zaha-hadid-architects-patrik-schumacher-ai-dalle-midjourney/.

Bayomi, N., El Kholy, M., Fernandez, J.E. et al. (2022). Building Envelope Object Detection Using YOLO Models. In: *Proceedings of the 2022 Annual Modeling and Simulation Conference, ANNSIM 2022*. doi: 10.23919/ANNSIM55834.2022.9859463.

Bhamare, D.K., Saikia, P., Rathod, M.K. et al. (2021). A Machine Learning and Deep Learning Based Approach to Predict the Thermal Performance of Phase Change Material Integrated Building Envelope. *Building and Environment* https://doi.org/10.1016/j.buildenv.2021.107927.

Buratti, C., Lascaro, E., Palladino, D., and Vergoni, M. (2014). Building Behavior Simulation by Means of Artificial Neural Network in Summer Conditions. *Sustainability (Switzerland)* 6 (8): https://doi.org/10.3390/su6085339.

Chen, Y. and Chen, Z. (2000). A Neural-Network-Based Experimental Technique for Determining z-Transfer Function Coefficients of a Building Envelope. *Building and Environment* 35 (3): https://doi.org/10.1016/S0360-1323(99)00010-4.

Cheng, Z., Yoshinobu, C., Martin, K. et al. (2020). *Generative Design Tool for Modular Buildings*. Gensler.

Chokwitthaya, C., Zhu, Y., Mukhopadhyay, S., and Collier, E. (2020). Augmenting Building Performance Predictions During Design Using Generative Adversarial Networks and Immersive Virtual Environments. *Automation in Construction* https://doi.org/10.1016/j.autcon.2020.103350.

Deb, C., Dai, Z., and Schlueter, A. (2021). A Machine Learning-Based Framework for Cost-Optimal Building Retrofit. *Applied Energy* https://doi.org/10.1016/j.apenergy.2021.116990.

Duong, P. (2022). NBBJ. *Drawn to Design* https://doi.org/10.1515/9783035624670-047.

Emunds, C., Pauen, N., Richter, V. et al. (2022). SpaRSE-BIM: Classification of IFC-Based Geometry via Sparse Convolutional Neural Networks. *Advanced Engineering Informatics* https://doi.org/10.1016/j.aei.2022.101641.

Frey, B.J. and Dueck, D. (2007). Clustering by Passing Messages Between Data Points. *Science* 315 (5814): https://doi.org/10.1126/science.1136800.

Goldberg, D.E. (1989). *Genetic Algorithms in Search, Optimization, and Machine Learning*. Reading, MA: *Addison Wesley*.

Goodfellow, I.J., Pouget-Abadie, J., Mirza, B.X.M. et al. (2014). Generative Adverserial Nets. *Advances in Neural Information Processing Systems*.

Gossard, D., Lartigue, B., and Thellier, F. (2013). Multi-Objective Optimization of a Building Envelope for Thermal Performance Using Genetic Algorithms and Artificial Neural Network. *Energy and Buildings* 67: 253–260. https://doi.org/10.1016/j.enbuild.2013.08.026.

Han, Y., Fan, C., Geng, Z. et al. (2020). Energy Efficient Building Envelope Using Novel RBF Neural Network Integrated Affinity Propagation. *Energy* 209: https://doi.org/10.1016/j.energy.2020.118414.

Han, J.M., Ang, Y.Q., Malkawi, A., and Samuelson, H.W. (2021). Using Recurrent Neural Networks for Localized Weather Prediction with Combined Use of Public Airport Data and On-Site Measurements. *Building and Environment* https://doi.org/10.1016/j.buildenv.2021.107601.

He, Q., Li, Z., Gao, W. et al. (2021). Predictive Models for Daylight Performance of General Floorplans Based on CNN and GAN: A Proof-of-Concept Study. *Building and Environment* https://doi.org/10.1016/j.buildenv.2021.108346.

Huang, C.Z., Yao, G., Wang, J. et al. (2022). Accelerated Environmental Performance-Driven Urban Design with Generative Adversarial Network. *Building and Environment* 224: 109575.

Hussien, A., Khan, W., Hussain, A. et al. (2023). Predicting Energy Performances of Buildings' Envelope Wall Materials via the Random Forest Algorithm. *Journal of Building Engineering* https://doi.org/10.1016/j.jobe.2023.106263.

Kheiri, F. (2021). Optimization of Building Fenestration and Shading for Climate-Based Daylight Performance Using the Coupled Genetic Algorithm and Simulated Annealing Optimization Methods. *Indoor and Built Environment* https://doi.org/10.1177/1420326X19888008.

Kim, C.H., Kim, M., and Song, Y.J. (2021). Sequence-to-Sequence Deep Learning Model for Building Energy Consumption Prediction with Dynamic Simulation Modeling. *Journal of Building Engineering* https://doi.org/10.1016/j.jobe.2021.102577.

Kim, M.K., Cremers, B., Liu, J. et al. (2022). Prediction and Correlation Analysis of Ventilation Performance in a Residential Building Using Artificial Neural Network Models Based on Data-Driven Analysis. *Sustainable Cities and Society* 83: 103981. https://doi.org/10.1016/j.scs.2022.103981.

Krogh, A. (2008). What Are Artificial Neural Networks? *Nature Biotechnology* https://doi.org/10.1038/nbt1386.

Kuchukov, Roman. 2021. NeuroArch: Architectural Imagery of Artificial Intelligence. https://towardsdatascience.com/neuroarch-ai-imagery-eng-1b9e1d11944a

LeCun, Y., Bengio, Y., and Hinton, G. (2015). Deep Learning. *Nature* 521 (7553): 436.

Liu, Y., Colburn, A., and Inanici, M. (2020). Deep Neural Network Approach for Annual Luminance Simulations. *Journal of Building Performance Simulation* https://doi.org/10.1080/19401493.2020.1803404.

Lu, Y., Wei, W., Geng, X. et al. (2022). Multi-Objective Optimization of Building Environmental Performance: An Integrated Parametric Design Method Based on Machine Learning Approaches. *Energies* 15 (9): 7031. https://doi.org/10.3390/en15197031.

Lu, C., Li, S., Junhua, G. et al. (2023). A Hybrid Ensemble Learning Framework for Zero-Energy Potential Prediction of Photovoltaic Direct-Driven Air Conditioners. *Journal of Building Engineering* https://doi.org/10.1016/j.jobe.2022.105602.

McNeel. 2010. "Grasshopper Generative Modeling for Rhino."

Midjourney Inc. 2022. Midjourney. https://www.midjourney.com/home/?callbackUrl=%2Fapp%2F.

Miller, C., Kathirgamanathan, A., Picchetti, B. et al. (2020). The Building Data Genome Project 2, Energy Meter Data From the ASHRAE Great Energy Predictor III Competition. *Science Data* 7: 368. https://doi.org/10.1038/s41597-020-00712-x.

Minsky, M.L. and Papert, S. (1969). *Perceptrons, Expanded Edition An Introduction to Computational Geometry*. MIT Press.

Moon, J.W., Lee, J.H., and Kim, S. (2014). Evaluation of Artificial Neural Network-Based Temperature Control for Optimum Operation of Building Envelopes. *Energies* 7 (11): https://doi.org/10.3390/en7117245.

Ngarambe, J., Duhirwe, P.N., Quang, T.V. et al. (2023). Coupling Convolutional Neural Networks with Gated Recurrent Units to Model Illuminance Distribution from Light Pipe Systems. *Building and Environment* 237: https://doi.org/10.1016/j.buildenv.2023.110276.

OpenAI. 2023. OpenAI-DALL.E 2. https://openai.com/dall-e-2.

Qiu, C., Yi, Y.K., Wang, M., and Yang, H. (2020). Coupling an Artificial Neuron Network Daylighting Model and Building Energy Simulation for Vacuum Photovoltaic Glazing. *Applied Energy* https://doi.org/10.1016/j.apenergy.2020.114624.

Qorbani, M.A., Dalirani, F., Rahmati, M., and Hafezi, M.R. (2022). A Deep Convolutional Neural Network Based on U-Net to Predict Annual Luminance Maps. *Journal of Building Performance Simulation* https://doi.org/10.1080/19401493.2021.2004229.

Revit (2021). *Generative Design Primer*. United States: Revit.

Rombach, R., Patrick Esser, and Contributors. 2022. Stable Diffusion. https://stablediffusionweb.com/.

Ronneberger, O., Fischer, P., and Brox, T. (2015). U-Net: Convolutional Networks for Biomedical Image Segmentation. In: *Lecture Notes in Computer Science (Including Subseries Lecture Notes in Artificial Intelligence and Lecture Notes in Bioinformatics)*. https://doi.org/10.1007/978-3-319-24574-4_28.

Rumelhart, D.E., Hinton, G.E., and Williams, R.J. (1986). Learning Representations by Back-Propagating Errors. *Nature* 323 (6088): https://doi.org/10.1038/323533a0.

Rutten, D. (2013). Galapagos: on the Logic and Limitations of Generic Solvers. *Archit Design* 83: 132–135.

Saryazdi, S., Ebrahimi, M., Etemad, A. et al. (2022). Data-Driven Performance Analysis of a Residential Building Applying Artificial Neural Network (ANN) and Multi-Objective Genetic Algorithm (GA). *Building and Environment* https://doi.org/10.1016/j.buildenv.2022.109633.

Urresti, A., Campos-Celador, A., and Sala, J.M. (2019). Dynamic Neural Networks to Analyze the Behavior of Phase Change Materials Embedded in Building Envelopes. *Applied Thermal Engineering* 158: https://doi.org/10.1016/j.applthermaleng.2019.113783.

Wang, T.C., Liu, M.Y., Zhu, J.Y. et al. (2018). High-Resolution Image Synthesis and Semantic Manipulation with Conditional GANs. *Proceedings of the IEEE Computer Society Conference on Computer Vision and Pattern Recognition* https://doi.org/10.1109/CVPR.2018.00917.

Wang, J., Mae, M., and Taniguchi, K. (2022). Uncertainty Modeling Method of Weather Elements Based on Deep Learning for Robust Solar Energy Generation of Building. *Energy and Buildings* 266: 112115. https://doi.org/10.1016/j.enbuild.2022.112115.

Wong, S.L., Wan, K.K.W., and Lam, T.N.T. (2010). Artificial Neural Networks for Energy Analysis of Office Buildings with Daylighting. *Applied Energy* 87 (2): 551–557. https://doi.org/10.1016/j.apenergy.2009.06.028.

Wu, A.N., Stouffs, R., and Biljecki, F. (2022). Generative Adversarial Networks in the Built Environment: A Comprehensive Review of the Application of GANs Across Data Types and Scales. *Building and Environment* 223: 109477.

6

Efficient Parametric Design-Space Exploration with Reinforcement Learning-Based Recommenders

Md Shariful Alam and Tomás Méndez Echenagucia

Department of Architecture, University of Washington, Seattle, WA, USA

Introduction

Advancements in technology and the emergence of simulation tools have transformed the design process, enabling architects to predict the performance of designs before execution. This shift from intuitive cognition to data-driven design has led to more accurate and confident design solutions. The use of parametric models (Gu, Yu, and Behbahani 2021) further enhances the process by generating multiple design alternatives within a defined design space (Ritter, Geyer, and Borrmann 2013), which encompasses a vast range of options for exploration. By considering the entire design space and analyzing various design alternatives, designers can avoid costly expenses and achieve better performance outcomes in the early stages of the design process.

Exploring the entire design space manually can be overwhelmingly tedious for a design team. Therefore, optimization becomes necessary to identify the best design option (Rahmani Asl et al. 2014). Finding a design solution that satisfies functional requirements and environmental objectives while optimizing efficiency and lowering costs is the aim of optimization. Various algorithms, such as the genetic algorithm, inspired by natural selection, are widely used for architectural optimization (Echenagucia 2014). These algorithms strategically iterate over different solutions, assessing their fitness based on predefined criteria such as energy efficiency and structural stability. However, these optimization processes prioritize quantitative outcomes and may generate solutions that are functionally superior but esthetically or spatially less appealing. This approach neglects the qualitative aspects of design options (Saldana Ochoa et al. 2021). The pure optimization approach is considered an oversimplification of the design problem, as it overlooks the designer's preferences and personal biases. Designers seek to achieve the best possible compromise between their preferences and performance results, which may be difficult with conventional optimization techniques.

Another limitation of existing computational optimization approaches is the time-consuming nature of performance simulations, particularly for computationally intensive tasks. As a result, optimizing a large design space can take hours or even days, consuming significant time and resources. To speed up the design optimization procedure, surrogate models are being widely used (Mueller and Ochsendorf 2015). These models can rapidly predict a design's performance without requiring a complete simulation for each iteration. A collection of previously assessed designs and their accompanying performance measures are used to train machine learning (ML) models. Once trained, these models can quickly approximate performance outcomes (Wortmann et al. 2015), speeding up the optimization process. However, accurate predictions require a substantial number of simulations to prepare the training set for the surrogate model, especially when dealing with vast design spaces.

Designers face a significant challenge when navigating large design spaces, but researchers have made remarkable progress by incorporating ML algorithms. To gain an overall understanding of the vast design space generated, a study implemented Combinatorial Equilibrium Modeling (CEM) (Ohlbrock and Schwartz 2016) and clustered design options using self-organizing maps (SOM). Visualizing clusters with the assistance of the Uniform Manifold Approximation and Projection algorithm (UMAP) (Fuhrimann et al. 2018) provided insights into the design space. Another study (Saldana Ochoa et al. 2021) followed a similar approach but also sought to incorporate the designer's understanding of non-quantifiable aspects. By including human designers' preferences in their proposed framework, they introduced qualitative limitations alongside the quantitative ones. In the application of the five-step design framework, Saldana Ochoa et al. (2021) utilized it to explore the design of a stadium, which is both structurally sound and looks good, while Bertagna et al. (2021) used the same process to revisit an existing structure. In the case of the existing structure, they generated additional options using CEM and clustered them using SOM to obtain a low-dimensional representation of the design space. The arrangement of design options in a two-dimensional grid proved beneficial for considering multiple criteria such as structural, daylight, and radiance analysis.

There are two main approaches to incorporating user preferences in the multiobjective optimization process. First, users can adjust the weightings between objectives during a multi-objective search. Second, users can choose which designs to consider for each generation (Simons, Parmee, and Gwynllyw 2010). Reeh (2019) achieved the design of a single-family home using a genetic algorithm-based optimization approach that allows users to filter design possibilities after each iteration. The non-dominated sorting genetic algorithm (NSGA) (Mohapatra et al. 2015) allowed users to personalize the optimization process to align with their preferences in decision-making. (Harding and Brandt-Olsen (2018) developed the "Biomorpher" grasshopper plug-in based on a similar approach, grouping similar design options, and presenting them in an interactive dashboard to assist designers in filtering out undesired options. This approach employed interactive evolutionary computation (IEC) (Takagi 2001) to achieve design solutions that satisfy both performance and esthetic preferences. To incorporate the designer's qualitative measures Yi (2019) proposed a framework that derives numerical measurements for esthetic preferences through a survey, where the participants vote for their preferred option in an interactive dashboard created using the Grasshopper plug-in Human UI ("Human UI" 2016).

As researchers delve into innovative methods for design space exploration, they are actively seeking collaborations with diverse experts in built environment studies. Unlocking the potential of design computing and ML is the hope behind these collaborations. While multiobjective optimization processes have been proposed in previous studies, an unexplored avenue with significant potential lies in utilizing recommender systems (Ricci, Rokach, and Shapira 2022). These systems, akin to those recommending products or media content, can be employed to suggest design options, alleviating users from the intricate complexities of comprehending the entire design space. This approach enables stress-free exploration while aligning with users' intentions.

Reinforcement learning-based recommender systems (Choi et al. 2018) present a pioneering paradigm among various recommender systems utilized on websites. Diverging from conventional collaborative or content-based filtering techniques (Techlabs 2021), which heavily rely on exhaustive user information for effective suggestions, reinforcement learning-based systems offer a compelling solution. Unlike traditional methods that often demand users' personal details or prolonged data collection periods, these systems rapidly grasp user preferences through interactive experiences, addressing the "cold start" challenge (Lika, Kolomvatsos, and Hadjiefthymiades 2014). By leveraging reinforcement learning principles, these systems swiftly acquire accurate insights, ensuring impartial recommendations devoid of biases related to demographics or background. This streamlined yet potent approach has contributed to the surging popularity of reinforcement learning-based recommender systems. Such systems operate ethically, concentrating on providing superior recommendations while steering clear of commercial biases. The integration of this tool into parametric design exploration is anticipated to herald an exciting era of participatory design and uninhibited exploration.

This chapter presents a framework that utilizes AI models to address limitations in the current design process. The framework comprises two subdivisions, which are applied to find a suitable design solution for a four-story office building in Seattle, evaluating annual energy consumption using EnergyPlus. The first subdivision quickly learns performance outcomes through dimensionality reduction and clustering, while the interactive dashboard allows users to provide feedback and receive new design suggestions from a reinforcement learning-based recommender system. This approach enables efficient exploration of the design space with the goal of generating high-performing and visually appealing solutions.

Methodology

In the first section of the study, a design space is created, and ML algorithms are employed to cluster all the design options effectively. This clustering process ensures that buildings with similar performance analyses are grouped together. This step is crucial as it sets the foundation for the second section, where a reinforcement learning-based recommender system is implemented. In the second section, the focus is on the implementation and customization of the reinforcement learning algorithm to achieve a design solution that satisfies both functional objectives and esthetic appeal. A reward function is designed to prioritize high-performing alternatives while incorporating the designer's esthetic preferences. This customization allows the algorithm to guide the designer toward design options that excel in both functional and esthetic aspects. A design dashboard is created to facilitate the exploration of the extensive design space. The reinforcement learning algorithm is trained to understand user preferences through interaction with the dashboard.

Section 01: Clustering Design Options

Design Space Generation

The Design Space comprises 6000 four-storied design options with varying lengths and widths, ranging from 10 to 50 m (see Table 6.1). The building type is a four-storied "mid-rise apartment" ("Commercial Reference Buildings" n.d.) with the ground floor serving as a retail store. The ground floor has the highest window-to-wall ratio (WWR), while the upper floors have different WWRs. The north and south facades of the apartment portion are divided into a 5 × 3 grid, allowing for a maximum of 5 windows on each floor on each side. The east and west facades are divided into a 3 × 3 grid, allowing for a maximum of 3 separate windows on each floor on each side. In total, the building can have 48 window segments (see Figure 6.2). The presence of windows in each segment depends on the design option parameters.

A pandas DataFrame (McKinney and others 2011) with 6000 rows and 98 columns is created (see Table 6.1), representing unique design options. The first 25 columns correspond to window positions on the north facade, while columns 15–23, 24–38, and 39–47 represent window positions for the west, south, and east facades, respectively. Each window position is assigned a unique decimal value indicating the WWR and size, with zero, indicating no window and non-zero values ranging between 0.3 and 0.7. Columns 49 and 50 represent the lengths and widths of the design options, while columns 50 through the end define the depth of shades (see Figure 6.1). The DataFrame allows for shade depths of 0 for windows, except for segments with a WWR of zero, where the shade depth is also set to zero to avoid bias.

Table 6.1 Building characteristics for the main Design Space.

Building characteristics	Values
Building width	Range (10—50 m) (east-west)
Building length	Range (10—50 m) (north-south)
Window segments (East-west)	3 × 3
Window segments (North-South)	5 × 3
Floor-to-floor height	3 m
Number of floors	4
Shade depth	Range (0–2.5 m) three-sided shade
Window sizes	Range (0–5 m)
Ground floor WWR	0.6
Surrounding context	Not considered
DataFrame configuration	
Number of parameters	98
Amount of data points	6000

Methodology | 117

	North facade 00—14	West facade 15—23	South facade 24—38	East facade 39—47	Length	Width	North shade 50—64	West shade 65—73	South shade 74—88	East shade 89—97
	0 ... 14	15 ...23	24 ... 38	39 ... 47	48	49	50 ... 64	65 ...73	74 ... 88	89 ...97
32459	0.4 ... 0	0 ... 0.4	0.3 ... 0	0.7 ... 0	0.4	0	0 ... 0	0.5 ...0.7	0 ... 0	0 ... 0
82397	0.7 ... 0.4	0 ... 0.4	0 ... 0.7	0.7 ... 0.3	0	0	0.3 ... 0	0 ...0.7	0.3 ... 0.6	0.5 ...0.6
1702	0.6 ... 0	0 ... 0	0.5 ... 0.5	0 ... 0.5	0.7	0	0.6 ... 0	0.7 ... 0.6	0.6 ... 0	0 ... 0
52330	0 ... 0.7	0.6 ... 0.7	0 ... 0.3	0 ... 0.5	0	0.6	0.5 ... 0	0.4 ... 0.5	0 ... 0.3	0.4 ... 0 ... 0.5
87482	0.6 ... 0	0 ... 0.5	0 ... 0	0.6 ... 0	0.7	0	0 ... 0	0 ... 0	0 ... 0	0 ... 0

Figure 6.1 Data structure of the main Design Space.

Table 6.2 Sample data frame of the main Design Space.

	0	1	2	3	4	5	6	7	8	9	10	11	12	13	14	15	16	17
4754	0	0	0.5	0.4	0	0	0.4	0	0	0	0	0.5	0	0.4	0.3	0	0.3	0.3
1091	0.7	0.6	0	0	0.4	0.5	0	0	0.7	0.4	0.7	0	0	0.5	0.5	0.7	0.5	0
2984	0.6	0	0.5	0.5	0.6	0.3	0.3	0.5	0	0.6	0	0	0	0	0.7	0.7	0.7	0
4506	0.7	0.3	0	0.3	0.5	0.6	0	0.3	0	0	0.7	0	0	0	0	0	0	0
4968	0	0	0	0.7	0	0	0.3	0	0	0	0.7	0.7	0.6	0	0	0.5	0.5	0

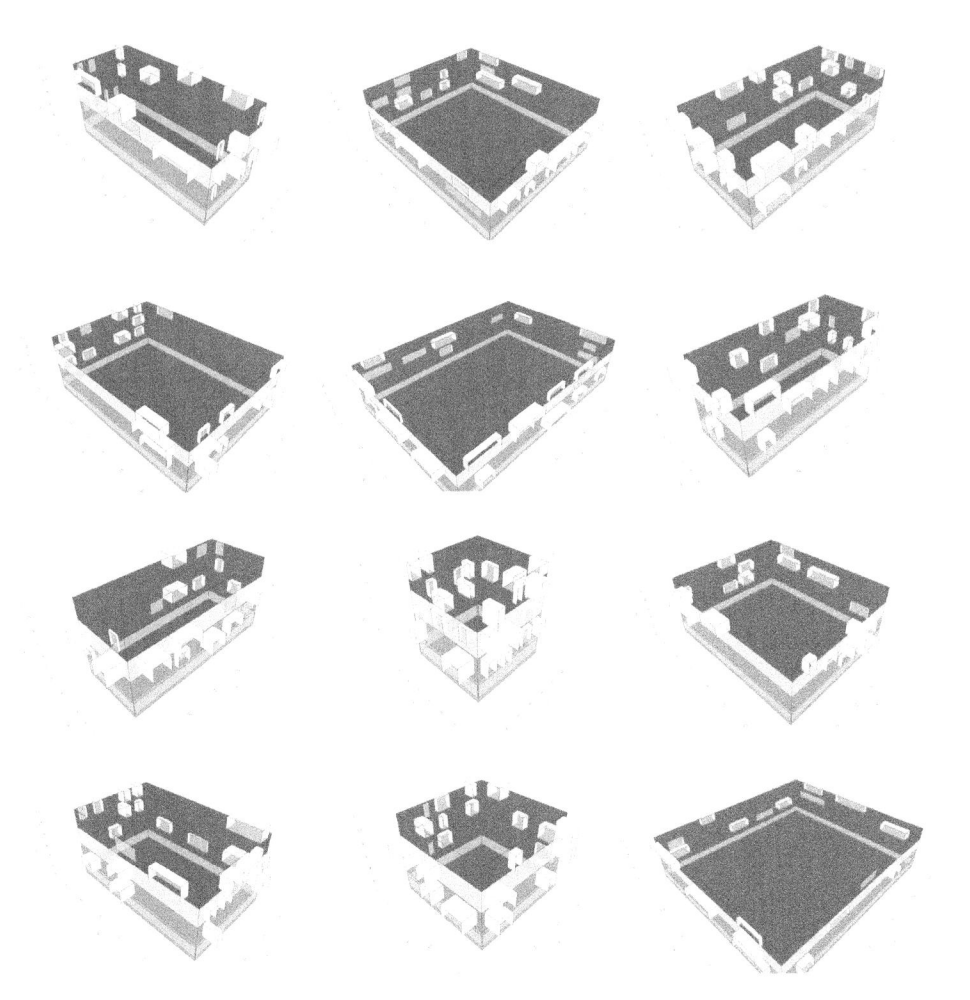

Figure 6.2 Randomly selected 12 design options from the main Design Space.

Performance Evaluation

To recommend design options with lower annual energy consumption, the algorithm needs to know the annual energy consumption of all the 6000 design options in the generated design space. However, simulating all 6000 design options would be extremely time-consuming. To address this issue, the study employs a novel approach where the performance outcome of only 20% of the design options is learned, and this information is used to approximate the performance outcome of all other design options. The performance outcome considered is the annual energy consumption (in kWh) for heating, cooling, and lighting. EnergyPlus (version 22-2-0) is used for the simulations, and the whole process is conducted in Python (version 3.9). The authors utilize an external Python library called "Compas eplus" (Echenagucia [2022] 2023) to communicate with EnergyPlus, developed by the second author of this chapter. The geometries are generated using Python scripts, which are then converted into an EnergyPlus-readable IDF format to generate the outcomes. Table 6.3 provides the properties that were fixed for the building during the simulation which is kept the same for the whole study.

Clustering Design Options

The primary goal is to cluster similar design options to identify the clusters that are preferred by designers during interaction, allowing the algorithm to show more design options from those specific clusters. To understand designers' preferences, their position in the design space needs to be analyzed, and nearby similar options must be identified for future recommendations. Euclidean distances between different design options can help determine the proximity of data points. The effectiveness of the clustered output depends on the given dataset. In the current dataset, each design has 98 features, resulting in 98-dimensional data points. Having high-dimensional data points with a relatively low number of data instances can lead to the "curse of dimensionality" (Verleysen and François 2005). This phenomenon presents challenges, such as increased computational complexity, decreased model performance, and data sparsity. To address these issues, it is crucial to reduce the dimensions of the dataset before using it for clustering purposes.

Dimensionality Reduction

The study investigated dimensionality reduction methods and found t-SNE (t-Distributed Stochastic Neighbor Embedding) (van der Maaten and Hinton 2008) ensuring effective

Table 6.3 Simulation configuration followed for all studies.

Simulation configuration	Values
Building type	DOE midrise apartment
Location	Seattle
Wall	Typical Insulated Steel Framed Exterior Wall-R16
Roof	Generic Roof
Floor	Generic Interior Floor
Window	Generic Double Pane
Simulation outcome unit	Kilowatt-hour (kWh)/year

simulation. t-SNE is a widely used nonlinear technique, creating a probability distribution to cluster similar data points and achieve distinct separations between clusters in lower-dimensional space. The Scikit-learn library's TSNE model was used, with hyperparameter adjustments to improve cluster separation (perplexity: 30, early exaggeration: 12). After reducing the data points to three-dimensional representations using the TSNE dimensionality reduction method, the team employed Python's Plotly library (Dabbas 2021) to visualize the outcomes. The reduced dimension data points appeared to be distributed in a large sphere (see Figure 6.3), which posed challenges for density-based clustering methods that were initially considered for grouping the data points. The structure of the data frame contributed to the difficulty in achieving effective clustering. Different parameters have different levels of influence on the performance outcome, which should be informed to the data frame before reducing the dimension.

Adding Weights Method
Scikit-learn Linear regression model (Su, Yan, and Tsai 2012) is utilized to find out the weights of different columns. To examine the accuracy of the weights, the team visualized data points in lower dimensions. By only simulating randomly selected 20% of the data points from the entire design space (1200 design options) and using their performance outcomes to train the linear regression model, we obtained weights that effectively modified the data frame, leading to densified groups of data points. Visualizing these modified data points in a three-dimensional space showed effective clustering (see Figure 6.3).

Now, instead of simulating all the design options, the team only simulated data points near the centroid of the created groups, considering them good representatives of their respective clusters. It was observed that the performance outcomes of other data points in each group deviated very little from the outcome of the data point close to the centroid. Thus, we assumed the performance outcomes of all data points in a cluster to be the same as that of the centroid data point. This assumption resulted in a low "prediction error."

The mean absolute error (MAE) (Willmott and Matsuura 2005) was calculated for each data point while using this framework, and the percentage of the actual value predicted wrong represented the final MAE. The MAE for all clusters was summed and divided by the number of clusters to calculate the average MAE for the entire clustering method. The average MAE is considered as the "prediction error," and was found to be 1.1. This means that the performance prediction for any data point can be approximately 98.9% to 101.1% of its actual outcome.

Figure 6.3 Data points visualization in the lower dimension. (Left: without adding any weights; Middle: After adding weights; Right: clusters by Meanshift clustering).

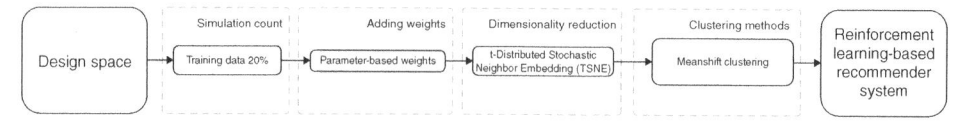

Figure 6.4 Proposed framework.

Clustering Method

In this study, considering that the dimensionality reduction processes aim to densify data points into smaller groups, the Meanshift clustering method was chosen for further investigations (see Figure 6.4). Meanshift is a density-based clustering algorithm known for its ability to identify clusters of varying shapes and sizes (Derpanis 2005). One of its major advantages is the adaptive determination of the number of clusters by adjusting the bandwidth parameter. By manipulating the bandwidth value, the granularity of the clustering results can be controlled, resulting in different numbers of clusters. In this study, a bandwidth value of 0.003 was utilized, which produced a total of 49 clusters (see Figure 6.3).

Section 02: Reinforcement Learning-Based Recommender System

In the second section of the study, the clustered design options and their corresponding performance outcomes are utilized to create a design dashboard using Compas ("COMPAS" n.d.) and Plotly (Dabbas 2021). This design dashboard is accessible online without the need to install any software. The dashboard provides a three-dimensional model of various design options from the design space, allowing designers to view and interact with the designs from different angles.

Process Explanation

Incorporating reinforcement learning (Kaelbling, Littman, and Moore 1996) into the design dashboard allowed us to strategically extract the designer's preferences. Reinforcement learning is a type of ML where an agent learns from its interactions with the user and makes decisions that align with the user's preferences. The agent constantly learns from its environment through trial and error, maximizing the rewards it receives for each interaction. The process begins with the agent displaying a random design option to the designer. Three buttons are provided on the dashboard: "like," "unlike," and "slide" (see Figure 6.6). If the designer clicks "like," the cluster to which the design option belongs is rewarded with a positive value. Conversely, if the designer dislikes the option, the reward is a negative value. Sliding the option results in a reward of zero.

The rewards received are used to update the q-value (also known as the action-value function) of each cluster. Each cluster, along with all designs within that cluster, has a preassigned q-value before any interactions begin. These q-values are inversely mapped to the performance outcomes, indicating that higher annual energy consumption leads to lower q-values. The performance outcomes are mapped from 100 to 0 for this system, where a cluster with the highest annual energy consumption per square meter has a q-value of 0, and the cluster with the lowest annual energy consumption per square meter has a value of 100. After each interaction, the q-values are updated based on the user's feedback, enabling the system to adapt and better align with the designer's preferences.

Methodology

Reward Function

The quantitative value of the user's feedback is denoted as the reward (R). A function is established to determine the appropriate reward, which can be positive or negative, for the system based on the user's interaction with the displayed design option. This function takes into account two constants, alpha (α) and gamma (γ), along with the reward (R) and the previous q-value. The old q-value is then updated with the new value obtained from this reward function (see Equation 1). This update equation is known as the Bellman equation (Barron and Ishii 1989), a fundamental concept in reinforcement learning. The study simplifies the Bellman equation by presenting only one design option in each iteration, resulting in a single state to consider. If multiple options were displayed simultaneously, the algorithm would need to calculate probabilities based on the q-values to estimate user preferences, which is not explored in this chapter.

Bellman equation for incorporated reinforcement learning

$$f(r) = (1-\alpha) \times Q + \alpha \times (R + \gamma \times Q) \tag{6.1}$$

α = learning rate
γ = discount factor
R = reward defined by β
Q = Previous q-value

Constants/Hyperparameters

The exploration process in the design dashboard involves four predefined constants that allow designers to customize their experience strategically:

Learning Rate (alpha (α))   This hyperparameter represents the learning rate, which controls the impact of recent interactions on the new q-value compared to past interactions. A higher alpha value gives more weight to recent preferences, allowing designers to adapt and change their preferences over time. Designers need to define the alpha value before starting the exploration process, and it typically ranges between 0 and 1.

Discount Factor (gamma (γ))   The gamma (γ) value is included to facilitate multistate reinforcement learning in the future, although it may not have a significant impact on single-state reinforcement learning. Gamma determines the algorithm's speed in aiming for options with greater q-values. It ensures that designers do not get stuck in a specific set of design options where their q-values may decrease over time. Like the learning rate, gamma also takes a value between 0 and 1, and designers must assign it before the exploration process begins.

Exploration Exploitation Trade-off Epsilon (ε)   When the user provides feedback, the agent has two options: it can either randomly select a cluster to show design options or choose the cluster with the highest q-value. To prevent excessive jumping across the design space, the system restricts the search to nearby clusters. The epsilon (ε) constant determines the likelihood of random exploration. In the Python script, an if function is used to compare a randomly generated number between 0 and 1 with epsilon (ε). If the random number is less than epsilon, the system selects a random nearby cluster. Higher epsilon (ε) values increase the chance of random selection, while lower values favor the exploitation of preferred options. The value of epsilon can be adapted over time, allowing users to have less exploration as they gain more experience with the design space.

Priority Trade-off (beta (β)) The constant beta (β) in the reinforcement learning process determines how much the agent prioritizes the user's preferences over the preassigned q-values. It is a value between 0 and 1, where a higher beta value means that the user's preferences have more influence on the agent's decisions. In other words, if the beta is higher, the user's feedback of "like" for a design option will have a greater impact on the agent's recommendation for future designs. This aspect sets the proposed reinforcement learning-based recommender system apart from traditional systems. In conventional algorithms, the main focus is to increase the number of "likes" for individual design options. The suggested system, however, goes beyond that objective. It tries to advise designers on both preferred design alternatives and clusters with high performance.

Reward Alteration with Alpha (α) and Gamma (γ) The reward's magnitude after a positive interaction affects the number of hits required to suppress the highest-performing design option. Determining the perfect reward value for exploration depends on the interrelationship between beta (β) and other constants. The reward function considers all four constants (alpha, gamma, epsilon, and beta) to strike a balance and guide the design exploration process, considering trade-offs. Understanding this interplay is essential in deriving an effective reward function for personalized design exploration. Figure 6.5 illustrates this relationship. The team conducted an investigation to examine how the assigned rewards relate to the number of iterations required to surpass the highest q-value, considering different values of alpha (α) and gamma (γ). It was observed that lower initial reward values result in more iterations for a cluster with the lowest q-value to surpass the highest q-value. It was found that the reward should be greater than 100 to avoid an almost infinite number of iterations for a cluster with a q-value of 0 to surpass a q-value of 100. To account for the possibility that the cluster with the lowest q-value could be the one designer prefer, Beta (β) is employed to specify a suitable reward(R) value for the system, eliminating the need for designers to repeatedly click "like" to express their preferences.

Function Determines beta(β) A function has been created to construct a Pareto frontier, which maps reward values (varying from 100 to 200) on the *x*-axis of the graph to the number of "likes" necessary to attain a q-value of one hundred of the cluster with the least q-value on the y-axis. A Pareto Frontier is a distribution of optimal solutions, which helps to understand the trade-off between multiple objectives. Here the team focuses to investigate the way to compromise the number of iterations for different reward values. The function utilizes the same Bellman equation used in the algorithm to derive the number of "likes" needed (Eq. 6.1). The exploration factor (epsilon, ε) is set to 0 to eliminate exploration effects and solely focus on the frontier.

The function can construct the Pareto frontier with various combinations of alpha (α) and gamma (γ) values. It runs before the exploration process begins, using preassigned values of alpha, gamma, and beta. Beta (β) is important in establishing the amount of "likes" required to give preference to clusters with moderate or reduced q-values, as well as in defining an acceptable reward function. To illustrate, let's discuss a system with gamma 0.01 and alpha

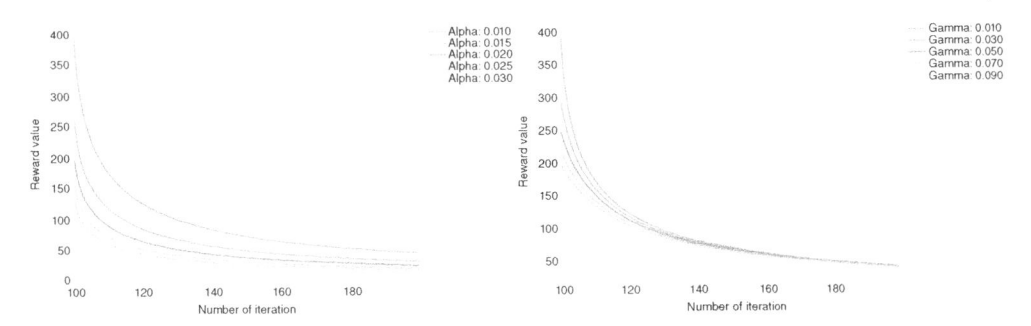

Figure 6.5 Changes in reward value with the number of interactions for different alpha(right) and gamma(left) values.

0.01. The function is used to calculate the number of "likes" for reward values ranging from 100 to 200, resulting in a range of 41 to 395. By multiplying this range (354) by beta (0.6), we obtain the desired number of "likes" (nearly 212). The corresponding reward value can then be determined from the Pareto frontier.

Design Dashboard

The team opted for Plotly, a Python library (Dabbas 2021) with integration into Dash (Hossain et al. 2019), instead of the commonly used Human UI plugin for creating the dashboard. Unlike the dashboard created using the Human UI plugin, which is limited to access within Grasshopper, the dashboard produced by Plotly is accessible via any web browser. Moreover, the Plotly dashboard offers enhanced integration options and greater flexibility in its functionality. The dashboard features a 3D model of the design option, interactive buttons for user input, a line chart illustrating performance changes in kWh, and pixelated images of selected design options. Eight scatter plots below the 3D perspective help visualize changes after each interaction, with the first row showing individual data points and the second row representing clusters as single data points (see Figure 6.6).

1) **First row, first column chart:** In order to determine if closely aligned data points are clustered together, this chart colors data points according to their cluster number.
2) **First row, second column chart:** The changes in q-values after each repetition are seen in this graph. It excludes the values that were initially allocated and simply shows the changes in the q-values. The q-value for every data point in a cluster is the same.
3) **First row, third column chart:** This graph displays the actual performance results of individual data points (annual energy consumption per square meter (kWh)). No remapping was done.
4) **First row, fourth column chart:** This chart highlights the displayed data point by marking it black and keeping the rest of it white. By clicking on any data point, a pixelated image of the selected design option appears, facilitating exploration in the lower-dimensional space.
5) **Second row, first column chart:** The standard deviation of the average performance outcome across all clusters is color mapped in this graph. It shows which subset of the data has performance outcomes that are substantially different from the mean.

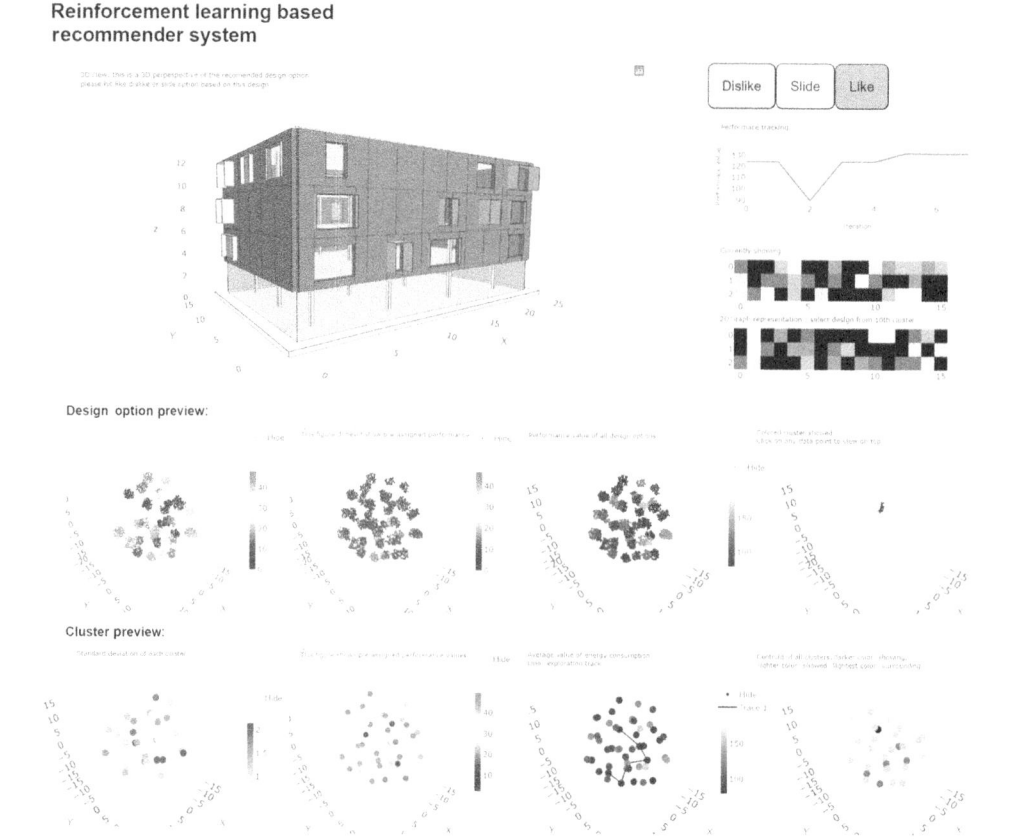

Figure 6.6 Design Dashboard (after 7 iterations).

6) **Second row, second column chart:** Showing preassigned q-values for each cluster, this graph reveals the discrepancy between assigned q-values and average performance outcomes.
7) **Second row, third column chart:** This graph contains a line that represents maneuvering in the design space after the last interaction and shows the average yearly energy usage per square meter for each cluster. Proper reinforcement learning functioning is indicated if the line consistently moves toward warmer-colored clusters.
8) **Second row, fourth column chart:** The current design option's origin cluster is marked in black, whereas previously visited clusters are tinted in gray. It is possible to trace the exploration of the design space and comprehend the algorithm's success by looking at nearby clusters to the present one, which are similarly gray and offer information about possible future steps.

Discussion

Indeed, while our study presents a promising framework that combines a recommender system with design space exploration, the true measure of its effectiveness lies in obtaining feedback from designers. While there are several advantages to the proposed framework employing dimensionality reduction, clustering, and reinforcement learning-based recommender systems, there are also a number of limitations that need to be resolved in further studies.

- **Generalizability to Different Simulation Outcomes:** The current investigations focused on predicting the EnergyPlus outcome, specifically the yearly energy consumption per square meter for cooling, heating, and lighting. It is crucial to determine how well the proposed clustering-based performance prediction method would work in approximating other different types of performance outcomes, such as indoor air quality, daylighting, or thermal comfort.
- **Balancing Visual and Performance Outcome Differences while Clustering:** In this framework, clustering assumes that design options with different performance outcomes will also exhibit visual differences. To enhance the efficiency of the proposed framework, it is beneficial to cluster design options based on both visual and performance outcome differences.
- **Applicability to Different Building Types and Contexts:** The study explored a "mid-rise apartment" building, with randomly varying window sizes in different orientations. However, this approach may not directly apply to all types of apartment buildings or other building typologies.
- **Addressing Designer Subjectivity and Biases:** The mental state and subjective preferences of designers can influence the learning process of the reinforcement learning algorithm. Addressing individual biases and preferences to provide personalized and unbiased design recommendations requires further research and consideration.

The dashboard was carefully developed and made available online through the Google Cloud service, enabling global user engagement. While it offers valuable functionality, there is recognition of the need for improvements in usability and comprehensiveness. The main focus was on showcasing the potential of reinforcement learning-based recommender systems in design space exploration, with plans to refine and improve the dashboard based on user feedback and further research.

Conclusion

This study introduces a pioneering approach to exploring vast design spaces by integrating human and machine intelligence to generate high-performing and visually appealing design solutions. Unlike previous research relying on guided optimizations, our study employs a reinforcement learning-based recommender system that learns from designer interactions to suggest design options aligned with their preferences while minimizing annual energy consumption. To achieve effective recommendations, the algorithm needs to learn the performance outcomes of various design options. Recognizing the time-intensive nature of simulating all possibilities, we developed a framework that approximates performance outcomes by learning from a subset of the dataset. Remarkably, by simulating only 20% of the dataset, we achieved accurate predictions of the remaining design options' performance.

We used powerful ML algorithms to rapidly and effectively explore broad design areas, focusing on yearly energy usage as a vital indicator due to its intricate connection with numerous design aspects. This innovative approach leverages design computation and artificial intelligence to address an important problem in the field, resulting in fast and accurate predictions that showcase its sophistication and intelligence. Moreover, this process contributes to sustainability efforts by significantly reducing computation time and encourages widespread participation in design decision-making through the interactive design dashboard.

References

Barron, E.N. and Ishii, H. (1989). The Bellman Equation for Minimizing the Maximum Cost. *Nonlinear Analysis: Theory, Methods & Applications* 13 (9): 1067–1090. https://doi.org/10.1016/0362-546X(89)90096-5.

Bertagna, F., D'Acunto, P., Ohlbrock, P.O., and Moosavi, V. (2021). Holistic Design Explorations of Building Envelopes Supported by Machine Learning. *Journal of Facade Design and Engineering* 9 (April): 31–46. https://doi.org/10.7480/jfde.2021.1.5423.

Choi, Sungwoon, Heonseok Ha, Uiwon Hwang, Chanju Kim, Jung-Woo Ha, and Sungroh Yoon. 2018. "Reinforcement Learning Based Recommender System Using Biclustering Technique." arXiv. https://doi.org/10.48550/arXiv.1801.05532.

"Commercial Reference Buildings." n.d. Energy. Gov. . https://www.energy.gov/eere/buildings/commercial-reference-buildings.

"COMPAS." n.d. COMPAS, A computational framework for collaboration and research in Architecture, Engineering, Fabrication, and Construction. https://compas.dev/.

Dabbas, E. (2021). *Interactive Dashboards and Data Apps with Plotly and Dash: Harness the Power of a Fully Fledged Frontend Web Framework in Python – No JavaScript Required*. Packt Publishing Ltd.

Derpanis, K.G. (2005). Mean Shift Clustering. *Lecture Notes* 32: 1–4.

Echenagucia, Tomás. 2014. "Computational Search in Architectural Design." https://doi.org/10.6092/polito/porto/2543137.

Echenagucia, Tomas Mendez. (2022)2023. "Compas_eplus." Python. https://github.com/tmsmendez/compas_eplus.

Fuhrimann, Lukas, Vahid Moosavi, Patrick Ole Ohlbrock, and Pierluigi D'Acunto. 2018. *Data-Driven Design: Exploring New Structural Forms Using Machine Learning and Graphic Statics*.

Gu, N., Rongrong, Y., and Behbahani, P.A. (2021). Parametric Design: Theoretical Development and Algorithmic Foundation for Design Generation in Architecture. In: *Handbook of the Mathematics of the Arts and Sciences* (ed. B. Sriraman), 1361–1383. Cham: Springer International Publishing https://doi.org/10.1007/978-3-319-57072-3_8.

Harding, J. and Brandt-Olsen, C. (2018). Biomorpher: Interactive Evolution for Parametric Design. *International Journal of Architectural Computing* 16 (June): 144–163. https://doi.org/10.1177/1478077118778579.

Hossain, S., Calloway, C., Lippa, D. et al. (2019). Visualization of Bioinformatics Data with Dash Bio. In: *Proceedings of the 18th Python in Science Conference*, 126–133. Austin, Texas: SciPy.

"Human UI." 2016. Text. Food4Rhino. January 31, 2016. https://www.food4rhino.com/en/app/human-ui.

Kaelbling, L.P., Littman, M.L., and Moore, A.W. (1996). Reinforcement Learning: A Survey. *Journal of Artificial Intelligence Research* 4 (May): 237–285. https://doi.org/10.1613/jair.301.

Lika, B., Kolomvatsos, K., and Hadjiefthymiades, S. (2014). Facing the Cold Start Problem in Recommender Systems. *Expert Systems with Applications* 41 (4, Part 2): 2065–2073. https://doi.org/10.1016/j.eswa.2013.09.005.

van der Maaten, L. and Hinton, G. (2008). Viualizing Data Using T-SNE. *Journal of Machine Learning Research* 9 (November): 2579–2605.

McKinney, W. and others(2011). Pandas: A Foundational Python Library for Data Analysis and Statistics. *Python for High Performance and Scientific Computing* 14 (9): 1–9.

Mohapatra, P., Nayak, A., Kumar, S., and Tiwari, M.K. (2015). Multi-Objective Process Planning and Scheduling Using Controlled Elitist Non-Dominated Sorting Genetic Algorithm. *International Journal of Production Research* 53 (6): 1712–1735. https://doi.org/10.1080/00207543.2014.957872.

Mueller, C. and Ochsendorf, J. (2015). Combining Structural Performance and Designer Preferences in Evolutionary Design Space Exploration. *Automation in Construction* 52 (April): https://doi.org/10.1016/j.autcon.2015.02.011.

Ohlbrock, P.O. and Schwartz, J. (2016). Combinatorial Equilibrium Modeling. *International Journal of Space Structures* 31 (August): https://doi.org/10.1177/0266351116660799.

Rahmani Asl, M., Bergin, M., Menter, A., and Yan, W. (2014). *BIM-Based Parametric Building Energy Performance Multi-Objective. Optimization.* 2: https://doi.org/10.52842/conf.ecaade.2014.2.455.

Reeh, Chris. 2019. "Generative Suburban Frameworks: Emerging Architect-Guided Optimization Workflows Within Suburban Mass Production." Theses from the M. Arch. Program, May. https://digitalcommons.unl.edu/marchthesis/2.

Ricci, F., Rokach, L., and Shapira, B. (2022). Recommender Systems: Techniques, Applications, and Challenges. In: *Handbook, edited by Francesco Ricci, Lior Rokach, and Bracha Shapira* (ed. R. Systems), 1–35. New York, NY: Springer US https://doi.org/10.1007/978-1-0716-2197-4_1.

Ritter, F., Geyer, P., and Borrmann, A. (2013). The Design Space Exploration Assistance Method: Constraints and Objectives. In: *Proceedings of the 13th International Conference on Construction Applications of Virtual Reality, 30-31 October 2013, London, UK.* https://api.semanticscholar.org/CorpusID:55912374.

Saldana Ochoa, K., Ohlbrock, P.O., D'Acunto, P., and Moosavi, V. (2021). Beyond Typologies, beyond Optimization: Exploring Novel Structural Forms at the Interface of Human and Machine Intelligence. *International Journal of Architectural Computing* 19 (3): 466–490. https://doi.org/10.1177/1478077120943062.

Simons, C.L., Parmee, I.C., and Gwynllyw, R. (2010). Interactive, Evolutionary Search in Upstream Object-Oriented Class Design. *IEEE Transactions on Software Engineering* 36 (6): 798–816. https://doi.org/10.1109/TSE.2010.34.

Su, X., Yan, X., and Tsai, C.-L. (2012). Linear Regression. *WIREs Computational Statistics* 4 (3): 275–294. https://doi.org/10.1002/wics.1198.

Takagi, H. (2001). Interactive Evolutionary Computation: Fusion of the Capabilities of EC Optimization and Human Evaluation. *Proceedings of the IEEE* 89 (9): 1275–1296. https://doi.org/10.1109/5.949485.

Techlabs, Maruti. 2021. "What Are the Types of Recommendation Systems?" MLearning.Ai (blog). August 18, 2021. https://medium.com/mlearning-ai/what-are-the-types-of-recommendation-systems-3487cbafa7c9.

Verleysen, M. and François, D. (2005). The Curse of Dimensionality in Data Mining and Time Series Prediction. In: *Computational Intelligence and Bioinspired Systems* (ed. J. Cabestany, A. Prieto, and F. Sandoval), 758–770. Lecture Notes in Computer Science. Berlin, Heidelberg: Springer https://doi.org/10.1007/11494669_93.

Willmott, C.J. and Matsuura, K. (2005). Advantages of the Mean Absolute Error (MAE) over the Root Mean Square Error (RMSE) in Assessing Average Model Performance. *Climate Research* 30 (1): 79–82. https://doi.org/10.3354/cr030079.

Wortmann, T., Costa, A., Nannicini, G., and Schroepfer, T. (2015). Advantages of Surrogate Models for Architectural Design Optimization. *AI EDAM* 29 (4): 471–481. https://doi.org/10.1017/S0890060415000451.

Yi, Y.K. (2019). Building Facade Multi-Objective Optimization for Daylight and Aesthetical Perception. *Building and Environment* 156 (June): 178–190. https://doi.org/10.1016/j.buildenv.2019.04.002.

7

Multi-Level Optimization of UHP-FRC Sandwich Panels for Building Façade Systems

Pooya Darghiasi[1], Anil Baral[1], Bahram Abediniangerabi[1], Atefe Makhmalbaf[2] and Mohsen Shahandashti[1]

[1] Department of Civil Engineering, The University of Texas at Arlington, Arlington, TX, USA
[2] School of Architecture, The University of Texas at Arlington, Arlington, TX, USA

Introduction

Commercial and residential buildings consume about 39% of the total U.S. energy consumption in 2021 (U.S. EIA 2022). This energy use is expected to increase by 0.3% every year until 2050 (U.S. EIA 2020). To minimize the negative environmental impacts of these buildings, it is necessary to employ potential energy-efficient designs and methods in the architectural, engineering, and construction (AEC) industry (Abediniangerabi, Shahandashti, and Makhmalbaf 2020; Shahandashti et al. 2017). The amount of energy consumed in buildings is influenced by various factors, such as, the physical characteristics of the building, climate and weather conditions, building operations, maintenance practice, and building orientation and layout (Abediniangerabi and Shahandashti 2022). In particular, façade systems and buildings envelopes play a crucial role in managing the heating and cooling loads of buildings, thereby significantly influencing the energy performance. In addition, façade systems are supposed to provide support for the exterior walls and ensure their stability against various environmental loads such as wind, rain, and snow. In recent years, there has been considerable research dedicated to examining the optimal design of façade systems from various perspectives, including but not limited to energy efficiency, cost-effectiveness, and structural integrity. However, only a few studies have taken into account the interaction of the façade systems' design parameters on multiple and perhaps competing performance-based objectives in buildings at different levels. The design of façade systems has been studied mainly from two different aspects: building level and assembly level. At the building level, the design variables of façade systems are selected to improve the whole-building performance criteria such as building's energy consumption, indoor thermal and visual comfort (Al-Homoud 2005; Wang, Zmeureanu, and Rivard 2005; Cheng, Wang, and Zhang 2014; Ruiz et al. 2014). While at the assembly level, the panel's design variables are selected based on improving other criteria such as serviceability, weight, and blast resistance (Khalkhali, Khakshournia, and Nariman-Zadeh 2014; Garrido et al. 2019; Wang, Li, and Sun 2020;

Artificial Intelligence in Performance-Driven Design: Theories, Methods, and Tools, First Edition.
Edited by Narjes Abbasabadi and Mehdi Ashayeri.
©2024 John Wiley & Sons Inc. Published 2024 by John Wiley & Sons Inc.

Shobeiri 2021). This Chapter presents a framework that enables the selection of optimal design parameters for façade systems, considering multiple performance-based objectives such as energy efficiency, cost-effectiveness, and structural performance at two levels, simultaneously. The following subsection provides an overview of recent advancements in the design optimization of façade systems from various perspectives. Additionally, the limitations of these studies will be discussed, and a proposed solution to address these gaps will be presented.

Building Façade Design Optimization

Different techniques and approaches help decision-makers find optimal building façade system design alternatives (Wetter 2019; Abediniangerabi, Makhmalbaf, and Shahandashti 2022). While some performance criteria, such as the building's energy efficiency and financial aspects, are mainly addressed at the building level (Shi et al. 2016), some other aspects, such as the structural performance of the building's components, are investigated at the assembly level to fulfill the building's serviceability requirements (Bedon et al. 2019). Optimizing building façade systems could be a single-or-multi-objective problem that deals with at least two competing goals (e.g. building energy consumption and indoor thermal comfort) (Diakaki, Grigoroudis, and Kolokotsa 2008; Stavrakakis et al. 2012). In the literature, various methods have been used to optimize the building façade systems at the building or assembly levels.

At the building level, the implementation of passive design strategies has been thoroughly investigated and recommended in recent years in the context of improving the energy-efficient design of buildings (Bui et al. 2020; Abediniangerabi, Makhmalbaf, and Shahandashti 2021). Double-skin façade systems (Hensen, Bartak, and Drkal 2002; Shameri et al. 2011; Anđelković et al. 2012; Darkwa, Li, and Chow 2014) ventilated photovoltaics (PV) systems (Shahsavar et al. 2011; Athienitis et al. 2018), PV wall-mounted multi-layer façade systems (Peng et al. 2013; Li et al. 2019), dynamic insulation materials (DIMs) (Imbabi 2012; Menyhart and Krarti 2017; Koenders, Loonen, and Hensen 2018), and innovative high-performance sandwich panels (Abediniangerabi et al. 2018; Abediniangerabi et al. 2019; Mahdi et al. 2021) are among those passive design strategies for improving building energy efficiency. These approaches offer more cost-effective solutions than active solutions, which incur higher investment costs and have higher embodied energy (Ramesh, Prakash, and Shukla 2010; Chastas, Theodosiou, and Bikas 2016). To optimize the design parameters of façade systems at building level, researchers have employed various methods and techniques. For example, Coley and Schukat (2002), Wang Zmeureanu, and Rivard (2005), Ioannou and Itard (2015), Kämpf et al. (2010), Hamdy, Hasan, and Siren (2011), Yu et al. (2015), Hamdy et al. (2013), and Ferrara et al. (2014) used the genetic algorithm — a search technique that mimics the process of natural selection and genetics to find the optimal solution to a problem — to select optimum design parameters for façade systems (e.g. material properties, openings' size, and position, insulation thickness) to improve energy efficiency, thermal or visual comfort, and cost effectiveness. Stavrakakis et al. (2012) used surrogate models and designed a genetic algorithm to select the optimum values for the size and U-value of the windows, and the shading's size to improve thermal comfort. Surrogate models can provide faster results and reduce computational costs by approximating a complex system behavior using statistical or machine learning techniques. Fesanghary, Asadi, and

Gheem (2012) employed harmony search algorithms — which mimic the process of finding a harmonious musical chord to solve a problem — to select the optimum material properties for façade systems to minimize the building's energy consumption and improve the thermal comfort of buildings. Ruiz et al. (2014) aimed to select the best design parameters for walls, roof insulation, glazing, and window frames to minimize energy consumption and life cycle cost using Tabu search which is a metaheuristic optimization algorithm that uses a memory-based search mechanism to efficiently explore the solution space and find the optimal solution. Furthermore, Delgarm et al. (2016) developed a multi-objective optimization framework through the genetic algorithm, coupled with a whole-building energy simulation model, to explore the effect of various architectural parameters (e.g. building orientation, window size, and overhang specification) on a multi-story office building's energy consumption. Lin et al. (2016) substituted a building's energy simulation model with regression models to provide the optimal configurations for an office building envelope, including construction material, window size and layout, and sunshade type, to minimize the energy use and construction cost of the building.

In addition to the performance criteria at the building level, façade systems must also meet structural criteria, such as serviceability, which is usually investigated at the assembly level (Bedon et al. 2019). At the assembly level, façade systems (i.e. concrete sandwich panels) are typically investigated using experiments and numerical simulations to provide insights for the designers (Bedon et al. 2019). For example, Wang et al. (2020) used Kriging surrogate models and NSGA-II (non-dominated sorting genetic algorithm) to optimize the face sheet displacement and blast resistance of a 300 mm × 300 mm sandwich panel based on results of an experimental study and a numerical model. In another study, Khalkhali et al. (2014) employed the hybrid finite element model (ANSYS) and NSGA-II algorithm to solve a multi-objective optimization problem and find trade-off design points that minimize the structure's weight and displacement for a corrugated core sandwich panel. Moreover, Garrido et al. (2019) used a direct multi-search method to improve the structural serviceability, thermal resistance, acoustic performance, and environmental performance by selecting the optimum design variables panel's material properties, number of inner webs, total panel width, and core thickness. Table 7.1 exemplifies the objectives, parameters, and methods used for optimizing façade systems at the building and assembly levels.

According to Table 7.1, there are various objectives, parameters, and methods used in optimizing façade systems with respect to different performance-based aspects of buildings. For instance, at building levels researchers have aimed at optimizing the façade systems, mainly by reducing a building's energy use, maximizing thermal comfort or reducing a building's life cycle cost. There is also a growing interest in optimizing the façade systems at assembly level considering objectives such as structural serviceability, thermal resistance, blast resistance, and environmental performance of the panels. At both levels, different design parameters and optimization methods are utilized, and their selection depends on the specific nature of the problem. Although the design optimization of façade systems has been thoroughly investigated at two separate levels, only a few studies have investigated the interaction between multiple competing objectives across multiple levels in buildings. For example, Brown and Mueller (2016) have investigated how building layouts can affect the energy performance of buildings using a finite element structural modeling and building energy simulations. Krem et al. (2013) studied the effect of building morphology (the location of the structural cores or walls and the building's layout) on the energy performance of a high-rise building in different climate zones. Furthermore, Cauteren et al. (2022) proposed

Table 7.1 Examples of studies in the optimization of façade systems at the building level and assembly level.

Level	Researcher(s)	Objective(s)	Parameters	Method(s)
Building Level	Al-Homoud (2005, 2009)	Energy use	Absorptance, glass area, emittance, U-value	Direct search
	Cheng et al. (2014)	Room temperature	Specific heat of the building's internal envelope	Direct search
	Bouchlaghem and Letherman (1990)	Thermal comfort	Thermophysical properties of building component, windows size and location, windows shading, building layout, thicknesses, surface treatment of the enclosing envelope, weight, and surface area of partitions	Simplex method
	Hasan et al. (2008)	Building's Life cycle cost	The thickness of the insulation material	Hybrid Hooke–Jeeves and Particle swarm optimization algorithm
	Stazi et al. (2012)	Life cycle cost wall system	Wall thickness, material, and window type	Factorial plan technique
	Gong et al. (2012)	Minimum thermal load	Insulation thickness, type of window, shading, and orientation	Orthogonal method
	Ruiz et al. (2014)	Building's energy use and life cycle cost	Insulation thickness and material type of openings	Tabu search
	Coley and Schukat (2002)	Annual building energy use	Type of window, type of wall type, and area of the window in wall and roof	Genetic algorithm
	Wang et al. (2005)	Life cycle energy	Building's orientation and material types	Genetic algorithm
	Ioannou and Itard (2015)	Building's energy use	Windows', walls', roofs', and floors' U-value	Genetic algorithm
	Kämpf et al. (2010)	Absorbed energy by the corresponding surface	The shape of the building with consistent volume	Genetic algorithm
	Hamdy et al. (2011)	Thermal comfort and Energy use	Window size and corresponding U-value, size of shading	Genetic algorithm
	Stavrakakis et al. (2012)	Thermal comfort	Window position and size of the opening	Genetic algorithm based on surrogate models

Reference	Objective	Design Variables	Method
Yu et al. (2015)	Energy consumption and thermal comfort	Area, orientation, heat transfer coefficient of wall and window	Genetic algorithm
Fesanghary et al. (2012)	Building's life cycle cost and CO_2 emission	Materials of wall system and type of glazing	Harmony search algorithm
Gossard et al. (2013)	Energy use and thermal comfort	Wall and roof thermophysical properties	Genetic algorithm coupled with artificial neural network
Magnier and Haghighat (2010)	Thermal comfort and energy consumption	The thickness of concrete, HVAC set points and window size	TRNSYS (transient system simulation tool) coupled with artificial neural networks
Ferrara et al. (2014)	Energy consumption and life cycle cost	Insulation thickness, type of glazing, and shading systems	Genetic algorithm
Azari et al. (2016)	Building energy use and life cycle environmental impact	Insulation material, window type, window frame material, wall thermal resistance, and window-to-wall ratios	Hybrid artificial neural network and genetic algorithm
Ascione et al. (2019)	Primary energy consumption, energy-related global cost, and discomfort hours	Set point temperature, thermo-physical properties of envelope properties, window type, and building orientation	Genetic algorithm
Zhang et al. (2013)	Energy use intensity (EUI)	Rood and wall Insulation thickness, glazing, and infiltration	Statistical surrogate modeling and genetic algorithm
Wang et al. (2020)	Blast resistance of panel	Thickness and density of the panel's core layers	Kriging modeling and NSGA_II algorithm
Khalkhali et al. (2014) [Assembly Level]	Structure weight and displacement	Panel's face thickness, core member thickness, the distance between face sheets, and order of corrugation	Hybrid finite element model (ANSYS) and NSGA-II algorithm
Shobeiri (2021)	Weight, boundary reaction force, and energy absorption	Core thickness, number and height of unit cells, stiffener configuration	Topology optimization based on finite element analysis (ABAQUS)
Murthy et al. (2006)	Bending stiffness and strength	Core to skin weight ratio	Gradient-based optimization
Garrido et al. (2019)	Structural serviceability, thermal resistance, acoustic performance, cost, environmental performance	Material properties, number of inner webs, total panel width, and core thickness	Direct multi-search method

a multi-objective optimization framework to determine the optimum design of hybrid steel or timber structures while considering environmental impact and financial budget.

Despite the advancements in the design optimization of concrete sandwich panels, there is still a gap in the literature regarding the structural performance of building façade systems, specifically multi-layer UHP-FRC sandwich panels, while considering the building's energy efficiency and life cycle cost. Façade systems are expected to withstand various environmental loads, such as wind loads causing lateral deflections. In addition, these systems are subject to seasonal temperature variations within their layers, causing the thermal bowing effect, thus intensifying the lateral deflections. Modeling the structural response of the concrete sandwich panels simultaneously with other performance criteria at the building level, such as energy use and life-cycle costs, is challenging due to the limitations of simulation models. Several software programs simulate the energy performance, life-cycle cost, and structural performance of building components using different modeling techniques. For example, whole-building energy simulation programs, such as TRNSYS and EnergyPlus, use the conduction transfer function (CTF) to calculate the conduction heat transfer in building cooling/heating loads and energy calculations in buildings (Li et al. 2009; Delcroix et al. 2012). At the assembly level, the finite element method (FEM) is usually used by programs, such as COMSOL Multiphysics and ANSYS, to solve the related partial differential equations (PDEs) for calculating the responses of a model. Although these programs provide valuable benefits, they may not provide enough information to investigate simultaneous interactions between different performance criteria at different levels. Statistical surrogate models offer a promising approach to solve multi-objective optimization problems by substituting the simulation models and providing the opportunity to evaluate the different performance criteria from different levels simultaneously. Surrogate models can estimate the behavior of a complex system or process by using a simpler mathematical model that is computationally efficient in order to simplify the resolution of multi-objective optimization problems.

This chapter proposes a surrogate-based multi-level multi-objective optimization framework for optimizing the UHP-FRC sandwich panel for the building's façade system from structural, energy efficiency, and financial aspects by (1) constructing polynomial regression surrogate models using input-output data generated from a finite element and a whole-building simulation model, and (2) utilizing the non-dominated and crowding distance sorting genetic algorithm (NSGA-II) to extract the Pareto front solutions as a decision-making tool to enable making a trade-off between the competing performance criteria.

Methodology

A surrogate-based multi-level optimization framework is proposed to optimize the design variables of UHP-FRC façade systems, considering the interdependency between multiple objectives such as structural performance of panels, energy efficiency, and the life-cycle cost of building. UHP-FRC façade panels are multi-layer sandwich façade systems with two structural wythes (i.e. UHP-FRC) and an insulation layer (i.e. expanded polystyrene) in between. Fiber content, insulation thickness, and building orientation are selected as the design variables to optimize structural performance, thermal performance, and life cycle cost of the UHP-FRC façade system for a prototype building model derived from the US Department of Energy's (DOE) commercial building reference models, located in Houston,

Methodology | 135

Texas. The DOE's prototype buildings provide complete descriptions for whole building energy models such as EnergyPlus to simulate the energy performance of the building (US DOE 2022).

Figure 7.1 presents the proposed framework to optimize building façade systems (i.e. UHP-FRC panel) concerning building energy performance, structural performance, and the life-cycle cost of the façade system.

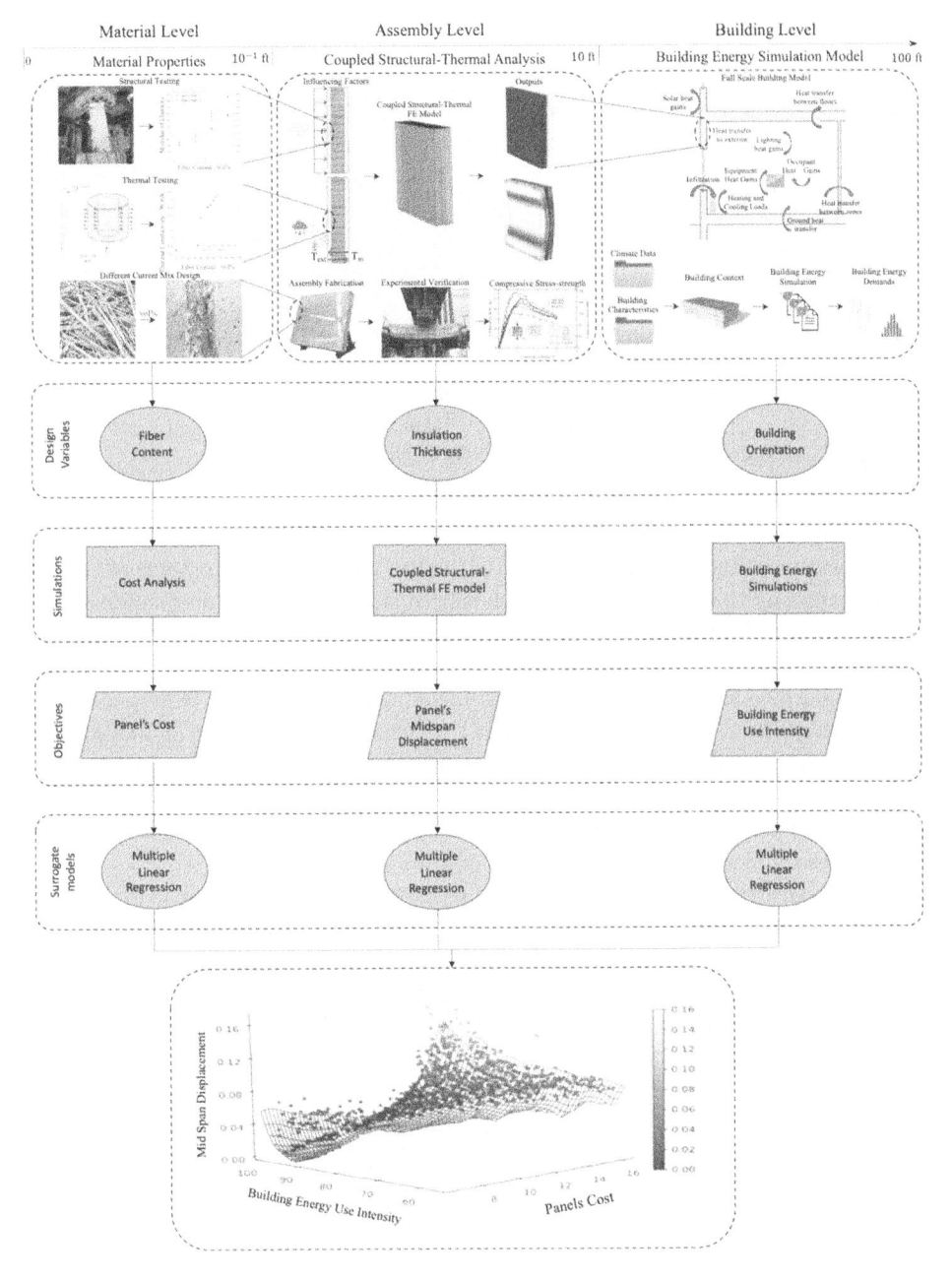

Figure 7.1 The proposed framework to optimize energy performance, structural performance, and the life-cycle cost of building façade systems. Source: Mahlebashieva/Adobe Stock; The Constructor.

The thermal and mechanical properties of the UHP-FRC are modeled for different mix designs as a dependent factor of the fiber content. Façade assemblies' structural response (e.g. maximum midspan displacement) and thermal response (e.g. thermal resistivity) with different mix designs and configurations are numerically estimated using a coupled heat transfer and structural finite element model. Multiple combinations of decision variables within the decision space are used as inputs to the simulation model to estimate the desired outputs. To evaluate how the panel's thermal performance affects the building, the estimated thermal resistivity derived from the finite element model is utilized as input for a whole-building energy simulation model, enabling the estimation of energy use for different building orientations. The life cycle cost of façade systems with different configurations is also determined. Three surrogate models are constructed to approximate the response surface of the interdependent objectives at three different levels (assembly and building): (1) midspan displacement, (2) building EUI, and (3) life cycle cost. Furthermore, to allow making a trade-off between the competing and yet interdependent objectives, Pareto front solutions are extracted by applying the NSGA-II algorithm as a multi-objective decision-making tool to find a set of efficient choices for design variables. The following subsections describe the finite element model, building energy simulations, panel cost analysis, surrogate models, and the details and assumptions used for each model.

Midspan Displacements and Thermal Resistivity of UHP-FRC Panels

Thermo-Mechanical Properties of UHP-FRC, Model's Boundary Conditions, and Finite Element Model Specifics

This study assumes that the building uses 3.05 m (10 ft)*0.91 m (3 ft)×20.32 cm (8 inches) UHP-FRC panels for the façade system, which is fixed at both ends, and no rotation or displacement for the panel at the end connections is allowed. Figure 7.2 illustrates the 3D schematic view of the UHP-FRC panel used in the numerical finite element model of this study. The thermo-mechanical properties for the constituent materials of the UHP-FRC panel used in the finite element model are provided in Table 7.2. To investigate the effect of fiber content on panels' responses (i.e. midspan displacement and thermal resistivity), correlations between the fiber content and required material properties such as thermal conductivity, specific heat, and elastic modulus are obtained from published experiments in the literature and used in the simulations (Małek et al. 2021a,b).

For the boundary condition, the exterior temperature is considered colder than the interior temperature to trigger the maximum midspan displacement in the same direction that the wind load causes. It is assumed that the building is located in Houston, Texas. In this case, the interior temperature would be the neutral room temperature: 25°C (77°F) (Pasut et al. 2013), and the exterior temperature is presumed to be the coldest recorded temperature in Houston, Texas, from 2010 to 2020: −7°C (20°F) (National Oceanic and Atmospheric Administration 2020). Furthermore, a uniform lateral wind load is calculated based on ASCE/SEI 7-16 and is applied to the panel. The following equation determines the design wind load in buildings (ASCE/SEI 7-16 2017):

$$P_s = \lambda k_{zt} P_{s30} \tag{7.1}$$

where λ is the adjustment factor for the height of the building, k_{zt} is the topographic factor, and P_{s30} is the ASCE 7-16's simplified design wind load in an urban or suburban area.

Methodology 137

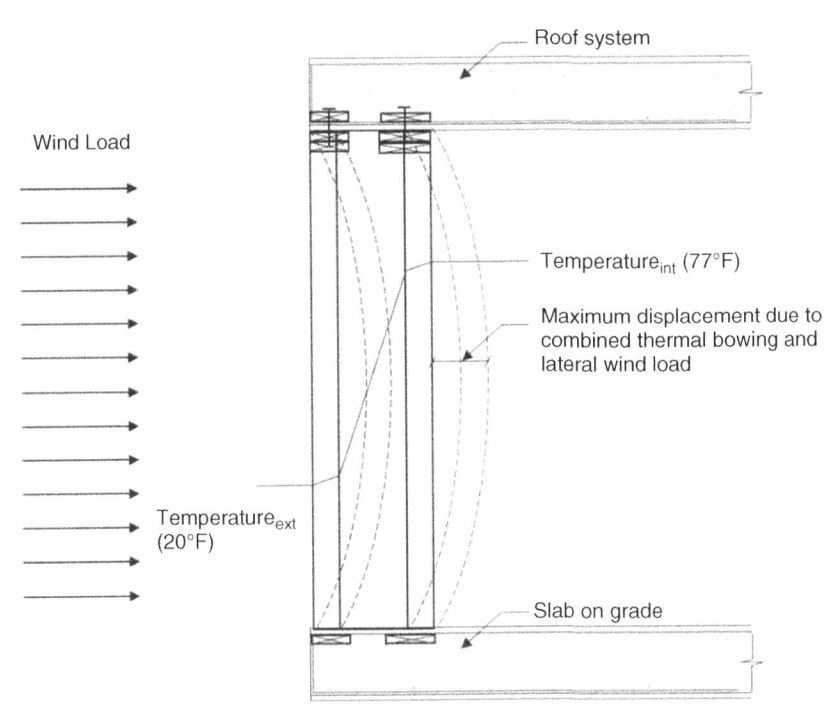

Figure 7.2 Wind force resisting system.

Table 7.2 Thermo-mechanical properties of the UHP-FRC panel for the finite element model.

Material	Properties	Value	Reference
Insulation	Thermal Conductivity (W/m k)	0.0058	Abediniangerabi et al. (2018)
	Specific Heat (J/kg K)	645	Abediniangerabi et al. (2018)
	Density (kg/m^2)	28	Abediniangerabi et al. (2018)
	Elastic Modulus (MPA)	200,000	Yucel et al. (2003)
	Poison ratio	0.3	Yucel et al. (2003)
	Coefficient of Thermal Expansion (CTE) for (1/K)	$63*10^{(-6)}$	Yucel et al. (2003)
UHP-FRC	Thermal conductivity (W/m K)	$0.1017*F* + 1.8803$	Małek et al. (2021a)
	Specific heat (J/kg K)	$0.0491*F + 1.9749$	Małek et al. (2021a)
	Density (kg/m^2)	2403	Abediniangerabi et al. (2018)
	Elastic Modulus	$2.3e5*(F^3) - 6.9e5*(F^2) + 8.3e5*(F) + 3.15e7$	Małek et al. (2021b)
	Poisson ratio	0.12	Małek et al. (2021b)
	CTE for (1/K)	$1.475*10^{(-6)}$	Jawdhari and Fam (2020)

[*] F, fiber content (%).

To extract the relevant load and adjustment factors from ASCE 7-16, the building's geometry is considered to match a DOE prototype small office building with a 10-degree roof angle and 3.05 m (10-ft) height located in a flat spot in Houston, Texas. As a result, a maximum wind load of 1.6 kPa (33 PSF) has been calculated and applied to the panel based on a wind speed of 60.8 m/s (136 mph), which corresponds to approximately a 7% probability of exceedance in 50 years.

To consider different scenarios for the material properties and panels' geometry, the fiber content is assumed to range from 0% to 2%, and insulation thickness from 19.05 mm (0.75 inches) to 101.6 mm (4 inches) with a total thickness of 203.2 mm (8 inches) for the panel. To create a pool of random numbers for fiber content and insulation thickness (the inputs of the simulation model), an uniform distribution function was used for the fiber content to generate 100 random numbers from 0% to 2%, and a deterministic approach was used for the insulation layer thickness to obtain practical values for the insulation layer with one-half-inch growth increments from 19.05 mm (0.75 inches) to 101.6 mm (4 inches). Then 100 samples from all possible combinations of fiber content and insulation thickness were selected using the Latin hypercube sampling method. The UHP-FRC panel (Figure 7.3) is then simulated 100 times within the finite element model for the selected combinations of fiber content and insulation thickness to construct the midspan displacement surrogate model using polynomial regression.

Coupled Structural-Thermal Model at the Assembly Level

Coupled structural mechanics and heat transfer physics in façade systems are complex phenomena (Abediniangerabi, Shahandashti, and Makhmalbaf 2021). This complexity is due to the instantaneous effect of the heat transfer on the structural behavior of panels that results in the thermal-bowing impact on the panel (Jawdhari and Fam 2020). Thermal bowing, especially when combined with other environmental loads, such as wind load, could be in large amounts and result in structural failures (Tomlinson and Fam 2014). Therefore, it is crucial to consider the thermal-bowing effects of panels when evaluating their structural

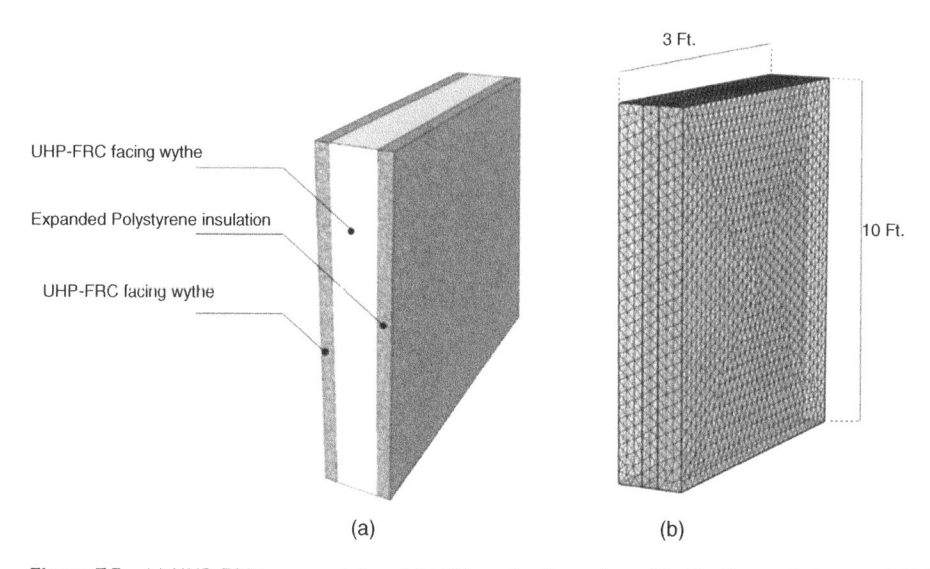

Figure 7.3 (a) UHP-FRC base model and (b) 3D meshed panel used in the thermal-structural finite element model.

performance. To this end, a numerical multi-physics model—coupled structural mechanics and heat transfer was implemented to simulate the impact of the panel's geometry and material properties on the instantaneous thermal and structural performance of the panel at the assembly level. Figure 7.4 illustrates the proposed finite element model to solve the multi-physics model. First, a three-dimensional model of the UHP-FRC façade panel was constructed to represent the panel for different scenarios for insulation thickness and concrete fiber contents. This study utilized a three-layer panel, illustrated in Figure 7.3, with the dimensions of 3.05 m (10 feet) in length, 0.91 m (3 feet) in width, and 20.32 cm (8 inches) in depth. The finite element model of the panel contained 16 boundaries, 28 edges, and 16 vertices. The panel's geometry was created using COMSOL software's built-in geometry tools. To ensure accuracy, suitable material properties for each layer were assigned according to

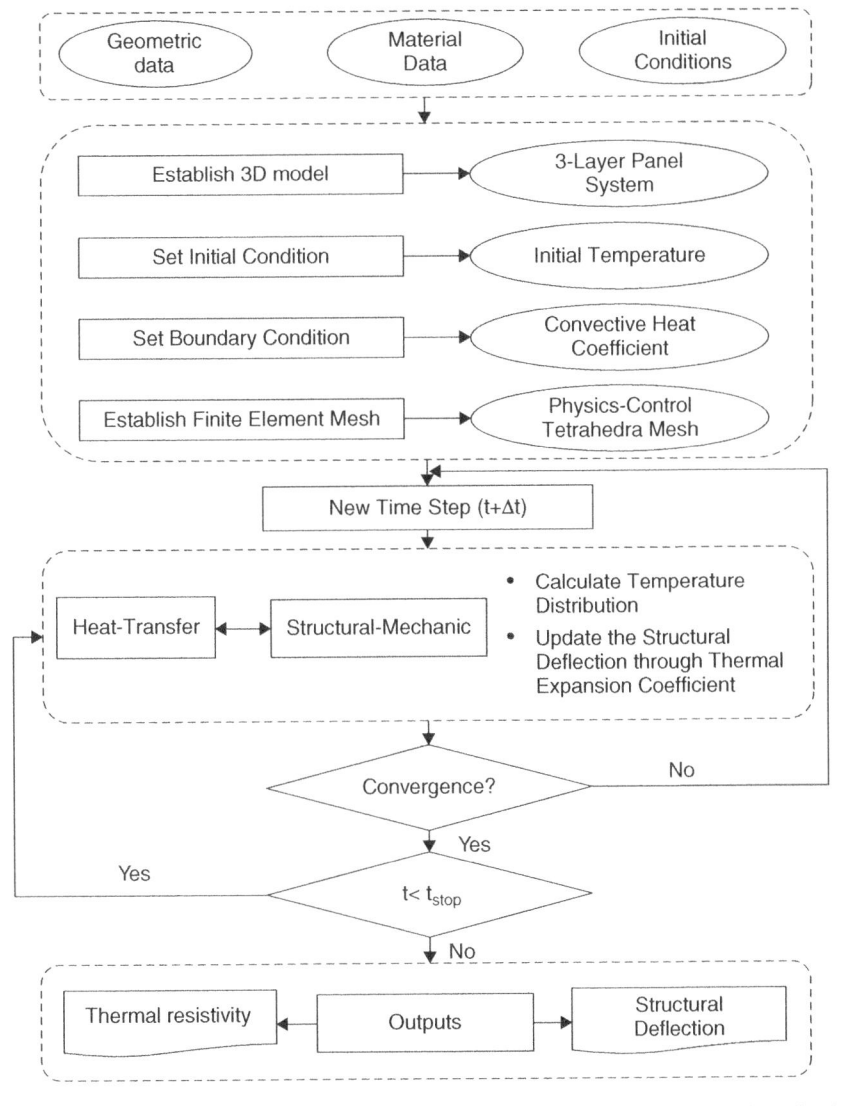

Figure 7.4 The proposed finite element model to solve the coupled structural mechanics and heat-transfer model of the UHP-FRC façade panel.

the details given in Table 7.2. The authors defined the sandwich panel's boundary conditions, including interior and exterior temperatures, as well as wind loads as described in the previous section. After constructing the geometry, material properties, and boundary conditions, the model mesh was created. This study employed a physics-controlled mesh with a normal element size. This feature allows the mesh to adapt automatically based on the local physics and solution requirements of the problem. This approach ensures that the elements were small enough to accurately capture the local physics of the problem while not being too small to unnecessarily increase the computational cost of the simulation. Ultimately, the completed mesh consisted of 19,373 domain elements, 6930 boundary elements, and 476 edge elements. The governing (PDEs) for coupled structural-mechanic and heat-transfer physics were defined in the model to be solved in COMSOL software. The midspan displacement and the thermal resistivity (R-value) of the UHP-FRC panels were extracted from the solutions for different combinations of fiber contents and insulation thicknesses. The thermal resistivity solutions for the panels were used as input to a whole building energy simulation model to estimate the energy use of the building with UHP-FRC panels, as will be explained in the next section. Based on the input-output data generated from the finite element model, implemented in COMSOL Multiphysics software, the midspan displacement of the panel will be approximated using polynomial regression. Further details about the governing equations and boundary conditions of the finite element model and the approach used to simulate the whole building energy intensity are presented in the following sections of this Chapter.

Governing Equations of the Structural–Thermal Finite Element Model

To solve the coupled structural–thermal problem, first, the thermal model solves heat transfer equations to determine the temperature distribution within the panel's layers at the assembly level based on the temperature difference between the exterior and interior layers. Simultaneously, the calculated temperature distribution, obtained from the thermal model, is passed to the structural mechanics model to determine the midspan displacement of the panel due to combined thermal bowing and lateral structural load (i.e. wind load).

The heat-transfer model is based on the conservation of energy law, meaning that the inflow and outflow of energy should be the same per unit of time (Hawileh and Naser 2012). The following three-dimensional equation describes the heat-transfer model in SI unit:

$$\rho c \frac{\partial T}{\partial t} = k \left(\frac{\partial^2 T}{\partial x^2} + \frac{\partial^2 T}{\partial y^2} + \frac{\partial^2 T}{\partial z^2} \right) + Q \tag{7.2}$$

where ρ is the material density (kg/m^3), T is the temperature (°K), c is the specific heat coefficient (J/kg°K), k is the material's conductivity (W/m°K), and Q is the generated heat per unit of material (W/m^3) (all units are in SI).

The thermal boundary condition is described with the following equation in SI unit (Jawdhari and Fam 2020):

$$-k\, \partial T / \partial u = h\_o \left(T\_object - T\_air \right) + h\_air \left(T\_object - T\_air \right) \tag{7.3}$$

where u is the direction of heat transfer, h_o and h_air are the heat transfer coefficients of solid object and fluid, respectively (W/m^2 K), and T_object and T_air are the temperatures of a solid object and air, respectively (°K) (all units are in SI).

To solve the heat-transfer model using the FEM, the three-dimensional heat-transfer equation is discretized into an ordinary differential equation (ODE) as follows (Jawdhari and Fam 2020):

$$D\bar{t} + K\bar{t} = \bar{q} \qquad (7.4)$$

where $\bar{t}$ is the nodal temperature vector, $\bar{q}$ is the heat vector input, and K, and D are the symmetric matrices generated by the finite element model for the heat conduction/convective and heat capacity, respectively.

As the temperature changes through the panel's system material, the solid object will react by changing volume. When the structure is fixed, the volume change in the material will result in thermal stress causing deformations in the structure (Jeon, Muliana, and Saponara 2014). For a linear elastic material, the thermal strain is determined below:

$$\varepsilon = \alpha \left(T - T\_ref \right) \qquad (7.5)$$

where ε is the thermal strain, T is the nodal temperature, and T_ref is a reference temperature.

As the temperature is computed in the heat-transfer model, one-order higher discretization is used in the structural mechanic model to obtain the proportional strains from the calculated temperature.

Based on a conservative assumption, a fully composite contact between panels is modeled in the finite element model as it results in higher stress within the component (Pozo 2018). Assuming a fully composite interaction between panel layers is a conservative assumption for thermal bowing because it assumes that the layers of the panel act as a single unit under thermal loads. When a panel is subjected to a temperature change, each layer of the panel will expand or contract according to its own CTE. If the layers are not fully bonded to each other, or if there are gaps between the layers, they can expand or contract more freely, which can lead to less stresses and lateral deformations in the panel. Furthermore, this study assumed that the connectors inside the panel have a negligible effect on thermal and structural performance. However, it is possible to simulate the connectors to further evaluate their influence on thermal and structural performance.

Energy Performance of the UHP-FRC Panels at the Building Level

One of the outputs of the coupled structural–thermal model at the assembly level is the thermal resistivity (*R*-value) for different panel configurations (i.e. fiber content and insulation thickness). These values are extracted for the solutions of the finite element model and used in building energy simulations of the UHP-FRC façade panel at the building level. Building energy calculations are carried out using physics-based simulations at the whole building level to determine the normalized annual energy uses (i.e. EUI) for an office building with UHP-FRC façade panels. The physics-based simulation program takes input as a description of the building, including the geometry, construction materials, lighting, and occupancy schedules, and combines it with local weather information to determine the thermal loads as well as the system responses to these loads (i.e. building energy use). In this study, the surface heat fluxes of a prototype building were computed using the CTF method, implemented in EnergyPlus, to determine the energy use of the building. A DOE prototype small office building was selected to represent the building context for the simulations. Figure 7.5

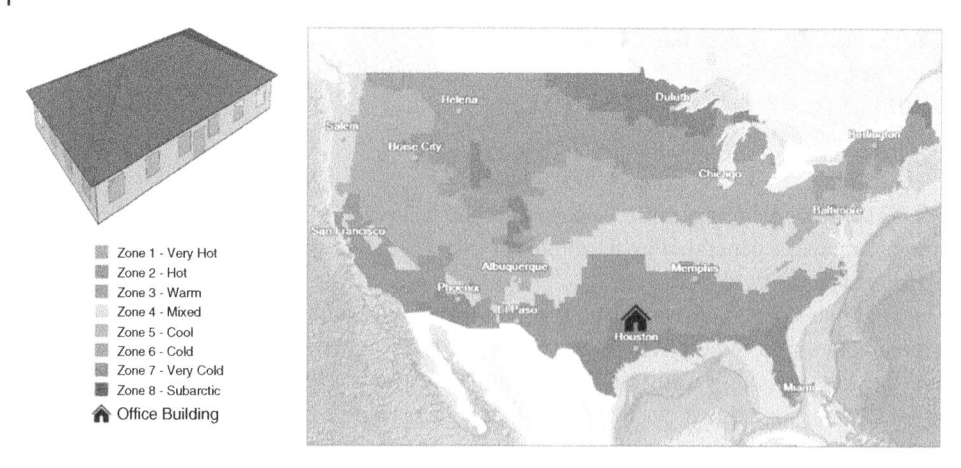

142 | 7 Multi-Level Optimization of UHP-FRC Sandwich Panels for Building Façade Systems

Figure 7.5 DOE office building and its location. Source: US DOE 2022/U.S. Department of Energy/Public domain.

illustrates the schematic design of the office building and its location in the US. To conduct simulations in EnergyPlus, the authors obtained the small office DOE prototype building from the US DOE website. The input file of the prototype building can be modified to reflect changes in building characteristics. In order to incorporate the thermal resistance of the panels in the building energy simulations, the input file of the building was modified for each scenario using the IDF editor in EnergyPlus software. The thermal resistivity of the panel was obtained from the heat-transfer finite element model in COMSOL to be used in the building energy simulations considering multiple combinations of decision variables (i.e. fiber content and insulation thickness). At the building level, building orientation is assumed as the only design variable affecting the building energy usage. Since the building model has a symmetrical design, building orientation ranging from 0 to 180° is considered in the simulations. Other inputs, such as occupancy level, lighting level, and infiltration rates, are assumed according to ANSI/ASHRAE/IES Standard 90.1. Furthermore, the building operation schedule is considered to be constant during simulations. Figure 7.6 illustrates the overview of the described methodology to calculate the building energy intensity using the estimated thermal resistivity of the panel in the finite element model.

Life Cycle Cost Analysis of the UHP-FRC Panels

The life cycle cost analysis of the UHP-FRC façade panels with different fiber contents and insulation thicknesses is carried out using net present value (NPV) analysis considering the material cost, fabrication cost, and transportation cost (i.e. panel delivery cost from fabrication site) over the life cycle of the panels. UHP-FRC panels are used as exterior walls of the office building with a gross wall area of 240.12 m^2 which requires total 261 panels with the assumed dimensions. The steel fiber used for the UHP-FRC façade panels is a Type V (ASTM A850—standard specification for steel bars, carbon-manganese, merchant quality with 50 KSI [345 MPA] yield point), continuously deformed, 38.1 mm (1–1/2 inches) long with 1.143 mm (0.045 inches) diameter. The gravimetrical fiber contents range from 0% to 2%. The thickness of the insulation layer (i.e. EPS) ranges from 19.05 mm (0.75 inches) to 101.6 mm

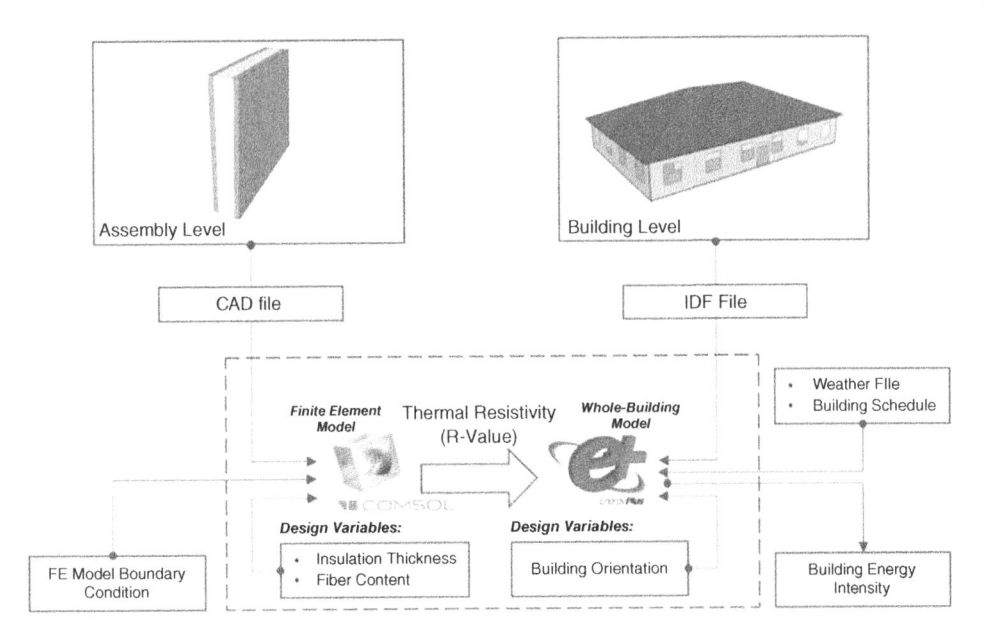

Figure 7.6 The overview of the methodology to calculate building energy intensity using computed thermal resistivity of the panel in the finite element model.

(4 inches). Since the thickness of the panel is assumed to be constant (i.e. 20.32 cm [8 inches]), an increase in the insulation layer's thickness will decrease the panel's outer and inner structural layers. Therefore, a thinner insulation layer will increase the structural performance of the panel but decrease the panel's energy performance. In contrast, having thicker insulation will improve the thermal performance of the panel, but it will reduce the structural strength of the panel. Table 7.3 shows the cost data used in the life cycle cost analysis of the panels for an office building in Houston, Texas. The unit cost for steel fiber, concrete mix, EPS insulation, and panel fabrication cost is obtained from the RSMeans (2020).

In Table 7.4, various panel configurations for a specific building are compared in terms of their material cost, fabrication cost, transportation cost, and total cost. The material cost of each panel is based on the cost of ready-mix concrete and fiber, and the fabrication cost is assumed to be $3.15. To transport the panels, a heavy haul truck with a capacity of 22 tons is assumed to deliver them 10 miles from the fabrication site to the construction site. The

Table 7.3 Cost data inputs and assumptions.

Cost components	Unit	Cost	Reference
Ready mix concrete	m^3	$210.56	RSmeans (2020)
EPS	m^3	$3.06	RSmeans (2020)
Steel fiber	kg	$2.71	RSmeans (2020)
Panel fabrication	Each	$3.15	RSmeans (2020)
Transportation cost	Mile	$7.5	Local rates — Houston, Texas

Table 7.4 Material cost, fabrication cost, and transportation cost of panels.

Configuration	Structural layer thickness (mm)	Structural layer volume (m³)	Insulation layer thickness (mm)	Insulation layer Volume (m³)	Material cost for a total of 261 panels	Fabrication cost for a total of 261 panels	Weight of each panel (kg)	Number of panels delivered by truck	Rounds of delivery	Delivery cost	Total cost
1	184.2	0.15	19.05	0.015	$15,039	$822.15	771.57	28	10	$1,500	$17,361
2	177.8	0.15	25.4	0.023	$14,749	$822.15	744.96	29	9	$1,350	$16,921
3	165.1	0.14	38.1	0.031	$14,164	$822.15	691.75	31	9	$1,350	$16,336
4	152.4	0.13	50.8	0.046	$13,580	$822.15	638.54	34	8	$1,200	$15,603
5	139.7	0.11	63.5	0.054	$12,998	$822.15	585.33	37	8	$1,200	$15,019
6	127	0.11	76.2	0.061	$12,413	$822.15	532.13	41	7	$1,050	$14,284
7	101.6	0.08	101.6	0.084	$11,246	$822.15	425.7	51	6	$900	$12,969

local transportation cost for panels is estimated to be $7.5 per mile. Due to the weight of the panels, the capacity of the truck limits the number of panels that can be delivered. Using thicker structural layers with concrete increases the weight of the panels, and as a result, more trips are required to deliver them to the construction site. For instance, delivering panels with 7.25 inches of structural layers to the selected building will require 10 rounds of delivery at a cost of $1500. On the other hand, panels with 4 inches of structural layers require only 6 rounds of delivery, which will cost $900.

Net Present Value

NPV is used to estimate the impact of fiber content and insulation layer thickness on the life cycle cost of the panels. A life span of 20 years is assumed for the UHP-FRC façade panels due to EPS insulation's shorter service life (Alam et al. 2017). A discount rate of 0.25%, set by the Board of Governors of all 12 Federal Reserve Banks for the year 2021 (Board of Governors of the Federal Reserve System 2021), is used for the analysis. The response surface of the life cycle cost of panels is approximated using a polynomial regression model concerning the decision variables, which are fiber content and insulation thickness.

Surrogate Models

The surrogate models are usually developed to approximate the behavior of a complex system or process using a simpler and computationally efficient mathematical model. The surrogate model construction involves selecting an appropriate approximation method such as polynomial regression, radial basis functions, or artificial neural networks.

The selection of surrogate models depends on various factors such as the type of input and output variables, the complexity of the model, the accuracy required, the available computational resources, and the type of optimization problem being solved. This study utilized polynomial regression models to estimate the response because they are computationally efficient, meaning they take less time and resources to build and assess. This feature makes them valuable for use in cases where simulation models are time-consuming or computationally expensive to run (Hastie et al. 2009; Shahandashti et al. 2022; Darghiasi Baral, and Shahandashti 2023). The input and output data for each objective (i.e. midspan displacement, energy use, panel costs) were obtained for 100 sample inputs following the procedures outlined in previous sections. The process of constructing the surrogate model involved splitting the data into training (80%) and testing sets (20%), choosing the degree of the polynomial regression model, conducting regression analysis using the training data, evaluating the model using the testing data, refining the model, and finally using the model to predict the system's response for new input parameters. The quality of the surrogate model is validated using statistical metrics such as the coefficient of determination (R-squared), and root mean square error (RMSE). The validated surrogate model can then be used in a multi-objective optimization framework to select the best subset of design parameters that improve all objectives as well as to identify the interdependency between design variables. It should be noted that the surrogate models, developed in this study, have limitations in terms of their applicability. These models are only valid within the range of input variables for which they were developed, and it is not recommended to extrapolate beyond these limits. Figure 7.7 shows the described methodology used to develop the surrogate model for buildings' EUI and midspan displacements.

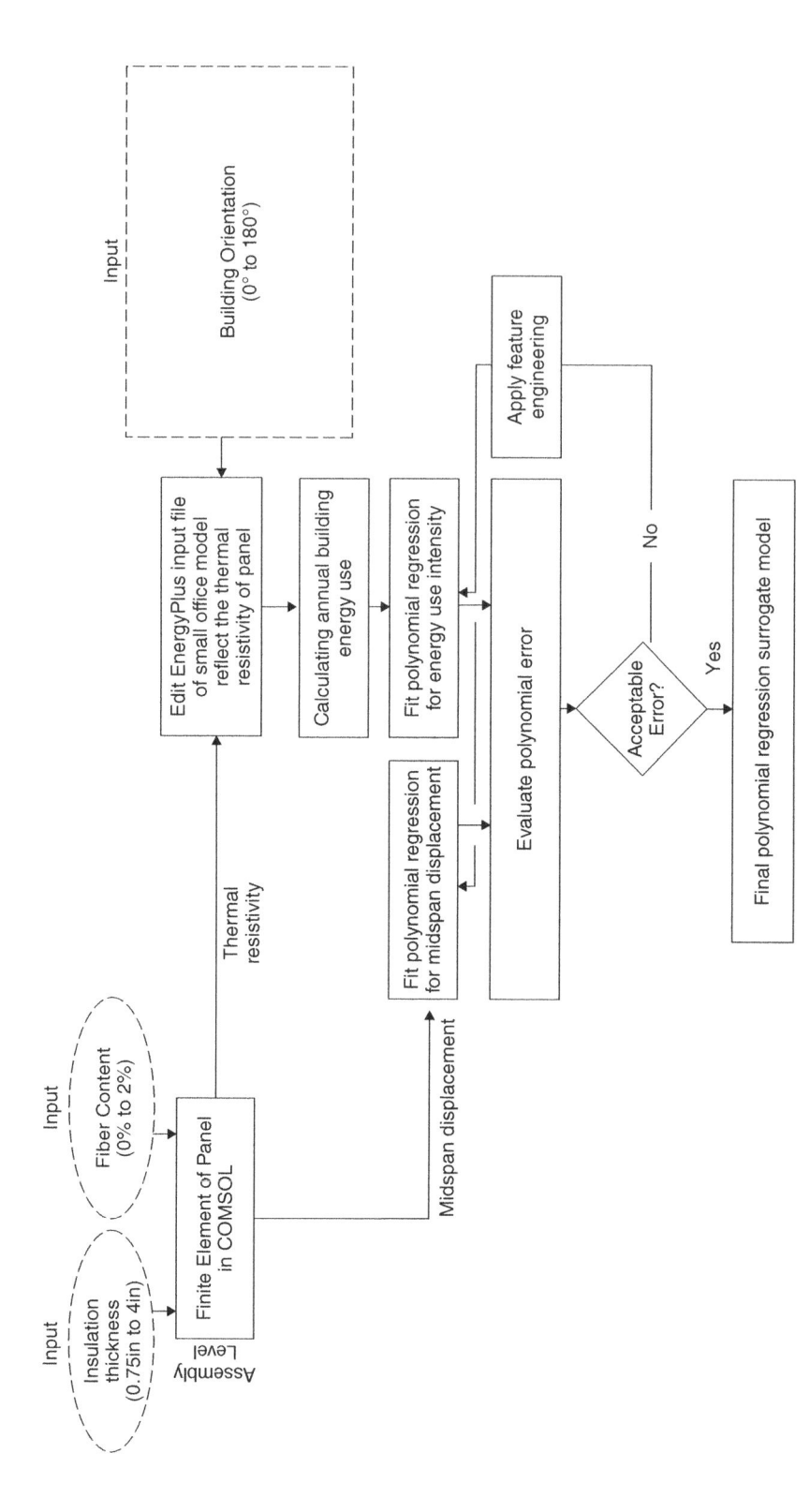

Figure 7.7 Methodology used to construct the surrogate model for EUI and midspan displacement.

Multi-objective Optimization Algorithm

Multi-objective optimization is a mathematical optimization problem involving more than one objective function that should be optimized simultaneously (Gunantara 2018). This section discusses utilizing a multi-objective optimization framework to obtain the best solutions that improve structural performance, building energy use, and panel costs by taking into account various design variables such as insulation thickness, fiber content, and building orientation. The proposed multi-objective optimization function can be posed mathematically as:

$$\text{Minimize } F(x) = |d_1(x), e_2(x), c_3(x)|^T \tag{7.6}$$

$$\text{Subjected to}: \begin{cases} g(x) \leq 0 \\ h(x) = 0 \end{cases}$$

where $F(x)$ is the list of objective functions, $d_1(x) e_2(x)$, and $c_3(x)$ are the objective function representing midspan displacement, building energy use, and life cycle cost; x represents the vector of design variables, i.e. insulation thickness, fiber content, and building orientation; $g(x)$ represents the inequality constraint, and $h(x)$ represents the equality constraint limiting the value of design variables. The solution to the multi-objective function can be obtained using the Pareto method or scalarization (Weck and Kim 2004). Scalarization combines multi-objective functions using weights, which is not suitable for dealing with competing objective functions (Gunantara 2018). The Pareto method is used when a compromise solution (trade-off) for different objectives is to be represented as a Pareto optimal front (POF) (Deb and Gupta 2005; Delgarm et al. 2016). The Pareto front is a set of non-dominated solutions in which no objective can be improved without degrading at least one other objective. Non-dominated solutions are optimal in all respects and are not outperformed by any other solution in the population, whereas dominated solutions can be improved in at least one objective without affecting performance in other objectives. Pareto front solutions provide decision-makers with insight into a trade-off among objectives, allowing them to choose optimal solutions based on the Pareto frontier solutions and their own judgment.

In this chapter, the non-dominated and crowding distance sorting genetic algorithm (NSGA-II) is employed to find a set of non-dominated or optimal solutions (Pareto front) for the three competing objectives discussed in this chapter. NSGA-II is a genetic algorithm that is inspired by the process of natural selection and genetics in biological organisms to find the Pareto front of a problem. Genetic algorithms are a class of algorithms that use selection, crossover, and mutation operations on a population of potential solutions to search for optimal solutions to a given problem (Holland 1992; Mirjalili 2019). The NSGA-II framework used in this study is shown in Figure 7.8.

First, The NSGA-II algorithm generates an initial population of solutions, which are then sorted based on their non-dominated status. Non-dominated solutions are those that are not dominated by any other solutions in the population. After sorting, NSGA-II assigns each solution a crowding distance value, which measures the density of solutions around that particular solution. Solutions with higher crowding distances are preferred since they are less dense, and the algorithm aims to maintain diversity in the population.

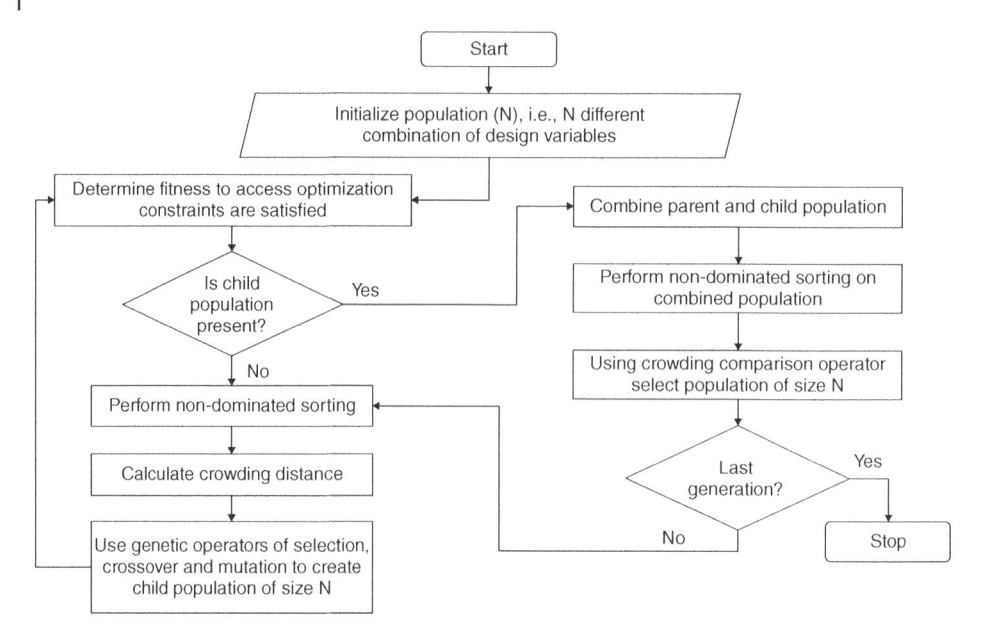

Figure 7.8 Overview of non-dominated and crowding distance sorting genetic algorithm (NSGA-II). Source: Adapted from NSGA-II Deb 2001.

Next, NSGA-II selects parents for the next generation using a combination of tournament selection and crowding distance selection. The selected parents are then used to create offspring solutions using crossover and mutation operators. The offspring are added to the population, and the sorting and crowding distance assignment process is repeated. NSGA-II continues this process until a stopping criterion is met, such as reaching a maximum number of generations or finding a satisfactory Pareto front. In general, the population size for NSGA-II is set between 50 and 200, and the maximum number of generations is set to 100 and 300 multiplied by the number of decision variables (Deb et al. 2002). In this study, the population in the NSGA-II algorithm was set to 100, and the maximum number of generations was set to 200 multiplied by the number of variables in the objective functions, as suggested by Delgarm et al. (2016). The constraints of the optimization problems are defined to be the upper limit and lower limit of the input variables that are used to construct the surrogate models.

Results and Discussion

Surrogate Models

Surrogate models were developed to represent the whole-building energy simulation model, finite element model, and panel cost analysis results. The finite element model, described in the methodology section, was executed in COMSOL software, to simulate the midspan displacement and the thermal resistivity of the panel. The simulations were carried out for 100 data samples that corresponded to different insulation thicknesses and fiber contents as explained in the previous section. Figure 7.9 illustrates an example output for the finite element simulation model for insulation thickness of 80 mm, and fiber content of 1.5%.

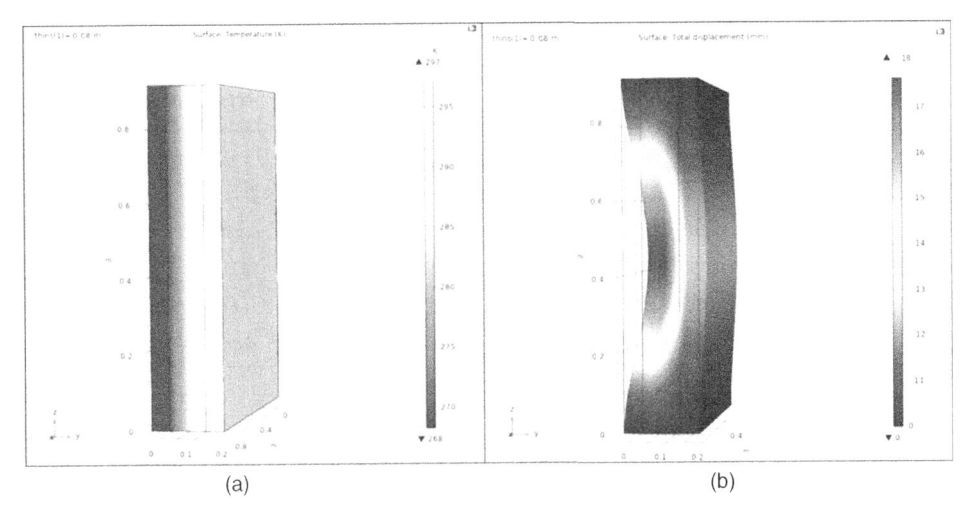

Figure 7.9 (a) Temperature distribution in the panel, and (b) Midspan displacement; insulation thickness: 80 mm, Fiber content: 1.5%, thermal resistivity: 8.08 K m^2/W, midspan deflection: 18 mm.

Following each simulation, the thermal resistivity results that were obtained from the finite element simulation model were utilized in the input file of EnergyPlus to simulate the EUI of the building, as described in the methodology. The input file of EnergyPlus is a text file that specifies the building geometry, construction materials, HVAC systems, lighting systems, schedules, weather data, and other parameters required to simulate the energy performance of the building. The authors updated the building's input file using the EnergyPlus IDF editor to reflect the thermal resistivity of the panel that was obtained from the finite element model. The EnergyPlus simulations were conducted 100 times for all the thermal resistivities obtained from the finite element model and different building orientations from 0° to 180°, to simulate the EUI of the building. The building EUI was obtained from the EnergyPlus output report, which provides a summary of the key results, including the annual energy consumption, peak demand, and energy intensity.

The simulation results showed that the minimum and maximum midspan displacements were 17.42 mm and 22.34 mm within the decision space, respectively. The finite element model results show that the midspan displacement of the panel improves by 22% when the concrete's fiber content in the panel's facing wythes increases from 0% to 2% and the insulation thickness of the panel decreases from 101.6 mm (4 inches) to 19.05 mm (0.75 inches)—due to the use of materials with higher mechanical strength in the panel. In contrast, this improvement in the midspan displacement decreases the thermal resistivity from 18.42 K m^2/W to 4.06 K m^2/W in the panel. Based on the whole building energy simulation model results, this drop in the thermal resistivity of panels increases the building's EUI by approximately 3.4%. Table 7.5 summarizes the input/output ranges for the simulation models.

Figure 7.10 visualizes the midspan displacement of the panel and EUI of the building for all 100 simulations within the finite element model at the assembly level and the whole building energy simulation model at the building scale. The results show that the panel's midspan displacement ranges from 17.42 mm to 22.34 mm, and the building EUI ranges from 276.29 MJ/m^2 to 285.91 MJ/m^2.

7 Multi-Level Optimization of UHP-FRC Sandwich Panels for Building Façade Systems

Table 7.5 Simulation model's input and output ranges.

	Parameters	Minimum value	Maximum value
Input	Insulation thickness (mm)	19.05 mm	101.6 mm
	Fiber content (%)	0%	2%
	Building orientation (degree)	0°	180°
Output	Panel's midspan displacement	17.42 mm	22.34 mm
	Panel's thermal resistivity	18.42 K m^2/W	4.06 K m^2/W
	Building EUI	276.29 MJ/m^2	285.91 MJ/m^2

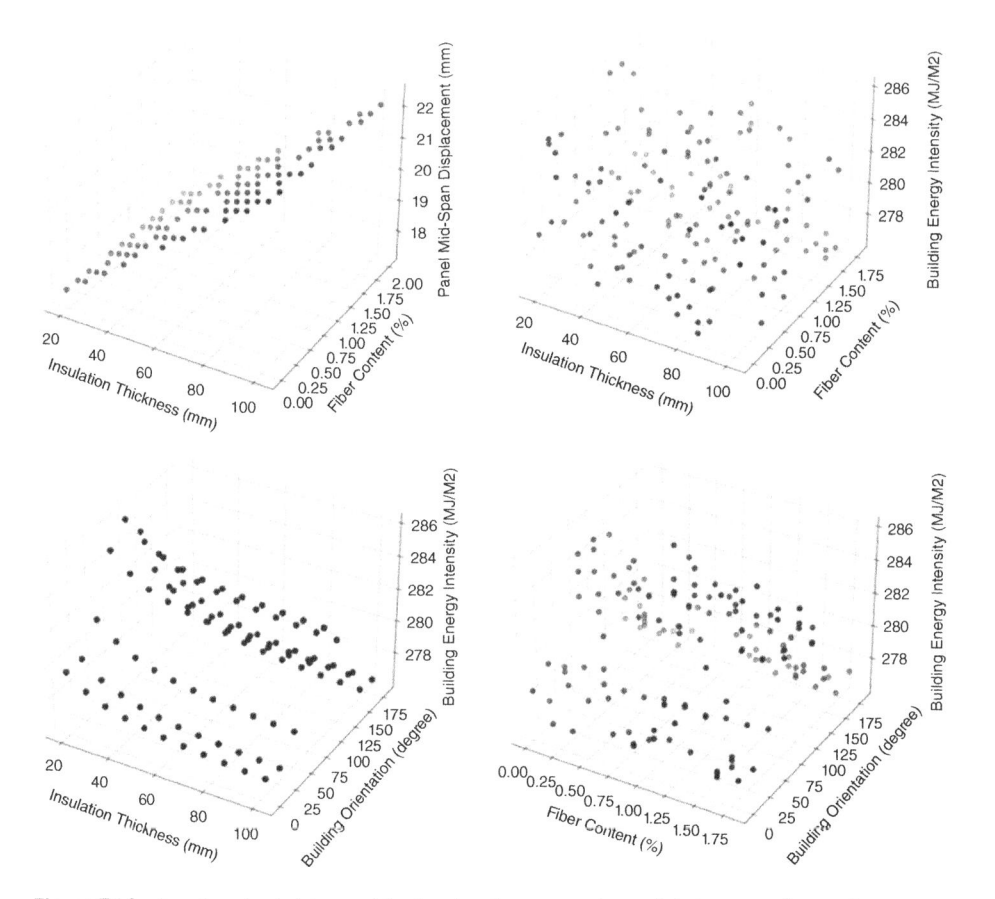

Figure 7.10 Input–output data used to develop the surrogate models to approximate the response surfaces.

Moreover, the life cycle cost of the panels with the different design configurations (i.e. insulation thickness and fiber content) was calculated over 20 years of the life cycle. The life cycle cost of the panels included the material cost, fabrication cost, and transportation cost for panels. Table 7.6 shows the input/output data ranges used in the life cycle cost analysis.

Table 7.6 Input and output ranges for the NPV analysis.

	Items	Unit	Minimum value	Maximum value
Input	Insulation thickness	mm	19.05	101.6
	Fiber content	%	0	2
Output	Weight	kg/panel	193.1	350.0
	Material and fabrication cost	$/each	46.50	60.82
	Rounds of delivery	round	6	10
	Delivery cost	$/total	900	1500
	Total panel cost	$/whole building	13,036.21	17,374.64
	Panels' NPV	$/whole building	74,428.98	79,538.49

Table 7.7 Surrogate models to approximate the response surface of the objective functions.

Objective function	Decision variables	Approximate response surface	Adjusted R^2	RMSE
Midspan displacement (mm)	Fiber content % (f), insulation thickness (mm) (t)	$0.057*t - 0.106*f + 16.55$	0.97	0.7 (mm)
Building energy use (MJ/m^2)	Fiber content % (f), insulation thickness (mm) (t), building orientation degree (°)	$0.000535*t^2 - 0.094*t + 0.00098*f + 5.66*\sin(o) + 280.15$	0.81	1.13 (MJ/m^2)
Life cycle cost — NPV ($)	Fiber content % (f), insulation thickness (mm) (t)	$-52.02*t + 6377.96*f + 18318.1$	0.99	38.7 ($)

Finally, a regression analysis was conducted on the pool of input-output data to construct the surrogate models for the targeted objective functions. Table 7.7 presents the developed surrogate models for approximating the response surfaces of the three objective functions. The surrogate models were validated using testing the (20% of the dataset) based on the RMSE. The low RMSE values for the regression models suggest that the surrogate models can effectively replace the simulation models with a high degree of accuracy. The validity of surrogate models is limited to the specific data ranges for which they were developed.

Pareto Front Solutions

This section provides the Pareto optimal solutions for the bi-objective and triple-objective problems. To investigate the interaction between two objectives, all possible combinations of objectives (i.e. building EUI, midspan displacement, and life cycle cost) are chosen. Figure 7.11a represents the Pareto-optimal solution for the building EUI and midspan displacement. Based on the findings, the panel's structural performance will worsen as its energy efficiency improves. The Pareto front obtained from bi-objective optimization of

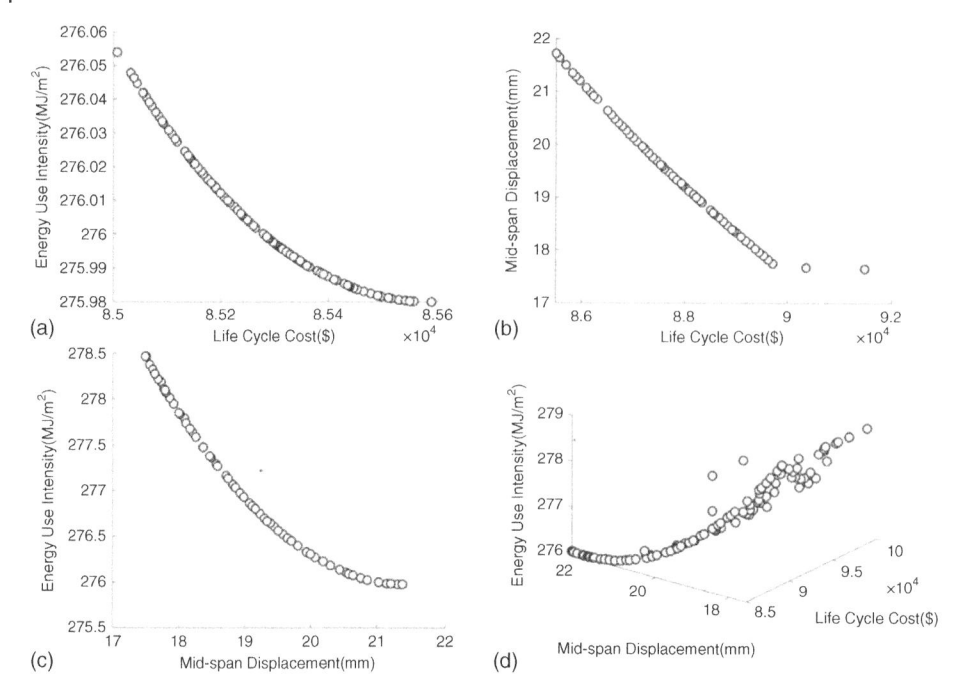

Figure 7.11 Pareto front for bi-objective and tri-objective optimization.

midspan displacement and life cycle cost reveals the trade-off between the two objectives (Figure 7.11b). Similar observations were made for the bi-objective optimization problem involving building EUI and the life cycle cost of the façade system (Figure 7.11c). The result of the triple-objective minimization is shown in Figure 7.11d. It can be noted from Figure 7.11d that it is impossible to minimize all three objective functions together as all three objectives conflict with one another. However, it allows designers to find a set of efficient choices to make trade-offs within the decision space. The findings suggest that relying solely on one building-level criterion, such as energy use when choosing design parameters for façade systems may lead to the underperformance of such systems in other aspects such as structural serviceability or financial considerations. This indicates that a holistic approach to façade design optimization, which considers the interdependency between multiple objectives across various levels, is necessary to ensure that the overall performance of the system is optimized. In other words, decisions should not be made based on one objective alone, but rather on a combination of objectives that reflect the needs and goals of different stakeholders involved in the design process. Such an approach would result in more efficient and effective façade systems that are better suited to meet the requirements for building energy efficiency, while also ensuring that structural and financial considerations are taken into account.

Conclusion

This chapter introduced a multi-level multi-objective surrogate-based optimization framework to enable the performance-based design optimization of building façade systems considering the interdependency between multiple objectives at different levels. The proposed framework simultaneously considered structural and thermal as well as the financial performance of UHP-FRC sandwich panels for building façade systems as dependent factors of material mix designs and assembly configuration variables. Pareto front solutions were extracted by applying a non-dominated and crowding distance sorting genetic algorithm (NSGA-II) as a decision-making tool to find a set of efficient choices for design variables to facilitate trade-offs between the structural performance, building energy use, and life-cycle cost of the façade panels. It is important to note that the surrogate models constructed in this study are only valid within the data ranges that they are developed and should not be extrapolated beyond the range of input variables for which they were developed. In addition, this study considered sandwich panels under the assumption of full compositeness without any connectors, future research can explore more realistic composite levels and include the panels' connectors in the simulation model. This may result in requiring more computational resources, especially for the finite element models. It is also of interest to extend the scope of the proposed approach by including more design variables in the system such as window-to-wall ratio, shading devices, type and placement of glazing, building layout, and seismic loads, as well as considering the uncertainty associated with them to find more realistic and reliable solutions.

In conclusion, this chapter proposed an approach that takes into account multiple objectives at different levels, allowing designers to consider the interdependency between various design factors to optimize the overall performance of the façade systems based on a holistic approach. This approach would lead to the development of more efficient and effective façade systems to satisfy the energy efficiency requirements of buildings, while simultaneously taking into account the structural and financial constraints of the system.

References

Abediniangerabi, B. and Shahandashti, M. (2022). Early-Stage Advisory System for Energy-Conscious Design of Building Façade Systems. *Construction Research Congress* 195–204.

Abediniangerabi, B., Shahandashti, M., Bell, B. et al. (2018). Building Energy Performance Analysis of Ultra-High-Performance Fiber-Reinforced Concrete (UHP-FRC) Façade Systems. *Energy and Buildings* 174: 262–275.

Abediniangerabi, B., Shahandashti, M., Bell, B. et al. (2019). Assembly-Scale and Whole-Building Energy Performance Analysis of Ultra-High-Performance Fiber-Reinforced Concrete (UHP-FRC) Facade Systems. In: *International Interactive Symposium on Ultra-High-Performance Concrete*, vol. Vol. 2, no. 1. Iowa State University Digital Press.

Abediniangerabi, B., Shahandashti, S.M., and Makhmalbaf, A. (2020). A Data-Driven Framework for Energy-Conscious Design of Building Facade Systems. *Journal of Building Engineering* 29: 101172.

Abediniangerabi, B., Makhmalbaf, A., and Shahandashti, M. (2021). Deep Learning for Estimating Energy Savings of Early-Stage Facade Design Decisions. *Energy and AI* 5: 100077.

Abediniangerabi, B., Shahandashti, M., and Makhmalbaf, A. (2021). Coupled Transient Heat and Moisture Transfer Investigation of Facade Panel Connections. *Journal of Engineering, Design and Technology* 19 (3): 758–777.

Abediniangerabi, B., Makhmalbaf, A., and Shahandashti, M. (2022). Estimating Energy Savings of Ultra-High-Performance Fibre-Reinforced Concrete Facade Panels at the Early Design Stage of Buildings Using Gradient Boosting Machines. *Advances in Building Energy Research* 16 (4): 542–567.

Alam, M., Singh, H., Suresh, S., and Redpath, D.A.G. (2017). Energy and Economic Analysis of Vacuum Insulation Panels (VIPs) Used in Non-domestic Buildings. *Applied Energy* 188: 1–8.

Al-Homoud, M.S. (2005). A Systematic Approach for the Thermal Design Optimization of Building Envelopes. *Journal of Building Physics* 29 (2): 95–119.

Al-Homoud, M.S. (2009). Envelope Thermal Design Optimization of Buildings with Intermittent Occupancy. *Journal of Building Physics* 33 (1): 65–82.

American Society of Civil Engineers (ASCE 7-16) (2017). *Minimum Design Loads and Associated Criteria for Buildings and Other Structures*. American Society of Civil Engineers.

Anđelković, A.S., Cvjetković, T.B., Đaković, D.D., and Stojanović, I.H. (2012). The Development of Simple Calculation Model for Energy Performance of Double Skin Façades. *Thermal Science* 16 (Suppl. 1): 251–267.

Ascione, F., Bianco, N., Mauro, G.M., and Napolitano, D.F. (2019). Building Envelope Design: Multi-objective Optimization to Minimize Energy Consumption, Global Cost and Thermal Discomfort. Application to Different Italian Climatic Zones. *Energy* 174: 359–374.

Athienitis, A.K., Barone, G., Buonomano, A., and Palombo, A. (2018). Assessing Active and Passive Effects of Façade Building Integrated Photovoltaics/Thermal Systems: Dynamic Modelling and Simulation. *Applied Energy* 209: 355–382.

Azari, R., Garshasbi, S., Amini, P. et al. (2016). Multi-objective Optimization of Building Envelope Design for Life Cycle Environmental Performance. *Energy and Buildings* 126: 524–534.

Bedon, C., Honfi, D., Machalická, K.V. et al. (2019). Structural Characterisation of Adaptive Facades in Europe–Part I: Insight on Classification Rules, Performance Metrics and Design Methods. *Journal of Building Engineering* 25: 100721.

Board of Governors of the Federal Reserve System (US), (2021) The Discount Window and Discount Rate. https://www.federalreserve.gov/monetarypolicy/discountrate.htm, retrieved on 31 December 30, 2021.

Bouchlaghem, N.M. and Letherman, K.M. (1990). Numerical Optimization Applied to the Thermal Design of Buildings. *Building and Environment* 25 (2): 117–124.

Brown, N.C. and Mueller, C.T. (2016). Design for Structural and Energy Performance of Long Span Buildings Using Geometric Multi-Objective Optimization. *Energy and Buildings* 127: 748–761.

Bui, D.-K., Nguyen, T.N., Ghazlan, A. et al. (2020). Enhancing Building Energy Efficiency by Adaptive Façade: A Computational Optimization Approach. *Applied Energy* 265: 114797.

Cauteren, D., Ramon, D., Stroeckx, J. et al. (2022). Design Optimization of Hybrid Steel/Timber Structures for Minimal Environmental Impact and Financial Cost: A Case Study. *Energy and Buildings* 254: 111600.

Chang, S.-w., Castro-Lacouture, D., and Yamagata, Y. (2020). Decision Support for Retrofitting Building Envelopes Using Multi-Objective Optimization Under Uncertainties. *Journal of Building Engineering* 32: 101413.

Chastas, P., Theodosiou, T., and Bikas, D. (2016). Embodied Energy in Residential Buildings-Towards the Nearly Zero Energy Building: A Literature Review. *Building and Environment* 105: 267–282.

Cheng, R., Wang, X., and Zhang, Y. (2014). Analytical Optimization of the Transient Thermal Performance of Building Wall by Using Thermal Impedance Based on Thermal-Electric Analogy. *Energy and Buildings* 80: 598–612.

Chow, T.T., Fong, K.F., He, W. et al. (2007). Performance Evaluation of a PV Ventilated Window Applying to Office Building of Hong Kong. *Energy and Buildings* 39 (6): 643–650.

Coley, D.A. and Schukat, S. (2002). Low-Energy Design: Combining Computer-Based Optimization and Human Judgement. *Building and Environment* 37 (12): 1241–1247.

Darghiasi, P., Baral, A., and Shahandashti, M. (2023). Estimation of Road Surface Temperature Using NOAA Gridded Forecast Weather Data for Snowplow Operations Management. *Journal of Cold Regions Engineering* 37 (4): 04023018.

Darkwa, J., Li, Y., and Chow, D.H.C. (2014). Heat Transfer and Air Movement Behaviour in a Double-Skin Façade. *Sustainable Cities and Society* 10: 130–139.

Deb, K. (2001). *Multi-Objective Optimization Using Evolutionary Algorithms*. Chichester, England: John Wiley & Sons, Ltd.

Deb, K. and Gupta, H. (2005). Searching for Robust Pareto-Optimal Solutions in Multi-objective Optimization. In: *International Conference on Evolutionary Multi-criterion Optimization*, 150–164. Berlin, Heidelberg: Springer.

Deb, K., Pratap, A., Agarwal, S., and Meyarivan, T.A.M.T. (2002). A Fast and Elitist Multiobjective Genetic Algorithm: NSGA-II. *IEEE Transactions on Evolutionary Computation* 6 (2): 182–197.

Delcroix, B., Kummert, M., Daoud, A., and Hiller, M.D.E. (2012). Conduction Transfer Functions in TRNSYS Multizone Building Model: Current Implementation, Limitations and Possible Improvements. *Proceedings of SimBuild* 5 (1): 219–226.

Delgarm, N., Sajadi, B., Delgarm, S., and Kowsary, F. (2016). A Novel Approach for the Simulation-Based Optimization of the Buildings Energy Consumption Using NSGA-II: Case Study in Iran. *Energy and Buildings* 127: 552–560.

Diakaki, C., Grigoroudis, E., and Kolokotsa, D. (2008). Towards a Multi-objective Optimization Approach for Improving Energy Efficiency in Buildings. *Energy and Buildings* 40 (9): 1747–1754.

Ferrara, M., Fabrizio, E., Virgone, J., and Filippi, M. (2014). A Simulation-Based Optimization Method for Cost-Optimal Analysis of Nearly Zero Energy Buildings. *Energy and Buildings* 84: 442–457.

Fesanghary, M., Asadi, S., and Geem, Z.W. (2012). Design of Low-Emission and Energy-Efficient Residential Buildings Using a Multi-Objective Optimization Algorithm. *Building and Environment* 49: 245–250.

Garrido, M., Madeira, J.F.A., Proença, M., and Correia, J.R. (2019). Multi-objective Optimization of Pultruded Composite Sandwich Panels for Building Floor Rehabilitation. *Construction and Building Materials* 198: 465–478.

Gong, X., Akashi, Y., and Sumiyoshi, D. (2012). Optimization of Passive Design Measures for Residential Buildings in Different Chinese Areas. *Building and Environment* 58: 46–57.

Gossard, D., Lartigue, B., and Thellier, F. (2013). Multi-objective Optimization of a Building Envelope for Thermal Performance Using Genetic Algorithms and Artificial Neural Network. *Energy and Buildings* 67: 253–260.

Gunantara, N. (2018). A Review of Multi-objective Optimization: Methods and its Applications. *Cogent Engineering* 5 (1): 1502242.

Hamdy, M., Hasan, A., and Siren, K. (2011). Impact of Adaptive Thermal Comfort Criteria on Building Energy Use and Cooling Equipment Size Using a Multi-objective Optimization Scheme. *Energy and Buildings* 43 (9): 2055–2067.

Hamdy, M., Hasan, A., and Siren, K. (2013). A Multi-stage Optimization Method for Cost-Optimal and Nearly-Zero-Energy Building Solutions in Line with the EPBD-Recast 2010. *Energy and Buildings* 56: 189–203.

Hasan, A., Vuolle, M., and Sirén, K. (2008). Minimisation of Life Cycle Cost of a Detached House Using Combined Simulation and Optimisation. *Building and Environment* 43 (12): 2022–2034.

Hastie, T., Tibshirani, R., Friedman, J.H., and Friedman, J.H. (2009). *The Elements of Statistical Learning: Data Mining, Inference, and Prediction*, vol. Vol. 2. New York: Springer.

Hawileh, R.A. and Naser, M.Z. (2012). Thermal-Stress Analysis of RC Beams Reinforced with GFRP Bars. *Composites Part B: Engineering* 43 (5): 2135–2142.

Hensen, J., Bartak, M., and Drkal, F. (2002). Modeling and Simulation of a Double-Skin Facade System. *ASHRAE Transactions* 108 (2): 1251–1259.

Holland, J.H. (1992). Genetic Algorithms. *Scientific American* 267 (1): 66–73.

Imbabi, M.S.-E. (2012). A Passive–Active Dynamic Insulation System for All Climates. *International Journal of Sustainable Built Environment* 1 (2): 247–258.

Ioannou, A. and Itard, L.C.M. (2015). Energy Performance and Comfort in Residential Buildings: Sensitivity for Building Parameters and Occupancy. *Energy and Buildings* 92: 216–233.

Jawdhari, A. and Fam, A. (2020). Thermal-Structural Analysis and Thermal Bowing of Double Wythe UHPC Insulated Walls. *Energy and Buildings* 223: 110012.

Jeon, J., Muliana, A., and La Saponara, V. (2014). Thermal Stress and Deformation Analyses in Fiber Reinforced Polymer Composites Undergoing Heat Conduction and Mechanical Loading. *Composite Structures* 111: 31–44.

Kämpf, J.H., Montavon, M., Bunyesc, J. et al. (2010). Optimisation of Buildings Solar Irradiation Availability. *Solar Energy* 84 (4): 596–603.

Khalkhali, A., Khakshournia, S., and Nariman-Zadeh, N. (2014). A Hybrid Method of FEM, Modified NSGAII and Topsis for Structural Optimization of Sandwich Panels with Corrugated Core. *Journal of Sandwich Structures & Materials* 16 (4): 398–417.

Koenders, S.J.M., Loonen, R.C.G.M., and Hensen, J.L.M. (2018). Investigating the Potential of a Closed-Loop Dynamic Insulation System for Opaque Building Elements. *Energy and Buildings* 173: 409–427.

Krem, M., Hoque, S.T., Arwade, S.R., and Breña, S.F. (2013). Structural Configuration and Building Energy Performance. *Journal of Architectural Engineering* 19 (1): 29–40.

Li, X.Q., Chen, Y., Spitler, J.D., and Fisher, D. (2009). Applicability of Calculation Methods for Conduction Transfer Function of Building Constructions. *International Journal of Thermal Sciences* 48 (7): 1441–1451.

Li, M., Ma, T., Liu, J. et al. (2019). Numerical and Experimental Investigation of Precast Concrete Facade Integrated with Solar Photovoltaic Panels. *Applied Energy* 253: 113509.

Lin, Y.-H., Tsai, K.-T., Lin, M.-D., and Yang, M.-D. (2016). Design Optimization of Office Building Envelope Configurations for Energy Conservation. *Applied Energy* 171: 336–346.

Magnier, L. and Haghighat, F. (2010). Multiobjective Optimization of Building Design Using TRNSYS Simulations, Genetic Algorithm, and Artificial Neural Network. *Building and Environment* 45 (3): 739–746.

Mahdi, S., Mohamed Ali, M.S., Sheikh, A.H. et al. (2021). An Investigation into the Feasibility of Normal and Fibre-Reinforced Ultra-High Performance Concrete Multi-cell and Composite Sandwich Panels. *Journal of Building Engineering* 41: 102728.

Małek, M., Jackowski, M., Łasica, W., and Kadela, M. (2021a). Influence of Polypropylene, Glass and Steel Fiber on the Thermal Properties of Concrete. *Materials* 14 (8): 1888.

Małek, M., Jackowski, M., Łasica, W. et al. (2021b). Mechanical and Material Properties of Mortar Reinforced with Glass Fiber: An Experimental Study. *Materials* 14 (3): 698.

Menyhart, K. and Krarti, M. (2017). Potential Energy Savings from Deployment of Dynamic Insulation Materials for US Residential Buildings. *Building and Environment* 114: 203–218.

Mirjalili, S. (2019). Genetic Algorithm. In: *Evolutionary Algorithms and Neural Networks*, 43–55. Cham: Springer.

Murthy, O., Munirudrappa, N., Srikanth, L., and Rao, R.M.V.G.K. (2006). Strength and Stiffness Optimization Studies on Honeycomb Core Sandwich Panels. *Journal of Reinforced Plastics and Composites* 25 (6): 663–671.

National Oceanic and Atmospheric Administration, NOAA National Centers for Environmental Information., "Global Summary of the Year". (2020).

Pasut, W., Zhang, H., Arens, E. et al. (2013). Effect of a Heated and Cooled Office Chair on Thermal Comfort. *HVAC & R Research* 19 (5): 574–583.

Peng, J., Lin, L., Yang, H., and Han, J. (2013). Investigation on the Annual Thermal Performance of a Photovoltaic Wall Mounted on a Multi-layer Façade. *Applied Energy* 112: 646–656.

Pozo, F. (2018). *On Thermal Bowing of Concrete Sandwich Wall Panels with Flexible Shear Connectors."* PhD Dissertation. Utah State University.

Ramesh, T., Prakash, R., and Shukla, K.K. (2010). Life Cycle Energy Analysis of Buildings: An Overview. *Energy and Buildings* 42 (10): 1592–1600.

RSMeans, Heavy Construction Cost Data (2020). *Norwell*. MA: RSMeans.

Ruiz, P.A., Martín, J.G., Lissén, J.M.S. et al. (2014). An Integrated Optimisation Method for Residential Building Design: A Case Study in Spain. *Energy and Buildings* 80: 158–168.

Shahandashti, S.M., Abediniangerabi, B., Bell, B., and Chao, S.H. (2017). Probabilistic Building Energy Performance Analysis of Ultra-high-Performance Fiber-Reinforced Concrete (UHP-FRC) Façade System. *Computing in Civil Engineering* 2017: 223–230.

Shahandashti, M., Mattingly, S., Darghiasi, P. et al. (2022). *Snowplow Operations Management System. No. FHWA/TX-22/5-6996-01-1*. Texas Department of Transportation. Research and Technology Implementation Office.

Shahsavar, A., Salmanzadeh, M., Ameri, M., and Talebizadeh, P. (2011). Energy Saving in Buildings by Using the Exhaust and Ventilation Air for Cooling of Photovoltaic Panels. *Energy and Buildings* 43 (9): 2219–2226.

Shameri, M.A., Alghoul, M., Sopian, K., M. et al. (2011). Perspectives of Double Skin Façade Systems in Buildings and Energy Saving. *Renewable and Sustainable Energy Reviews* 15 (3): 1468–1475.

Shi, X., Tian, Z., Chen, W. et al. (2016). A Review on Building Energy Efficient Design Optimization From the Perspective of Architects. *Renewable and Sustainable Energy Reviews* 65: 872–884.

Shobeiri, V. (2021). Design Optimization of Sandwich Panels Under Impact Loads. *Engineering Optimization* 53 (9): 1632–1650.

Stavrakakis, G., Zervas, P.L., Sarimveis, H., and Markatos, N. (2012). Optimization of Window-Openings Design for Thermal Comfort in Naturally Ventilated Buildings. *Applied Mathematical Modelling* 36 (1): 193–211.

Stazi, F., Mastrucci, A., and Munafò, P. (2012). Life Cycle Assessment Approach for the Optimization of Sustainable Building Envelopes: An Application on Solar Wall Systems. *Building and Environment* 58: 278–288.

Tomlinson, D. and Fam, A. (2014). Experimental Investigation of Precast Concrete Insulated Sandwich Panels with Glass Fiber-Reinforced Polymer Shear Connectors. *ACI Structural Journal* 111 (3).

U.S. Department of Energy (DOE) (2022). Commercial Prototype Building Models (2021). https://www.energycodes.gov/prototype-building-models.

U.S. Energy Information Administration. Annual energy outlook 2020 with projections to 2050 (2020). https://www.eia.gov/todayinenergy/detail.php?id=42635#

U.S. Energy Information Administration. (2022) "How much energy is consumed in U.S. buildings?". https://www.eia.gov/tools/faqs/faq.php?id=86&t=1

Wang, Z. and Rangaiah, G.P. (2017). Application and Analysis of Methods for Selecting an Optimal Solution From the Pareto-optimal Front Obtained by Multiobjective Optimization. *Industrial & Engineering Chemistry Research* 56 (2): 560–574.

Wang, W., Zmeureanu, R., and Rivard, H. (2005). Applying Multi-objective Genetic Algorithms in Green Building Design Optimization. *Building and Environment* 40 (11): 1512–1525.

Wang, E., Li, Q., and Sun, G. (2020). Computational Analysis and Optimization of Sandwich Panels with Homogeneous and Graded Foam Cores for Blast Resistance. *Thin-Walled Structures* 147: 106494.

Weck, O. and Kim, I.Y. (2004). Adaptive Weighted Sum Method for Bi-objective Optimization. In: *45th AIAA/ASME/ASCE/AHS/ASC Structures, Structural Dynamics & Materials Conference*, 1680.

Wetter, M. (2019). A view on future building system modeling and simulation. In: *Building performance simulation for design and operation*, 631–656. Routledge.

Yu, W., Li, B., Jia, H. et al. (2015). Application of Multi-objective Genetic Algorithm to Optimize Energy Efficiency and Thermal Comfort in Building Design. *Energy and Buildings* 88: 135–143.

Yucel, K.T.Y., Basyigit, C., and Ozel, C. (2003). Thermal Insulation Properties of Expanded Polystyrene as Construction and Insulating Materials. In: *15th Symposium in Thermophysical Properties*, 54–66.

Zhang, R., Liu, F., Schoergendorfer, A. et al. (2013). Optimal Selection of Building Components Using Sequential Design via Statistical Surrogate Models. In: *Proceedings of Building Simulation*, 2584–2592.

8

Decoding Global Indoor Health Perception on Social Media Through NLP and Transformer Deep Learning

Mehdi Ashayeri

School of Architecture, College of Arts and Media, Southern Illinois University Carbondale, Carbondale, IL, USA

Introduction

Social media platforms offer a valuable data source for capturing perceptions and subjective matters within built environments. They enable participation, interaction, and open communication, allowing diverse stakeholders to express different narratives and viewpoints (Yue et al. 2022). Research shows that social media strongly influences how people see their lives and the world around them, which in turn affects their overall well-being (Greco and Polli 2021). According to Marshal McLuhan (Fen 1969; McLuhan 1994), media technologies act as extensions of human senses and cognition, which in turn reshape our interactions with our environment. Social media further offers a platform for public discussions on many topics. Its real-time insights into what many people think and do make it a valuable resource for research (Diaz et al. 2016). Additionally, the wealth of data available on social media represents a primary source for exploring people's opinions, sentiments, emotions, and life's experiences (Bollen, Mao, and Zeng 2011). As a result, most recently, monitoring and evaluating public perception through social media has become a crucial approach in environmental research.

The influence of social networks and the internet on environmental activism is evident. Within the activist community, social networks can serve as a means to cope with the absence of a formal system of laws and regulations in their initiatives (Sullivan and Xie 2009). The feedback received through social networks can either positively reinforce ecosystem governance or have a negative impact, potentially compromising it. As a result, social feedback plays a pivotal role in determining the solutions towards sustainability and whether interventions are perceived as just and supported by multiple stakeholders (Dawson et al. 2017). The presence of social feedback can also influence the fulfillment of ecological outcomes (Dawson et al. 2017). Recent studies (Skill, Passero, and Francisco 2021) have delved into how social networks, specifically X, frame and discuss major environmental events, underscoring the significant role of digital platforms in shaping global environmental narratives.

In light of data scarcity challenges, social media has been a turn towards an unconventional yet rich data source in environmental health studies (Jiang et al. 2015; Lopez et al. 2019; Bazzaz et al. 2021; Chen and Wang 2021; Ghermandi et al. 2023). When people post their

Artificial Intelligence in Performance-Driven Design: Theories, Methods, and Tools, First Edition.
Edited by Narjes Abbasabadi and Mehdi Ashayeri.
©2024 John Wiley & Sons Inc. Published 2024 by John Wiley & Sons Inc.

experiences and observations on platforms such as X, they unintentionally provide real-time, public data that can identify environmental concerns overlooked by traditional metrics (Stefanidis et al. 2017). The integration of conventional (e.g. meteorological, land cover) and social media data has prompted significant scholarly interest in environmental health research. The combination of user feedback and established monitoring parameters accelerates the identification of critical pollution conditions within built environments (Montanaro et al. 2022). Social media's role as an "on-the-ground monitor" (Sachdeva and McCaffrey 2018) or a "social sensor" (Jiang et al. 2019) becomes evident in its ability to bridge the gap between data collection and real-world experiences. The idea of categorizing social media users based on their influence levels offers a new opportunity to amplify awareness about the air pollution and its impacts (Pramanik et al. 2020).

Various studies have demonstrated the significant correlations between social media feedback and air quality, ultimately contributing to the detection and monitoring of air pollution (e.g. Hswen et al. 2019). By analyzing sentiment in social media content, researchers have confirmed that social media provides a valuable tool for monitoring outdoor air pollution in urban areas (e.g. Jiang et al. 2019). The interplay between negative tweets and areas with higher air pollution illustrates the potential for social media data to serve as an informative indicator of environmental quality (Hswen et al. 2019). Beyond its role in identifying environmental concerns, social media exerts a tangible influence on air quality through its power to prompt action. Environmental discussions on social media platforms foster a bottom-up force that compels governments and policymakers to address pollution issues (Wang and Jia 2021). Furthermore, its role in decision-making and planning is evident (e.g. Kaplan and Haenlein 2010; Shelton, Poorthuis, and Zook 2015). These characteristics create a two-way impact – social media acts as both a source of information and a catalyst for change, driving public engagement and government intervention to mitigate health risks associated with air pollution.

Nowadays, advances in data-driven techniques have helped develop more reliable models for the human-centric design decision-makings through exploring textual data. Text mining as a data-driven approach is a technique that uses NLP framework allowing machines to understand the human language, primarily through transforming unstructured text into normalized and structured data suitable for analysis (Lewis and Jones 1996). Started in the 1950s (Shannon 1951; Chomsky 1957) at the intersection of linguistics and AI (Winograd 1972; Jurafsky and Martin 2009), NLP was initially distinguished from text information retrieval (IR) (Salton and McGill 1983; Manning, Raghavan, and Schütze 2008), which uses highly scalable statistics-based techniques to effectively index and search vast quantities of text (Nadkarni, Ohno-Machado, and Chapman 2011; Goodfellow, Bengio, and Courville 2016). Text mining can help collect adequate data in a timely and cost-efficiently manner (Abdulaali, Usman, and Hanafiah 2020).

Not for long, text mining based on review data collected through surveys has been used for indoor health studies particularly in workplaces (e.g. Moezzi and Goins 2011). With the widespread adoption of digital technologies and easier access to internet connections over the past two decades, performing text-mining on online reviews has gained popularity. This approach allows researchers to tap into a wider spectrum of real-world data and gain deeper insights across various fields (University of Liechtenstein et al. 2016; Antons et al. 2020; Romero-Silva and de Leeuw 2021). However, there still exists limited studies used such capabilities to explore occupant feedback on indoor health or indoor environmental quality (IEQ) metrics–including aural comfort, visual comfort, thermal comfort, and IAQ. Despite the substantial research efforts in the field of IEQ, our comprehensive review identified only five published studies that employed social media to investigate occupant feedback on indoor health indicators (e.g. Villeneuve and O'Brien 2020; Chinazzo 2021; Parkinson et al. 2021; Salamone et al. 2021; Ma et al. 2023).

When considering computational approaches, many health-related studies within the built environment predominantly use a non-linguistic approach, especially when analyzing behavioral mobility patterns derived from social media data (e.g. Broniatowski, Paul, and Dredze 2013; Hawelka et al. 2014; Jurdak et al. 2015; Paul and Dredze 2021). Yet, when it comes to linguistic-based techniques — namely NLPs — the majority still depend on traditional rule-based methods, such as lexicon-based techniques, to interpret human sentiments. In previous indoor health research, as referenced by aforementioned five studies, no linguistic-based models have been developed using either conventional machine learning (ML) or powerful ML techniques such as deep learning algorithms. There's a distinct discrepancy in utilizing deep learning techniques that can provide a richer understanding of the subject matter within its real-world context. Notably, the potential of emerging pre-trained models developed upon a large corpus of real-world textual data through transformer-based deep learning (Vaswani et al. 2017) remains largely untapped in the analysis of social media data for indoor health-focused studies.

This research aimed to explore occupants' sentiments regarding IAQ experiences in buildings during the early stages of the COVID. By developing NLP models for sentiment analysis, this chapter sought to capture the perceptions of building occupants feedback about IAQ issues at a time when they were spending considerably more time indoors than usual due to the stay-at-home orders. To obtain detailed contextual feedback on IAQ concerns during pre and post COVID eras, the present chapter employed the emerging deep learning technique, RoBERTa (Liu et al. 2019). This model, an extension of bidirectional encoder representations from transformers (BERT) introduced by Google AI in 2018 (Devlin et al. 2018), has been fine-tuned using a vast corpus of X data. BERT and its variants, like RoBERTa, represent a significant shift in the approach to sentiment analysis on large-scale social media datasets. This chapter extracted geo-tagged data from X database posted by users worldwide during the first year of the pandemic (2020) and compared it with the baseline (2019).

Literature Review

Social Media and Urban Life: Theories, Challenges, and Opportunities

The emergence of digital media has undeniably revolutionized the way we interact, communicate, and consume information. Marshal McLuhan, in his seminal work "Understanding Media: The Extension of Man," (McLuhan 1994) delves into the profound impact of media on society, asserting that "the medium is the message." McLuhan's ideas set the groundwork for understanding the digital age, where various media platforms have flourished. His insights reveal that the medium through which content is delivered shapes and influences our perceptions and understanding of that content. For instance, a message conveyed through television would have a different impact than the same message delivered through print media.

Clay Shirky, in his book "Here Comes Everybody: The Power of Organizing Without Organizations," (Shirky 2008) explores the impact of digital media on social organization and activism. He emphasizes that digital tools have democratized the ability to organize and collaborate without traditional hierarchical structures. Social media platforms have empowered individuals to mobilize for social causes and amplify their voices on a global scale. One of the significant impacts of digital media, as highlighted by Shirky, is the rise of online communities and collaborative efforts. People with shared interests and goals can now connect and collaborate across borders, transcending physical limitations, fostering vibrant discussions, knowledge-sharing, and mutual assistance among members.

Moreover, the concept of "user-generated content" (UGC) (Bardhan et al. 2010) has gained prominence in the digital era, blurring the line between producers and consumers of information. This phenomenon has democratized content creation, allowing diverse voices to be heard, and challenging the traditional media's monopoly on information dissemination. Bloggers, vloggers, and social media influencers have emerged as influential figures with dedicated audiences, reshaping the media landscape. The "real-time" nature of digital media enables rapid and widespread dissemination of information, bringing attention to critical issues and facilitating international solidarity. However, the fast-paced nature of information sharing can also lead to the spread of misinformation and rumors, highlighting the importance of media literacy and critical thinking in the digital age.

Amid the numerous benefits of digital media, it is essential to acknowledge and address the challenges it poses. Neil Postman's book "Amusing Ourselves to Death: Public Discourse in the Age of Show Business" (Postman 2006) sheds light on the role of entertainment in shaping public discourse. Postman's argument emphasizes how the integration of entertainment values into news and information mediums has led to a decline in serious public discourse. In the digital media age, where attention-grabbing content often takes precedence, Postman's ideas become even more relevant. Misinformation and fake news have become concerning issues in the digital landscape, facilitated by the ease of sharing information online, leading to misinformation campaigns and social unrest. Navigating this vast digital landscape demands media literacy and critical thinking to discern fact from fiction.

Furthermore, Arthur Miller's profound work "The Assault on Privacy: Computers, Data Banks, and Dossiers" (Miller 1971) raises pressing concerns about unregulated data collection in the digital age. Mass surveillance and constant monitoring infringe upon individuals' rights to maintain personal boundaries and autonomy. The pervasive nature of data collection enables potential misuse, leading to manipulation, discrimination, or unwarranted surveillance, eroding trust between users and digital platforms. Miller's insights underscore the urgency of addressing privacy implications in the digital landscape. As data accumulates at an unprecedented scale, personal information becomes vulnerable to unauthorized access and misuse. Large-scale data breaches can have severe repercussions on national security, economic stability, and social cohesion. To safeguard privacy in the digital age, robust regulatory frameworks and ethical practices must hold data collectors accountable. Transparency, consent-based data collection, and empowering users with control over their data are essential for preserving privacy while embracing digital media's potential.

In his influential work "Emergence: The Connected Lives of Ants, Brains, Cities, and Software" (Johnson 2001), Steve Johnson explores the emergence of complex systems from seemingly simple interactions. Employing the analogy of a city as a "pattern in time," he highlights the gradual and interconnected growth of cities, driven by the collective actions and interactions of its inhabitants. Similarly, digital media has evolved through dynamic interactions among internet users, utilizing diverse technological tools to establish social media platforms, blogs, online forums, and digital content sharing as integral aspects of modern life. These transformations have significantly impacted communication, information access, and societal engagement. By drawing parallels between the emergent nature of cities and the evolution of digital media, the latter's development emerges as a dynamic and interconnected process, offering valuable insights into its transformative effects on society. Rooted in collective contributions and interactions within the ever-evolving online ecosystem, digital media's origin mirrors the organic emergence of cities through interactions among individuals and their environment. This connection becomes increasingly apparent when contrasting the growth of digital media with the natural emergence of cities, underscoring the profound interplay between human interaction and technological advancement.

Considering the benefits and challenges of digital media, social media platforms offer intriguing opportunities to understand our cities. Despite concerns over misinformation and privacy infringement, these platforms reflect urban life and interactions. The data they generate provide insights into urban behaviors, patterns, and human perceptions aiding urban planning and policymaking. Social media data enables researchers to gauge public sentiment, analyze social networks, and identify trends impacting urban life. Moreover, digital interconnectedness fosters global collaborations among urban practitioners, facilitating knowledge-sharing and collective efforts toward sustainable solutions. However, ethical considerations are crucial in utilizing social media data, ensuring privacy protection, and avoiding biases. Embracing this digital frontier with ethical principles and rigorous research methodologies will shape a more sustainable and resilient urban future.

Methods for Computing Social Media Data in Environmental Studies

Through the lens of big data analytics, data-driven techniques, and extensive realm of social media data, this chapter highlights two analytical approaches stand out: Social Mobility (or Behavioral Patterns) and Linguistics, often referred to as NLP. Each method presents its own unique advantages and challenges, allowing researchers to explore the nuanced dimensions of human-environment interactions.

Computing Behavioral (Mobility) Patterns

Despite the multitude of subjective opinions shared on social media, platforms like X have been instrumental in understanding the mobility patterns of people for public health and epidemiological studies (e.g. Bisanzio et al. 2020; Zhang et al. 2021; Chan, Cheung, and Erduran 2023). Mobility patterns derived from social media platforms are a treasure trove of spatiotemporal data. These patterns allow researchers and policymakers to discern where individuals travel, how often, and during which times. By understanding these movements, decision-makers can make inferences about health trends in urban populations. E.g., the density of movement can indicate areas of potential disease spread or areas where air quality might impact public health (Salathé et al. 2012). Although behavioral analysis offers concrete data points on the geographical location of social media users for facilitating targeted interventions and informed urban planning decisions (Hawelka et al. 2014), they may lack the context and reasoning behind users' movements, making it challenging to perceive their intentions or environmental attitudes (Shelton et al. 2014).

From a methodological standpoint, numerous advanced techniques have been developed to analyze mobility patterns derived from social media data. One particularly effective approach involves quantifying dispersion through the Radius of Gyration (rg) of movements and subsequently integrating these findings into a Spatial Autoregressive (SAR) model

(Box 8.1). This serves to elucidate the intricate relationships between various urban explanatory variables and observed movement patterns. (Mohammadi and Taylor 2017) employed this method to comprehend the relationships between urban mobility and energy dynamics, though it hasn't been extensively used in epidemic and health research. A preprint by (Kishore et al. 2021) utilized an autoregressive model, distinct from the SAR model for a nationwide public health study.

Box 8.1 General spatiotemporal approach for behavioral analysis of social media data

Step 1. Calculation of Radius of Gyration (*rg*):
The Radius of Gyration (*rg*) for an individual *i* at time *t* is given by:

$$rg(t) = \sqrt{\frac{\sum_{j=1}^{N_i} w_{ij} \cdot d_{ij}^2}{\sum_{j=1}^{N_i} w_{ij}}}$$

where:

- N_i is the total number of geotagged tweets (locations) of individual *i* during time period *t*.
- w_{ij} is the weight associated with each location *j* of individual *i*. The weight can be determined based on the significance or importance of each location, or set to 1 if all locations have equal importance.
- d_{ij} is the Euclidean distance between the centroid of individual *i* and the geotagged location *j*.
- Calculation of Centroid for individual *i*: The centroid coordinates $\text{lat}_{\text{cent}_i}$ and $\text{long}_{\text{cent}_i}$ for individual *i* are computed as follows:

$$\text{lat}_{\text{cent}_i} = \frac{1}{N_i} \sum_{j=1}^{N_i} \text{lat}_{ij}$$

$$\text{long}_{\text{cent}_i} = \frac{1}{N_i} \sum_{j=1}^{N_i} \text{long}_{ij}$$

- Calculation of Euclidean Distance d_{ij}: The Euclidean distance d_{ij} between the centroid and each geotagged location *j* of individual *i* is calculated as follows:

$$d_{ij} = \sqrt{\left(\text{lat}_{\text{cent}_i} - \text{lat}_{ij}\right)^2 - \left(\text{long}_{\text{cent}_i} - \text{long}_{ij}\right)^2}$$

Step 2. Development of Spatial Autoregressive Model:
The SAR model aims to model the spatial relationship between a variable y_i for individual *i* and the neighboring values of the variable. The model can be represented as follows:

$$y_i = \rho \sum_{j=1}^{N_i} w_{ij} y_j + \alpha \cdot rg_i + \beta X_i + \varepsilon_i$$

where:

- y_i is the value of the variable of interest (e.g., mobility behavior) for individual i.
- ρ is the spatial autocorrelation coefficient, representing the influence of neighboring values on y_i.
- w_{ij} is the spatial weight associated with the relationship between individual i and its neighboring individual j, capturing spatial autocorrelation. It can be based on different criteria, such as inverse distance weighting or contiguity-based weights.
- y_j is the value of the variable for neighboring individual j.
- α is the coefficient representing the influence of the Radius of Gyration (rg) for individual i.
- rg_i is the Radius of Gyration for individual i calculated earlier.
- β is the coefficient vector representing the influence of exogenous variables X_i on y_i.
- ε_i is the error term.
- $\rho \sum_{j=1}^{N_i} w_{ij} y_j$ represents the spatially lagged variable of interest for individual i (the dependent variable for neighboring individuals j).

Computing Linguistics: Evolution of NLP Analysis

This section provides a brief overview of the evolution of NLP analysis historically with emerged categories in the field, along with the pioneering papers influenced each category (Table 8.1):

Statistical: Statistical approaches brought data-driven methods to NLP, utilizing probabilities and frequencies to capture patterns in language. Hidden Markov Models (HMMs) and n-gram models were widely used to capture sequential dependencies in text. These statistical concepts for NLP analysis have been significantly influenced by (Shannon 1948).

Lexicons: The early approaches to NLP heavily relied on lexicon-based methods, which focused on building dictionaries and rules to process text. One prominent example (Harris 1954) is the use of part-of-speech tagging and syntactic parsing based on manually crafted grammar rules. Sentiment analysis leverages various types of lexicons to extract and understand emotions and opinions from textual data as listed. Sentiment Lexicons contain words or phrases along with their associated sentiment scores, indicating whether they

Table 8.1 Evolution of NLP analysis and early papers.

Modeling method	Year	Paper title	References
Statistical	1948	A Mathematical Theory of Communication	Shannon (1948)
Lexicon	1954	Distributional Structure	Harris (1954)
Traditional	1997	Long Short-Term Memory	Hochreiter and Schmidhuber (1997)
Deep Learning	1998	Gradient-Based Learning Applied to Document Recognition	Lecun et al. (1998)
Transformer Deep Learning	2017	Attention is all You Need	Vaswani et al. (2017)

express positive, negative, or neutral sentiments. Examples include AFINN, SentiWordNet, and Valence Aware Dictionary and sEntiment Reasoner (VADER); Emotion Lexicons associate words with specific emotions such as joy, sadness, fear, anger, and surprise. These lexicons are used in emotion recognition tasks. Examples include NRC Emotion Lexicon and WordEmotion; Subjectivity Lexicons categorize words as subjective, or objective based on their likelihood of expressing opinions or emotions. They are valuable in sentiment analysis tasks to differentiate between subjective and objective content. Domain-specific Lexicons focus on words and expressions specific to particular industries or fields. Researchers can create customized lexicons for domain-specific sentiment analysis, enhancing accuracy for specialized contexts. Noun–Verb Lexicons provide information about the semantic roles and relationships between nouns and verbs, supporting tasks such as semantic role labeling and co reference resolution. The number of sentiment categories and the number of words per category in each lexicon can vary significantly based on the specific lexicon and its intended use. Table 8.2 provides some examples of popular sentiment lexicons, along with their sentiment categories and approximate word counts per category. The numbers provided are approximate and may vary depending on the version or source of the lexicon.

Table 8.2 Comparison of sentiment lexicons—sentiment categories and word counts per category.

Lexicon	Sentiment categories	Words per category	Author/ref.
Affective Norms for English Words (AFINN)	Positive, Negative	Approximately 2477 positive words, 4768 negative words	Finn Årup Nielsen
SentiWordNet	Positive, Negative, Neutral	Over 155,000 words (varying proportions per category)	Andrey Breslav, JuliaSoft S.r.l.
Valence Aware Dictionary and sEntiment Reasoner (VADER)	Positive, Negative, Neutral, Compound	Approximately 7500 lexical features	Hutto and Gilbert (2014)
NRC Emotion Lexicon	Anger, Fear, Sadness, Joy, Disgust, Surprise, Anticipation, Trust, Positive, Negative	Over 14,000 words (varying proportions per category)	Saif M. Mohammad, Peter D. Turney
WordEmotion	Joy, Fear, Sadness, Anger, Disgust, Surprise, Trust, Anticipation	Over 8000 words (varying proportions per category)	Isabella Poggi, Andrea Venerosi, et al.
Bing Liu's Opinion Lexicon (AFINN-111)	Positive, Negative	2477 positive words, 4765 negative words	Bing Liu
MPQA Subjectivity Lexicon	Subjective, Objective	Around 6000 words (varying proportions per category)	Theresa Wilson, Janyce Wiebe
Harvard General Inquirer	Multiple categories for different emotions, cognitive states, and language types	Over 11,000 words (distributed across various categories)	Philip J. Stone, Dexter C. Dunphy

Machine Learning: With the advent of ML in NLP, researchers began employing ML algorithms that could automatically learn patterns from textual data. In the early stages, Ratnaparkhi (Ratnaparkhi 1996) utilized MaxEnt models for part-of-speech tagging. Concurrently, Magerman (Magerman 1995) explored decision trees for parsing. Rabiner (Rabiner 1989) integrated HMMs for tasks in speech recognition. SVMs, as demonstrated by Joachims (1998), were found effective for text categorization. Lafferty, McCallum, and Pereira (2001) introduced Conditional Random Fields (CRF) for sequence segmentation and labeling. The utility of Naive Bayes for text classification was validated by McCallum and Nigam (1998). Boosting algorithms, particularly the BoosTexter system, were examined by Schapire and Singer (2000) for text categorization. Daelemans et al. (2002) advocated for memory-based learning, presenting TiMBL as an exemplar. Collins (2002)synthesized the perceptron approach with HMMs, optimizing sequence modeling. And k-Nearest Neighbors (kNNs) (Yang and Liu 1999) method was used as a viable technique for classification tasks. Collectively, these seminal works laid the foundation for subsequent advancements in NLP.

Conventional Deep Learning: Deep learning, a branch of ML based on deep artificial neural networks (ANNs), has extensively transformed the NLP field. This approach heralded a paradigm shift in NLP by employing ANNs with multiple layers to autonomously learn hierarchical features from textual data. Within this context, Long Short-Term Memory (LSTM) networks were introduced as a significant advancement (Hochreiter and Schmidhuber 1997). Subsequently, the concept of bidirectional processing (Schuster and Paliwal 1997), which laid the foundation for Bidirectional Long Short-Term Memory (BiLSTM) networks, was introduced. Additionally, Convolutional Neural Networks (CNNs) (Lecun et al. 1998) have been prominently utilized. These architectural innovations, including the pioneering concept of LSTM and the bidirectional capabilities of BiLSTM, have played a pivotal role in propelling NLP analysis forward. LSTM networks excel in capturing sequential information inherent to text, while BiLSTM networks, through their bidirectional processing, further enhance the understanding of context. CNNs adeptly exploit local patterns. This collective progress underscores the significant impact of deep learning on advancing NLP analysis.

Transformer Deep Learning: In NLP, a "Transformer" refers to a specific type of deep learning architecture designed to handle sequential data, such as language. The transformer architecture is particularly well-suited for NLP tasks because it addresses some limitations of previous models like RNNs, particularly LSTMs, and CNNs, which struggle to capture long-range dependencies in sequences due to their sequential processing nature. Transformers revolutionized NLP with their self-attention mechanism, enabling the capture of long-range dependencies in text. The "Attention Is All You Need" paper (Vaswani et al. 2017) introduced the transformer architecture, paving the way for models like BERT (Devlin et al. 2018), GPT (Generative Pre-trained Transformer) (Radford et al. 2018), RoBERTa (Liu et al. 2019), Text-To-Text Transfer Transformer (T5) (Raffel et al. 2019), and more. While both BERT and BiLSTM use bidirectional processing, they have different architectural foundations (transformer vs. LSTM) and serve different purposes. BERT is primarily used for contextualized word embeddings and various NLP tasks like text classification, question answering, and more. BiLSTM, on the other hand, is a recurrent architecture designed for sequence modeling tasks.

Most but not all transformer-based methods in NLP involve a pre-training phase. Pre-training is a key characteristic of transformer architectures and has become a fundamental approach for improving the performance of various NLP tasks. In pre-training, a transformer model is trained on a large corpus of text to learn contextualized representations of words, phrases, and sentences. This pre-trained model captures rich linguistic patterns and relationships from the data. After pre-training, the model can be fine-tuned on specific downstream NLP tasks, such as text classification, named entity recognition, and machine translation. Pre-training is crucial because it allows models to acquire a strong foundation of language understanding, which can then be fine-tuned for specific tasks with relatively smaller amounts of task-specific labeled data. This has led to significant improvements in the effectiveness and efficiency of various NLP applications.

Model	Year	Pre-training	Architecture	Objective	Author/Ref.
Word2Vec	2013	Shallow, static embeddings	Continuous Bag of Words (CBOW) and Skip-gram	Predicting context words	Mikolov et al. (2013a)
ELMo	2018	Deep, contextual embeddings	BiLSTM with character CNNs	Bidirectional word embeddings	Peters et al. (2018)
BERT	2018	Deep, bidirectional context	Transformer	Masked language model	Devlin et al. (2018)
GPT-1	2018	Deep, unidirectional context	Transformer, Generative	Autoregressive language model	Radford et al. (2018)
RoBERTa	2019	Deep, bidirectional context	Transformer	Masked language model	Liu et al. (2019)
GPT-2	2019	Deep, unidirectional context	Transformer, Generative	Autoregressive language model	Radford et al. (2019)
T5	2019	Deep, text-to-text framework	Transformer	Text-to-text conversion	Raffel et al. (2019)
GPT-3	2020	Deep, few-shot learning	Transformer, Generative	Multitask, few-shot learning	Brown et al. (2020)
ELECTRA	2020	Deep, bidirectional context, modified pre-training task	Transformer, Discriminator	Effective language representations	Clark et al. (2020)

"Shallow" and "Deep" refers to the depth of the neural network architecture used in each model.

Materials and Methods

Data Query

In this study, we picked X as the source for social media data because (a) X users send short messages that are limited to 280 characters, therefore people sentiment is conveyed through a short text communication; (b) X offers API key to access the entire historical data; and

(c) many studies have used X as the primary social media platform for the human-centered explorations (Pilař et al. 2019), particularly health-related explorations in the built environment, and this is evident by a recently published comprehensive review by (Chen and Wang 2021). In this research, we extracted data for two consecutive years: 2019 and 2020 to compare pre and post COVID sentiments on IAQ. We utilized the tweepy package in Python (Roesslein 2020), combined with our X API v2 key, to extract historical data. For implementing data acquisition, we identified a cluster of terms related to the IAQ, including "indoor pollution concentrations," "indoor PM2.5," "indoor exposure," "indoor air pollution," "indoor air circulation," "dehumidifier," "indoor virus," "indoor airborne," as well as "indoor air quality" itself. These terms were queried based on exact phrases, which identified tweets that included only these terms within the posted comments to highlight IAQ scopes. To avoid bots, we only implemented data acquisition based only on verified X accounts.

Text Preprocessing

Before feeding any text data into the model, it underwent a comprehensive preprocessing pipeline to ensure consistency and remove any noise. Table 8.3 lists 12 methods applied to implement data preprocessing.

Text Tokenization

Before feeding data into the model, it's imperative to convert the raw texts into a format the machine can understand (Jurafsky and Martin 2009; Manning et al. 2014). This process is known as tokenization. Alongside the RoBERTa model, we initialized its corresponding

Table 8.3 Methods applied for data pre-processing.

Removal/Fixation	Tasks
URLs	All URLs, regardless of the protocol (HTTP or HTTPS), were extracted and eliminated
Mention and Hashtag	Mentions (e.g., '@username') and hashtags (e.g., '#trending') were identified and removed.
Email Address	Any detected email addresses were extracted
HTML Tags	All HTML tags embedded in the text were stripped out
Numerical Data	Pure numerical data were identified and removed
Contraction	Common contractions like "don't" and "can't" were expanded to "do not" and "cannot" respectively
Characters	Special characters, excluding apostrophes, were removed
Case Normalization	The entire text corpus was converted to lowercase for consistency
Stop Words	Common English words, which don't typically contain important significance, were filtered out
Lemmatization	Words were transformed to their base or dictionary form to ensure consistency in representation
Short Word	To further refine the data, words that have less than three characters were removed
Space Normalization	All multiple white spaces were converted into a single space

tokenizer, which is adept at breaking down input sequences into tokens compatible with the model. This tokenizer not only segments texts into words or sub-words but also ensures that the sequences are appropriately formatted with special tokens that the RoBERTa architecture requires. This action uses the RoBERTa tokenizer from the transformers library, splitting the preprocessed text into individual tokens. The RoBERTa tokenizer may even further split some words into smaller sub-word units, which can be helpful for handling out-of-vocabulary words and improving model generalization. For RoBERTa base models, the maximum sequence length is capped at 512 tokens.

Text Summarization

For entries surpassing a specified token count of 510, we implemented a summarization technique. This limit of 510 tokens is set to account for the two special tokens, including the "Classifier" (CLS) and "Separator" (SEP), which are often added in transformer models. When these special tokens are included, the total token count becomes 512, which aligns with the maximum input length for models like BERT and RoBERTa – (CLS) Token is often added to the beginning of a sequence. In models like BERT, the representation of this token (after passing through the transformer layers) is used for classification tasks.

(SEP) Token is used to separate different segments in a sequence. E.g., for a task that requires understanding two sentences in relation to each other, the input might look like: (CLS) Sentence 1 (SEP) Sentence 2 (SEP) — We used a summarization technique using the bidirectional and auto-regressive transformers (BART) model. This transformer-based sequence-to-sequence model, developed by facebook AI (Lewis et al. 2019), is fine-tuned for text summarization with weights from facebook/bart-large-cnn. This approach ensures that extended text inputs are condensed while preserving their core sentiment and content.

Generating Co-occurrence Matrix

Co-occurrence Matrix represents how often two terms appear together within a specific context (e.g. within the same document, sentence, or window of n words) (Deerwester et al. 1990). Each cell in the matrix shows the frequency with which the terms represented by the corresponding row and column appear together. Both rows and columns in the dataset correspond to terms. This matrix is useful for understanding relationships between terms, semantic analyses, or word embeddings (Mikolov et al. 2013b). We used co_occurrence_matrix() function to craft a co-occurrence matrix from a given set of text tokens. Utilizing a sliding window approach, the function evaluates how frequently two tokens appear within a specified vicinity of one another. By default, a window size of five was chosen, considering five tokens before and after the current token under scrutiny.

Sentiment Analysis and Classification

We employed the RoBERTa model, a variant of the BERT model, for sentiment analysis. Given the nature of our data, originating from X, it was crucial to employ a model that comprehends the nuances and semantics of tweets, which often differ from conventional textual data due to brevity, slang, and other platform-specific linguistic attributes. To this end, we chose the version of RoBERTa that was specifically pre-trained on a sentiment analysis task using the "cardiffnlp/twitter-roberta-base-sentiment" weights (Barbieri et al. 2020).

This specialized version of RoBERTa is adept at capturing the underlying sentiment of tweets, which can often be layered and subtle. Each processed text input was fed into the RoBERTa-based sentiment analysis pipeline. The model's output provided a sentiment label ("Negative", "Neutral", or "Positive") along with a confidence score. It's worth noting that any text exceeding the token threshold was first summarized before sentiment classification, ensuring it fit within the model's token limit. Ultimately, the dataset is augmented with sentiment labels and their corresponding confidence scores as new columns.

Visualizations

Embedding Visualization

To provide a deeper insight into the underlying linguistic representations formed by the RoBERTa model, we applied a methodology for creating embedding visualization. Embedding visualization in NLP refers to the graphical representation of word or sentence embeddings (Mikolov et al. 2013b). Embeddings are dense vector representations of words or sentences that capture their semantic meaning in a multi-dimensional space (Pennington, Socher, and Manning 2014). Given the high-dimensionality of these vectors (e.g., 768 dimensions for a base RoBERTa model), visualizing them directly is not feasible. Therefore, we used dimensionality reduction techniques to project these vectors into a lower-dimensional space (typically 2D or 3D) for visualization. We proceeded with the following steps to create embedding visualizations:

(a) RoBERTa Model Loading: We initialized the base RoBERTa model using the pre-trained weights ("cardiffnlp/twitter-RoBERTa-base-sentiment"); (b) Embedding Extraction: For the extraction of embeddings, a developed a function, extract_embeddings(). This function handles a list of preprocessed texts and extracts embeddings corresponding to each text. These embeddings were derived from the last hidden state of the base RoBERTa model, which encapsulates the semantic representation of the entire input sequence. Each text, upon tokenization and appropriate padding, was fed into the RoBERTa model to obtain its embedding; (c) *K*-means Clustering on Embeddings: Before diving into clustering, it was imperative to determine the optimal number of clusters. For this purpose, we implemented the elbow method (Ketchen and Shook 1996). Specifically, *K*-means, clustering, (MacQueen 1967) was executed iteratively for a range of cluster numbers (from 1 to 9 in this study). For each iteration, the inertia (or within-cluster sum of squares) (Thorndike 1953) was computed and captured. The distortions were subsequently plotted against the range of cluster numbers to visualize the "elbow," which indicates the optimal number of clusters. This was a user-informed decision where the point of inflection (the "elbow") is the recommended value for the number of clusters. Once the optimal number of clusters was determined and input by the user, *K*-means clustering was applied to segment the embeddings into distinct clusters (Lloyd 1982); (d) Dimensionality Reduction with t-SNE: To visualize the high-dimensional embeddings in a 2D space, we employed t-SNE (t-distributed Stochastic Neighbor Embedding) (van der Maaten and Hinton 2008). This method reduces the dimensionality of the data while preserving local structures. In our study, t-SNE was parameterized with two components for a 2D projection, and we allowed for adjustable perplexity to account for different data densities; and (e) 2D Visualization with Clusters: After dimensionality reduction, the

2D embeddings were visualized using a scatter plot, where data points were color-coded based on their respective clusters.

Attention Score Visualization (Attention Map) and Interpretation

To garner insights into the model's internal operations and to understand its interpretation of input text, attention score visualization is employed. Attention visualization in transformer text analysis like RoBERTa is a graphical representation that helps to interpret and understand how attention mechanisms operate within the model while processing a given text (Vig 2019). In transformer models, the attention mechanism is a fundamental component that allows the model to weigh the significance of different parts of the text when generating a representation for it. This mechanism enables the model to focus more on certain words while paying less attention to others, depending on the context. It allows for the examination of the relationships and interactions between words and how these relationships evolve through the layers of the network. Such visualizations are crucial for interpreting model behavior, diagnosing potential issues, and potentially improving the model's performance by gaining a deeper understanding of its operation. In this research, the focus of the analysis was directed towards a text excerpt concerning the relevance of IAQ to human health particularly during the pandemic, using a random tweet pulled from the platform.

The attention scores in the model explain the focus level allocated to various tokens during the processing of a specific token, with higher scores denoting stronger relationships or relevance among considered tokens. Typically, tokens exhibit higher attention scores towards immediate neighbors or tokens within the same phrase or clause, elucidating local dependencies. The interpretation of these scores begins with Self-Attention, where tokens primarily focus on themselves, illustrating a core facet of the model's attention mechanism. Progressing, Neighboring Token Attention takes role, showing higher scores between adjacent tokens or those within the same phrase, reflecting local contextual understanding. The narrative extends to Special Token Attention, where attention to (CLS) often contributes to a global text representation, while attention to (SEP) marks sentence boundaries or transitions, acting as textual delineators in the model's narrative. In some cases, Distributed Attention arises where tokens spread attention across multiple other tokens, displaying a broader contextual grasp and capturing long-term dependencies essential for semantic understanding. The narrative further traverses through Layer-wise Variation in the transformer architecture, where initial layers capture basic syntactic relationships, but as one ascend through layers, more abstract or semantic relationships get unveiled, creating a comprehension gradient from syntactic to semantic understanding. Finally, the narrative culminates with Visualization, where graphical portrayals provide intuitive insights into the model's internal narrative, offering a sturdy framework for understanding text interpretation by the model, spotlighting specific topics or domains, and availing a diagnostic lens for model behavior analysis and potential refinement avenues.

In attention visualization in RoBERTa, the architecture is often composed of multiple layers, commonly 12, each with its own set of attention scores. These layers, referred to as leaders in this context, play a crucial role in understanding the hierarchical processing and extraction of features from the input text at various levels of abstraction. Each layer potentially learns to attend to different aspects of the text, building increasingly complex representations as the information ascends through the layers. When interpreting the visualization, examining the attention scores at each layer provides insight into the model's focus at that particular level of abstraction. For instance, lower layers might focus on basic syntactic relationships, while higher layers may capture more abstract or semantic relationships. The visualization of attention across these layers can be observed through heatmaps or directed graphs, which depict the strength and direction of attention between words in the text. By comparing the attention patterns across layers, one can gauge how the model's understanding of the text evolves, and which layers are crucial for capturing certain types of relationships. The attention visualizations serve as a powerful tool for dissecting and interpreting the multi-layered attention mechanism within the transformer model, providing a clearer understanding of how the model processes and derives meaning from the input text. The bertviz package in Python was utilized to generate attention visualizations.

Results and Discussion

In our data query, we extracted 131,651 tweets for 2019 and 234,104 tweets for 2020. This represents an 80% increase in the number of tweets related to IAQ from one year to the next. Such a significant uptick suggests heightened public engagement and concern regarding air quality inside buildings, particularly during the pandemic (Morawska and Cao 2020; Allen and Ibrahim 2021). This could be attributed to people spending more time indoors due to lockdowns and safety measures (Flaxman et al. 2020; Nicola et al. 2020), making them more aware and sensitive to their immediate environment and the quality of air they breathe. Our sentiment analysis spanning 2019–2020 further highlighted distinct shifts in sentiment score percentages (Table 8.4). In 2019, 32.71% of the content related to IAQ subjects was negative, 48.89% neutral, and 18.40% positive. By 2020, negative sentiments increased by 5.15–37.86%. Neutral sentiments decreased to 46.31%, a reduction of 2.58%. Positive sentiments declined by 2.57–15.83%. These shifts suggest a trend towards more negative and fewer positive sentiments in 2020 compared to 2019. The widespread stay-at-home directives in 2020, leading to higher indoor occupancy, could potentially explain these outcomes. Further investigations would also be beneficial to understand the underlying causes and broader implications of these year-to-year shifts in sentiment distribution.

In the comparative analysis of word cloud graphs for 2019 and 2020 (Figure 8.1), a distinct shift in the frequency and nature of keywords associated with sentiments towards IAQ was observed. The word clouds, categorized into negative, neutral, and positive sentiments, provide a visual representation of the public discourse surrounding IAQ during these two years. A notable surge in certain keywords in 2020, possibly triggered by the COVID-19 pandemic, reflects a heightened public awareness and concern regarding IAQ. For instance, terms like "poorly ventilated," "poor ventilation," "poor air," "very poor," "COVID19," "virus," became more prevalent in the negative sentiment category, potentially indicating an increased

Table 8.4 Global sentiment scores on IAQ obtained from RoBERTa sentiment analysis for 2019 and 2020.

Year	Negative (%)	Neutral (%)	Positive (%)
2019	28.1	56.9	15.0
2020	37.9	46.3	15.8

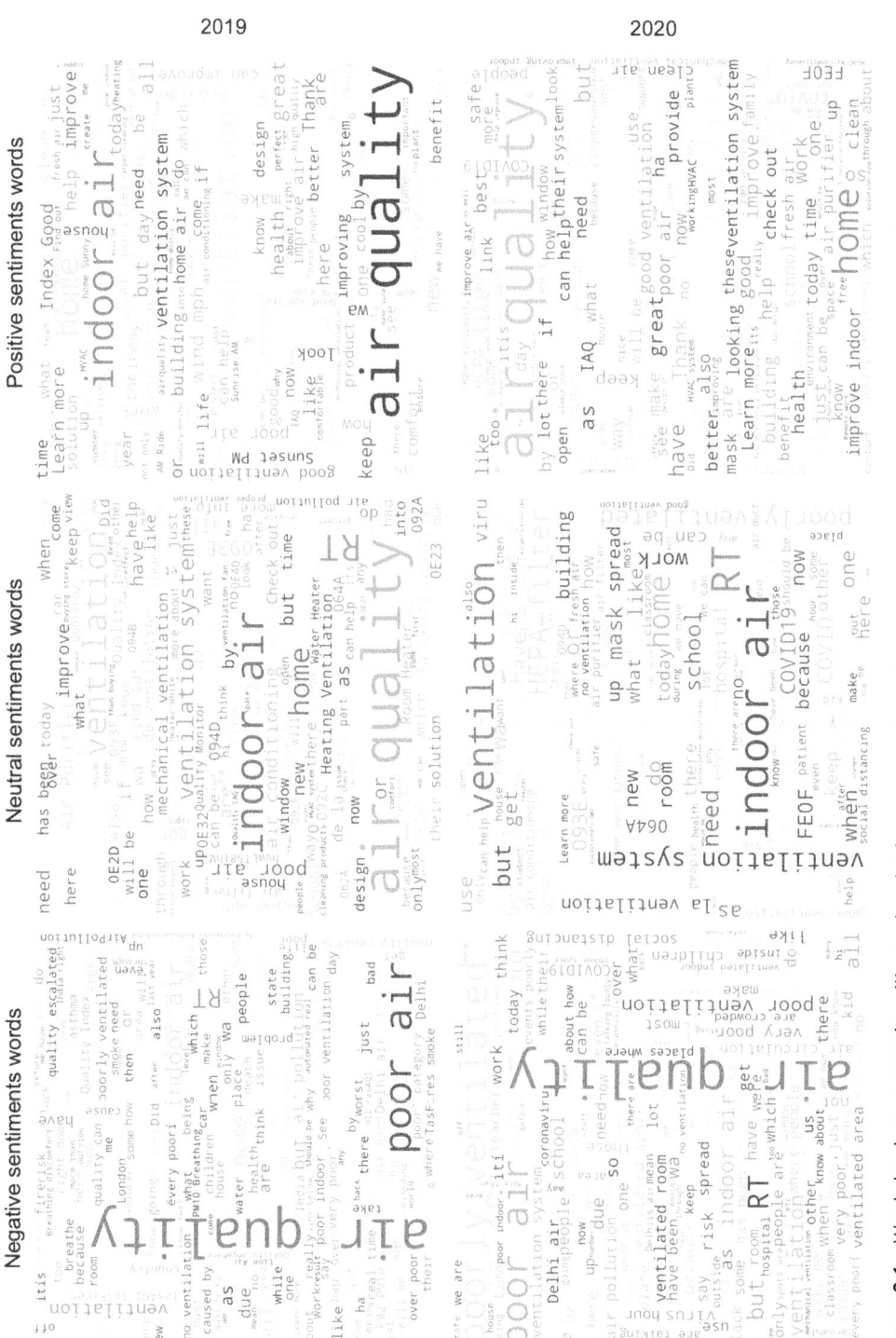

Figure 8.1 Word cloud representations illustrating the frequency and prominence of keywords associated with sentiments (Negative, Neutral, and Positive) towards IAQ for the years 2019 (top row) and 2020 (bottom row). The variation in keyword prevalence across the two years reflects the evolving public discourse on IAQ, notably influenced by the COVID-19 pandemic.

apprehension about air quality amidst the pandemic. This analysis underscores the dynamic nature of public sentiment and its responsiveness to global health crises. The pandemic has evidently steered the narrative around IAQ, urging a blend of concern and proactive discourse within the community. Such insights are instrumental in understanding public perception and can guide policymakers, stakeholders, and health experts in addressing IAQ issues, thereby contributing to enhanced public health measures and community well-being.

Figure 8.2 presents confidence distributions (histograms) for each sentiment category — negative, neutral, and positive — across the years 2019 and 2020. In 2019, the graph shows that the distribution of confidence values peaked at between 80% and 90% for both negative and neutral sentiments, while it peaked at between 50% and 60% for positive sentiments. This suggests that the model was considerably more certain in its classification of negative and neutral sentiments in 2019 compared to positive ones. Such a trend might reflect a more distinct or consistent usage of language patterns associated with negative and neutral sentiments in the sampled data for that year. It also raises questions about the factors contributing to this increased clarity and the potential nuances in language that rendered positive sentiment classifications with a lower confidence. In 2020, the distribution for negative and neutral sentiments remained the same as the year 2019, while the distribution for positive sentiments maintained a fairly constant trend post a confidence level of 50%, indicating that the challenges in classifying positive sentiments with higher confidence persisted into 2020. This might be because of a persisting lexical ambiguity or the prevalence of nuanced expressions in positive sentiment language that the model found challenging to decipher with high certainty. Further analysis may unveil more intricate linguistic patterns or external factors that could have influenced the model's performance in sentiment classification over the observed period.

In order to determine the optimal number of clusters for t-SNE plots for both the years 2019 and 2020, an elbow graph was constructed based on the sum of squared distances, facilitating the identification of a point where the reduction in inertia begins to diminish.

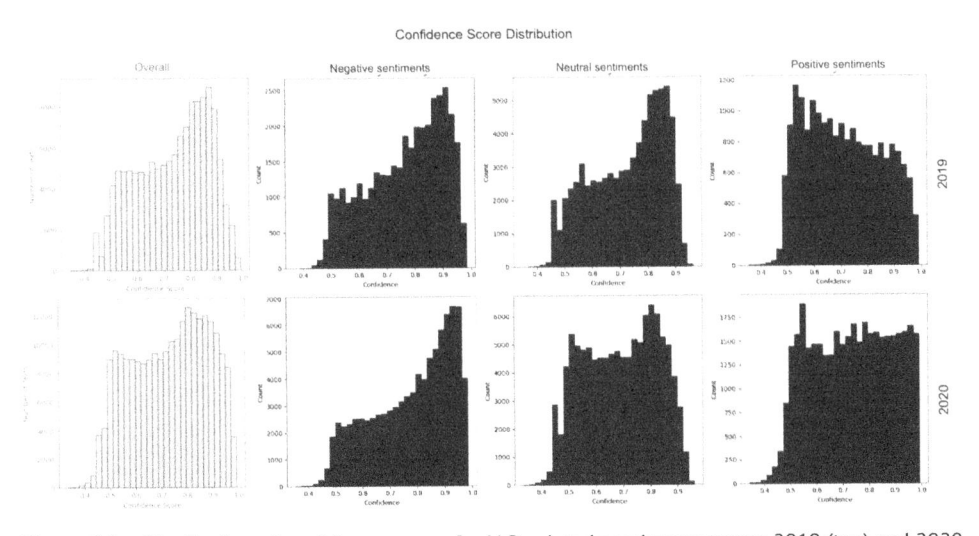

Figure 8.2 Distribution of confidence scores for IAQ-related sentiments across 2019 (top) and 2020 (bottom), shown both overall (left) and across sentiment categories: Negative, Neutral, and Positive (right).

176 | *8 Decoding Global Indoor Health Perception on Social Media Through NLP and Transformer Deep Learning*

This point, often referred to as the "elbow point," signifies a balance between minimizing within-cluster variance and limiting the number of clusters. The analysis identified that nine clusters (referred to as the "nine-cutter") were the most effective in capturing the inherent structure of the data for both years, thus providing a harmonized and robust segmentation for subsequent analysis (Figure 8.3). Following the determination of the optimal number of clusters, a t-SNE analysis was employed on the sentiment embeddings obtained from the RoBERTa model, which was trained on the corpus of X data pertaining to IAQ for 2019 and 2020 (Figure 8.4). The t-SNE technique was instrumental in reducing the dimensionality of the sentiment embeddings while preserving the local structure of the data, making it an ideal precursor to the clustering analysis. The subsequent k-means clustering, utilizing the pre-determined nine-cluster solution, unveiled distinct sentiment clusters within the two-dimensional t-SNE space. This configuration illustrated a demarcation of sentiment trends across the two years, thereby aiding in a deeper understanding of public sentiment dynamics regarding IAQ over the examined period.

Figures 8.5 and 8.6 showcase the attentiveness mechanism of the RoBERTa model while processing an actual sample text pulled from X platform twitted on 2020: "Poor indoor air quality can lead to the spread of airborne infectious diseases." Figure 8.5 illustrates a model-view perspective, exhibiting the attention patterns across all layers of the transformer

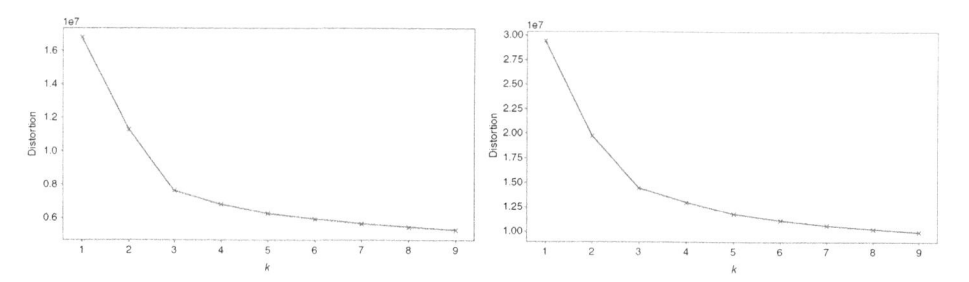

Figure 8.3 Elbow graph illustrating the sum of squared distances for different numbers of k-means clusters, indicating an optimal cluster count of nine for the year 2019 (left) and 2020 (right).

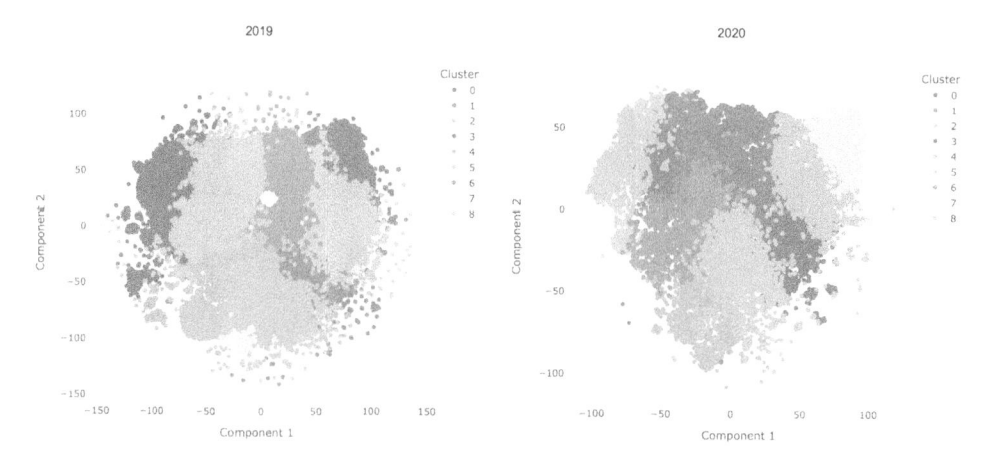

Figure 8.4 t-SNE visualization of RoBERTa-derived sentiment embeddings segmented by k-means clustering for the years 2019 (left) and 2020 (right), demonstrating the distribution and grouping of sentiments in a two-dimensional space.

Results and Discussion | 177

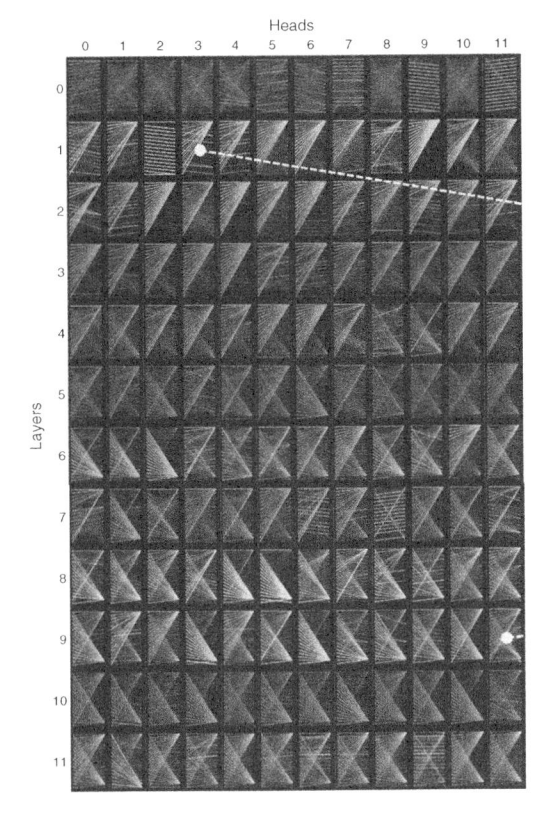

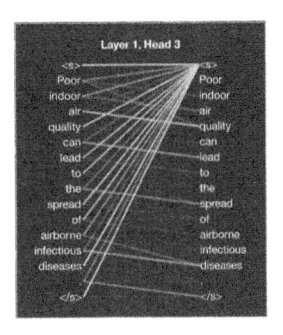

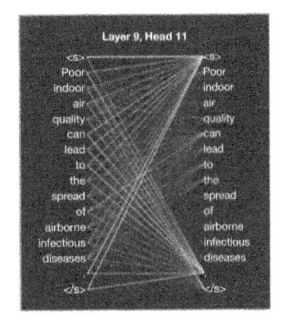

Figure 8.5 Model-view visualization depicting the progression of attention patterns across all layers (0–11) of the RoBERTa model while analyzing IAQ sentiments.

architecture from 0 to 11. Initial layers predominantly display localized attention, concentrating on adjacent tokens to capture syntactic relations. As the narrative advances through layers, a broader semantic comprehension is depicted through more distributed attention patterns, reflecting the model's deepening understanding of contextual relationships within the text. Figure 8.6 transitions to a head-view perspective, providing a more granular insight into individual attention heads within a selected layer. Each head, potentially learning different textual features, collectively contributes to the model's ability to grasp diverse syntactic and semantic relations across tokens. Notably, special tokens, (CLS) and (SEP), serve crucial roles in global sentence representation and sentence boundary demarcation, respectively. Together, these visualizations elucidate the intricate dynamics of how the RoBERTa model interprets text, shedding light on the complex inter-token relationships. This graphical representation forms a robust foundation for understanding the underlying mechanisms driving transformer-based models in analyzing sentiments pertaining to IAQ, thereby enriching our methodology in environmental health research leveraging NLP frameworks.

Figure 8.7 depicts Neuron Activation Heatmap. This graph showcases the attention scores across different tokens in the input text, within the first attention head of the first layer of the "RoBERTa-base" model. Each cell in the heatmap indicates the attention score between a pair of tokens, illustrating how each token attends to every other token in the phrase "Poor indoor air quality can lead to the spread of airborne infectious diseases." The color

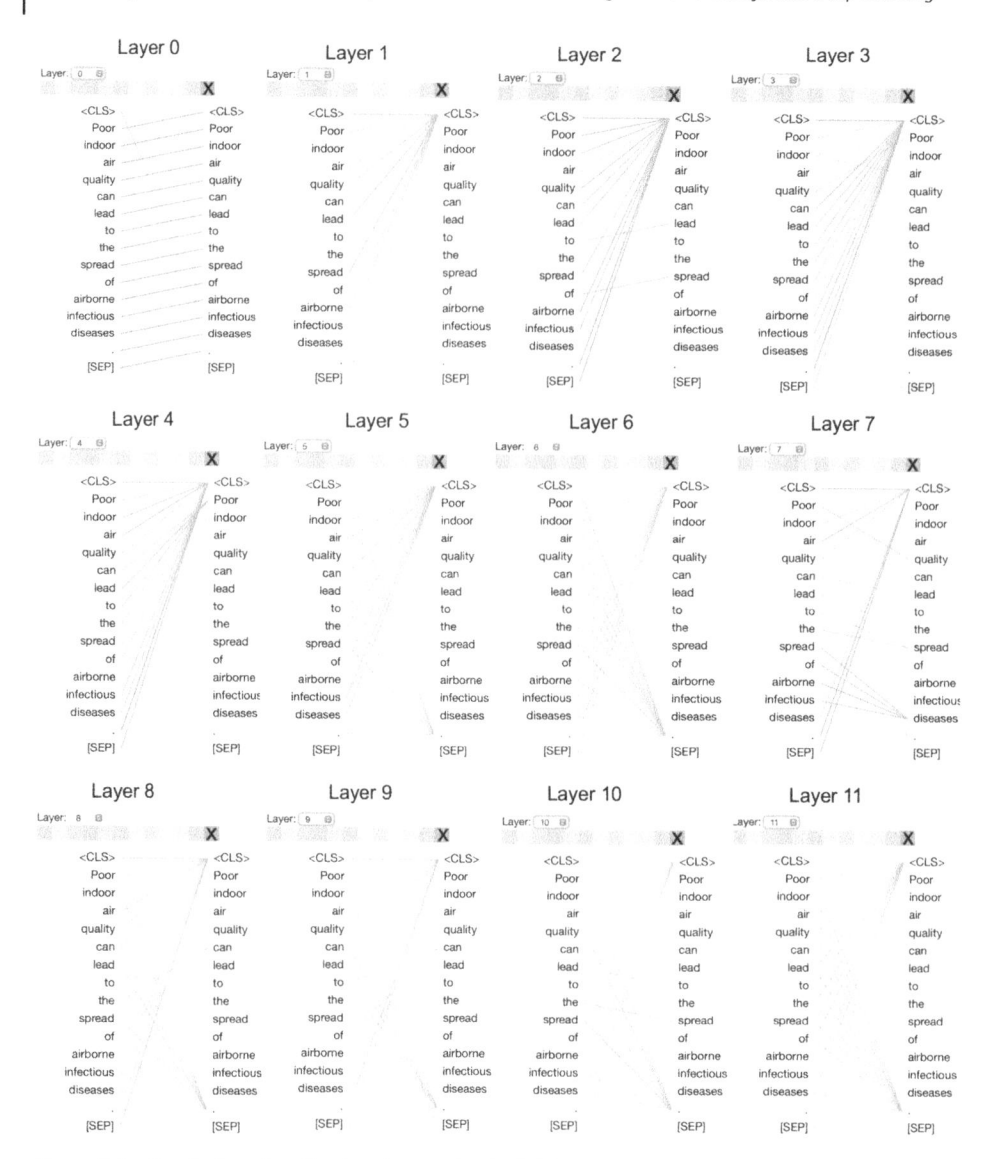

Figure 8.6 Head-view visualization showcasing individual attention heads within a selected layer, unraveling diverse inter-token relationships in the analysis of IAQ sentiments.

intensity — ranging from cool (low attention scores) to warm (high attention scores) — reflects the magnitude of attention each token receives from others.

Conclusion

This chapter delved into the intersection of digital media, communication technologies, and environmental health to better understand modern cities, particularly focusing on IAQ amidst the global pandemic. Utilizing the transformative capabilities of NLP through the RoBERTa algorithm, a significant shift in public perception regarding IAQ was uncovered

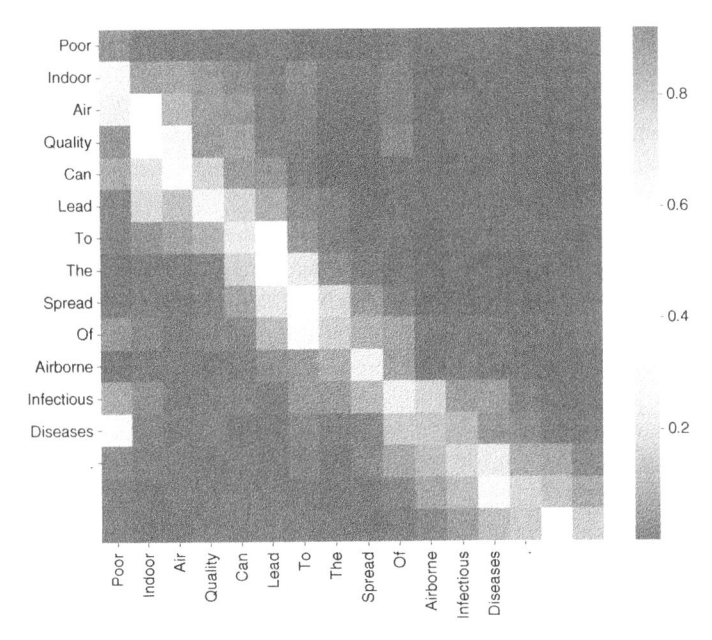

Figure 8.7 Heatmap displaying attention scores between tokens in the first attention head of "RoBERTa-base" model's first layer, highlighting how tokens attend to each other in assessing IAQ and disease spread.

between the years 2019 and 2020. This analysis, based on real-world feedback harvested from the X platform, highlighted a notable increase in negative perceptions towards IAQ following the enforcement of stay-at-home orders. The findings accentuate the potential of employing social media analytics in environmental health research, offering a novel lens to evaluate and adapt to rapidly changing global circumstances like the COVID-19 pandemic. This exploration also underscores the urgency for architects, urban planners, and policymakers to prioritize IAQ in their design and policy considerations to better align with public sentiment and health recommendations. Moving forward, the application of advanced NLP techniques on a larger scale could significantly contribute to a more nuanced understanding of urban health challenges, thereby guiding more effective, data-driven decision-making in urban planning and environmental health strategies.

References

Abdulaali, H.S., Usman, I.M.S., and Hanafiah, M.M. (2020). Online Review Analysis of Perceived Indoor Environmental Quality (IEQ) at Former Green Certified Hotels in Kuala Lumpur, Malaysia. *Journal of Xi'an University Of Architecture & Technology* 14: 659–670.

Allen, J.G. and Ibrahim, A.M. (2021). Indoor Air Changes and Potential Implications for SARS-CoV-2 Transmission. *The Journal of American Medical Association* 325 (20): 2112. https://doi.org/10.1001/jama.2021.5053.

Antons, D., Grünwald, E., Cichy, P., and Salge, T.O. (2020). The Application of Text Mining Methods in Innovation Research: Current State, Evolution Patterns, and Development Priorities. *R&D Management* 50 (3): 329–351. https://doi.org/10.1111/radm.12408.

Barbieri, F., Camacho-Collados, J., Neves, L., and Espinosa-Anke, L. (2020). TweetEval: Unified Benchmark and Comparative Evaluation for Tweet Classification. *arXiv* http://arxiv.org/abs/2010.12421.

Bardhan, I.R., Demirkan, H., Kannan, P.K. et al. (2010). An Interdisciplinary Perspective on IT Services Management and Service Science. *Journal of Management Information Systems* 26 (4): 13–64. https://doi.org/10.2753/MIS0742-1222260402.

Bazzaz, A., Sepideh, M.H., Kashani, E.M., and Jameii, S.M. (2021). Big Data Analytics Meets Social Media: A Systematic Review of Techniques, Open Issues, and Future Directions. *Telematics and Informatics* 57 (March): 101517. https://doi.org/10.1016/j.tele.2020.101517.

Bisanzio, D., Kraemer, M.U.G., Bogoch, I.I. et al. (2020). Use of Twitter Social Media Activity as a Proxy for Human Mobility to Predict the Spatiotemporal Spread of COVID-19 at Global Scale. *Geospatial Health* 15 (1): https://doi.org/10.4081/gh.2020.882.

Bollen, J., Mao, H., and Zeng, X.-J. (2011). Twitter Mood Predicts the Stock Market. *Journal of Computational Science* 2 (1): 1–8. https://doi.org/10.1016/j.jocs.2010.12.007.

Broniatowski, D.A., Paul, M.J., and Dredze, M. (2013). National and Local Influenza Surveillance Through Twitter: An Analysis of the 2012–2013 Influenza Epidemic. Edited by Tobias Preis. *PLoS One* 8 (12): e83672. https://doi.org/10.1371/journal.pone.0083672.

Brown, Tom B., Benjamin Mann, Nick Ryder, Melanie Subbiah, Jared Kaplan, Prafulla Dhariwal, Arvind Neelakantan, et al. 2020. "Language Models Are Few-Shot Learners." https://doi.org/10.48550/ARXIV.2005.14165.

Chan, H.-Y., Cheung, K.K.C., and Erduran, S. (2023). Science Communication in the Media and Human Mobility during the COVID-19 Pandemic: A Time Series and Content Analysis. *Public Health* 218 (May): 106–113. https://doi.org/10.1016/j.puhe.2023.03.001.

Chen, J. and Wang, Y. (2021). Social Media Use for Health Purposes: Systematic Review. *Journal of Medical Internet Research* 23 (5): e17917. https://doi.org/10.2196/17917.

Chinazzo, G. (2021). Geographical Distribution of the Sources of IEQ Complaints: An Analysis through Text-Mining of Online Job Reviews. *Journal of Physics: Conference Series* 2069 (1): 012176. https://doi.org/10.1088/1742-6596/2069/1/012176.

Chomsky, N. (1957). *Syntactic Structures*. De Gruyter https://doi.org/10.1515/9783112316009.

Clark, Kevin, Minh-Thang Luong, Quoc V. Le, and Christopher D. Manning. 2020. "ELECTRA: Pre-Training Text Encoders as Discriminators Rather Than Generators." https://doi.org/10.48550/ARXIV.2003.10555.

Collins, M. (2002). Discriminative Training Methods for Hidden Markov Models: Theory and Experiments with Perceptron Algorithms. In: *Proceedings of the ACL-02 Conference on Empirical Methods in Natural Language Processing—EMNLP'02*, vol. Vol. 10, 1–8. Association for Computational Linguistics https://doi.org/10.3115/1118693.1118694.

Daelemans, W., van der Sloot, K., Zavrel, J., and van den Bosch, A.P.J. (2002). *TiMBL: Tilburg Memory Based Learner*, vol. Vols. 3–10. TILBURG: Faculteit Communicatie en Cultuur.

Dawson, N.M., Grogan, K., Martin, A. et al. (2017). Environmental Justice Research Shows the Importance of Social Feedbacks in Ecosystem Service Trade-Offs. *Ecology and Society* 22 (3): art12. https://doi.org/10.5751/ES-09481-220312.

Deerwester, S., Dumais, S.T., Furnas, G.W. et al. (1990). Indexing by Latent Semantic Analysis. *Journal of the American Society for Information Science* 41 (6): 391–407. https://doi.org/10.1002/(SICI)1097-4571(199009)41:6<391::AID-ASI1>3.0.CO;2-9.

Devlin, Jacob, Ming-Wei Chang, Kenton Lee, and Kristina Toutanova. 2018. "BERT: Pre-Training of Deep Bidirectional Transformers for Language Understanding." https://doi.org/10.48550/ARXIV.1810.04805.

Diaz, F., Gamon, M., Hofman, J.M. et al. (2016). Online and Social Media Data As an Imperfect Continuous Panel Survey. Edited by Cédric Sueur. *PLoS One* 11 (1): e0145406. https://doi.org/10.1371/journal.pone.0145406.

Fen, S.-N. (1969). Marshall McLuhan's 'Understanding Media'. *The Journal of Educational Thought (JET) / Revue de La Pensée Éducative* 3 (3): 161–180.

Flaxman, S., Mishra, S., Axel Gandy, H. et al. (2020). Estimating the Effects of Non-Pharmaceutical Interventions on COVID-19 in Europe. *Nature* 584 (7820): 257–261. https://doi.org/10.1038/s41586-020-2405-7.

Ghermandi, A., Langemeyer, J., Van Berkel, D. et al. (2023). Social Media Data for Environmental Sustainability: A Critical Review of Opportunities, Threats, and Ethical Use. *One Earth* 6 (3): 236–250. https://doi.org/10.1016/j.oneear.2023.02.008.

Goodfellow, I., Bengio, Y., and Courville, A. (2016). *Deep Learning*. In: *Adaptive Computation and Machine Learning*. Cambridge, Massachusetts: The MIT Press.

Greco, F. and Polli, A. (2021). Security Perception and People Well-Being. *Social Indicators Research* 153 (2): 741–758. https://doi.org/10.1007/s11205-020-02341-8.

Harris, Z.S. (1954). Distributional Structure. *WORD* 10 (2–3): 146–162. https://doi.org/10.1080/00437956.1954.11659520.

Hawelka, B., Sitko, I., Beinat, E. et al. (2014). Geo-Located Twitter as Proxy for Global Mobility Patterns. *Cartography and Geographic Information Science* 41 (3): 260–271. https://doi.org/10.1080/15230406.2014.890072.

Hochreiter, S. and Schmidhuber, J. (1997). Long Short-Term Memory. *Neural Computation* 9 (8): 1735–1780. https://doi.org/10.1162/neco.1997.9.8.1735.

Hswen, Y., Qin, Q., Brownstein, J.S., and Hawkins, J.B. (2019). Feasibility of Using Social Media to Monitor Outdoor Air Pollution in London, England. *Preventive Medicine* 121 (April): 86–93. https://doi.org/10.1016/j.ypmed.2019.02.005.

Hutto, C. and Gilbert, E. (2014). VADER: A Parsimonious Rule-Based Model for Sentiment Analysis of Social Media Text. *Proceedings of the International AAAI Conference on Web and Social Media* 8 (1): 216–225. https://doi.org/10.1609/icwsm.v8i1.14550.

Jiang, W., Wang, Y., Tsou, M.-H., and Xiaokang, F. (2015). Using Social Media to Detect Outdoor Air Pollution and Monitor Air Quality Index (AQI): A Geo-Targeted Spatiotemporal Analysis Framework with Sina Weibo (Chinese Twitter). Edited by Luís A. Nunes Amaral. *PLoS One* 10 (10): e0141185. https://doi.org/10.1371/journal.pone.0141185.

Jiang, J.-Y., Xue, S., Wang, W., and Young, S. (2019). Enhancing Air Quality Prediction with Social Media and Natural Language Processing. In: *Proceedings of the 57th Annual Meeting of the Association for Computational Linguistics*, 2627–2632. Florence, Italy: Association for Computational Linguistics https://doi.org/10.18653/v1/P19-1251.

Joachims, T. (1998). Text Categorization with Support Vector Machines: Learning with Many Relevant Features. *Machine Learning ECML-98*: 137–142.

Johnson, S. (2001). *Emergence: The Connected Lives of Ants, Brains, Cities, and Software*. New York: Scribner.

Jurafsky, D. and Martin, J.H. (2009). *Speech and Language Processing: An Introduction to Natural Language Processing, Computational Linguistics, and Speech Recognition*. In: *Prentice Hall Series in Artificial Intelligence*, 2nde. Upper Saddle River, NJ: Pearson Prentice Hall.

Jurdak, R., Zhao, K., Liu, J. et al. (2015). Understanding Human Mobility from Twitter. Edited by Ye Wu. *PLoS One* 10 (7): e0131469. https://doi.org/10.1371/journal.pone.0131469.

Kaplan, A.M. and Haenlein, M. (2010). Users of the World, Unite! The Challenges and Opportunities of Social Media. *Business Horizons* 53 (1): 59–68. https://doi.org/10.1016/j.bushor.2009.09.003.

Ketchen, D.J. Jr. and Shook, C.L. (1996). The Application of Cluster Analysis in Strategic Management Research: An Analysis and Critique. *Strategic Management Journal* 17 (6): 441–458. https://doi.org/10.1002/(SICI)1097-0266(199606)17:6<441::AID-SMJ819>3.0.CO;2-G.

Kishore, N., Taylor, A.R., Jacob, P.E. et al. (2021). The Relationship between Human Mobility Measures and SAR-Cov-2 Transmission Varies by Epidemic Phase and Urbanicity: Results from the United States." Preprint. *Epidemiology* https://doi.org/10.1101/2021.04.15.21255562.

Lafferty, J., McCallum, A., and Pereira, F. (2001). Conditional Random Fields: Probabilistic Models for Segmenting and Labeling Sequence Data. In: *ICML'01: Proceedings of the Eighteenth International Conference on Machine Learning*. Morgan Kaufmann Publishers Inc.

Lecun, Y., Bottou, L., Bengio, Y., and Haffner, P. (1998). Gradient-Based Learning Applied to Document Recognition. *Proceedings of the IEEE* 86 (11): 2278–2324. https://doi.org/10.1109/5.726791.

Lewis, D.D. and Jones, K.S. (1996). Natural Language Processing for Information Retrieval. *Communications of the ACM* 39 (1): 92–101. https://doi.org/10.1145/234173.234210.

Lewis, Mike, Yinhan Liu, Naman Goyal, Marjan Ghazvininejad, Abdelrahman Mohamed, Omer Levy, Ves Stoyanov, and Luke Zettlemoyer. 2019. "BART: Denoising Sequence-to-Sequence Pre-Training for Natural Language Generation, Translation, and Comprehension." https://doi.org/10.48550/ARXIV.1910.13461.

Liu, Yinhan, Myle Ott, Naman Goyal, Jingfei Du, Mandar Joshi, Danqi Chen, Omer Levy, Mike Lewis, Luke Zettlemoyer, and Veselin Stoyanov. 2019. "RoBERTa: A Robustly Optimized BERT Pretraining Approach." https://doi.org/10.48550/ARXIV.1907.11692.

Lloyd, S. (1982). Least Squares Quantization in PCM. *IEEE Transactions on Information Theory* 28 (2): 129–137. https://doi.org/10.1109/TIT.1982.1056489.

Lopez, B.E., Magliocca, N.R., and Crooks, A.T. (2019). Challenges and Opportunities of Social Media Data for Socio-Environmental Systems Research. *Land* 8 (7): 107. https://doi.org/10.3390/land8070107.

Ma, N., Zhang, Q., Murai, F. et al. (2023). Learning Building Occupants Indoor Environmental Quality Complaints and Dissatisfaction from Text-Mining Booking.Com Reviews in the United States. *Building and Environment* 237 (June): 110319. https://doi.org/10.1016/j.buildenv.2023.110319.

Maaten, L.v.d. and Hinton, G. (2008). Visualizing Data Using T-SNE. *The Journal of Machine Learning Research* 9 (2579–2605): 85.

MacQueen, J.B. (1967). Some Methods for Classification and Analysis of MultiVariate Observations. In: *Proceedings of the 5th Berkeley Symposium on Mathematical Statistics and Probability*, vol. Vol 1, 281–297. California: University of California Press.

Magerman, D.M. (1995). Statistical Decision-Tree Models for Parsing. In: *Proceedings of the 33rd Annual Meeting on Association for Computational Linguistics*, 276–283. Cambridge, MA: Association for Computational Linguistics https://doi.org/10.3115/981658.981695.

Manning, C.D., Raghavan, P., and Schütze, H. (2008). *Introduction to Information Retrieval*, 1st ed. Cambridge University Press https://doi.org/10.1017/CBO9780511809071.

Manning, C., Surdeanu, M., Bauer, J. et al. (2014). The Stanford CoreNLP Natural Language Processing Toolkit. In: *Proceedings of 52nd Annual Meeting of the Association for*

Computational Linguistics: System Demonstrations, 55–60. Baltimore, MA: Association for Computational Linguistics https://doi.org/10.3115/v1/P14-5010.

McCallum, A. and Nigam, K. (1998). A Comparison of Event Models for Naive Bayes Text Classification. In: *AAAI Conference on Artificial Intelligence*.

McLuhan, M. (1994). *Understanding Media: The Extensions of Man*, 1st MIT Presse. Cambridge, MA: MIT Press.

Mikolov, Tomas, Kai Chen, Greg Corrado, and Jeffrey Dean. 2013a. "Efficient Estimation of Word Representations in Vector Space." https://doi.org/10.48550/ARXIV.1301.3781.

Mikolov, Tomas, Ilya Sutskever, Kai Chen, Greg Corrado, and Jeffrey Dean. 2013b. "Distributed Representations of Words and Phrases and Their Compositionality." https://doi.org/10.48550/ARXIV.1310.4546.

Miller, A.R. (1971). *The Assault on Privacy: Computers, Data Banks, and Dossiers*. Berichte Der Universitaet von Michigan. Ann Arbor: University of Michigan Press.

Moezzi, M. and Goins, J. (2011). Text Mining for Occupant Perspectives on the Physical Workplace. *Building Research & Information* 39 (2): 169–182. https://doi.org/10.1080/09613218.2011.556008.

Mohammadi, N. and Taylor, J.E. (2017). Urban Energy Flux: Spatiotemporal Fluctuations of Building Energy Consumption and Human Mobility-Driven Prediction. *Applied Energy* 195 (June): 810–818. https://doi.org/10.1016/j.apenergy.2017.03.044.

Montanaro, T., Sergi, I., Basile, M. et al. (2022). An IoT-Aware Solution to Support Governments in Air Pollution Monitoring Based on the Combination of Real-Time Data and Citizen Feedback. *Sensors* 22 (3): 1000. https://doi.org/10.3390/s22031000.

Morawska, L. and Cao, J. (2020). Airborne Transmission of SARS-CoV-2: The World Should Face the Reality. *Environment International* 139 (June): 105730. https://doi.org/10.1016/j.envint.2020.105730.

Nadkarni, P.M., Ohno-Machado, L., and Chapman, W.W. (2011). Natural Language Processing: An Introduction. *Journal of the American Medical Informatics Association* 18 (5): 544–551. https://doi.org/10.1136/amiajnl-2011-000464.

Nicola, M., Alsafi, Z., Sohrabi, C. et al. (2020). The Socio-Economic Implications of the Coronavirus Pandemic (COVID-19): A Review. *International Journal of Surgery* 78 (June): 185–193. https://doi.org/10.1016/j.ijsu.2020.04.018.

Parkinson, T., Schiavon, S., de Dear, R., and Brager, G. (2021). Overcooling of Offices Reveals Gender Inequity in Thermal Comfort. *Scientific Reports* 11 (1): 23684. https://doi.org/10.1038/s41598-021-03121-1.

Paul, M. and Dredze, M. (2021). You Are What You Tweet: Analyzing Twitter for Public Health. *Proceedings of the International AAAI Conference on Web and Social Media* 5 (1): 265–272. https://doi.org/10.1609/icwsm.v5i1.14137.

Pennington, J., Socher, R., and Manning, C. (2014). Glove: Global Vectors for Word Representation. In: *Proceedings of the 2014 Conference on Empirical Methods in Natural Language Processing (EMNLP)*, 1532–1543. Doha, Qatar: Association for Computational Linguistics https://doi.org/10.3115/v1/D14-1162.

Peters, Matthew E., Mark Neumann, Mohit Iyyer, Matt Gardner, Christopher Clark, Kenton Lee, and Luke Zettlemoyer. 2018. "Deep Contextualized Word Representations." https://doi.org/10.48550/ARXIV.1802.05365.

Pilař, L., Stanislavská, L.K., Pitrová, J. et al. (2019). Twitter Analysis of Global Communication in the Field of Sustainability. *Sustainability* 11 (24): 6958. https://doi.org/10.3390/su11246958.

Postman, N. (2006). *Amusing Ourselves to Death: Public Discourse in the Age of Show Business*, 20th Anniversarye. New York, NY, USA: Penguin Books.

Pramanik, P., Mondal, T., Nandi, S., and Saha, M. (2020). AirCalypse: Can Twitter Help in Urban Air Quality Measurement and Who are the Influential Users? In: *Companion Proceedings of the Web Conference 2020*, 540–545. Taipei, Taiwan: ACM https://doi.org/10.1145/3366424.3382120.

Rabiner, L.R. (1989). A Tutorial on Hidden Markov Models and Selected Applications in Speech Recognition. *Proceedings of the IEEE* 77 (2): 257–286. https://doi.org/10.1109/5.18626.

Radford, Alec, Karthik Narasimhan, Tim Salimans, and Ilya Sutskever. 2018. "Improving Language Understanding with Unsupervised Learning." https://s3-us-west-2.amazonaws.com/openai-assets/research-covers/language-unsupervised/language_understanding_paper.pdf.

Radford, Alec, Jeffrey Wu, Rewon Child, David Luan, Dario Amodei, and Ilya Sutskever. 2019. "Language Models are Unsupervised Multitask Learners." https://cdn.openai.com/better-language-models/language_models_are_unsupervised_multitask_learners.pdf.

Raffel, Colin, Noam Shazeer, Adam Roberts, Katherine Lee, Sharan Narang, Michael Matena, Yanqi Zhou, Wei Li, and Peter J. Liu. 2019. "Exploring the Limits of Transfer Learning with a Unified Text-to-Text Transformer." https://doi.org/10.48550/ARXIV.1910.10683.

Ratnaparkhi, A. (1996). A Maximum Entropy Model for Part-of-Speech Tagging. *Proceedings of the Conference on Empirical Methods in Natural Language Processing* 1: 133–142. https://aclanthology.org/W96-0213.

Roesslein, Joshua. 2020. "Tweepy: Twitter for Python!" https://github.com/tweepy/tweepy.

Romero-Silva, R. and de Leeuw, S. (2021). Learning from the Past to Shape the Future: A Comprehensive Text Mining Analysis of OR/MS Reviews. *Omega* 100 (April): 102388. https://doi.org/10.1016/j.omega.2020.102388.

Sachdeva, S. and McCaffrey, S. (2018). Using Social Media to Predict Air Pollution during California Wildfires. In: *Proceedings of the 9th International Conference on Social Media and Society*, 365–369. Copenhagen Denmark: ACM https://doi.org/10.1145/3217804.3217946.

Salamone, F., Barozzi, B., Bellazzi, A. et al. (2021). Working from Home in Italy During COVID-19 Lockdown: A Survey to Assess the Indoor Environmental Quality and Productivity. *Buildings* 11 (12): 660. https://doi.org/10.3390/buildings11120660.

Salathé, M., Bengtsson, L., Bodnar, T.J. et al. (2012). Digital Epidemiology. Edited by Philip E. Bourne. *PLoS Computational Biology* 8 (7): e1002616. https://doi.org/10.1371/journal.pcbi.1002616.

Salton, G. and McGill, M.J. (1983). *Introduction to Modern Information Retrieval. McGraw-Hill Computer Science Series*. New York: McGraw-Hill.

Schapire, R. and Singer, Y. (2000). BoosTexter: A Boosting-Based System for Text Categorization. *Springer Link* 39: 135–168. https://doi.org/10.1023/a:1007649029923.

Schuster, M. and Paliwal, K.K. (1997). Bidirectional Recurrent Neural Networks. *IEEE Transactions on Signal Processing* 45 (11): 2673–2681. https://doi.org/10.1109/78.650093.

Shannon, C.E. (1948). A Mathematical Theory of Communication. *Bell System Technical Journal* 27 (3): 379–423. https://doi.org/10.1002/j.1538-7305.1948.tb01338.x.

Shannon, C.E. (1951). Prediction and Entropy of Printed English. *Bell System Technical Journal* 30 (1): 50–64. https://doi.org/10.1002/j.1538-7305.1951.tb01366.x.

Shelton, T., Poorthuis, A., Graham, M., and Zook, M. (2014). Mapping the Data Shadows of Hurricane Sandy: Uncovering the Sociospatial Dimensions of 'Big Data'. *Geoforum* 52 (March): 167–179. https://doi.org/10.1016/j.geoforum.2014.01.006.

Shelton, T., Poorthuis, A., and Zook, M. (2015). Social Media and the City: Rethinking Urban Socio-Spatial Inequality Using User-Generated Geographic Information. *Landscape and Urban Planning* 142 (October): 198–211. https://doi.org/10.1016/j.landurbplan.2015.02.020.

Shirky, C. (2008). *Here Comes Everybody: The Power of Organizing without Organizations*. New York: Penguin Press.

Skill, K., Passero, S., and Francisco, M. (2021). Assembling Amazon Fires through English Hashtags. Materializing Environmental Activism within Twitter Networks. *Computer Supported Cooperative Work (CSCW) 30* (5–6): 715–732. https://doi.org/10.1007/s10606-021-09403-6.

Stefanidis, A., Vraga, E., Lamprianidis, G. et al. (2017). Zika in Twitter: Temporal Variations of Locations, Actors, and Concepts. *JMIR Public Health and Surveillance* 3 (2): e22. https://doi.org/10.2196/publichealth.6925.

Sullivan, J. and Xie, L. (2009). Environmental Activism, Social Networks and the Internet. *The China Quarterly* 198 (June): 422–432. https://doi.org/10.1017/S0305741009000381.

Thorndike, R.L. (1953). Who Belongs in the Family? *Psychometrika* 18 (4): 267–276. https://doi.org/10.1007/BF02289263.

University of Liechtenstein, Debortoli, S., Müller, O. et al. (2016). Text Mining for Information Systems Researchers: An Annotated Topic Modeling Tutorial. *Communications of the Association for Information Systems* 39: 110–135. https://doi.org/10.17705/1CAIS.03907.

Vaswani, Ashish, Noam Shazeer, Niki Parmar, Jakob Uszkoreit, Llion Jones, Aidan N. Gomez, Lukasz Kaiser, and Illia Polosukhin. 2017. "Attention Is All You Need." https://doi.org/10.48550/ARXIV.1706.03762.

Vig, Jesse. 2019. "A Multiscale Visualization of Attention in the Transformer Model." https://doi.org/10.48550/ARXIV.1906.05714.

Villeneuve, H. and O'Brien, W. (2020). Listen to the Guests: Text-Mining Airbnb Reviews to Explore Indoor Environmental Quality. *Building and Environment* 169 (February): 106555. https://doi.org/10.1016/j.buildenv.2019.106555.

Wang, J. and Jia, Y. (2021). Social Media's Influence on Air Quality Improvement: Evidence from China. *Journal of Cleaner Production* 298 (May): 126769. https://doi.org/10.1016/j.jclepro.2021.126769.

Winograd, T. (1972). Understanding Natural Language. *Cognitive Psychology* 3 (1): 1–191. https://doi.org/10.1016/0010-0285(72)90002-3.

Yang, Y. and Liu, X. (1999). A Re-Examination of Text Categorization Methods. In: *Proceedings of the 22nd Annual International ACM SIGIR Conference on Research and Development in Information Retrieval*, 42–49. Berkeley, CA, USA: ACM https://doi.org/10.1145/312624.312647.

Yue, A., Mao, C., Chen, L. et al. (2022). Detecting Changes in Perceptions Towards Smart City on Chinese Social Media: A Text Mining and Sentiment Analysis. *Buildings* 12 (8): 1182. https://doi.org/10.3390/buildings12081182.

Zhang, L., Brikell, I., Dalsgaard, S., and Chang, Z. (2021). Public Mobility and Social Media Attention in Response to COVID-19 in Sweden and Denmark. *JAMA Network Open* 4 (1): e2033478. https://doi.org/10.1001/jamanetworkopen.2020.33478.

9

Occupant-Driven Urban Building Energy Efficiency via Ambient Intelligence

Narjes Abbasabadi[1] and Mehdi Ashayeri[2]

[1] Department of Architecture, School of Architecture, College of Built Environments, University of Washington, Seattle, WA, USA
[2] School of Architecture, College of Arts and Media, Southern Illinois University Carbondale, Carbondale, IL, USA

Introduction

Cities are major contributors to global energy consumption and associated emissions (IPCC 2014), with buildings being the primary energy consumers (US EPA 2017). To combat climate change, many cities worldwide, including those in the United States, have adopted climate action plans to achieve net-zero emissions by 2050. Human dimensions including occupancy, occupant behavior, and socioeconomic aspects are identified as strong drivers of energy use in buildings (Hong, D'Oca, Turner, et al. 2015; Abbasabadi and Ashayeri 2021; Harputlugil and de Wilde 2021). Therefore, considering the human aspects of energy use in the building's lifecycle, from design to operation, is crucial for effective design and management and ultimately contributes to meeting energy reduction goals and combating climate change as a global priority (Mata et al. 2022). Occupant monitoring, occupant modeling, and energy feedback systems are the key approaches for bringing humans into the process of urban building energy optimization and improving energy efficiency and energy management in cities and promoting sustainability and built environment decarbonization at scale (Happle, Fonseca, and Schlueter 2018; Laaroussi et al. 2020; Ali et al. 2021; Dabirian, Panchabikesan, and Eicker 2022).

Here, occupancy refers to occupant presence and absence schedule in the given space, whereas occupant behavior refers to occupant interactions with building systems (Happle, Fonseca, and Schlueter 2018 and Dabirian, Panchabikesan, and Eicker 2022). Psychological, sociological, and economic theories have been applied to understand interactions of occupants with one or multiple building energy systems (Heydarian et al. 2020), and many research studies executed on occupant behavior in buildings and cities and how they influence energy use (Salim et al. 2020).

There is a significant body of research on the impacts of human dimensions on energy consumption (D'Oca, Hong, and Langevin 2018; Harputlugil and de Wilde 2021). A review by D'Oca, Hong, and Langevin (2018) discusses the impact of human factors on building energy use across various stages of the building lifecycle, with different stakeholders involved. Designers need data, models, tools, and case studies to provide an evidence-based

Artificial Intelligence in Performance-Driven Design: Theories, Methods, and Tools, First Edition.
Edited by Narjes Abbasabadi and Mehdi Ashayeri.
©2024 John Wiley & Sons Inc. Published 2024 by John Wiley & Sons Inc.

understanding of the human dimensions of energy use in the planning and design stages. In the operational stage, occupants need to learn and understand the operation of building systems to achieve comfort and minimize energy use, while during the construction and regulation phases, it is important to understand how occupants use products from vendors and manufacturers. Policymakers need to provide regulations for the human-sensitive stream of data and better understand the impact of human dimensions on building energy use. In addition, many research studies exist on common approaches and tools for occupancy modeling (Yan et al. 2015; Harputlugil and de Wilde 2021; Dabirian, Panchabikesan, and Eicker 2022) and monitoring (Olivia and Christopher 2015; Dziedzic, Da, and Novakovic 2019). The design and planning phase often rely on modeling and simulation with limitations in data availability regarding dynamic human aspects resulting in uncertainty and discrepancy between predicted and measured energy data.

An iterative process can be followed to implement and integrate realistic occupancy and occupant behavior factors into building energy modeling platforms, including collecting data via occupant monitoring, developing occupancy and occupant behavior models, evaluating the model, and implementing it into design and energy simulation tools (Yan et al. 2015). Literature indicates the need to integrate behavioral rules into modeling and design frameworks, requiring data collection to gain insight into various design scenarios. In addition, literature on occupant behavior in building energy policy (BEP) has identified key questions and challenges related to building technical standards and regulations, building information policies, building energy incentives, and BEP evaluations and the way forward (Hu et al. 2020).

Occupant-related inputs are significant parameters that influence energy simulation accuracy at both the building and urban levels (Dabirian, Panchabikesan, and Eicker 2022). Modeling occupancy patterns that describe occupant presence or absence is a crucial first step in the stochastic modeling of occupant behavior and is critical to the energy modeling of buildings (Gaetani, Hoes, and Hensen 2016; Chen et al. 2022). In order to model occupant behavior, it is important to develop occupant presence and action models that describe the presence, absence, and movement of occupants in spaces, as well as various types of adaptive and nonadaptive behavior, such as adjusting blinds, opening windows, switching lights, and the use of appliances (Happle, Fonseca, and Schlueter 2018). Fixed occupant schedules have commonly been used in urban-scale building energy modeling due to a lack of dynamic occupancy data and to validate the predictions of developed models (Dabirian, Panchabikesan, and Eicker 2022; Dong et al. 2021; Happle, Fonseca, and Schlueter 2018). However, the proliferation of occupant-centric big data, such as IoT, sensor-based, and mobility data, has paved the way to model occupant behavior at a neighborhood, district, or city scale (Dabirian, Panchabikesan, and Eicker 2022). Datasets that cover occupancy data are classified into six distinct groups, that is, occupancy data, mobility data, crowdsourced environmental data, building performance and operational data, urban spatial data, and survey data (Salim et al. 2020). These datasets encompass various aspects of urban-scale occupant and mobility behavior. The process of data-driven modeling, which involves modeling occupant behaviors and energy usage, typically comprises several stages, including data acquisition, data cleaning and extraction, data aggregation and representation, data mining and machine learning, modeling, and interpretation (Salim et al. 2020).

Occupant monitoring is a promising tool for improving energy efficiency in buildings and cities and incorporating occupancy and occupant behavior into urban building energy optimization (Amasyali and El-Gohary 2021). With the rise of IoT devices such as smartphones, sensors, cameras, and radio-frequency identification devices (RFIDs), it has become possible to collect vast amounts of data for tracking people within buildings (Akkaya et al. 2015). Occupant monitoring systems, such as WiFi counts or sensors, allow building managers to gain insights into occupant behavior and adjust building systems accordingly to optimize energy use (Zhan and Chong 2021). Ambient Intelligence (AmI) systems, empowered by advances in Artificial Intelligence (AI) and Internet of Things (IoT) technologies, have shown potential for supporting flexible and adaptive user-centered operational environments and improving energy efficiency in buildings. Real-time energy monitoring systems through AmI systems enable the collection of occupancy-related data for a better understanding of energy use dynamics and designing future scenarios with possibilities for energy savings. However, as this is still an emerging area of research, there are gaps that need to be filled, and the impacts and applicability of these systems should be studied beyond a building level and extended to larger city scales.

The occupancy monitoring capability offers extensive opportunities to improve building energy consumption through smart HVAC control. Building energy management systems can monitor energy demand and usage patterns to achieve precise control of energy consumption, resulting in reduced energy costs and better control of building energy consumption (Franceschini and Neves 2022). Occupant behavior, including the setting of comfort criteria, operation of lighting, office equipment, space thermostat, and HVAC systems, can also be monitored to classify it into workstyles such as austerity, standard, and wastefulness, enabling the identification of areas where energy savings can be achieved. Plug load monitoring and related occupant behavior interventions can play a critical role in reducing building energy consumption (O'Brien et al. 2017).

A study by Anand, Cheong, and Sekhar (2022) analyzed the literature on occupancy monitoring and building system control methods, finding that occupancy is a key driver behind building system performance, and that incorrect occupant information can lead to wasted energy and poor Indoor Environmental Quality (IEQ). For occupancy-driven analysis, such as evaluating the performance of lighting sensors or HVAC demand in airport terminal buildings, agent-based occupant modeling approaches are useful to simulate the stochasticity in occupancy patterns (O'Brien et al. 2017). The monitoring data can be used to validate the accuracy of building energy models and simulations, which can sometimes exhibit a significant performance gap between predicted and actual energy use (Zhang, Wu, and Calautit 2022). Occupant monitoring can help cities achieve their energy efficiency goals by identifying and quantifying energy savings opportunities and enabling better access to this efficiency potential (U.S. Department of Energy, n.d.).

Additionally, providing occupants with feedback on their energy consumption has been shown to increase awareness and encourage more energy-efficient behavior (Laaroussi et al. 2020). Eco-feedback tools have been recognized as a useful tool within sociology and psychology to encourage behavioral change (McCalley and Midden 1998). In recent years, serious games (García et al. 2017) and mobile applications (Aliberti et al. 2017a) have been developed as energy efficiency feedback (EEF) tools to increase user awareness of energy consumption and reduce energy use. AmI-based EEF tools are designed to influence occupants' beliefs and attitudes toward energy use and potential savings through feedback systems (Axon 2016; Brummer 2018; Novak et al. 2018). By incorporating occupant monitoring into building management strategies, cities can reduce their overall energy consumption and contribute to a more sustainable future. In buildings where occupant-controlled electrical loads account for a large portion of whole-building demand, improvements in building performance are dependent on systems that can effectively influence the participation and actions of occupants (Konis, Orosz, and Sintov 2016). Automated building control systems have been proposed as a solution to reduce energy use for building operations, but these systems may result in less occupant control (Akkaya et al. 2015). To address this issue, a data-driven approach has been proposed to calculate and recommend an action plan to the occupant, making them aware of the impact of their behavior on increasing building energy efficiency without sacrificing comfort (Boulmaiz, Reignier, and Ploix 2022).

Innovation in the construction and use of buildings is essential to meet urgent energy reduction goals worldwide. Studies on nontechnical climate mitigation solutions (Mata et al. 2022) also suggest significant energy-saving and climate mitigation potentials through behavioral solutions as well as flexibility in demand, inadequate or adequate comfort levels, circular and sharing economy, social organizational innovations, and passive and active building operational solutions. However, most research is focused on technical aspects rather than on the social effects of occupant behavior on energy consumption in buildings (Harputlugil and de Wilde 2021). A more comprehensive approach is necessary, including interdisciplinary research and collaborations between various fields, to develop effective human-centered strategies for reducing energy consumption and achieving sustainable building performance.

Digital Twin (DT) technology has the potential to enhance building energy management and accelerate decarbonization in the built environment (Francisco, Mohammadi, and Taylor 2020; Bortolini et al. 2022; Huang, Zhang, and Zeng 2022). DT allows for the creation of a digital replica of a city's buildings, providing a powerful tool to simulate and visualize the entire system, conduct scenario analysis, and predict performance. Integration of DT with smart buildings and cities enables real-time planning and management of urban energy systems (Francisco, Mohammadi, and Taylor 2020). Furthermore, DT can provide real-time feedback to influence energy consumption patterns and promote community engagement (Axon 2016; Brummer 2018; Novak et al. 2018; Koroleva et al. 2019; Krietemeyer et al. 2021). However, there are gaps that limit the scalability of these models due to the novelty of the technology and data quality and availability (Lu et al. 2020; Agouzoul et al. 2021; Opoku et al. 2021).

This chapter provides a review of occupant-driven urban building energy monitoring, and data-driven approaches for improving energy efficiency awareness and reducing energy consumption in cities. Various techniques are discussed to better understand occupant behavior and predict energy use. Effective systems that can influence and encourage positive occupant actions are also highlighted as crucial for improving building performance. With a focus on an integrated socio-technical approach for better understanding energy use dynamics and energy reduction through behavioral aspects, the review concludes with an outlook on integrated modeling, monitoring, and feedback systems and explores the multilevel implications for decarbonization in buildings and cities. The chapter emphasizes a need for a holistic systems approach and developing DTs that remedy limitations regarding physics-based modeling and bringing occupants into the feedback loop via a socio-technical approach. The approaches covered span the building's lifecycle stages, from design and planning to policymaking and operation.

Occupancy and Building Energy Use

Definitions

Numerous studies have been conducted to create definitions, metrics, frameworks, data sources, methods, and tools to incorporate occupancy into building energy models and understand its impact on energy consumption (Yan et al. 2015; D'Oca, Hong, and Langevin 2018; Harputlugil and de Wilde 2021; Dabirian, Panchabikesan, and Eicker 2022). The International Energy Agency (IEA) Energy in the Buildings and Communities (EBC) Program has consolidated research studies on various modeling and simulation approaches for enhancing occupant-driven energy efficiency, including IEA EBC Annex 66 (Yan et al. 2017), which provides the definition and simulation of occupant behavior in buildings and procedures for occupant monitoring, IEA EBC Annex 53 (Yoshino, Hong, and Nord 2017), which discusses the total energy use in buildings with a focus on analysis and evaluation methods, and IEA EBC Annex 79 (O'Brien et al. 2020), which introduces main challenges and opportunities in the area of occupant-centric building design and operation.

IEA EBC Annex 81 (Fierro and Pauwels 2022) focuses on data-driven smart buildings and envisions a future world empowered by reliable and ubiquitous real-time data from buildings, enabling digital solutions to rapidly scale and widely disseminate energy efficiency knowledge within accessible software applications. Annex 81 report focuses on establishing standards, protocols, and procedures for low-cost, high-quality data capture, sharing, and utilization in buildings, with a particular emphasis on the potential of Software-as-a-Service innovation, data-driven building automation, and energy optimization (O'Neill and Wen 2022). To achieve a high level of accuracy on occupancy patterns at the individual building granularity, a yearlong empirical study is needed for collecting data through the deployment of a cluster of occupancy sensors and/or conducting surveys to collect information. However, this is not feasible for a large urban-scale exploration (e.g. it involves significant challenges, including equipment costs, installation labor costs, monitoring costs, and privacy issues).

An occupant-driven energy model explores human-related energy use, taking into account various factors, including occupancy and occupant behavior (Yoshino, Hong, and Nord 2017; Anand, Cheong, and Sekhar 2022; Dahlström, Broström, and Widén 2022; Franceschini and Neves 2022). Occupancy is defined based on several subfactors, including occupant presence/absence, estimation (number of occupants) and prediction (prediction in a future time window of occupancy), movement (transitions between rooms/zones), and activity (identification or prediction of a specific activity). Occupant behavior is defined as the occupant's interactions with building systems to meet their energy and comfort-related needs, and adaptive behaviors refer to behaviors such as clothing adjustment. In this context, interaction with building systems are window and door operation, blinds/solar shading operation, thermostat, or air-conditioning (cooling and heating systems) adjustment, artificial light control, and use of appliances. A review article by Happle, Fonseca, and Schlueter (2018) discusses the modeling of occupant behavior in urban-scale building energy models. The article defines occupant presence models, which are often called occupancy models, as models that "describe the presence, absence, and movement of occupants in spaces" (Happle, Fonseca, and Schlueter 2018). Therefore, based on this definition, occupancy can be understood as the state of being present in a space. Occupant presence models, which are often called occupancy models, describe the presence, absence, and movement of occupants in spaces. Occupant action models describe

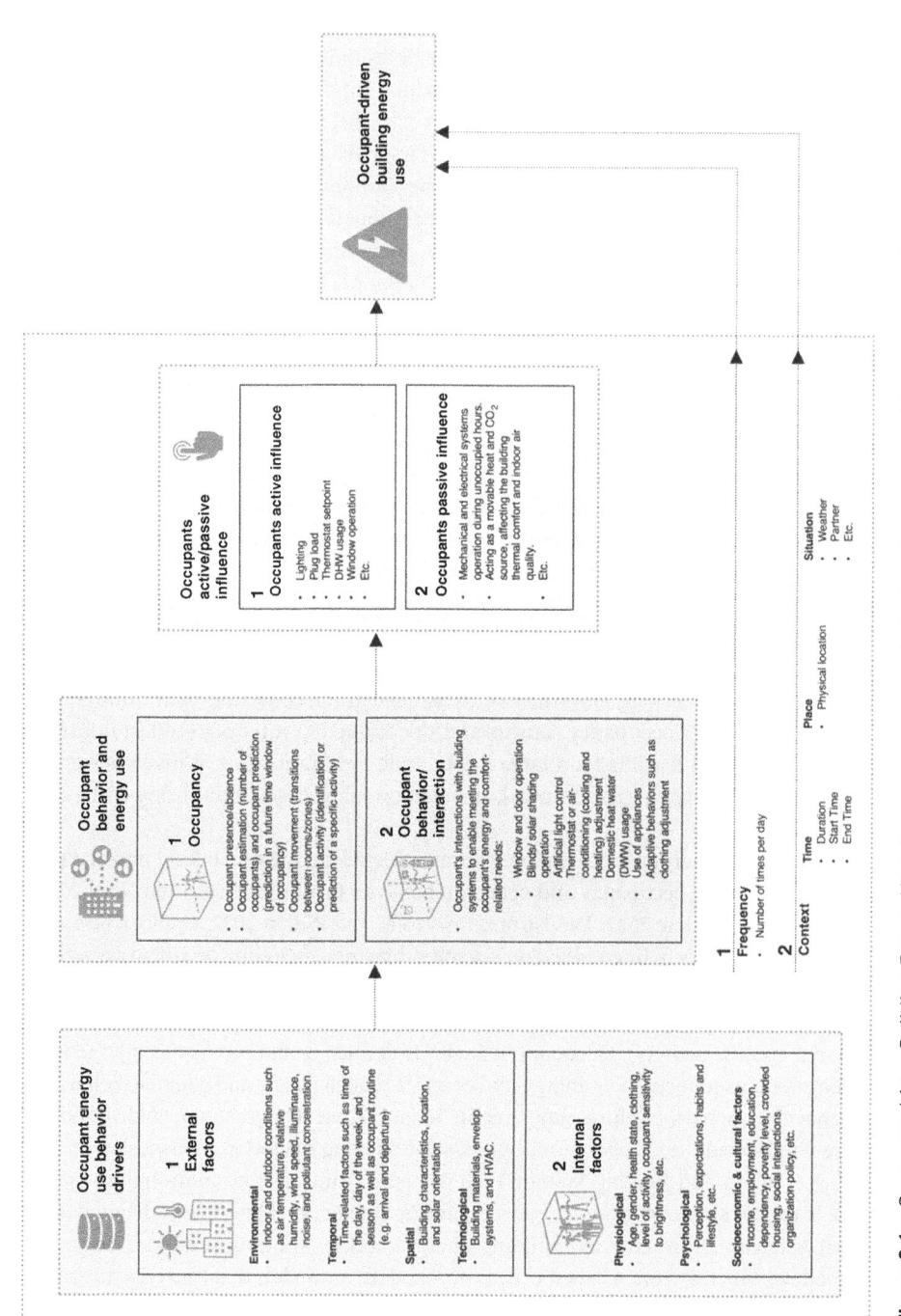

Figure 9.1 Occupant-driven Building Energy Use; Occupant energy use behavior drivers, occupant behavior classification, occupants active/passive influence.

various types of adaptive and nonadaptive behavior, such as adjusting blinds, opening windows, switching lights, and the use of appliances (Happle, Fonseca, and Schlueter 2018). The changes in design decisions based on knowledge of how occupants will use the building can significantly reduce energy consumption for heating, cooling, and lighting.

Occupancy and occupant behavior in buildings are governed by various driving factors and systems, which can be categorized into external and internal factors (Stazi and Naspi 2018). External factors include environmental, temporal, spatial, or technological variables, while internal factors include physiological, psychological, or socioeconomic factors (Hong, D'Oca, Turner, et al. 2015; Hong, D'Oca, Taylor-Lange, et al. 2015; Belafi, Hong, and Reith 2019). The need for comfort within the occupant's environment is identified as a primary driver of occupant energy-related behaviors (Yan et al. 2017), and it is associated with environmental factors and other influential factors such as contextual, physiological, and psychological factors (O'Brien and Gunay 2014; Pisello et al. 2016). The socioeconomic characteristics refer to income, employment, education, dependency, and social interactions (Abbasabadi and Ashayeri 2021). The Energy Cultures framework (He, Hong, and Chou 2021) evaluates behavior suggesting that consumer energy behavior can be comprehended by investigating the interactions between cognitive norms, material culture, and energy practices. The complexity of quantifying uncertain internal factors is challenging, so primarily occupant behavior models at a building scale have been developed relative to external factors and drivers.

Variation in building energy usage due to occupancy includes occupant active and passive interaction with building systems (Anand, Cheong, and Sekhar 2022). Active interactions include the actions taken to regulate the building systems by occupants, while passive interactions are connected to occupants' presence without any physical action performed to regulate the building system. Accurate information is needed to measure the active influence of occupants, but it is difficult to capture each energy-usage act with its associated contributing factor due to the high uncertainty of occupant behavior. Energy use variation due to occupant's passive interactions is determined based on the presence or absence of the occupant, which is denoted as occupied or unoccupied hours of building operation. Energy is wasted in large amounts when the mechanical and electrical systems operate inefficiently during unoccupied hours. Researchers have found that 26–65% of energy is used during unoccupied hours, and 19–28% is used for electricity and HVAC during nonfunctional weekends (Anand, Cheong, and Sekhar 2022). Thus, incorporating more realistic occupancy schedules in energy models is crucial. Occupant behaviors and activities are analyzed based on frequency and context, which includes time, place, and situation (Mo and Zhao 2021), and energy consumed in buildings is correlated with these factors (Laskari et al. 2022). Figure 9.1 illustrates occupant-driven building energy use, occupant energy use behavior drivers, occupant behavior classification, and occupants active/passive influence.

Occupant Monitoring Methods

Occupant monitoring, made possible by IoT devices such as smartphones, sensors, cameras, and RFIDs, is a promising tool for improving energy efficiency in buildings and cities (Akkaya et al. 2015). Occupant monitoring systems, such as WiFi counts or sensors, allow building managers to gain insights into occupant behavior and adjust building systems accordingly to optimize energy use (Zhan and Chong 2021). Advances in AI and IoT technologies have enabled the development of AmI systems that support user-centered operational environments and improve energy efficiency in buildings. Real-time energy monitoring systems through AmI systems enable the collection of occupancy-related data for a better understanding of energy use dynamics and designing future scenarios with possibilities for energy savings. The occupancy monitoring capability also offers extensive opportunities to improve building energy consumption through intelligent HVAC control, enabling precise control of energy consumption, resulting in reduced energy costs and better control of building energy consumption (Franceschini and Neves 2022). Occupant monitoring can help cities achieve their energy efficiency goals by identifying and quantifying energy savings opportunities and enabling better access to this efficiency potential.

Occupant monitoring methods refer to the techniques and tools used to collect data on the behavior of occupants in buildings. These methods are widely used to evaluate building technologies, assess energy performance, and improve IEQ. There are various methods to monitor occupant behavior in buildings, including physical monitoring, occupant investigation, and passive sensing techniques. The choice of method depends on the objectives of the study, the resources available, and the level of privacy required. Guidelines for the selection and set up of the monitoring approach are necessary, and the evaluation method should be made according to the objective of the evaluation. It is also essential to define the depth and nature of the study, audience, and resources available (Olivia and Christopher 2015).

Quantitative physical monitoring methods involve objective measurements such as physical sensing, which uses energy meters, indoor and outdoor environmental parameters (e.g. air temperature, relative humidity, illuminance, and pollutant concentration) measurements, and occupancy (occupant presence), and occupant behavior (their interaction with the building systems such as window operation) through sensors (Franceschini and Neves 2022). However, this method presents several challenges, including cost, privacy, and precision. Additionally, there is a need for occupant action monitoring and measurement of environmental variables simultaneously. It is also challenging to obtain unbiased data from occupants as they need to be unaware of being observed to avoid influencing their behavior. Organizational and legal restrictions, such as the Personal Data Protection Act, also pose challenges to this type of study. IEA EBC Appendix 66 provides comprehensive procedures for occupant monitoring (Yan et al. 2017). Occupancy monitoring methods are categorized into two main groups: (1) Observational studies; and (2) Experimental studies as follows (Anand, Cheong, and Sekhar 2022):

Occupant Monitoring Via Observational Studies

In-situ monitoring via observational studies of occupant behavior is one of the most effective and widely used research methods. It collects data on occupant behavior using smart sensors in the natural environment and, if appropriately designed and applied, can effectively avoid bias in the results (Du, Pan, and Yu 2020). In observational studies, sensors are used to passively monitor occupants' activities, attendance, and indoor environmental conditions. The monitoring period and the selection and placement of occupancy sensors can be determined based on seasonal variation (e.g. summer and winter) and building component usage type (e.g. windows and blinds). Observational studies could be further divided into two types: (1) occupant presence and equipment use, and (2) monitoring occupants' adaptive behavior.

Monitoring occupancy and plug loads combined are less reliant on building design than adaptive behavior (e.g. switching lights on/off and opening/closing windows).

Occupants' Presence and Their Equipment Usage
Occupant recognition involves various detectors such as Fitbit, motion sensors, CO_2 sensors, video cameras, information technology, and security-based systems such as GPS. Motion sensors are widely used for occupancy detection but cannot detect motionless occupants. They are reliable in measuring the occupancy transition state such as arrival, departure, and long transitional vacancy period. Using motion detectors and CO_2 sensors together can improve accuracy, but it can be challenging in zones with many CO_2 sources and sinks. Counting and identifying occupants using computer techniques can be tedious and costly in the long run. The most advanced choices for occupancy counting are GPS location and Wi-Fi-based methods, which are best for buildings with multiple entry points. Wi-Fi-based methods are economical and do not require additional infrastructure, but uniform sensor distribution is essential for accurate information, particularly for large-scale buildings. Passive Wi-Fi sensing methods can estimate occupant behavior and identify specific individuals while providing a certain level of privacy (Dziedzic, Da, and Novakovic 2019).

Monitoring Occupants' Adaptive Behavior
Monitoring occupants' adaptive behavior can provide valuable insights into energy usage patterns and motivations, such as adjusting lighting and thermostats or using fans and clothing to maintain thermal comfort. Traditional monitoring methods, such as manual observation and recording, can be costly, time-consuming, and limited in scope. Researchers have been exploring automated monitoring approaches, but some limitations, such as sensors' ability to differentiate between full and partial window opening, remain. Thermostat adjustments can be monitored through integrated sensors or set-point logs, and modern digital thermostats can collect and transfer data to a database. Cooling in buildings without air conditioning can be studied through opinion polls or plug-level energy data. Clothing can also affect thermal comfort, but observations and surveys may be needed when electronic sensing is not feasible. The choice of monitoring method should be tailored to the specific scenario and limitations of each approach.

Occupant Monitoring via Experimental Studies

Experimental studies are crucial in measuring occupant comfort conditions that affect behavior and play a vital role in understanding physiological and psychological influences on occupant behavior. These studies collect subjective responses and environmental parameters simultaneously in a controlled environment, such as a living laboratory. However, it is unclear whether generalized occupant behavioral models can be used for behavioral data collection, or if the data collection needs to be specific enough to account for the diversity of behavior, including different age groups, cultures, and genders. Therefore, an adequate number of subjects is needed and infrequent behavioral patterns that can occur daily or monthly must be measured in terms of duration and frequency. To determine acceptable sample sizes, power analysis can be used. While occupancy counting systems have pros and cons, computer vision-based systems with incorporated cameras are the most accurate systems. For example, a study conducted by (Kong et al. 2022) developed a series of occupancy sensing systems to track occupant behavior in indoor spaces. The study used three occupancy sensors to detect occupancy-based control (OBC) in two lab rooms, one used as the test lab and the other as a control lab with the same dimensions. Ten people were recruited to occupy each room, and data was collected using button switches. Comfort feedback and indoor environment preferences were collected during the test, and the energy consumption of HVAC systems in both rooms was monitored. Over a five-week test, the results showed that with OBC, HVAC energy could be saved.

Occupant-driven Energy Efficiency via Ambient Intelligence

Ambient Intelligence

AmI refers to the capability of an environment to sense, process, and respond to the needs and preferences of its occupants. AmI is a rapidly growing field that combines advances in AI, Internet of Things (IoT) technologies, sensing, and computing to create intelligent environments. AmI systems are characterized by their sensitivity, responsiveness, adaptability, transparency, ubiquity, and intelligence (Cook, Augusto, and Jakkula 2009). These features highlight the importance of context-aware computing, where the system can monitor and predict occupancy patterns and preferences such as lighting and temperature, and other factors that influence energy use to optimize energy consumption and occupant comfort. In addition, AmI can leverage ubiquitous computing (ubiComp) to provide users with access to robust and portable computing tools (Stavropoulos et al. 2015a). By integrating AI techniques, AmI can increase user comfort and decrease the intrusiveness of the system.

The performance and affordability of microcontrollers, wireless sensor networks, and other required devices play a critical role in enabling AmI systems to collect and process the necessary input data for AI algorithms (Stavropoulos et al. 2015a). Additionally, the use of actuators such as switches, motors, and other endpoints is essential in performing actions after the decision-making process. Recent technological advancements, such as the increasing popularity and low cost of smart meters, sensors, and actuators, have facilitated the application of AmI systems to increase occupant comfort and energy efficiency in buildings (Stavropoulos et al. 2015a). Machine learning techniques have been identified as having significant potential in enhancing the performance of AmI systems.

AmI applications are numerous and can be found in homes, offices, hospitals, transportation, and other areas. In the context of building energy efficiency, AmI has the potential to create occupant-driven systems that optimize energy use based on the needs and preferences of the occupants. This represents a departure from traditional building automation systems, which often rely on fixed schedules and setpoints that may not take into account the variability of occupancy and user behavior. By utilizing sensors and intelligent algorithms, AmI can monitor and predict occupancy patterns, lighting and temperature preferences, and other factors that influence energy use. The system can then adjust the building's infrastructure in real-time to optimize energy use and occupant comfort. Additionally, AmI can provide feedback to occupants on their energy use and encourage energy-saving behavior.

Real-time energy monitoring systems through AmI enable the collection of occupancy-related data for a better understanding of energy use dynamics and designing future scenarios with possibilities for energy savings. In office buildings, AmI can be particularly useful in optimizing lighting and temperature in different areas of the building based on occupancy. Residential buildings, on the other hand, can benefit from AmI's ability to optimize energy use and comfort in individual rooms based on the occupants' preferences. AmI systems have the potential to support flexible and adaptive user-centered operational environments and improve energy efficiency in buildings.

IEA EBC Annex 81 (Fierro and Pauwels 2022), a collaboration of 19 countries and over 50 organizations on data-driven smart buildings, aims to support the adoption of energy efficiency and demand flexibility strategies via data-driven tools and digitalization. This report focuses on how to standardize data collection and data use to gain insight into a better understanding of building operational patterns and accelerating energy performance in buildings in support of the decarbonization of the building sector (Candanedo and Athienitis 2022). IEA EBC Annex 81 investigates the potential of Software-as-a-Service innovation and data-driven automation, expanding a common software infrastructure to improve data accessibility under well-defined application program interfaces (APIs), deployed on edge-computing devices or the cloud or such as Apps on cellphone devices to reduce energy use in buildings and enable AI-driven energy optimization. The topical section on AI in smart buildings provides an overview of research and application papers contributed by the IEA EBC Annex 81 on the topic of AI in smart buildings (O'Neill and Wen 2022).

A review by Cook, Augusto, and Jakkula (2009) discusses AmI applications, and the challenges and opportunities faced by AmI researchers. Sensors are identified as a critical component of AmI, as they allow the algorithm to perceive the environment's conditions, which can be analyzed using AI techniques to control the environment to meet the algorithm's requirements. The focus of the review was on technologies that can sense, reason, and act. Motion sensors are used to detect the location of the user, allowing the system to better serve them by knowing their common preferences. Researchers recognize the challenges that arise when integrating AmI technologies, such as the need for awareness of the user's preferences, intentions, and identification of their needs (Cook, Augusto, and Jakkula 2009).

While there are challenges to the adoption of AmI systems, such as interoperability issues and privacy concerns related to the collection and use of occupant data, recent technological advancements, such as machine learning techniques, have increased the performance and affordability of AmI systems and their applicability for larger scales. However, as this is still an emerging area of research, there are gaps that need to be filled, and the impacts and applicability of these systems should be studied beyond a building level and extended to larger city levels to meet the goals of decarbonization and human health and well-being at scale. AmI represents an important area of research and development, and it has the potential to revolutionize the way we interact with the built environment, making buildings more efficient, and comfortable environments.

AmI-Based Energy Efficiency Feedback (EEF) Systems

AmI-based EEF tools have become a promising application in building energy efficiency. These tools provide occupants with real-time information about their energy consumption and encourage them to modify their behavior to reduce energy use. The integration of these tools with other building systems, such as lighting and HVAC, enables more sophisticated control strategies to be implemented, such as automatically adjusting the systems based on occupancy patterns. Researchers have conducted studies to understand the underlying behavior change for energy saving by examining insights from behavioral theories and persuasive system design (Koroleva, 2019). Eco-feedback tools have been recognized as a useful tool within sociology and psychology to encourage behavioral change (McCalley and Midden 1998). In recent years, serious games (García et al. 2017) and mobile applications (Aliberti et al. 2017a) have been developed as EEF tools to increase user awareness of energy consumption and reduce energy use.

EEF tools are designed to influence occupants' beliefs and attitudes toward energy use and potential savings through feedback systems (Axon 2016; Brummer 2018; Novak et al. 2018). A preferred choice is to utilize provisions in feedback about energy use to individuals and groups ("Chatzigeorgiou and Andreou 2021). These tools are defined as information presented during the interaction between the user and the product that encourages the user to adopt energy-saving strategies (McCalley and Midden 1998). For example, if an occupant is shown a comparison of their energy use, it may prompt them to want to control their consumption (Wood and Newborough 2007). One advantage of these tools is their ability to integrate with other building systems, providing a more comprehensive view of energy use in the building. Paone and Bacher (2018) conducted a study to evaluate how eco-feedback, social interaction, and gamification can influence building occupant behavior in fostering energy efficiency. The study found that codesigned and cocreated eco-feedback systems or interactive experiences such as games are an effective tool for reducing energy consumption. Another finding was that advanced control systems were accepted by the occupants because they improve the thermal comfort of the building and provide a perfect integration of energy and cost-saving strategies. When studying occupant's energy behavior, further analysis between behavioral change and technological improvement is needed to influence the energy effect of occupant behavior.

Studies have shown that energy savings among consumers can be stimulated by a designed behavior change system, and an integrated incentive model motivated users to adopt the proposed system to start changing their behavior. Koroleva (2019) conducted a study and used an experimental approach with a treatment and control group, which was later assessed by changes in energy consumption. The goal was to measure changes in attitudinal and behavioral measurements before and after exposure to the system. Three antecedents of behavior change – energy knowledge, perceived behavioral control, and behavioral intention were measured over a span of four months using a Shapiro–Wilk test. The results found that the developed visualizations were positively useful in all aspects and suggested that energy savings among consumers can be stimulated by a designed behavior change system. Also, an integrated incentive model motivated users to adopt the proposed system to start changing their behavior.

Another study (Stavropoulos et al. 2015b) developed an AmI application with the aim of reducing energy consumption and improving user comfort by intersecting multiple disciplines, including AmI, Automated Reasoning, Semantic Web Services, and Green Computing. The study utilized wireless sensors, actuator networks, and smart meters to collect environmental and energy data in a University building. Semantic annotations were added via web services, which allowed for the easy insertion of ontological entities using SAWSDL. The execution engine JESS was used to integrate expressiveness and defeasible logic, which corresponded with the reasoner SPINdle. The results showed a reduction in energy consumption of up to 4%, with the potential for higher reductions by collectively shutting down cooling units. However, managing reactive operation was a limitation in this study, and future research on hybrid agents could be beneficial.

Serious games and mobile applications have been developed as EEF tools to increase user awareness of energy consumption and reduce energy use. A study by García et al. (2017) developed a game using the CAFCLA framework, which enables the integration of multiple technologies for context awareness and social computing to address the challenges of promoting behavioral change for energy savings in public buildings. The game demonstrated how sensor network data can influence occupants' behavior in reducing energy use, while social interactions and competitiveness accelerate the desired outcome of energy savings. In addition to games, mobile applications have also been employed to increase user-awareness of energy consumption. Following a participatory approach, a study conducted by Aliberti et al. (2017a) developed a mobile application that promotes energy awareness for Smart Home monitoring. The study involved two online surveys and a focus group of 630 people. The study identified users and addressed topics such as consumer habits, perception and awareness of energy consumption, interest in energy efficiency, and relations with the energy provider. The outcome of the study was the development of FLEXMETER, an app that provides historical data for each energy vector and notifies consumers of their energy use while providing recommendations on the best times to turn on appliances.

Smart plug solutions that are designed to connect to electrical outlets and allow users to control the power to the connected devices remotely through a smartphone app or voice commands have also been proposed to promote behavioral change in building energy efficiency. These smart plugs can be used to turn on or off appliances, lights, and other devices, schedule their operation, or monitor energy consumption. Smart plugs typically use Wi-Fi or Bluetooth technology to communicate with other devices and can be integrated into a smart home ecosystem for more advanced automation and control. A study by (Himeur et al. 2022) employed a smart plug and a mobile application to promote behavioral change in building energy efficiency. The solution encouraged users to reduce energy consumption by performing energy-reducing actions, such as turning off the AC when leaving the room. The study recorded the monthly average of energy consumption two consecutive months before using the platform and one month after, along with several different scenarios. The results showed that using the platform led to energy savings of up to 68.03%. The savings were attributed to the recommendations generated to help end-users change their abnormal energy consumption habits.

Human-building interaction has become an increasingly important topic in the field of energy efficiency. A recent review by (Harputlugil and de Wilde 2021) evaluated the current state of research in this area, covering important issues, milestones, methodologies used, and building types analyzed in recent studies. The review highlighted that most eco-feedback research focuses solely on electricity feedback, and recommended longer study periods and larger sample sizes to achieve more reliable results in studies investigating eco-feedback. Furthermore, the study identified attention, learning, and motivation as three key behavioral mechanisms that must be considered for eco-feedback to be effective. Finally, the review emphasized the importance of the design of energy feedback tools in achieving effective eco-feedback.

AmI-based EEF tools in the form of eco-feedback tools, serious games, mobile applications, and smart plug solutions are some of the ways to promote occupant behavioral change in building energy efficiency. Although these solutions have been found effective, limitations such as privacy and cybersecurity issues, the accuracy of the sensors, and the bulkiness of the plug need to be addressed. In addition, there are limited EEF tools to allow for the exploration of occupant behavior across different scales and in real-time, as well as a solid behavior change system that supports human-centered energy reduction and stimulates energy savings (Koroleva et al. 2019; Krietemeyer et al. 2021). Another challenge is the need for user engagement. While EEF tools can provide occupants with real-time feedback on their energy use, they are only effective if occupants engage with the tools and modify their behavior accordingly. Available energy EEF tools have limitations in terms of being more technology-centered and less user-centered (Aliberti et al. 2017b). Therefore, it is important to design these tools in a way that is engaging and easy to use for occupants. Future work in this area may also benefit from advances in technology, further analysis between behavioral change and technological improvement, and hybrid agents. These solutions have the potential to promote occupant behavioral change and reduce energy consumption, resulting in energy-efficient buildings.

Occupant behavior is a key factor in the acceptance and application of technologies used in building design and retrofit. Case studies have demonstrated that occupant behavior influences the adaptability and implementation of building technologies (Yan et al. 2015). Previous studies have found that the perception of benefits, rather than the reduction of perceived barriers, is the strongest predictor of intention toward adopting renewable energy systems (Zhu and Dias 2021). Promotional strategies for renewable energy technologies, such as photovoltaic systems, should emphasize their environmental and financial benefits and innovativeness. Moreover, these strategies could be customized to consumer segments representing similar groups of like-minded people, rather than socio-demographic groups. To achieve stronger results in future studies, consistent predictors and measures for adoption, systematic collection of contextual variables, and compliance with reporting standards are recommended (Zhu and Dias 2021).

In terms of energy conservation, willingness to upgrade and openness to an energy conservation mindset was found to be the most critical features (Ghofrani, Zaidan, and Abulibdeh 2022). However, changing habits alone is not enough to save energy, and the use of interactive energy efficiency solutions such as smart controls, smart thermostats, and central control is necessary. A study on a smart building at an Australian university analyzed the impact of building automation and centralized control systems on energy consumption, indoor comfort, and productivity (Loengbudnark et al. 2022). The study found that perceived control increases comfort levels and occupants' satisfaction and has less impact on thermal and visual comfort. The perceived control had a positive effect on occupants' perceived productivity and using lighting system modifications led to a reduction in energy consumption. A study conducted by Soetedjo and Sotyohadi (2021) utilized IoT platforms to monitor and model occupancy-based energy consumption in real-time. The study found that automatic control of light and AC systems based on occupancy and room conditions significantly reduced building energy consumption. To promote thermally adaptive behaviors and comfort of office occupants while considering building energy consumption, a human and building interaction toolkit (HABIT) (Langevin, Wen, and Gurian 2016) was introduced.

In addition, behavioral and societal aspects are crucial in decision-making regarding energy technologies, as they influence their degree of acceptance and use. However, research on energy system modeling and analysis that considers these dimensions is relatively scarce (Huckebrink and Bertsch 2021). To improve the accuracy of energy system models for long-term projections with behavioral aspects, future research needs to identify which behavioral changes should be assessed and consider the technical characteristics of the energy demand process and various consumer socio-economic preferences (Huckebrink and Bertsch 2021).

Energy Efficiency via AmI Systems and Digital Twins Technology

The literature highlights the potential of DT technology to facilitate understanding of urban energy dynamics and accelerate decarbonization in the built environment (Francisco, Mohammadi, and Taylor 2020; Bortolini et al. 2022; Huang, Zhang, and Zeng 2022). DT technology is a promising approach to improving building energy efficiency, and it has been applied to various areas of the Architecture, Engineering, Construction, and Operations (AECO) sector (Pereira et al. 2021). DTs are virtual replicas of physical objects that integrate various types of data and can be used throughout the entire life cycle of physical objects (Deng, Zhang, and Shen 2021).

The development of DT for urban building energy models (UBEM) (Li et al. 2017) has the potential to transform building energy management and enhance energy efficiency. DT provides a powerful tool to create a digital replica of a city's buildings, which offers a new approach to simulate and visualize the entire system, conduct what-if scenario analysis, and predict system performance. DT leverages the increased availability of building performance data and open data initiatives to enhance monitoring, control, and decision-making through improved visualization and interaction with data. Additionally, DT's integration with emerging smart cities and city data offers an opportunity for real-time planning and management of urban energy (Francisco, Mohammadi, and Taylor 2020). Furthermore, DT as an effective tool can provide real-time feedback that can influence energy consumption patterns by changing underlying beliefs and attitudes regarding energy savings (Axon 2016; Brummer 2018; Novak et al. 2018), as well as promoting community engagement and stimulating energy savings (Koroleva et al. 2019; Krietemeyer et al. 2021). The ability of DT for incorporating urban complexities across time and scale through streaming data makes it a promising platform for intelligent urban energy management and decarbonization. However, there are knowledge gaps that limit the accuracy and scalability of these models due to the novelty of the technology and data quality and availability (Lu et al. 2020; Agouzoul et al. 2021; Opoku et al. 2021).

The advancements in digital tools have led to the development of Computer-Aided Design (CAD), Building Information Modeling (BIM), and Geographic Information Systems (GIS), which can be integrated with DTs. One of the challenges of dynamic urban simulations is the creation of 3D digital city models, but new approaches have been introduced that integrate publicly available datasets for developing 3D models (Katal et al. 2022). Energy-efficient building digital twins (BDTs) can be created using BIM and are the result of a "BIM+" approach (Wang et al. 2022). By using DT technology, it is possible to improve the energy footprint and asset performance of buildings (Jafari et al. 2020). In fact, a proposed energy distribution framework can be realized as a platform for energy customers to optimize their energy profiles, and this framework can be considered a product-service system (PSS) offered by energy suppliers (Mourtzis, Angelopoulos, and Panopoulos 2022). In another study, a predictive process-based framework was proposed for an early BIM energy-efficient design scenario using machine assistance for building designer support (Chen and Geyer 2022). The framework consisted of general design components, such as probabilistic surrogate modeling, ensemble modeling, and model interpretation, which provided coherent input variants' interpretation. Results show that an expected building energy efficiency range with intervention and input causes interpretation can be provided to building designers in an interactive process. While BIM is widely used for designing, constructing, operating, and maintaining buildings and infrastructures, it lacks the integration of generative algorithms or AI techniques (Stojanovski et al. 2022). To enable human-centered energy efficiency, there is a need to integrate AI into the process of analyzing building elements and environmental elements. For instance, with ML algorithms' capability to understand the symbolics of patterns, elements, and rules, AI can assist with processing large amounts of data. However, for effective processing, the data inputs should include hierarchical morphological structures for the AI to analyze the scale of the building, its elements, urban elements, landscape, and transportation flows (Stojanovski et al. 2022).

The use of DT technology has emerged as an effective approach to enhance building energy modeling and monitoring. In a recent study by Alanne and Sierla (2022), an overview of autonomous machine learning applications was presented, which highlighted the role of DTs as training environments in boosting the learning processes. Three main indicators, indoor comfort, energy efficiency, carbon footprint, and techno-economic viability, were identified as the key performance indicators in building energy modeling and monitoring. To achieve better performance, the study suggested that the outputs and prediction of asset management should be incorporated as state information to the reinforcement learning agent.

To conclude, DT technology is a promising approach to improving the energy efficiency of urban buildings. By creating virtual replicas of physical objects that integrate various types of data and can be used throughout the entire life cycle of buildings, it is possible to optimize energy profiles and improve asset performance (Deng, Zhang, and Shen 2021; Pereira et al. 2021; Wang et al. 2022). This approach provides a major lead for future research, which can help improve the efficiency and accuracy of building energy modeling and monitoring and promote the decarbonization of the built environment.

Conclusion

Incorporating human dimensions, such as occupancy and occupant behavior, is essential to achieve effective building design and management for mitigating climate change. To promote sustainability at scale, occupant monitoring, modeling, and feedback systems are crucial approaches. However, accurately representing occupancy patterns is a challenge, and occupancy is a significant source of uncertainty in predicting building energy use. Therefore, developing occupant models that describe the presence, absence, and movement of occupants in spaces is vital, and occupant-centric real-world data should be utilized to model occupant behavior. This chapter highlights the current state of research on the topic and the potential of occupant monitoring, AmI, and DT technology as a tool for improving energy efficiency in buildings and cities.

References

Abbasabadi, N. and Ashayeri, M. (2021). Socioeconomic Determinants of Public Health and Residential Building Energy Use in Chicago. In: *In UIA 2021 RIO: 27th World Congress of Architects*, 707–713. The Association of Collegiate Schools of Architecture (ACSA).

Agouzoul, A., Tabaa, M., Chegari, B. et al. (2021). Towards a Digital Twin Model for Building Energy Management: Case of Morocco. In: *Procedia Computer Science, The 12th International Conference on Ambient Systems, Networks and Technologies (ANT)/The 4th International Conference on Emerging Data and Industry 4.0 (EDI40) / Affiliated Workshops*, vol. 184 (January), 404–410. https://doi.org/10.1016/j.procs.2021.03.051.

Akkaya, K., Guvenc, I., Aygun, R. et al. (2015). IoT-based occupancy monitoring techniques for energy-efficient smart buildings. In: *2015 IEEE Wireless Communications and Networking Conference Workshops (WCNCW)*, 58–63. New Orleans, LA, USA: IEEE. https://doi.org/10.1109/WCNCW.2015.7122529.

Alanne, K. and Sierla, S. (2022). An Overview of Machine Learning Applications for Smart Buildings. *Sustainable Cities and Society* 76 (January): 103445. https://doi.org/10.1016/j.scs.2021.103445.

Ali, U., Shamsi, M.H., Hoare, C. et al. (2021). Review of Urban Building Energy Modeling (UBEM) Approaches, Methods and Tools Using Qualitative and Quantitative Analysis. *Energy and Buildings* 246 (September): 111073. https://doi.org/10.1016/j.enbuild.2021.111073.

Aliberti, A., Camarda, C., Ferro, V. et al. (2017a). A Participatory Design Approach for Energy-Aware Mobile App for Smart Home Monitoring. In: *SMARTGREENS*, 158–165.

Aliberti, A., Camarda, C., Ferro, V. et al. (2017b). A Participatory Design Approach for Energy-Aware Mobile App for Smart Home Monitoring. In: *Proceedings of the 6th International Conference on Smart Cities and Green ICT Systems*, 158–165. Porto, Portugal: SCITEPRESS - Science and Technology Publications https://doi.org/10.5220/0006299001580165.

Anand, P., Cheong, D., and Sekhar, C. (2022). A Review of Occupancy-Based Building Energy and IEQ Controls and Its Future Post-COVID. *Science of The Total Environment* 804 (January): 150249. https://doi.org/10.1016/j.scitotenv.2021.150249.

Amasyali, K. and El-Gohary, N.M. (2021). Real Data-Driven Occupant-Behavior Optimization for Reduced Energy Consumption and Improved Comfort. *Applied Energy* 302 (November): 117276. https://doi.org/10.1016/j.apenergy.2021.117276.

Axon, S. (2016). 'The Good Life': Engaging the Public with Community-Based Carbon Reduction Strategies. *Environmental Science & Policy* 66 (December): 82–92. https://doi.org/10.1016/j.envsci.2016.08.007.

Bortolini, R., Rodrigues, R., Alavi, H. et al. (2022). Digital Twins' Applications for Building Energy Efficiency: A Review. *Energies* 15 (19): 7002. https://doi.org/10.3390/en15197002.

Boulmaiz, F., Reignier, P., and Ploix, S. (2022). An Occupant-Centered Approach to Improve Both His Comfort and the Energy Efficiency of the Building. *Knowledge-Based Systems* 249 (August): 108970. https://doi.org/10.1016/j.knosys.2022.108970.

Brummer, V. (2018). Community Energy – Benefits and Barriers: A Comparative Literature Review of Community Energy in the UK, Germany and the USA, the Benefits It Provides for Society and the Barriers It Faces. *Renewable and Sustainable Energy Reviews* 94 (October): 187–196. https://doi.org/10.1016/j.rser.2018.06.013.

Candanedo, J.A. and Athienitis, A.K. (2022). Leveraging Data: A New Frontier in Building Modelling and Advanced Control. *Journal of Building Performance Simulation* 15 (4): 431–432. https://doi.org/10.1080/19401493.2022.2079827.

Chatzigeorgiou, I.M. and Andreou, G.T. (2021). A Systematic Review on Feedback Research for Residential Energy Behavior Change through Mobile and Web Interfaces. *Renewable and Sustainable Energy Reviews* 135 (January): 110187. https://doi.org/10.1016/j.rser.2020.110187.

Chen, J., Adhikari, R., Wilson, E. et al. (2022). Stochastic Simulation of Occupant-Driven Energy Use in a Bottom-up Residential Building Stock Model. *Applied Energy* 325 (November): 119890. https://doi.org/10.1016/j.apenergy.2022.119890.

Chen, X. and Geyer, P. (2022). Machine Assistance in Energy-Efficient Building Design: A Predictive Framework toward Dynamic Interaction with Human Decision-Making under Uncertainty. *Applied Energy* 307 (February): 118240. https://doi.org/10.1016/j.apenergy.2021.118240.

Cook, D.J., Augusto, J.C., and Jakkula, V.R. (2009). Ambient Intelligence: Technologies, Applications, and Opportunities. *Pervasive and Mobile Computing* 5 (4): 277–298. https://doi.org/10.1016/j.pmcj.2009.04.001.

Dabirian, S., Panchabikesan, K., and Eicker, U. (2022). Occupant-Centric Urban Building Energy Modeling: Approaches, Inputs, and Data Sources - A Review. *Energy and Buildings* 257 (February): 111809. https://doi.org/10.1016/j.enbuild.2021.111809.

Dahlström, L., Broström, T., and Widén, J. (2022). Advancing Urban Building Energy Modelling through New Model Components and Applications: A Review. *Energy and Buildings* 266 (July): 112099. https://doi.org/10.1016/j.enbuild.2022.112099.

Belafi, D., Zsofia, T.H., and Reith, A. (2019). A Library of Building Occupant Behaviour Models Represented in a Standardised Schema. *Energy Efficiency* 12 (3): 637–651. https://doi.org/10.1007/s12053-018-9658-0.

Deng, T., Zhang, K., and Zuo-Jun (Max) Shen. (2021). A Systematic Review of a Digital Twin City: A New Pattern of Urban Governance toward Smart Cities. *Journal of Management Science and Engineering* 6 (2): 125–134. https://doi.org/10.1016/j.jmse.2021.03.003.

D'Oca, S., Hong, T., and Langevin, J. (2018). The Human Dimensions of Energy Use in Buildings: A Review. *Renewable & Sustainable Energy Reviews* 81 (Journal Article): 731–742. https://doi.org/10.1016/j.rser.2017.08.019.

Dong, B., Liu, Y., Fontenot, H. et al. (2021). Occupant Behavior Modeling Methods for Resilient Building Design, Operation and Policy at Urban Scale: A Review. *Applied Energy* 293 (July): 116856. https://doi.org/10.1016/j.apenergy.2021.116856.

Du, J., Pan, W., and Cong, Y. (2020). In-Situ Monitoring of Occupant Behavior in Residential Buildings – a Timely Review. *Energy and Buildings* 212 (April): 109811. https://doi.org/10.1016/j.enbuild.2020.109811.

Dziedzic, J.W., Da, Y., and Novakovic, V. (2019). Indoor Occupant Behaviour Monitoring with the Use of a Depth Registration Camera. *Building and Environment* 148 (January): 44–54. https://doi.org/10.1016/j.buildenv.2018.10.032.

The U.S. Department of Energy "Energy Efficiency: Savings Opportunities and Benefits." n.d. Energy.Gov. . https://www.energy.gov/scep/slsc/energy-efficiency-savings-opportunities-and-benefits.

Fierro, G. and Pauwels, P. (2022). *Survey of Metadata Schemas for Datadriven Smart Buildings (Annex 81): Energy in Buildings and Communities Technology Collaboration Programme.* International Energy Agency, CSIRO https://pure.tue.nl/ws/portalfiles/portal/207017800/IEA_Annex_81_Survey_of_Metadata_Schemas.pdf.

Franceschini, P.B. and Neves, L.O. (2022). A Critical Review on Occupant Behaviour Modelling for Building Performance Simulation of Naturally Ventilated School Buildings and Potential Changes Due to the COVID-19 Pandemic. *Energy and Buildings* 258 (March): 111831. https://doi.org/10.1016/j.enbuild.2022.111831.

Francisco, A., Mohammadi, N., and Taylor, J.E. (2020). Smart City Digital Twin–Enabled Energy Management: Toward Real-Time Urban Building Energy Benchmarking. *Journal of Management in Engineering* 36 (2): 04019045. https://doi.org/10.1061/(ASCE)ME.1943-5479.0000741.

Gaetani, I., Hoes, P.-J., and Hensen, J.L.M. (2016). Occupant Behavior in Building Energy Simulation: Towards a Fit-for-Purpose Modeling Strategy. *Energy and Buildings* 121 (June): 188–204. https://doi.org/10.1016/j.enbuild.2016.03.038.

García, Ó., Alonso, R.S., Prieto, J., and Corchado, J.M. (2017). Energy Efficiency in Public Buildings through Context-Aware Social Computing. *Sensors (Basel, Switzerland)* 17 (4): 826. https://doi.org/10.3390/s17040826.

Ghofrani, A., Zaidan, E., and Abulibdeh, A. (2022). Simulation and Impact Analysis of Behavioral and Socioeconomic Dimensions of Energy Consumption. *Energy* 240 (February): 122502. https://doi.org/10.1016/j.energy.2021.122502.

Happle, G., Fonseca, J.A., and Schlueter, A. (2018). A Review on Occupant Behavior in Urban Building Energy Models. *Energy and Buildings* 174 (September): 276–292. https://doi.org/10.1016/J.ENBUILD.2018.06.030.

Harputlugil, T. and de Wilde, P. (2021). The Interaction between Humans and Buildings for Energy Efficiency: A Critical Review. *Energy Research & Social Science* 71: 101828. https://doi.org/10.1016/j.erss.2020.101828.

He, Z., Hong, T., and Chou, S.K. (2021). A Framework for Estimating the Energy-Saving Potential of Occupant Behaviour Improvement. *Applied Energy* 287 (April): 116591. https://doi.org/10.1016/j.apenergy.2021.116591.

Heydarian, A., McIlvennie, C., Arpan, L. et al. (2020). What Drives Our Behaviors in Buildings? A Review on Occupant Interactions with Building Systems from the Lens of Behavioral Theories. *Building and Environment* 179 (July): 106928. https://doi.org/10.1016/j.buildenv.2020.106928.

Himeur, Y., Alsalemi, A., Bensaali, F. et al. (2022). Techno-Economic Assessment of Building Energy Efficiency Systems Using Behavioral Change: A Case Study of an Edge-Based Micro-Moments Solution. *Journal of Cleaner Production* 331 (January): 129786. https://doi.org/10.1016/j.jclepro.2021.129786.

Hong, T., D'Oca, S., Taylor-Lange, S.C. et al. (2015). An Ontology to Represent Energy-Related Occupant Behavior in Buildings. Part II: Implementation of the DNAS Framework Using an XML Schema. *Building and Environment* 94 (December): 196–205. https://doi.org/10.1016/j.buildenv.2015.08.006.

Hong, T., D'Oca, S., Turner, W.J.N., and Taylor-Lange, S.C. (2015). An Ontology to Represent Energy-Related Occupant Behavior in Buildings. Part I: Introduction to the DNAs

Framework. *Building and Environment* 92 (October): 764–777. https://doi.org/10.1016/j.buildenv.2015.02.019.

Hong, T., Yan, D., D'Oca, S., and Chen, C.-f. (2017). Ten Questions Concerning Occupant Behavior in Buildings: The Big Picture. *Building and Environment* 114 (March): 518–530. https://doi.org/10.1016/j.buildenv.2016.12.006.

Hu, S., Yan, D., Azar, E., and Guo, F. (2020). A Systematic Review of Occupant Behavior in Building Energy Policy. *Building and Environment* 175 (May): 106807. https://doi.org/10.1016/j.buildenv.2020.106807.

Huang, W., Zhang, Y., and Zeng, W. (2022). Development and Application of Digital Twin Technology for Integrated Regional Energy Systems in Smart Cities. *Sustainable Computing: Informatics and Systems* 36 (December): 100781. https://doi.org/10.1016/j.suscom.2022.100781.

Huckebrink, D. and Bertsch, V. (2021). Integrating Behavioural Aspects in Energy System Modelling—A Review. *Energies* 14 (15): 4579. https://doi.org/10.3390/en14154579.

IPCC (2014). Climate Change 2014: Synthesis Report. Contribution of Working Groups I, II and III to the Fifth Assessment Report of the Intergovernmental Panel on Climate Change. In: (ed. IPCC). Geneva, Switzerland: https://doi.org/10.1017/CBO9781107415324.

Jafari, M.A., Zaidan, E., Ghofrani, A. et al. (2020). Improving Building Energy Footprint and Asset Performance Using Digital Twin Technology. *IFAC-PapersOnLine, 4th IFAC Workshop on Advanced Maintenance Engineering, Services and Technologies - AMEST 2020* 53 (3): 386–391. https://doi.org/10.1016/j.ifacol.2020.11.062.

Katal, A., Mortezazadeh, M., Wang, L.(.L.)., and Yu, H. (2022). Urban Building Energy and Microclimate Modeling – From 3D City Generation to Dynamic Simulations. *Energy* 251 (July): 123817. https://doi.org/10.1016/j.energy.2022.123817.

Kong, M., Dong, B., Zhang, R., and O'Neill, Z. (2022). HVAC Energy Savings, Thermal Comfort and Air Quality for Occupant-Centric Control through a Side-by-Side Experimental Study. *Applied Energy* 306 (January): 117987. https://doi.org/10.1016/j.apenergy.2021.117987.

Konis, K., Orosz, M., and Sintov, N. (2016). A Window into Occupant-Driven Energy Outcomes: Leveraging Sub-Metering Infrastructure to Examine Psychosocial Factors Driving Long-Term Outcomes of Short-Term Competition-Based Energy Interventions. *Energy and Buildings* 116 (March): 206–217. https://doi.org/10.1016/j.enbuild.2016.01.005.

Koroleva, K., Melenhorst, M., Novak, J. et al. (2019). Designing an Integrated Socio-Technical Behaviour Change System for Energy Saving. *Energy Informatics* 2 (S1): 30. https://doi.org/10.1186/s42162-019-0088-9.

Krietemeyer, B., Dedrick, J., Sabaghian, E., and Rakha, T. (2021). Managing the Duck Curve: Energy Culture and Participation in Local Energy Management Programs in the United States. *Energy Research & Social Science*, May, 102055 https://doi.org/10.1016/j.erss.2021.102055.

Laaroussi, Y., Bahrar, M., El Mankibi, M. et al. (2020). Occupant Presence and Behavior: A Major Issue for Building Energy Performance Simulation and Assessment. *Sustainable Cities and Society* 63 (December): 102420. https://doi.org/10.1016/j.scs.2020.102420.

Langevin, J., Wen, J., and Gurian, P.L. (2016). Quantifying the Human–Building Interaction: Considering the Active, Adaptive Occupant in Building Performance Simulation. *Energy and Buildings* 117 (April): 372–386. https://doi.org/10.1016/j.enbuild.2015.09.026.

Laskari, M., de Masi, R.-F., Karatasou, S. et al. (2022). On the Impact of User Behaviour on Heating Energy Consumption and Indoor Temperature in Residential Buildings. *Energy and Buildings* 255 (January): 111657. https://doi.org/10.1016/j.enbuild.2021.111657.

Li, W., Zhou, Y., Cetin, K. et al. (2017). Modeling Urban Building Energy Use: A Review of Modeling Approaches and Procedures. *Energy* 141 (December): 2445–2457. https://doi.org/10.1016/j.energy.2017.11.071.

Loengbudnark, W., Khalilpour, K., Bharathy, G. et al. (2022). Impact of Occupant Autonomy on Satisfaction and Building Energy Efficiency. *Energy and Built Environment* February, S2666123322000174. https://doi.org/10.1016/j.enbenv.2022.02.007.

Lu, Q., Parlikad, A.K., Woodall, P. et al. (2020). Developing a Digital Twin at Building and City Levels: Case Study of West Cambridge Campus. *Journal of Management in Engineering* 36 (3): 05020004. https://doi.org/10.1061/(ASCE)ME.1943-5479.0000763.

Mata, É., Kihila, J.M., Wanemark, J. et al. (2022). Non-Technological and Behavioral Options for Decarbonizing Buildings – A Review of Global Topics, Trends, Gaps, and Potentials. *Sustainable Production and Consumption* 29 (January): 529–545. https://doi.org/10.1016/j.spc.2021.10.013.

McCalley, L.T. and Midden, G.J.H. (1998). Computer Based Systems in Household Appliances: The Study of Eco-Feedback as a Tool for Increasing Conservation Behavior. In: *Proceedings. 3rd Asia Pacific Computer Human Interaction (Cat. No.98EX110)*, 344–349. https://doi.org/10.1109/APCHI.1998.704455.

Mo, Y. and Zhao, D. (2021). Application of Occupant Behavior Prediction Model on Residential Big Data Analysis. In: *Proceedings of the 8th ACM International Conference on Systems for Energy-Efficient Buildings, Cities, and Transportation*, 349–352. BuildSys' 21. New York, NY, USA: Association for Computing Machinery https://doi.org/10.1145/3486611.3491121.

Mourtzis, D., Angelopoulos, J., and Panopoulos, N. (2022). Development of a PSS for Smart Grid Energy Distribution Optimization Based on Digital Twin. *Procedia CIRP, Leading manufacturing systems transformation – Proceedings of the 55th CIRP Conference on Manufacturing Systems 2022* 107 (January): 1138–1143. https://doi.org/10.1016/j.procir.2022.05.121.

Novak, J., Melenhorst, M., Micheel, I. et al. (2018). Integrating Behavioural Change and Gamified Incentive Modelling for Stimulating Water Saving. *Environmental Modelling & Software* 102 (April): 120–137. https://doi.org/10.1016/j.envsoft.2017.11.038.

O'Brien, W., Gaetani, I., Carlucci, S. et al. (2017). On Occupant-Centric Building Performance Metrics. *Building and Environment* 122 (September): 373–385. https://doi.org/10.1016/j.buildenv.2017.06.028.

O'Brien, W. and Burak Gunay, H. (2014). The Contextual Factors Contributing to Occupants' Adaptive Comfort Behaviors in Offices – A Review and Proposed Modeling Framework. *Building and Environment* 77 (July): 77–87. https://doi.org/10.1016/j.buildenv.2014.03.024.

O'Brien, W., Wagner, A., Schweiker, M. et al. (2020). Introducing IEA EBC Annex 79: Key Challenges and Opportunities in the Field of Occupant-Centric Building Design and Operation. *Building and Environment* 178 (July): 106738. https://doi.org/10.1016/j.buildenv.2020.106738.

Olivia, G.-S. and Christopher, T.A. (2015). In-Use Monitoring of Buildings: An Overview and Classification of Evaluation Methods. *Energy and Buildings* 86 (January): 176–189. https://doi.org/10.1016/j.enbuild.2014.10.005.

O'Neill, Z. and Wen, J. (2022). Artificial Intelligence in Smart Buildings. *Science and Technology for the Built Environment* 28 (9): 1115–1115. https://doi.org/10.1080/23744731.2022.2125209.

Opoku, D.-G.J., Perera, S., Osei-Kyei, R., and Rashidi, M. (2021). Digital Twin Application in the Construction Industry: A Literature Review. *Journal of Building Engineering* 40 (August): 102726. https://doi.org/10.1016/j.jobe.2021.102726.

Paone, A. and Bacher, J.-P. (2018). The Impact of Building Occupant Behavior on Energy Efficiency and Methods to Influence It: A Review of the State of the Art. *Energies* 11 (4): https://doi.org/10.3390/en11040953.

Pereira, V., Santos, J., Leite, F., and Escórcio, P. (2021). Using BIM to Improve Building Energy Efficiency – A Scientometric and Systematic Review. *Energy and Buildings* 250 (November): 111292. https://doi.org/10.1016/j.enbuild.2021.111292.

Pisello, A.L., Castaldo, V.L., Piselli, C. et al. (2016). How Peers' Personal Attitudes Affect Indoor Microclimate and Energy Need in an Institutional Building: Results from a Continuous Monitoring Campaign in Summer and Winter Conditions. *Energy and Buildings* 126 (August): 485–497. https://doi.org/10.1016/j.enbuild.2016.05.053.

Salim, F.D., Dong, B., Ouf, M. et al. (2020). Modelling Urban-Scale Occupant Behaviour, Mobility, and Energy in Buildings: A Survey. *Building and Environment* 183 (October): 106964. https://doi.org/10.1016/j.buildenv.2020.106964.

Soetedjo, A. and Sotyohadi, S. (2021). Modeling of Occupancy-Based Energy Consumption in a Campus Building Using Embedded Devices and IoT Technology. *Electronics* 10 (18): 2307. https://doi.org/10.3390/electronics10182307.

Stavropoulos, T.G., Kontopoulos, E., Bassiliades, N. et al. (2015a). Rule-Based Approaches for Energy Savings in an Ambient Intelligence Environment. *Pervasive and Mobile Computing* 19 (May): 1–23. https://doi.org/10.1016/j.pmcj.2014.05.001.

Stazi, F. and Naspi, F. (2018). Triggers for Users' Behaviours. In: *Impact of Occupants' Behaviour on Zero-Energy Buildings* (ed. F. Stazi and F. Naspi), 19–29. SpringerBriefs in Energy. Cham: Springer International Publishing https://doi.org/10.1007/978-3-319-71867-5_4.

Stojanovski, T., Zhang, H., Frid, E. et al. (2022). Rethinking Computer-Aided Architectural Design (CAAD) – From Generative Algorithms and Architectural Intelligence to Environmental Design and Ambient Intelligence. In: *Computer-Aided Architectural Design. Design Imperatives: The Future Is Now*, vol. 1465 (ed. D. Gerber, E. Pantazis, B. Bogosian, et al.), 62–83. Communications in Computer and Information Science. Singapore: Springer Singapore https://doi.org/10.1007/978-981-19-1280-1_5.

US EPA, OAR. 2017. "Inventory of U.S. Greenhouse Gas Emissions and Sinks." Reports and Assessments. US EPA. February 8, 2017. https://www.epa.gov/ghgemissions/inventory-us-greenhouse-gas-emissions-and-sinks.

Wang, W., Guo, H., Li, X. et al. (2022). Deep Learning for Assessment of Environmental Satisfaction Using BIM Big Data in Energy Efficient Building Digital Twins. *Sustainable Energy Technologies and Assessments* 50 (March): 101897. https://doi.org/10.1016/j.seta.2021.101897.

Wood, G. and Newborough, M. (2007). Energy-Use Information Transfer for Intelligent Homes: Enabling Energy Conservation with Central and Local Displays. *Energy and Buildings* 39 (4): 495–503. https://doi.org/10.1016/j.enbuild.2006.06.009.

Yan, D., Hong, T., Dong, B. et al. (2017). IEA EBC Annex 66: Definition and Simulation of Occupant Behavior in Buildings. *Energy and Buildings* 156 (December): 258–270. https://doi.org/10.1016/j.enbuild.2017.09.084.

Yan, D., O'Brien, W., Hong, T. et al. (2015). Occupant Behavior Modeling for Building Performance Simulation: Current State and Future Challenges. *Energy and Buildings* 107 (November): 264–278. https://doi.org/10.1016/j.enbuild.2015.08.032.

Yoshino, H., Hong, T., and Nord, N. (2017). IEA EBC Annex 53: Total Energy Use in Buildings—Analysis and Evaluation Methods. *Energy and Buildings* 152 (October): 124–136. https://doi.org/10.1016/j.enbuild.2017.07.038.

Zhan, S. and Chong, A. (2021). Building Occupancy and Energy Consumption: Case Studies across Building Types. *Energy and Built Environment* 2 (2): 167–174. https://doi.org/10.1016/j.enbenv.2020.08.001.

Zhang, W., Yupeng, W., and Calautit, J.K. (2022). A Review on Occupancy Prediction through Machine Learning for Enhancing Energy Efficiency, Air Quality and Thermal Comfort in the Built Environment. *Renewable and Sustainable Energy Reviews* 167 (October): 112704. https://doi.org/10.1016/j.rser.2022.112704.

Zhu, Xianli, and Gabriela Prata Dias. 2021. "BEHAVE 2020-2021 – the 6th European Conference on Behaviour Change for Energy Efficiency," 294.

10

Understanding Social Dynamics in Urban Building and Transportation Energy Behavior

Narjes Abbasabadi

Department of Architecture, School of Architecture, College of Built Environments, University of Washington, Seattle, WA, USA

Introduction

Cities need to establish energy and carbon reduction targets to address climate change, a global priority. It's crucial to understand urban energy dynamics by considering the interactions among humans, resources, and built environments. This understanding can help alter energy consumption patterns and create more efficient, livable, and sustainable cities. However, modeling urban energy systems, a part of larger complex urban systems, comes with a high level of uncertainty. This uncertainty affects the reliability and applicability of urban energy studies in policy-making. The gap between real energy consumption and modeled predictions largely arises not from the thermodynamic behavior of energy consumption, but from overlooking dynamic human-related contexts.

Urban energy use of buildings and transportation is notably influenced by urban spatial patterns and socio-economic factors (Liu et al. 2019). Previous studies largely centered on the impacts of urban spatial factors such as urban density (Newman and Kenworthy 1989; Steemers 2003; Norman et al. 2006; Clark 2013), and building characteristics (Steemers 2003; Martins, Faraut, and Adolphe 2019). Conversely, human-centric determinants such as user behavior (Yu et al. 2011; Jia, Srinivasan, and Raheem 2017; Kim et al. 2017; Happle, Fonseca, and Schlueter 2018), and socio-economic factors (Yun and Steemers 2011; Büchs and Schnepf 2013; Wiedenhofer, Lenzen, and Steinberger 2013; Dagoumas 2014) are recognized as urban energy use drivers (Yang and Becerik-Gerber 2016; Carpino et al. 2018; Jazaeri, Gordon, and Alpcan 2019; Saha et al. 2019). Most past research explores and quantifies the impacts of occupancy on energy use in isolated individual buildings (Yang and Becerik-Gerber 2016; Carpino et al. 2018; Zahiri and Elsharkawy 2018; Jazaeri, Gordon, and Alpcan 2019) or at city or national scales through a top-down approach (Liu et al. 2019). A few studies (Huebner et al. 2015, 2016) explore a comparative analysis of building characteristics, socio-demographics, and appliances, alongside behavioral and attitudinal aspects. These analyses propose that building factors explain the majority of variability in residential

---

Artificial Intelligence in Performance-Driven Design: Theories, Methods, and Tools, First Edition.
Edited by Narjes Abbasabadi and Mehdi Ashayeri.
©2024 John Wiley & Sons Inc. Published 2024 by John Wiley & Sons Inc.

energy use, and when controlling for building characteristics, socio-demographic factors exhibit relatively slight explanatory power. Building size, household size, ownership, and heating season length were identified as significant predictors. Meanwhile, attitudinal factors were not deemed to be very significant predictors. Contrarily, other research (Zahiri and Elsharkawy 2018) posits that the occupants' socio-demographic characteristics significantly influence energy use, and inefficient building elements such as the building envelope result in excessive energy load for heating (Zahiri and Elsharkawy 2018). The influence of occupancy on energy use behavior has been modeled for designing new buildings and for retrofit purposes (Zahiri and Elsharkawy 2018).

Current urban-scale building energy models, based on existing studies and available tools, do not take into account occupancy features and occupant behavior, as these aspects are typically addressed only at the individual building level (Happle, Fonseca, and Schlueter 2018; Abbasabadi and Ashayeri 2019). These models mainly couple building archetypes with predetermined occupant behavior models based on the building occupancy types, which is a simplistic approach. Unlike the present models, there's a lack of models that incorporate a realistic socio-economic determinants for occupancy (Abbasabadi et al. 2019) or utilize person-based and stochastic occupant behavior modeling (Happle, Fonseca, and Schlueter 2018). Such progressive modeling approaches could potentially provide a more accurate picture of energy use patterns.

Past energy studies often simplify building occupancy to just the presence and number of occupants, broadly categorizing it as real-time occupancy or long-term occupancy (occupancy profile). Both types, with their fluctuations, play a role in energy efficiency (Yang and Becerik-Gerber 2016). Occupancy affects how building systems like lighting and appliances are used, contributes to heat gain through occupants' metabolism and activities, and influences HVAC loads when occupants interact with building components like adjusting windows and doors (Yang and Becerik-Gerber 2016).

Occupancy has also been examined in a broader sense by incorporating socio-economic factors into energy consumption models. For instance, a research by (Carpino et al. 2018) explored occupancy patterns based on five factors: household size, employment, education, age, and income categorizing them into high, medium, and low occupancy classes. Their results indicated that the low occupancy class had the least average energy use. In another study by (Jazaeri, Gordon, and Alpcan 2019), six common occupancy scenarios were modeled to understand energy dynamics. These scenarios include: (1) occupants with full-time jobs, (2) retired occupants or families with young children, (3) occupants who spend their afternoon outside the house, (4) occupants with part-time job in the morning, (5) occupants with a part-time job in the afternoon, and (6) occupants with a child that goes to school. The study concluded that occupancy patterns significantly impact annual building energy use, with scenarios having higher unoccupied periods showing lower energy demand.

Social relations also play a part in household energy behavior. A recent review by (Hargreaves and Middlemiss 2020) argues that targeting people through their social relations, rather than as isolated individuals, can alter energy consumption habits. For instance, social relations can influence household energy use, like heating and cooling loads, and even thermal-comfort levels. Acknowledging the social structure and its influence could pave the way for new policy approaches and interventions. The way people interact and the social influence they experience can also shape mobility and transportation energy usage patterns. While limited studies have explored the association between the SDPH and urban energy behavior in an integrated way that includes both urban building energy and transportation across urban zones is lacking. The impact of SDPH on city energy consumption remains unclear. Most existing studies focus either on individual building analysis or transportation energy, often relying on aggregated data and overlooking human-related factors. In this study, we aim for a more empirically-grounded analyses of how SDPH relates to urban energy behavior, taking into account both household building and transportation energy use in an integrated manner.

New advancements in information communication technologies, coupled with open data, significantly enhance our understanding of social dynamics in urban energy consumption, despite challenges arising from social and technological interactions (Abbasabadi and Mehdi Ashayeri 2017). Data-driven models, leveraging artificial intelligence and machine learning, are increasingly being utilized to understand socio-economic dynamics and occupancy patterns, as well as to predict future scenarios. Recently, machine learning algorithms like ANN, alongside other statistical models, have gained prominence in building occupancy modeling, including urban energy use (Abbasabadi and Ashayeri 2019), intra-urban exposure to ambient pollution modeling (Ashayeri et al. 2020), energy load optimization via HVAC and lighting control, occupant detection, people counting, movement tracking within specified areas, and learning user preferences to enhance occupant comfort levels (Saha et al. 2019).

This research integrates social health and occupancy factors into a unified urban model for building and transportation energy use, employing open data and an artificial intelligence-based approach using the ANN method. This method is further enriched with explanatory models through Garson, PDP, and Lek's profile approaches. This setup aids in developing an effective predictive model and unravelling complex patterns to understand the impact of each variable. Incorporating socio-economic and occupancy indicators facilitates a deeper insight into urban energy behavior across urban zones. An in-depth quantitative analysis is provided, exploring the intricate relationship between socio-spatial patterns and the primary facets of urban energy use — building and transportation, by employing various sensitivity analysis methods.

Methodology

In this methodological approach, an integrated model is developed to empirically investigate the impact of social health and occupancy factors on energy consumption in buildings and transportation sectors. The model encompasses a variety of variables: urban spatial patterns, building characteristics, occupancy details, socio-economic elements, and mobility and travel behaviors. By accounting for other variables, the methodology seeks to quantify the relative influence of social health and occupancy factors on urban energy behavior. This framework is developed to offer a comprehensive insight into the interplay between social health and occupancy through spatial disparity lenses and their collective effect on urban energy behavior.

Modeling Framework

A data-driven Urban Energy Use Modeling (UEUM) framework was established, employing the ANN machine learning algorithm for both predictive and explanatory models (Abbasabadi et al. 2019). This research primarily shares the findings from the explanatory model to discern the impact of social health and occupancy variables on energy use, while adjusting for other urban socio-spatial variables. A detailed outline of this framework, especially emphasizing the predictive model for multi-scale UEUM, is documented in (Abbasabadi et al. 2019) in the Applied Energy journal. Initially, the predictive model was utilized to estimate urban building energy use for buildings lacking energy use data. Utilizing a merged dataset of 58,205 buildings, the model projected the Energy Use Intensity (EUI) for 820,606 out-of-sample buildings in Chicago, with the necessary building characteristics data sourced from the Chicago Building Footprints (CBF) GIS-based dataset but lacking energy data. Concurrently, a travel demand model was constructed to estimate transportation energy use per household. Subsequently, an integrated model encompassing both building and transportation energy use was developed to simultaneously assess the two primary facets of urban energy use. This model also endeavored to analyze the contribution of each variable, encapsulating critical urban attributes like building characteristics, urban spatial patterns, occupancy features, and mobility and travel behaviors. This research leverages this model to explain the association between variables, clarifying the relative contribution of each and quantifying the effect of key urban attributes on energy use.

ANNs (Rosenblatt 1958) is believed as a versatile machine learning algorithm (Deng, Fannon, and Eckelman 2018; Abbasabadi and Ashayeri 2019) among other algorithms, were tested to enable capturing the complex and non-linear relationships between social health and energy dynamics across communities in the city. The ANN model, as a robust technique, enables capturing non-linear patterns of the complex data and provides the best results for integrated building and transportation energy modeling. Structuring the topology of the ANN networks and training highly efficient model, therefore, is a challenging task and is usually based on the rule of thumb approach. In the present research, we developed an automation script using nested for-loop (loop inside a loop) approach in *R* programming language to capture the best model in terms of performance. We used the cross-validation method, the fivefold, which according to the previous studies is known as an effective method (Amasyali and El-Gohary 2018; Moghadam et al. 2018).

Explanatory Model

The outcomes produced by the ANN, often termed as a "black box" model, can be challenging to interpret. However, several robust explanatory methods exist that can be coupled with neural networks to elucidate the workings of this black-box model (Olden, Joy, and Death 2004), enabling the interpretation of complex relationships identified (Gevrey, Dimopoulos, and Lek, 2003, 2006; Olden, Joy, and Death 2004; Fischer 2015). In this analysis, the Garson algorithm (Garson 1991; Fischer 2015), Lek's Profile (Gevrey, Dimopoulos, and Lek 2003, 2006), and PDP (Gevrey, Dimopoulos, and Lek 2003) are employed to assess the relative impact of each input variable on the energy use of urban buildings and transportation.

Data

The integrated model encompasses several key urban attributes such as building characteristics, urban spatial patterns, occupancy characteristics, and social health indicators. Various datasets have been utilized for this model, including the CBF dataset (Building Footprints [Current] 2015), Property Tax data from the Assessor's Office (Cook County Assessor Data 2019), Urban Sprawl data for the United States (Updated Urban Sprawl Data for the United States 2010), Socio-economic Indicators dataset (Census Data-Selected Socio-economic Indicators in Chicago, 2008–2012 2019), Chicago Energy Benchmarking dataset (City of Chicago 2016) (comprising 2,717 buildings larger than 50,000 ft^2), and Chicago Energy Usage dataset (City of Chicago 2010) (consisting of 65,378 buildings of all sizes). These datasets are used to predict the energy usage of buildings in Chicago for which energy data is not available.

Transportation data is sourced from the Chicago Regional Household Travel Tracker Survey by CMAP (Household Travel Survey 2016), Fuel Economy data (Fuel Economy 2019) from the US Department of Energy (DOE), and the Average Passenger Transportation Energy Intensity per mile from the US Department of Transportation (DOT) and Bureau of Transportation Statistics (BTS) (National Transportation Statistics 2019). Mobility factors like walkability, bikeability, and transit-oriented indices are obtained from the Walkability, Bikeability, Transit-Oriented Score dataset (Chicago Neighborhoods on Walk Score 2019). Additional details on data input, processing, and normality tests for integrated urban energy modeling of building and transportation components can be found in the research by (Abbasabadi et al. 2019).

The Urban Transportation Energy (UTE) model is developed using travel demand information alongside transportation EUI data for various travel modes. The travel demand modeling utilizes the latest Chicago Regional Household Travel Tracker Survey (Household Travel Survey 2016), encompassing daily travel details such as travel mode (car, bus, subway, rail transit, etc.), distance traveled, and vehicle manufacturing information (year, make, model). This survey includes data from 23,808 individuals residing in 10,552 households within the northeastern Illinois region, collected over one or two-day survey periods. The distance value indicates the direct line distance between origin and destination for each trip segment, based on actual location data. However, in the public dataset, location data is anonymized using the centroid of the resident census tract for privacy reasons.

The estimation of mode-based transportation energy use per household for light-duty vehicles and private cars is carried out using the Average Miles per Gallon (MPG) data from the Fuel Economy dataset provided by the DOE (Fuel Economy 2019). For public transit energy use estimation, the average passenger transportation energy intensity per mile from the DOT and BTS is utilized. This data, available in the National Transportation Statistics database (National Transportation Statistics 2019), gives the annual average transportation energy intensity per passenger. Additional details on transportation energy modeling are discussed in a research by (Abbasabadi et al. 2019) (Figures 10.1–10.3).

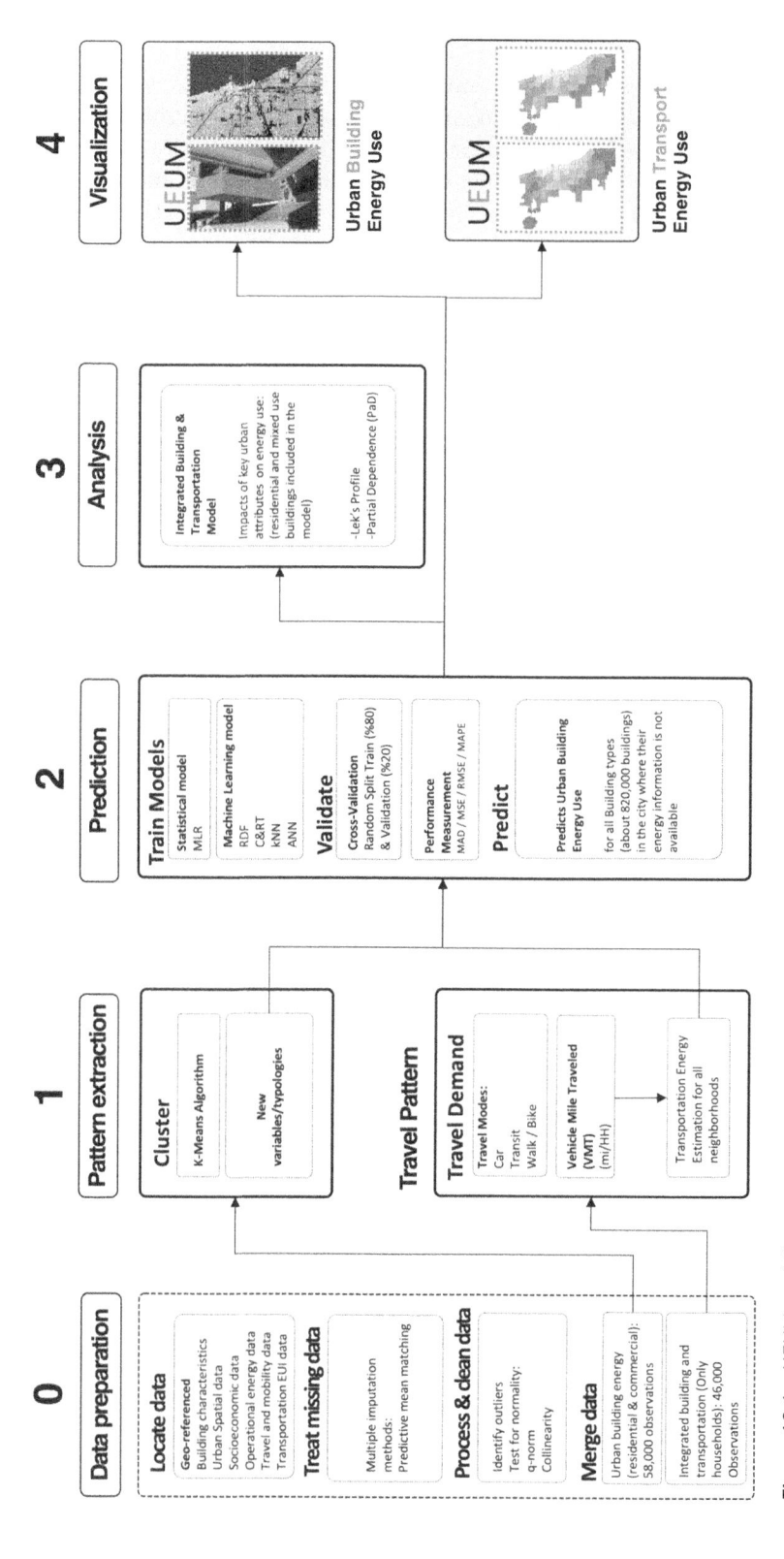

Figure 10.1 UEUM workflow.

Figure 10.2 Urban building energy use prediction and mapping for Chicago, IL.

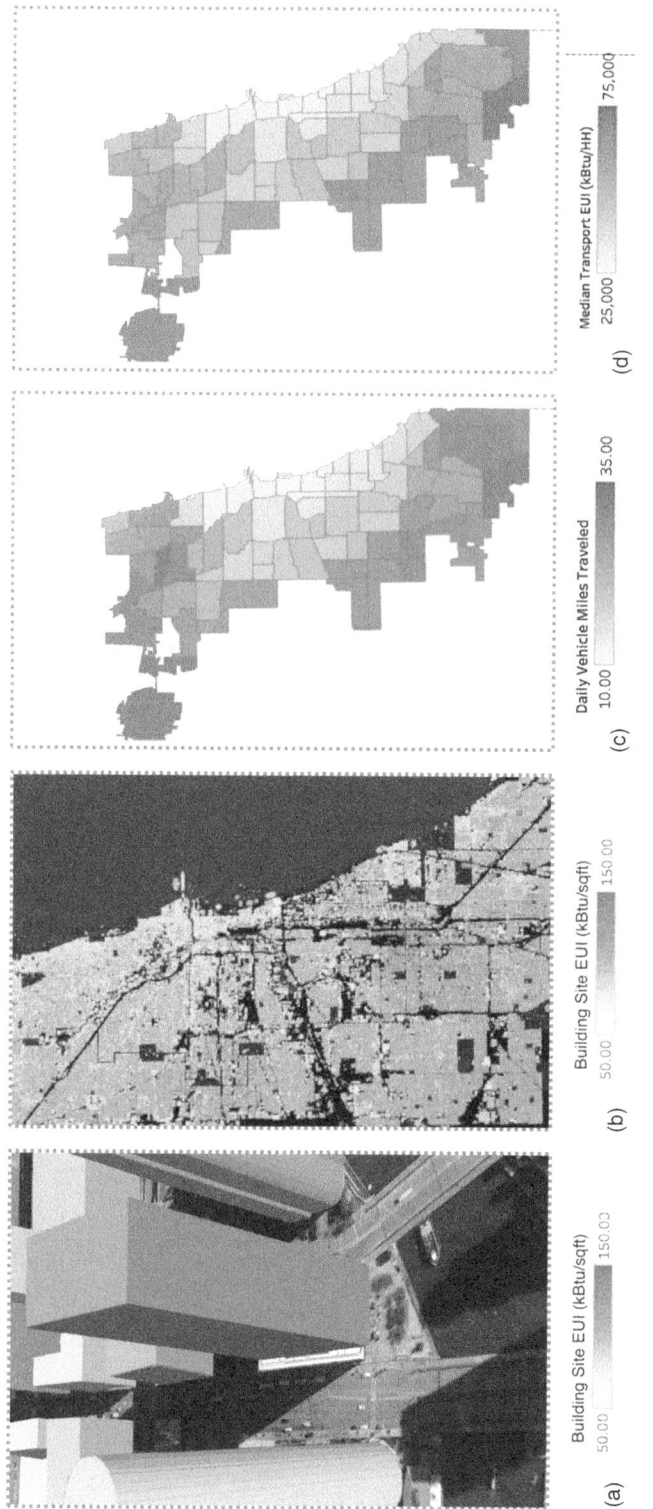

Figure 10.3 Multi-scale and multi-dimensional UEUM and visualization for Chicago, IL; (a, b) urban building energy use, (c) travel demand, and (d) transportation energy use.

Results and Discussion

Effects of Occupancy and Socio-economic Factors

In existing studies, occupancy's role in energy usage is often explored by examining various factors like employment, education, household size, income, and ownership, among other socio-demographic and behavior-related factors (Huebner et al. 2015, 2016). This research focused on several socio-economic and occupancy variables such as housing crowd, poverty level, unemployment, education, dependency, per capita income, household size, percentage of occupied units, and total occupants (TOC). We offer a detailed analysis of how these socio-economic and occupancy patterns interact with urban energy use behavior, focusing on both building and transportation sectors. Including these indicators enriches the modeling of integrated urban energy use, providing a clearer understanding of household energy demand patterns.

Variable Importance (VI)

The VI results indicate that the urban energy use in both buildings and transportation is significantly influenced by SDPH. As depicted in Figure 10.4, the Garson algorithm was utilized to display the relative contributions of each variable on building (Figure 10.4a) and transportation (Figure 10.4b) energy use, normalized between 0 and 1. Among the socio-economic indicators, income, unemployment, crowded housing (PHC), and total number of occupants were identified as major contributors to building EUI, following the building characteristics variables like building size, height, and year built. On the side of transportation EUI, household education level, poverty level, household dependency level, and income were identified as robust predictors, following essential variables like neighborhood features such as transit-oriented design, bikeability, and Vehicle Miles Traveled (VMT). Additionally, neighborhood walkability and distance to the Central Business District (CBD) were recognized as significant contributors to transportation energy use, with the unemployment factor following them. Urban spatial pattern determinants like distance to CBD and sprawl index were noted as predictors for both transportation and building EUI. However, their impact is relatively lower compared to other predictors such as building characteristics for building EUI prediction, and mobility indices like transit-oriented and bikeability indices of neighborhoods for transportation EUI prediction, as well as occupancy and socio-economic variables for predicting both building and transportation EUI.

Lek's Profile

The application of both Lek's profile and PDP methods (Gevrey, Dimopoulos, and Lek 2003) has been proven to be effective in enhancing the explanatory capabilities and interpretability of ANN beyond VI insights. Lek's profile method was integrated into the ANN model, and the outcomes are depicted in Figure 10.5. The profiles explain the relative contribution of each variable in the model while maintaining other variables at their constant values, assessing the impact on building and transportation energy use simultaneously. Six clusters were designated within Lek's profile encompassing all variables; these include building characteristics, urban spatial patterns, occupancy, socio-economic factors, and mobility and travel patterns. The results elucidate the influence of changes in input variables on the building

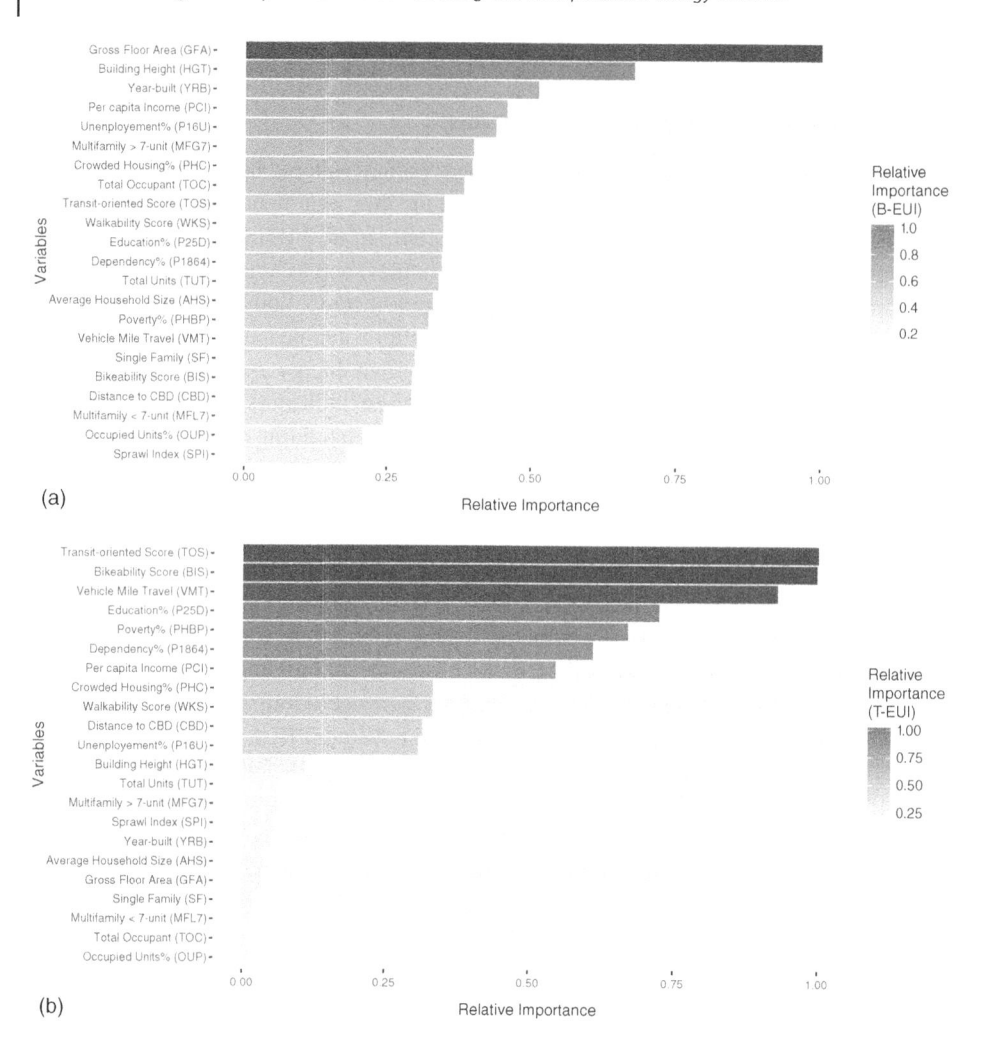

Figure 10.4 Variable importance plot in the integrated model; (a) building EUI and (b) transportation EUI. Source: Abbasabadi et al. (2019).

site EUI and transportation EUI. The findings from Lek's profile resonate with those from the Garson algorithm. Building attributes such as size and height emerge as paramount factors affecting building energy use, whereas neighborhood attributes like transit-oriented design, walkability, and bikeability, alongside location, significantly influence transportation EUI. Occupancy and socio-economic factors are identified as strong predictors for both building and transportation energy use. Moreover, building-related characteristics such as height and size also impact transportation energy use, albeit to a varying degree. The data suggests that urban energy consumption in both buildings and transportation is substantially affected by urban spatial configurations and socio-economic factors.

The profiles depicted in Figure 10.5 show the relationship between Per-Capita (household) Income (PCI) and EUI for buildings and transportation, with other variables held constant at their mean values (indicated in red). Three distinct income ranges are evident in the building site EUI profile: $0–$64,000, $64,000–$75,000, and above $75,000. Notably, the most

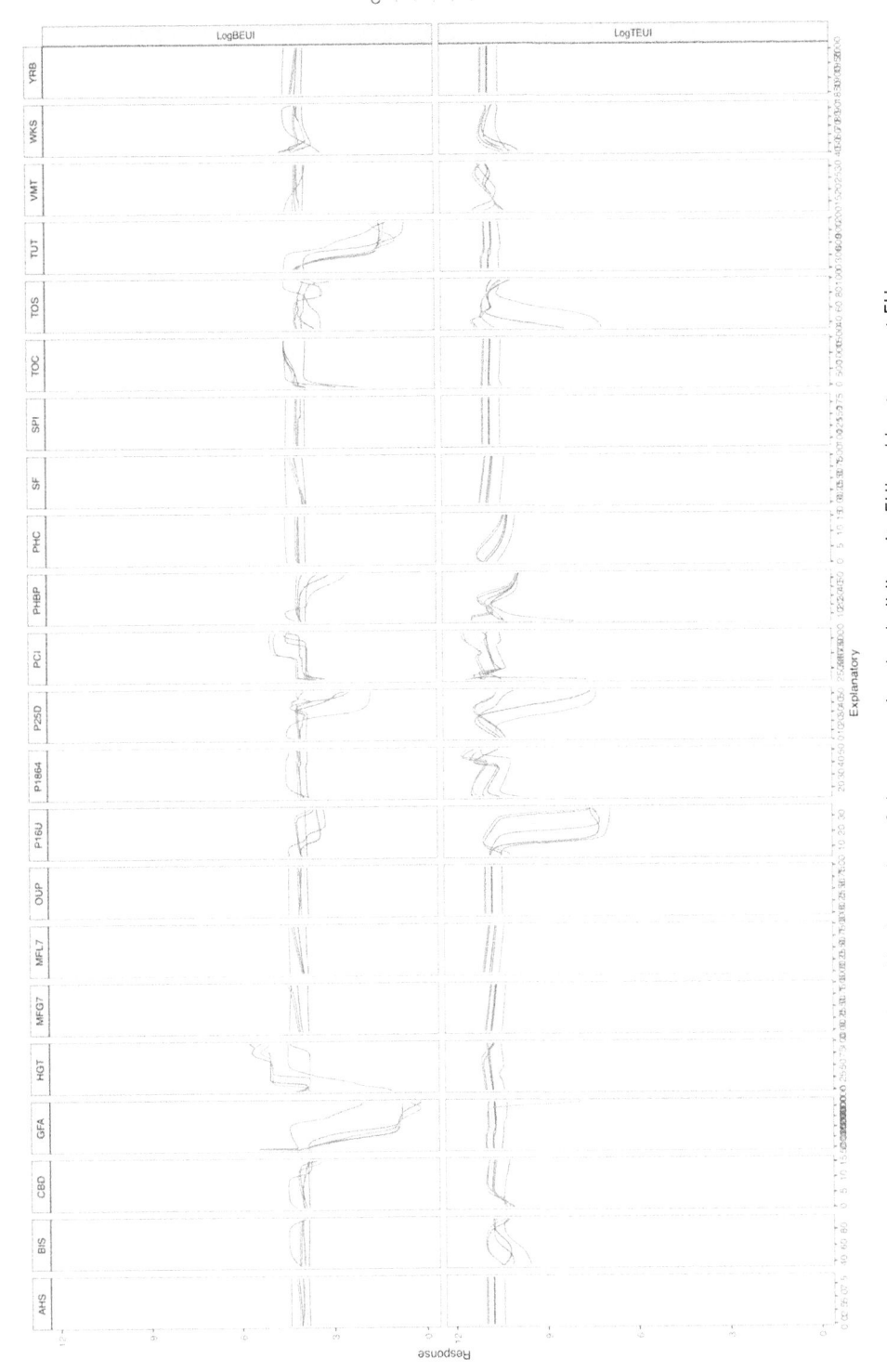

Figure 10.5 Lek's profile of all variables with six number of clusters against log building site EUI and log transport EU.

noticeable variation occurs within the second range ($64,000–$75,000). The pattern for transportation EUI mirrors that of building EUI, albeit with a less noticeable variation. In essence, the model reveals a peak in building energy use at a PCI of $75,000, with a comparable yet subtler trend in transportation energy use. This trend suggests a propensity for higher-income households to exhibit elevated energy consumption, corroborating findings from earlier studies examining the influence of income on building (Jazaeri, Gordon, and Alpcan 2019) and transportation (Zhang and Ding 2017) energy use.

Moreover, the Lek's profile indicates that the TOC variable interacts more with the Building Site EUI at higher levels, as depicted in Figure 10.5, whereas it shows a diminished interaction with Transportation EUI as TOC increases. This behavior suggests that an increase in TOC may correspond to an increased presence at home. The PHC variable, representing the percentage of rooms occupied by more than one person, is another notable factor. The sensitivity of both response variables, Building Site EUI and Transportation EUI, to the PHC variable is similar, yet the trends differ as illustrated in Figure 10.4. The Building Site EUI shows increased interaction at higher levels of PHC, whereas the Transportation EUI exhibits a polynomial interaction with PHC, peaking at 75% occupancy. The most pronounced interaction for Transportation EUI occurs between 75% and 90% occupancy. In conclusion, akin to prior socio-economic indicators, the PHC variable is a crucial factor in refining urban energy use models. The Dependency Variable (P1864) demonstrates a notable positive interaction with Building Site EUI between 40% and 43%, while the interaction experiences significant variations between 0% to 13.5% and 43% to 46.5% on the Transportation EUI profile. This variable manifests a non-linear interaction with both Building Site EUI and Transportation EUI profiles, albeit with a higher magnitude of interaction on the Transportation EUI. In addition, the household dependency is a strong predictor to determine urban energy use patterns, particularly for transportation energy use.

The results obtained herein confirm the importance of occupancy and socio-economic variables in previous studies such as (Carpino et al. 2018) which examines occupancy patterns based on five factors including (1) household size, (2) employment, (3) education, (4) age, and (5) income parameters. They categorized these aspects according to high, medium, and low occupancy classes, finding that the low occupancy class had the least average energy use. In another study by Zahiri and Elsharkawy (2018), the occupancy factor was incorporated in energy use model of a council housing tower block in London for retrofit purposes, highlighting the impact of occupants' socio-demographic traits on energy use. Earlier investigations, such as (Yang and Becerik-Gerber 2016), delved into the mechanisms by which occupancy and socio-economic factors affect energy use. They noted how the presence and number of occupants influence building energy demand, affecting the usage of building systems like lighting and appliances. Occupants' activities and metabolism contribute to heat gain, while their interactions with building components like adjusting openings, windows, and doors affect HVAC loads. However, a differing viewpoint is presented in studies by Huebner et al. (2015, 2016), asserting that the influence of occupancy, socio-demographics, and occupants' behavior and attitudes is considerably less compared to building characteristics. According to their findings, it's primarily building factors like size, household size, and ownership that account for the majority of the variability in residential energy use, while socio-demographic factors offer limited explanatory power and aren't significant predictors.

Figures 10.6 and 10.7 present heat maps from the 2D PDP analysis, created from the ANN model, illustrating the modeled relationship between socio-economic factors and distance to

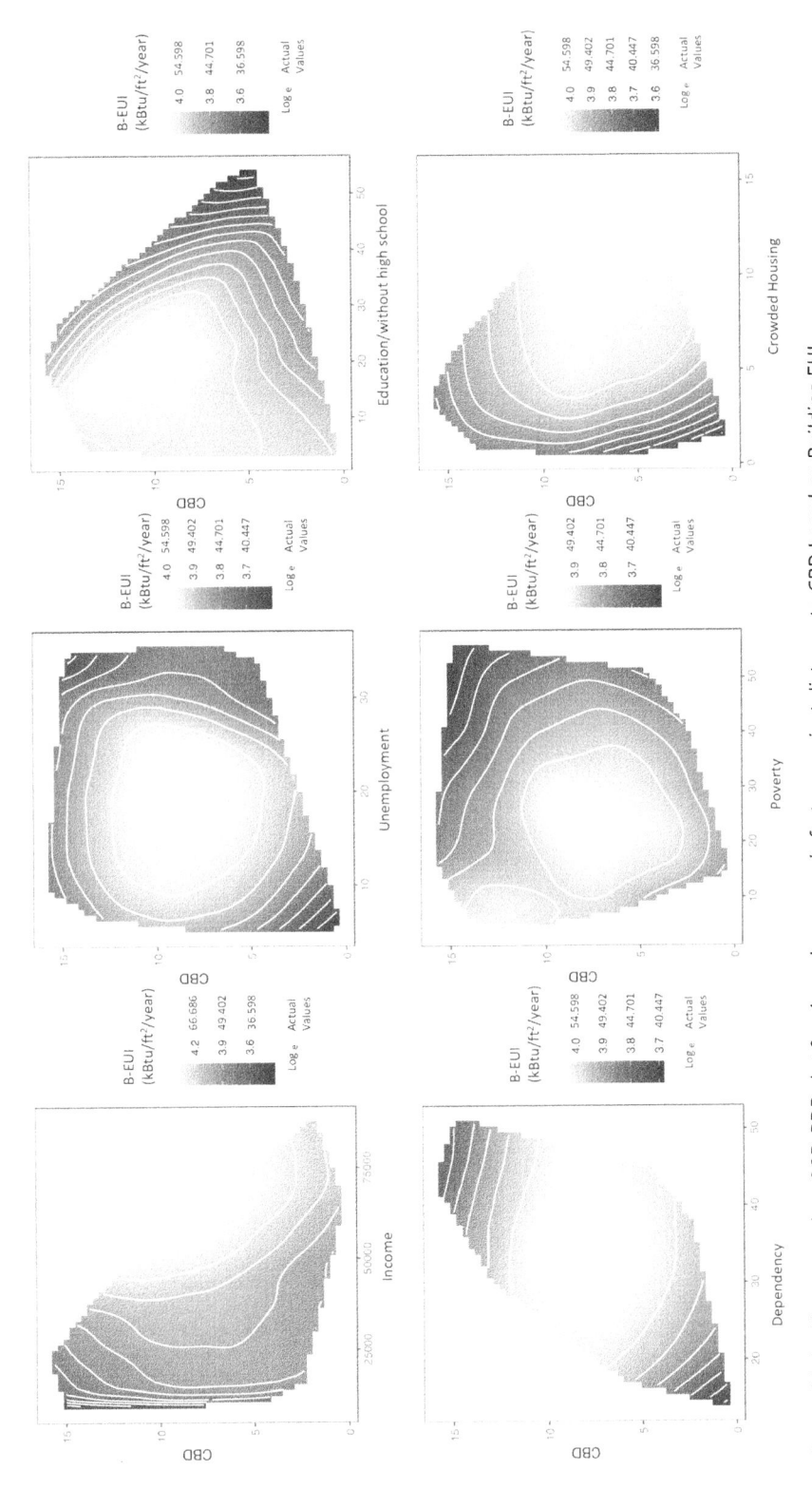

Figure 10.6 Heat-map plot of 2D-PDP plot for six socio-economic factors against distance to CBD based on Building EUI.

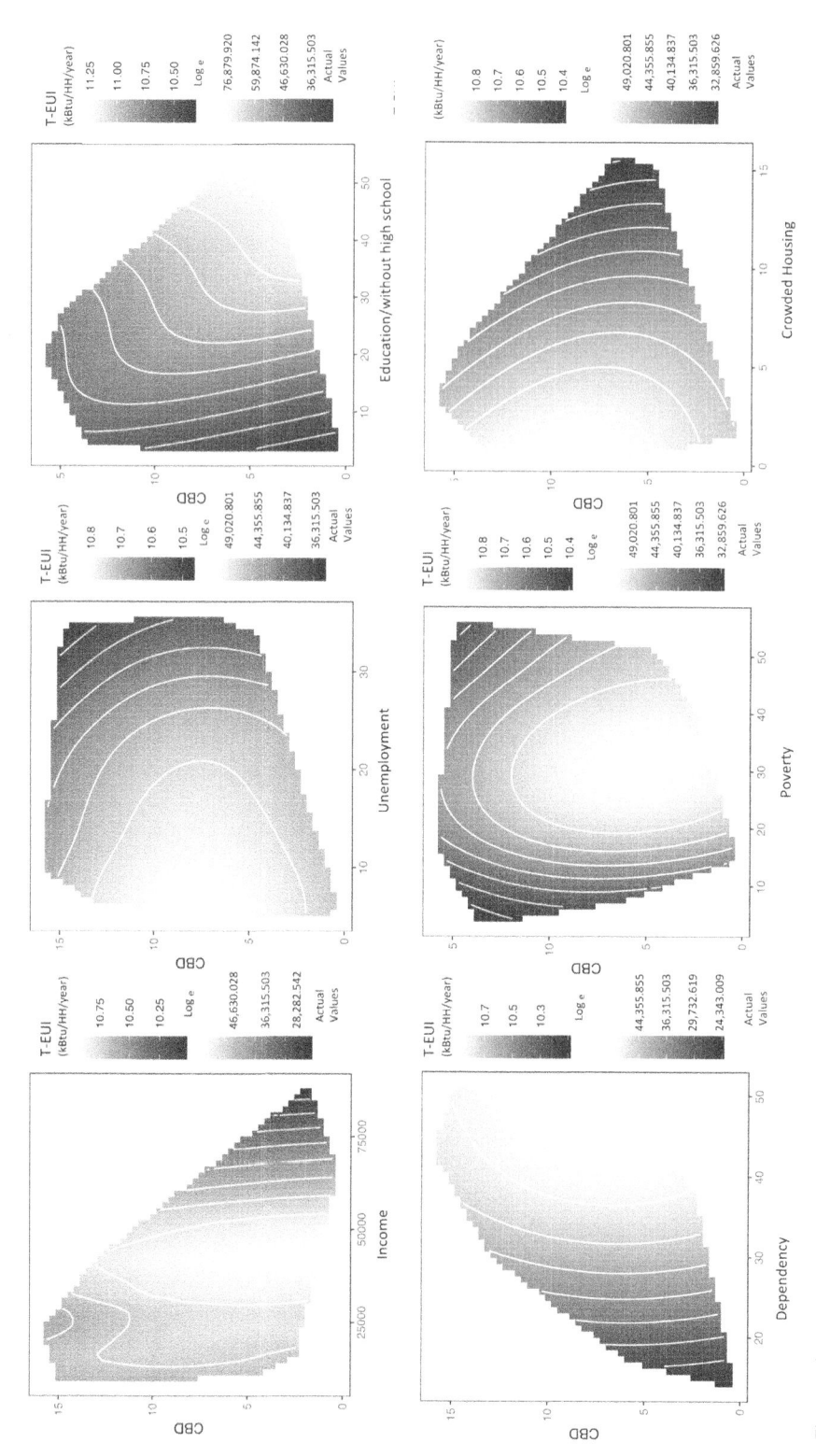

Figure 10.7 Heat-map plot of six socio-economic factors against distance to CBD based on transportation EUI.

the CBD with respect to urban building and transportation Energy Use Intensities (EUIs), respectively. The plots suggest that the effects of the variables on the model's predictions are not uniform across their range. The impact on energy use appears to be modulated by the residential building locations, for which the distance to the CBD serves as a representative metric.

Specifically, regarding the income factor, for buildings located 5–10 miles away from the business center, occupied by households with incomes ranging from $50,000 to $75,000; the model predicts a higher Building Energy Use Intensity (B-EUI). On the other hand, households residing 2.5–10 miles away from the CBD, with incomes ranging from $35,000 to $50,000, are associated with higher Transportation Energy Use Intensity (T-EUI) predictions by the model. This analysis offers insights into how socio-economic and spatial factors might be correlated with urban energy consumption, as estimated by the ANN model.

In addition, the unemployment factor displays distinct patterns in its relation to B-EUI and T-EUI, across varying distances from the CBD. Notably, a higher unemployment rate paired with buildings situated 7.5–10 miles away from the CBD appears to correspond with elevated predictions of B-EUI. Conversely, the distance range of 5–10 miles from the CBD showcases more pronounced predicted T-EUI values. Furthermore, the Poverty variable illustrates a notable effect on B-EUI, especially when buildings are situated within a 5–10 miles range from the CBD. For T-EUI, the impact of the Poverty variable appears more pronounced within the broader range of 2.5–10 miles from the CBD. The analysis also indicates a relationship between the percentage of PHC variable and B-EUI, particularly for buildings located 3–10 miles away from the CBD. However, for T-EUI, the impact seems to exhibit a different pattern, warranting further examination to understand the nuanced interactions better.

Moreover, the interaction between Poverty, CBD, and B-EUI reveals distinct patterns at two specific points; when Poverty index is below 10 and when it is 20, with CBD distances of about 12.5 and 7.5 miles, respectively (Figure 10.6). These spikes suggest conditions where the model predicts higher B-EUI, particularly associating lower poverty levels at certain distances from the CBD with higher predicted B-EUI. These spikes could represent different urban zones where socio-economic factors and geographical location lead to variations in predicted building energy use. Regarding T-EUI in Figure 10.7, a notable spike is observed when poverty is at 30 and CBD distance is at 5 miles, indicating a condition where the model predicts increased T-EUI. This specific association of poverty level and CBD distance with higher predicted T-EUI could represent a particular urban zone where socio-economic factors and proximity to the business district contribute to the variation in predicted transportation energy consumption. Understanding these patterns is crucial for exploring the interplay of socio-economic and spatial factors on UTE consumption, providing a foundation for informed energy conservation and urban planning initiatives.

The observed patterns suggest that household unemployment may influence building occupancy levels, as it affects the presence of occupants within buildings (Yang and Becerik-Gerber 2016). Increased presence at home typically leads to higher energy demands for heating, cooling, lighting, and appliance usage. Existing literature supports a positive relationship between employment factors and building energy demand (Jazaeri, Gordon, and Alpcan 2019). However, the non-linear pattern observed in the case of Chicago hints at a positive relationship up to a certain point, after which it appears to become negative.

The impacts of occupancy is explored in exaisting literature. For example, Jazaeri, Gordon, and Alpcan (2019) modeled six common occupancy scenarios, including (1) occupants with full-time jobs, (2) retired occupants or families with young children, (3) occupants spending afternoons outside, (4) occupants with morning part-time jobs, (5) occupants with afternoon part-time jobs, and (6) families with school-going children in order to assess building energy use, and conclude that occupancy patterns significantly affect annual building energy use, with scenarios depicting higher unoccupied periods showing lower energy demand.

In this chapter, the PDP and Lek's profile methods were employed to delve into the impact of occupancy, mobility, and socio-economic disparities on urban energy use patterns, resonating with findings from previous studies (Yang and Becerik-Gerber 2016; Carpino et al. 2018; Jazaeri, Gordon, and Alpcan 2019; Saha et al. 2019). Contrary to earlier works that investigated the impacts of occupancy on energy use within individual buildings (Yang and Becerik-Gerber 2016; Carpino et al. 2018; Jazaeri, Gordon, and Alpcan 2019; Saha et al. 2019) or at city or national scales through a top-down approach (Liu et al. 2019), or those that focused on a single transportation factor (Murat and Ceylan 2006; Zhang and Zhao 2017), this work seeks to bridge a gap by providing an integrated analysis of both building and transportation energy concurrently. Augmented by methodological approaches, this research utilized an artificial intelligence-based approach, specifically the ANN method enriched with an in-depth explanatory model using Garson, Lek's profile, and PDP, to unveil complex patterns and better understand how each variable contributes to the model. The endeavor here was to comprehend the effect of a wide range of socio-economic indicators on urban energy use behavior. Our findings underscore that urban energy consumption, encompassing both building and transportation sectors, is significantly influenced by spatial and socio-economic factors, corroborating earlier findings (Liu et al. 2019). It is elucidated that urban spatial patterns can significantly influence energy consumption by altering occupant behavior and transportation habits.

Conclusion

The main objective of this chapter was to explore the impact of socio-economic dynamics of public health on building and transportation energy use patterns. This research, utilizing ANN modeling augmented by Garson, Lek's profile, and PDP methods, pointed out that social health, occupancy, and mobility patterns are among the important determinants of urban building energy use. The findings showed that all the studied socio-economic factors related to public health have a meaningful relationship with urban energy behavior, covering both building and transportation energy use. However, household income stood out as a more significant factor affecting urban energy use, highlighting its central role in this context. On the other hand, the other socio-economic factors showed a weaker association with urban energy use, indicating a graded influence among the factors. This analysis helps provide a clearer understanding which is useful for discussing more energy-efficient urban frameworks while considering the socio-economic and public health variables involved. Through this endeavor, the chapter aim to contribute to the larger discussion on sustainable urban development by examining the complex interaction between socio-economic factors and urban energy consumption.

References

Abbasabadi, N. and Mehdi Ashayeri, J.K. (2017). Towards an Adaptive Urbanism beyond Hard Control: The Theories of Johnson and Lefebvre. In: *Architectural Research Addressing Societal Challenges*, 1ste, vol. Vol. 1, 257–262. London, UK: CRC Press/Taylor & Francis Group https://www.taylorfrancis.com/.

Abbasabadi, N. and Ashayeri, M. (2019). Urban Energy Use Modeling Methods and Tools; A Review and an Outlook for Future Tools. *Building and Environment* 106270. https://doi.org/10.1016/j.buildenv.2019.106270.

Abbasabadi, N., Ashayeri, M., Azari, R. et al. (2019). An Integrated Data-Driven Framework for Urban Energy Use Modeling (UEUM). *Applied Energy* 253 (November): 113550. https://doi.org/10.1016/j.apenergy.2019.113550.

Amasyali, K. and El-Gohary, N.M. (2018). A Review of Data-Driven Building Energy Consumption Prediction Studies. *Renewable and Sustainable Energy Reviews* 81: 1192–1205. https://doi.org/10.1016/j.rser.2017.04.095.

Ashayeri, M., Abbasabadi, N., Heidarinejad, M., and Stephens, B. (2020). Predicting Intraurban PM2.5 Concentrations Using Enhanced Machine Learning Approaches and Incorporating Human Activity Patterns. *Environmental Research* November: 110423. https://doi.org/10.1016/j.envres.2020.110423.

Büchs, M. and Schnepf, S.V. (2013). Who Emits Most? Associations Between Socio-Economic Factors and UK Households' Home Energy, Transport, Indirect and Total CO2 Emissions. *Ecological Economics* 90 (June): 114–123. https://doi.org/10.1016/j.ecolecon.2013.03.007.

"Building Footprints (Current)." 2015. Chicago Data Portal. 2015. https://data.cityofchicago.org/Buildings/Building-Footprints-current-/hz9b-7nh8?category=Buildings&view_name=Building-Footprints-current.

Carpino, C., Fajilla, G., Gaudio, A. et al. (2018). Application of Survey on Energy Consumption and Occupancy in Residential Buildings. An Experience in Southern Italy. In: *Energy Procedia, ATI 2018—73rd Conference of the Italian Thermal Machines Engineering Association, 148 (August)*, 1082–1089. https://doi.org/10.1016/j.egypro.2018.08.051.

"Census Data-Selected Socioeconomic Indicators in Chicago, 2008–2012." 2019. Chicago Data Portal. 2019. https://data.cityofchicago.org/Health-Human-Services/Census-Data-Selected-socioeconomic-indicators-in-C/kn9c-c2s2.

"Chicago Neighborhoods on Walk Score." 2019. Walk Score. 2019. https://www.walkscore.com/IL/Chicago.

City of Chicago (2010). Energy Usage 2010, City of Chicago, Data Portal. *City of Chicago, Environment & Sustainable Development.* 2010: https://data.cityofchicago.org/Environment-Sustainable-Development/Energy-Usage-2010/8yq3-m6wp.

City of Chicago (2016). Chicago Energy Benchmarking-2016 Data Reported in 2017, City of Chicago, Data Portal. *City of Chicago, Environment & Sustainable Development* 2016: https://data.cityofchicago.org/Environment-Sustainable-Development/Chicago-Energy-Benchmarking-2016-Data-Reported-in-/fpwt-snya.

Clark, T.A. (2013). Metropolitan Density, Energy Efficiency and Carbon Emissions: Multi-Attribute Tradeoffs and Their Policy Implications. *Energy Policy* 53: 413–428. https://doi.org/10.1016/j.enpol.2012.11.006.

Cook County Assessor Data (2019). Cook County Government. *Open Data* 2019: https://datacatalog.cookcountyil.gov/.

Dagoumas, A. (2014). Modelling Socio-Economic and Energy Aspects of Urban Systems. *Sustainable Cities and Society* 13 (October): 192–206. https://doi.org/10.1016/j.scs.2013.11.003.

Deng, H., Fannon, D., and Eckelman, M.J. (2018). Predictive Modeling for US Commercial Building Energy Use: A Comparison of Existing Statistical and Machine Learning Algorithms Using CBECS Microdata. *Energy and Buildings* 163: 34–43. https://doi.org/10.1016/j.enbuild.2017.12.031.

Fischer, A. (2015). How to Determine the Unique Contributions of Input-Variables to the Nonlinear Regression Function of a Multilayer Perceptron. *Ecological Modelling* 309–310 (August): 60–63. https://doi.org/10.1016/j.ecolmodel.2015.04.015.

"Fuel Economy." 2019. U.S. of Energy. 2019. https://www.fueleconomy.gov/.

Garson, G.D. (1991). Interpreting Neural-Network Connection Weights. *AI Expert* 6 (4): 46–51.

Gevrey, M., Dimopoulos, I., and Lek, S. (2003). Review and Comparison of Methods to Study the Contribution of Variables in Artificial Neural Network Models. *Ecological Modelling* 160 (3): 249–264. https://doi.org/10.1016/S0304-3800(02)00257-0.

Gevrey, M., Dimopoulos, I., and Lek, S. (2006). Two-Way Interaction of Input Variables in the Sensitivity Analysis of Neural Network Models. *Ecological Modelling* 195 (1–2): 43–50. https://doi.org/10.1016/j.ecolmodel.2005.11.008.

Happle, G., Fonseca, J.A., and Schlueter, A. (2018). A Review on Occupant Behavior in Urban Building Energy Models. *Energy and Buildings* 174 (September): 276–292. https://doi.org/10.1016/J.ENBUILD.2018.06.030.

Hargreaves, T. and Middlemiss, L. (2020). The Importance of Social Relations in Shaping Energy Demand. *Nature Energy* 5 (3): 195–201. https://doi.org/10.1038/s41560-020-0553-5.

"Household Travel Survey." 2016. Chicago Metropolitan Agency for Planning (CMAP). 2016. http://www.cmap.illinois.gov/data/transportation/travel-survey.

Huebner, G.M., Hamilton, I., Chalabi, Z. et al. (2015). Explaining Domestic Energy Consumption—The Comparative Contribution of Building Factors, Socio-Demographics, Behaviours and Attitudes. *Applied Energy* 159 (December): 589–600. https://doi.org/10.1016/j.apenergy.2015.09.028.

Huebner, G., Shipworth, D., Hamilton, I. et al. (2016). Understanding Electricity Consumption: A Comparative Contribution of Building Factors, Socio-Demographics, Appliances, Behaviours and Attitudes. *Applied Energy* 177 (September): 692–702. https://doi.org/10.1016/j.apenergy.2016.04.075.

Jazaeri, J., Gordon, R.L., and Alpcan, T. (2019). Influence of Building Envelopes, Climates, and Occupancy Patterns on Residential HVAC Demand. *Journal of Building Engineering* 22 (March): 33–47. https://doi.org/10.1016/j.jobe.2018.11.011.

Jia, M., Srinivasan, R.S., and Raheem, A.A. (2017). From Occupancy to Occupant Behavior: An Analytical Survey of Data Acquisition Technologies, Modeling Methodologies and Simulation Coupling Mechanisms for Building Energy Efficiency. *Renewable and Sustainable Energy Reviews* 68 (February): 525–540. https://doi.org/10.1016/j.rser.2016.10.011.

Kim, Y.-S., Heidarinejad, M., Dahlhausen, M., and Srebric, J. (2017). Building Energy Model Calibration with Schedules Derived from Electricity Use Data. *Applied Energy* 190 (March): 997–1007. https://doi.org/10.1016/j.apenergy.2016.12.167.

Liu, X., Jinpei, O., Chen, Y. et al. (2019). Scenario Simulation of Urban Energy-Related CO_2 Emissions by Coupling the Socioeconomic Factors and Spatial Structures. *Applied Energy* 238 (March): 1163–1178. https://doi.org/10.1016/j.apenergy.2019.01.173.

Martins, T.A.d.L., Faraut, S., and Adolphe, L. (2019). Influence of Context-Sensitive Urban and Architectural Design Factors on the Energy Demand of Buildings in Toulouse, France. *Energy and Buildings* 190 (May): 262–278. https://doi.org/10.1016/j.enbuild.2019.02.019.

Murat, Y.S. and Ceylan, H. (2006). Use of Artificial Neural Networks for Transport Energy Demand Modeling. *Energy Policy* 34 (17): 3165–3172. https://doi.org/10.1016/j.enpol.2005.02.010.

"National Transportation Statistics." 2019. United States Department of Transportation, Bureau of Transportation Statistics. 2019. https://www.bts.gov/topics/national-transportation-statistics.

Newman, P.W.G. and Kenworthy, J.R. (1989). Gasoline Consumption and Cities. *Journal of the American Planning Association* 55 (1): 24–37. https://doi.org/10.1080/01944368908975398.

Norman, J., MacLean, H.L., M. ASCE, and Kennedy, C.A. (2006). Comparing High and Low Residential Density: Life-Cycle Analysis of Energy Use and Greenhouse Gas Emissions. *Journal of Urban Planning and Development* 2006: 10–21. https://doi.org/10.1061/(ASCE)0733-9488(2006)132:1(10).

Olden, J.D., Joy, M.K., and Death, R.G. (2004). An Accurate Comparison of Methods for Quantifying Variable Importance in Artificial Neural Networks Using Simulated Data. *Ecological Modelling* 178 (3–4): 389–397. https://doi.org/10.1016/j.ecolmodel.2004.03.013.

Rosenblatt, F. (1958). The Perceptron: A Probabilistic Model for Information Storage and Organization in the Brain. *Psychological Review* 65 (6): 386–408. https://doi.org/10.1037/h0042519.

Saha, H., Florita, A.R., Henze, G.P., and Sarkar, S. (2019). Occupancy Sensing in Buildings: A Review of Data Analytics Approaches. *Energy and Buildings* 188–189 (April): 278–285. https://doi.org/10.1016/j.enbuild.2019.02.030.

Steemers, K. (2003). Energy and the City: Density, Buildings and Transport. *Energy and Buildings* 35 (1): 3–14. https://doi.org/10.1016/S0378-7788(02)00075-0.

Torabi, M., Sara, J.T., Mutani, G., and Lombardi, P. (2018). A GIS-Statistical Approach for Assessing Built Environment Energy Use at Urban Scale. *Sustainable Cities and Society* 37 (February): 70–84. https://doi.org/10.1016/J.SCS.2017.10.002.

Updated Urban Sprawl Data for the United States (2010). National Cancer Institute. *Geographic Information Systems & Science for Cancer Control* 2010: https://gis.cancer.gov/tools/urban-sprawl/.

Wiedenhofer, D., Lenzen, M., and Steinberger, J.K. (2013). Energy Requirements of Consumption: Urban Form, Climatic and Socio-Economic Factors, Rebounds and Their Policy Implications. *Energy Policy* 63 (December): 696–707. https://doi.org/10.1016/j.enpol.2013.07.035.

Yang, Z. and Becerik-Gerber, B. (2016). How Does Building Occupancy Influence Energy Efficiency of HVAC Systems? In: *Energy Procedia, CUE 2015—Applied Energy Symposium and Summit 2015: Low Carbon Cities and Urban Energy Systems*, vol. 88 (June), 775–780. https://doi.org/10.1016/j.egypro.2016.06.111.

Yu, Z., Fung, B.C.M., Haghighat, F. et al. (2011). A Systematic Procedure to Study the Influence of Occupant Behavior on Building Energy Consumption. *Energy and Buildings* 43 (6): 1409–1417. https://doi.org/10.1016/j.enbuild.2011.02.002.

Yun, G.Y. and Steemers, K. (2011). Behavioural, Physical and Socio-Economic Factors in Household Cooling Energy Consumption. *Applied Energy* 88 (6): 2191–2200. https://doi.org/10.1016/j.apenergy.2011.01.010.

Zahiri, S. and Elsharkawy, H. (2018). Towards Energy-Efficient Retrofit of Council Housing in London: Assessing the Impact of Occupancy and Energy-Use Patterns on Building Performance. *Energy and Buildings* 174 (September): 672–681. https://doi.org/10.1016/j.enbuild.2018.07.010.

Zhang, J. and Ding, W. (2017). Prediction of Air Pollutants Concentration Based on an Extreme Learning Machine: The Case of Hong Kong. *International Journal of Environmental Research and Public Health* 14 (2): 114–114. https://doi.org/10.3390/ijerph14020114.

Zhang, M. and Zhao, P. (2017). The Impact of Land-Use Mix on Residents' Travel Energy Consumption: New Evidence from Beijing. *Transportation Research Part D: Transport and Environment* 57 (December): 224–236. https://doi.org/10.1016/j.trd.2017.09.020.

11

Building Better Spaces: Using Virtual Reality to Improve Building Performance

Azadeh Omidfar Sawyer[1] and Kynthia Chamilothori[2]

[1] School of Architecture, Carnegie Mellon University, Pittsburgh, PA, USA
[2] Human-Technology Interaction, Industrial Engineering and Innovation Sciences, Eindhoven University of Technology, Eindhoven, The Netherlands

Introduction

Design decisions in architecture transform and shape relations between individuals, communities, and environments and are central in forming the experience of our daily lives, most of which are spent in built environments. At the same time, these design decisions are a crucial factor in climate change and the depletion of natural resources, with the building sector being responsible for 40% of the global annual carbon dioxide emissions in 2018 (International Energy Agency 2019). As a result, there is a growing urgency and responsibility for researchers, practitioners, and stakeholders in the building sector to make the most of available resources and create spaces that are energy efficient, as well as comfortable and pleasant for their occupants. As stated by Lam and Ripman, already in the 1970s, "we can no longer afford to waste space and energy so lavishly to produce such pitiful, pitiless environments."

The initial design phase plays a crucial role in shaping the overall performance of buildings. Decisions made during this stage of building design, such as massing, building orientation, layout, and material selection, greatly impact the energy efficiency, indoor environmental quality (IEQ), and functionality of the building (Jalaei and Jrade 2015). By considering building performance early on, designers can make informed decisions that lead to more efficient and sustainable buildings. At the same time, in order to design buildings that are not only energy efficient but also comfortable and pleasant for their occupants, it is necessary to pinpoint these qualities. The field of building performance examines specifically the relationship between design decisions, IEQ, and energy efficiency. IEQ refers to the physical and psychological aspects of the indoor environment that affect the comfort, health, and well-being of the building's occupants (Rohde et al. 2020). On the other hand, energy efficiency targets the ways by which we can reduce the energy consumption and environmental impact of a building (Omer 2009). For some of these aspects, such as energy consumption or thermal comfort, the relationship between design characteristics and building performance is well established and can be quantified through widely accepted metrics and design

Artificial Intelligence in Performance-Driven Design: Theories, Methods, and Tools, First Edition.
Edited by Narjes Abbasabadi and Mehdi Ashayeri.
© 2024 John Wiley & Sons Inc. Published 2024 by John Wiley & Sons Inc.

standards. Other performance aspects, especially those related to occupant satisfaction and wellbeing, for example, the occupant's aesthetic experience (de Wilde 2019) or the beneficial effects of positive sensorial stimuli (Rohde et al. 2020), are less clear and lack established metrics. As a result, architects are concerned about qualitative design aspects being dismissed in favor of quantitative design targets regarding energy and indoor climate (Petersen et al. 2014).

Collecting qualitative and quantitative information about a design proposal, as well as comparing various design variants, is a core element of the early design process (Purup and Petersen, 2020). Interviews with practicing architects by Purup and Petersen (2020) show that the quantitative information collected in the early design process includes building performance simulation outcomes relating to code compliance or financial analyses, while a key part of qualitative information is imagining the occupants experience. One of the few methods that can integrate information about both quantitative and qualitative building performance aspects during the design process is the use of immersive virtual environments, which enable designers to depict quantitative outcomes such as thermal, daylight, acoustic, or energy performance (Bahar et al. 2014; Vorländer et al. 2015; Keshavarzi, Caldas, and Santos 2021) and also experience an occupant's viewpoint and share this with clients (Purup and Petersen 2020;

Virtual environments consist of several key elements: a computer-generated 3D model or scene, a display, an interaction tool (such as a controller, mouse, or keyboard), and software that coordinates and brings all these components together. The display can be either monoscopic (a single image) or stereoscopic (3D) and can take different forms, such as smartphones, head-mounted displays, or projection-based screens. Virtual environments can be categorized into immersive and non-immersive, depending on the degree to which the possible actions of a user in the virtual environment, such as looking around or interacting with the environment, are similar to those in the real world (Slater 2009) and replace physical reality (Cummings and Bailenson 2016). A wide field of view, stereoscopy, and tracking of the user movements have been found to be central in giving the user the sense of being located in the virtual environment (Cummings and Bailenson 2016), while a wide field of view, tracking of the user's head movements, head-mounted display, and use of a first-person view are the minimum technical requirements for the user to experience their virtual body as their own (Spanlang et al. 2014). Current immersive virtual reality systems consist of head-mounted Virtual Reality (VR) displays or Cave Automatic Virtual Environment (CAVE) systems, which can provide stereoscopic visual input that corresponds to the user's head movements (Slater 2009). Head-mounted VR displays have become increasingly popular due to their low cost, wider range of application, and accessibility for the general public compared to CAVE systems and are thus the focus of this chapter.

The integration of VR technology in architectural design, research, and education is growing rapidly in both academic and industry settings. The use of VR in the built environment during the last decade can be categorized into three key areas relating to construction, i.e. construction safety, construction equipment, and construction project management, and three key areas relating more broadly to building performance, i.e. architectural and engineering design, human behavior and perception, and engineering education (Zhang et al. 2020). In the industry, VR is most commonly used for design review and stakeholder engagement (Purup and Petersen 2020), as it enables an immersive and interactive environment that allows for more effective collaboration and communication among stakeholders. Similarly, VR plays a crucial role in the initial design process by enabling designers to explore and interact with design variants (Purup and Petersen 2020) and make effective design decisions, as well as identify any potential issues before construction. For example, as discussed in later sections, VR has been used to illustrate the energy consumption of different lighting solutions in a first-person view, influencing up to 30% of participants in changing their design choices to the desired ones according to building performance targets (Carneiro, Aryal, and Becerik-Gerber 2019), or to allow teams of designers and engineers to conduct a joint design review and identify errors among the installation, structure, and architecture 3D models of the same project (Zaker and Coloma 2018). The ability of VR to emulate an occupant's viewpoint has also led to its widespread use in research related to building performance, as it allows for the collection of subjective, physiological, and behavioral responses toward simulated indoor environments in controlled conditions, providing a deeper understanding of the user's experience in a space. Examples in this domain include empirical investigations on window size (Moscoso et al. 2022) or view access (Abd-Alhamid et al. 2020) and their effects on occupant responses, as well as interactions between sensory modalities, such as visual and thermal perception (Chinazzo et al. 2021; Vittori, Pigliautile, and Pisello 2021). Lastly, VR is valuable in education by creating a sense of presence for its users by eliminating the barrier between the students and the display, i.e. creating "the perceptual illusion of non-mediation" (Lombard and Ditton 1997). The illusion of VR appears to benefit certain aspects of building performance education, enabling students to effectively participate in design-related tasks, including analysis, synthesis, and evaluation.

Although the use of VR is increasing rapidly across various fields, the concept itself is not new. VR has been in development for several decades and early forms of VR have been used in many fields, such as entertainment, military training, and medicine for years. However, even though the use of VR is growing in popularity, it is not widely used in architectural practice, research, and education. At the same time, it presents a valuable tool for designers, researchers, and educators in the field, allowing them to envision, investigate, and communicate both quantitative and qualitative building performance aspects. The aim of this chapter is to illustrate the possibilities and limitations of VR for building performance, particularly in relation to the initial design process, and inspire its further use in the field as a tool that can uniquely depict both quantitative and experiential aspects of a design. To this end, this chapter presents a narrative review of current applications of VR related to the early design process by focusing on the use of VR in building design, research on occupant wellbeing and satisfaction, design education, and client engagement. In this work, we define the "initial design process" as the exploratory design phase, during which the design team explores and improves different design options until consolidating them into a final design variant with input from stakeholders (Purup and Petersen 2020). The presented studies were selected with the aim to offer insights into the experience and effects of using VR in the context of building performance, including both quantitative and qualitative analyses of the responses of VR users, and to present a wide range of relevant uses of this technology.

Applications of Virtual Reality in Building Performance

Virtual Reality for Improving Building Design through Integrated Performance Data

The integration of building design and performance evaluation is an ongoing challenge due to the lack of seamless communication between design tools and building performance simulation tools (Purup and Petersen 2020), making it particularly difficult to connect numerical performance data with the experiential qualities of the space. Graphical representation of analysis output has been found to be the most important feature for the usability of building performance tools for engineers and architects (Attia et al. 2012). Similarly, building performance simulation tools have been criticized for not being accessible to architects in terms of their usability and output visualization (Weytjens et al. 2011). Additionally, current energy data visualization techniques, such as graphs and charts, have limited effectiveness in communicating information between users and their buildings, as they do not fully consider their user's three-dimensional environment or their interactions (Haefner et al. 2014).

VR technology, which has been suggested as a valuable tool to represent the experiential qualities of architectural design (Zobel 1995), can be very promising in this regard. By incorporating real-time performance values into the design process using VR technology, designers can better understand the relationship between design choices and their impact on lighting, energy use, and overall spatial quality. The use of VR technology integrated with performance data has the potential to greatly enhance energy visualization by enabling immersive visual data exploration, which allows the representation of data in a higher dimension, multiple perspectives, and an efficient way of navigating and interacting with complex sets of data.

Various methods have been developed to connect simulation data to the experiential qualities of spaces. For example, Haefner et al. (2014) created a VR system to interactively visualize data on user behavior and energy use in public buildings. The authors created a VR office room with sensors, automation devices, and energy consumers that was projected in a low-cost VR system and could display energy consumption data in real time, allowing users to interact with the data through gesture. In addition, Several studies have combined visualizations of design choices regarding electric lighting and the corresponding building performance simulation data, combining real-time photorealistic renderings of various luminaire parameters and false-color illuminance maps (Natephra et al. 2017) or electric lighting controls and visualizations of the corresponding energy consumption and illuminance levels (Carneiro, Aryal, and Becerik-Gerber 2019). The combination of these qualitative and quantitative information seen from a first-person perspective seems to be very effective for design feedback and for identifying areas that need improvement (Natephra et al. 2017). Carneiro et al. (2019) found that such visualizations were easily understood, and particularly those regarding energy consumption had a positive impact on participants' decision-making, with 30% of participants changing their design choices to those supported by the visualization after their VR experience and more than 70% of participants reporting that they reconsidered their design choices after being presented with this information. This research highlights the potential of information visualization as a tool to support informed design decisions. However, as will be discussed further in the next section, it is important to note that scenes presented with current VR display capabilities are inherently visually comfortable and lack any other sensory information (such as thermoception, which means that it is not possible to feel thermally uncomfortable from solar heat gains of sunlight shown in VR) and thus user behavior and decisions in VR cannot be directly generalized to real-world conditions. An interesting approach regarding the depiction of discomfort glare even in the limited dynamic range of current VR displays is the use of additional sensory modalities, such as through auditory or haptic feedback, to provide information to the user regarding the presence of (expected) glare phenomena in the VR scene (May et al. 2020).

Using a similar approach, this time regarding façade systems rather than electric lighting, current research by Dr. Omidfar Sawyer at the Carnegie Mellon University (CMU) School of Architecture focused on the façade design of the new University of Pittsburgh Medical Center Presbyterian Hospital in Pittsburgh, PA (Figure 11.1). In this sponsored collaborative research project between CMU, HGA, and University of Toronto, the team at CMU created a real-time VR framework for testing and comparing different façade design options to test the impact of design changes on energy use, daylight, and shadows. Performance data was displayed for each design option, allowing the VR user to observe how each design option was performing while being fully immersed in it (Figure 11.1, left). Additionally, the team incorporated multiple design options within the immersive space, each with their respective energy and lighting performance data, allowing them to compare the options side by side (Figure 11.1, right). Through this immersive experience, they discovered that although the energy savings between the some of the options were relatively similar (11% vs. 14%), the experiential qualities of the spaces were noticeably distinct. This method enabled the research team to choose the best design option after experiencing each one and being fully informed about its performance, ensuring that the design was human-centric, energy-efficient, and optimized for patients' needs. However, it is important to highlight challenges, such as the cost of the headset and the need for high-performance computer equipment capable of high-quality rendering, as well as challenges associated with assessing visual discomfort related to glare. As other researchers have pointed out (Natephra et al. 2017), the CMU research team also experienced limitations regarding transferring data from modeling and simulation software, such as Rhinoceros and Climate Studio, to VR. A significant challenge is that the existing workflow is limited to 3D geometry, while non-geometric data, including light values and materials, must be recreated manually. Similarly, combining accurate building performance data with indoor space visualizations in VR currently requires the use of multiple programs, for example, the 3D modeling, energy performance simulations, lighting performance simulations, and scene visualization in VR all take place in different software and might also require additional plug-ins to act as interfaces between these different platforms (Carneiro, Aryal, and Becerik-Gerber 2019). This limitation greatly restricts the designers' ability to transfer complex geometries and accurately represent the building's behavior.

After over a decade of VR use in architectural design and research, there is still a lack of standardization in creating immersive VR environments, making it challenging to compare

Figure 11.1 Illustration of VR framework developed at the Carnegie Mellon University School of Architecture to allow both displaying building performance data and experiencing the indoor scene. The system can be used to display a specific façade design (left) or multiple façade design options (right) side by side in the same room, with performance data on the wall and 3D energy consumption information in front of each façade option for comparison. Source: Azadeh Omidfar Sawyer & Mohammad Reza Takallouie.

results from previous studies and integrate different design solutions. In addition to the need for interoperability between design and VR tools, additional scientific knowledge is necessary to identify the most effective ways of presenting quantitative performance data in the VR, as current applications use different approaches such as object overlays (Natephra et al. 2017) or figures embedded in the VR scene (Figure 11.1). While the studies discussed in this section offer valuable insights, acknowledging their limitations is also important. Firstly, a few studies test the effectiveness of building performance visualizations in VR, and as they make use of very specific workflows and visualizations, additional research is necessary to confirm and generalize these findings. A systematic investigation of the effectiveness of different ways of visualizing and interacting with information in VR as well as the challenges in creating such building performance visualizations would greatly advance knowledge in this field. Additionally, a majority of these studies have primarily focused on college students within a restricted age range (Haefner et al. 2014; Carneiro, Aryal, and Becerik-Gerber 2019), limiting the generalizability of the findings to broader demographic groups and to real-world applications with design stakeholders. Lastly, whenever design choices in VR are informed by both data visualizations and the experience of the design solution, it is necessary to further establish the limits of generalizing human behavior and preferences in VR with those in real-world conditions.

Virtual Reality for Building Design Reviews and Education in Architecture and Engineering

A core aspect of the design process is the design review, which includes the "argumentative consolidation" of design variants, where members of the design team and stakeholders discuss design options and take joint decisions regarding the final design proposal (Purup and Petersen 2020). The conventional approach to designing a building can be complex and often fragmented with many disconnected workflows and tools used by various team members, conflicting objectives, and ineffective communication between the different stakeholders (Bullinger et al. 2010). More than a decade ago, the use of VR was suggested as a way to overcome these challenges and to improve communication and collaboration between stakeholders by providing a full-scale functional prototype (Bullinger et al. 2010), and today design teams use this technology both internally and to illustrate the design to clients (Purup and Petersen 2020). A systematic literature review by Horvat et al. (2022) showed that the core functionalities of existing applications of VR for design reviews in architecture, engineering, and construction industry are the representation, navigation, and manipulation of the immersive environment. The manipulation of the immersive environment can either be conducted within preset parameters, such as by switching between predetermined lighting conditions, or by directly editing the virtual environment and its objects. Additional functionalities include collecting information related to the user's experience in the virtual environment, such as recording their interaction with the scene. Lastly, Horvat et al. (2022) found that a number of VR applications allow collaboration by providing synchronous access to multiple users, showing the users' position, providing the option of a single user controlling the other users' viewpoint, allowing collaborative synchronous manipulation, and offering (often verbal-only) communication between users.

According to Horvat et al. (2022), current commercial applications that support the use of VR for design reviews include Enscape, IrisVR, AutodeskVR, Siemens NX VR, TechViz, NVIDIA Holodeck, and 3DEXPERIENCE, which can differ in the functionalities they provide. For example, only Enscape offers the possibility to manipulate the lighting or to generate objects, but it does not currently allow multiple users, which all other commercial applications do (Horvat et al. 2022). In addition to these commercial applications, researchers have developed various VR-based applications that aim to support design teams during the early design stages. For example, Podkosova et al. (2022) introduced a collaborative framework called BIMFLexi-VR, connecting a parametric component developed in Grasshopper/Rhinoceros to a VR environment. The modeling component performed optimized structural calculations, while the VR environment visualized the results. This flexible framework allows users to change design parameters directly in VR and observe the modified design and its associated performance metric in real time. The goal of this framework was to provide an intuitive platform for exploring design options and to facilitate collaborative decision-making. In a real-life case study, Zaker and Coloma (2018) used VR in a building design review, including a team of nine designers and engineers with little or no prior experience with VR. The participants examined two models in VR, one containing the structure and mechanical, electrical, and plumbing systems, and one containing the architecture model. The use of both models was reported to help identify misalignments between the two disciplines. Participants appreciated the sensation of "being inside the building," but also questioned how practical the use of VR would be for their daily practice, raising concerns about the ease of creating the VR scenes and the costs associated with the VR-related software and equipment. Moreover, participants recommended using VR to present designs to clients, for collaboration with other teams and internal design review.

VR has also been used successfully for participatory design sessions involving citizens in urban design projects. In a real-life case study, researchers built a VR model to represent an urban project in Chile and performed structured interviews with members of the community, showing them first technical drawings and 3D renderings and then the 3D model shown in VR (Loyola et al. 2019). Although the experimental procedure might have introduced order effects, qualitative analysis of the participants' comments suggests a higher level of spatial understanding in VR, with participants being able to identify particular elements in the design more easily in VR compared to when using technical drawings and 3D renderings. The researchers conclude that VR seems to be effective in representing urban design projects in participatory design processes, particularly for people who are unfamiliar with traditional architectural representations, such as technical drawings (Loyola et al. 2019). In another application of VR in urban participatory design in collaboration with the municipality of The Hague in the Netherlands, 76 city residents experienced simulated design alternatives of a park shown either in VR or on a computer (van Leeuwen et al. 2018). Seeing design variants in VR or a computer did not influence the participants' confidence in their design-related decisions or their accuracy in recalling differences between the variants, although they could better recall the objects they had seen. However, participants reported being more concentrated and feeling more present in the design variants when experiencing the scenes in VR compared to the computer. The authors note that the higher participant engagement in decision-making when experiencing the design variants in VR was very important for the municipality as a reason to invest in VR technologies with the aim to stimulate citizen participation (van Leeuwen et al. 2018).

VR environments have shown promising results in improving spatial perception compared to 3D models shown on a computer display both in studies involving mainly practitioners and students of architecture (Paes, Arantes, and Irizarry 2017) and in studies with laypeople (de Klerk et al. 2019). In a study examining the performance of CAD designers in finding flaws in a complex engineering model, designers found almost 10% more design flaws when using immersive VR compared to viewing the model on a screen (Wolfartsberger, 2019). Although the sample size in this study was small (16 participants), these outcomes are promising. At the same time, it is worth noting that participants reported feeling a degree of isolation from the rest of the team when using the head-mounted display, and would like the possibility to see them while being immersed in VR (Wolfartsberger 2019). Regarding the challenges of using VR in the architecture and construction industry, Prabhakaran et al. (2022) identified nine key topics through a systematic literature review. Four of those regard the development of the VR application and include the required programming, the modeling of the virtual content, the difficulties regarding the inter-operability of software and data involved in generating the VR environment, and the lack of multi-sensory integration. The next three challenges regard the necessary resources, such as the necessary equipment and infrastructure, the related costs, and the lack of professional skills that are necessary to create and use a VR environment. Lastly, the authors point out possible ethical issues, such as privacy and security concerns, as well as the implications of VR use for health and safety, including possible physical, physiological, and psychological effects.

VR has gained value not only in facilitating design reviews, communication, and engagement in architecture, engineering, and construction industry, but also in academia as it has shown to increase student engagement and support cognitive skills in remembering and understanding spatial and visual information (Jensen and Konradsen 2018). Try et al. (2021) examined the use of VR technology in their civil engineering laboratory course to enhance students' learning. The study found that VR-aided learning was more preferred than video-aided learning approach with regard to interactivity, cognitive interest, ease of understanding content, and support for learning. While VR-aided learning was comparatively less preferable than instructor-aided learning, it was viewed as better in terms of cognitive interest and accessibility. In architecture, the exploration of a design project in VR has been shown to increase the understanding of the space in self-reported evaluations of students (Loures Brandão et al. 2018). Similarly, a study conducted by Lucas (2018) on the impact of head-mounted VR environments on student understanding of wood frame construction showed improvements in the students' perception of space, materials of construction, and components of assemblies when using VR compared to traditional learning materials, with the greatest benefit found in understanding the components of construction. Moreover, the three-dimensional perception of a design (i.e. judgments related to height, length, and depth) was found to be more accurate when the design was shown in VR compared to a computer screen (Paes, Irizarry, and Pujoni 2021). In another study by Yang and Lee (2020) where eight fashion designers were asked to sketch on paper and in VR to solve a specific design task suggests that using VR has a significant impact on cognitive processes when designing. The study used a think-aloud protocol and coded all actions reported by the designers. The results showed that the two conditions did not differ in the time required to complete the design task. However, participants were found to spatially inspect their design more often and to make fewer depiction-related actions in VR. In addition, participants' thinking styles were found to differ between the two conditions, with a lower proportion of analysis thinking in VR sketching compared to traditional sketching. The level of detail and representations of new ideas in the final sketches were also noticeably reduced in the sketches using VR compared to paper. According to the authors, the lower level of detail in the final sketches along with the higher occurrence of inspecting the design show a more global thinking style when sketching in VR (Yang and Lee 2020). It is worth noting that the effectiveness of VR technology in enhancing learning outcomes may depend on the students' familiarity with the equipment and the limitations of the VR implementation (Schnabel and Kvan, 2003). In a study comparing the performance of architecture students in a task involving the manipulation of complex 3D objects in a 2D computer representation, 3D computer representation, and 3D immersive VR, students understood the volume of the studied objects better in the two 3D representations. However, their overall performance in the task was substantially lower in the 3D VR condition, which the authors attribute to the students' lack of familiarity with the VR equipment and the limitations of the VR implementation. Overall, in the context of design education, VR seems to provide a unique sense of scale, which has been noted by architects as fundamental knowledge that is "commonly lacking in architecture students and difficult to convey" (de Klerk et al. 2019). This full-body experience of a design appears to be related to a more global processing style (Yang and Lee 2020), an improved spatial understanding (Jensen and Konradsen 2018; Loures Brandão et al. 2018) and a better overview of overall design components (Lucas 2018). In combination with the increased student engagement seen with VR, we can expect a growing use of this technology in design education, with potential transformative effects in design solutions due to the aforementioned new thinking and designing process enabled by this technology. However, as the use of VR (albeit in fashion design) was also shown to lead to design solutions showing a lower level of detail and fewer new ideas (Yang and Lee 2020), it is important to examine further the effects of VR use on design outputs and to exercise caution when applying it in design education, complementing its use with existing educational methods. As emphasized by Lege and Bonner, to effectively integrate VR into education it becomes critical to develop a well-defined pedagogical justification and measurable student outcomes (Lege and Bonner 2020).

In addition to high-end VR equipment, another interesting technology for education applications is low-cost smartphone-based VR headsets, where a smartphone is used to display stereoscopic scenes that are seen through a handheld VR display. In one of Dr. Chamilothori's courses at the Eindhoven University of Technology, smartphone-based VR is used to allow students to simultaneously experience the same 360° virtual scene and discuss their sense of presence in the virtual environment. This exercise has been a consistently engaging and motivating activity for the students (Figure 11.2). Although limited in their technical capabilities and the degree of interaction they provide, smartphone-based VR headsets offer an opportunity to reduce the costs of high-end equipment and make use of smartphone devices that many students already own.

While VR presents a unique opportunity to offer students an interactive and immersive learning experience, there are also barriers to their widespread use, such as the aforementioned high costs in equipment and human resources to develop and maintain VR applications, and the need for users to be familiar with the technology to achieve the intended outcomes. In addition, students might experience the same VR environment differently, reporting for example feeling unsafe or experiencing cybersickness (Jensen and Konradsen 2018). Undergraduate students using VR headsets have been found to experience more severe symptoms of cybersickness compared to those using desktop displays, highlighting the importance of developing strategies to alleviate cybersickness in virtual environments (Yildirim 2020). Similarly, students with visual disabilities can be excluded

Figure 11.2 Students using smartphone-based VR headsets in class to experience and discuss the sense of presence in virtual environments in the Eindhoven University of Technology course "Environmental Psychology" (MSc Program Human-Technology Interaction, School of Industrial Engineering and Innovation Sciences). Source: Kynthia Chamilothori (Chapter author).

from educational activities involving VR. Such differences in student access to and experience of VR-based educational content can create issues of equity in the classroom (Jensen and Konradsen 2018). Eye safety is also another concern when using VR displays, particularly regarding potential damage to the retina from exposure to blue light (i.e. blue light hazard). This concern becomes more relevant as VR usage becomes increasingly common in industry and education, with expected increases in display luminance range and usage (Leontopoulos, Leontopoulos, and Knoop 2023). Recent studies suggest that current displays do not pose a concern, but caution that this could change depending on advances in display technology capabilities (Leontopoulos, Leontopoulos, and Knoop 2023). In addition to these challenges, achieving an effective process that is suitable for widespread implementation of VR in the design review process requires the improvement of various aspects, including fine-tuning the height and inter-pupillary distance of VR users, examining the advantages and disadvantages of giving users more control over their movements and interaction in VR, and testing the use of standalone VR equipment (Loyola et al. 2019). Moreover, in the context of VR in architectural education, there are also challenges in integrating VR into the traditional design process and workflows, which can result in resistance to change and difficulties in collaboration between team members. While studies show that VR enhances students' learning experiences, there is a concern that it may replace other forms of learning, such as hands-on experience and interaction with physical models, which are essential in architectural design and research. Therefore, while VR has potential benefits, its integration in the design review and process requires careful consideration of its limitations and its full effectiveness and usefulness in terms of enhancing learning and improving outcomes should be thoroughly studied.

Virtual Reality for Research on Building Occupant Comfort and Well-Being

The increasing accessibility and capabilities of commercially available VR headsets have also led to a growing interest in the use of VR for research on occupant responses. Research using scale models and full-scale prototypes is complex, costly, and in many cases challenging, and thus the low cost, experimental control, mobility, and ease in presenting multiple stimuli offered by VR is particularly promising. To illustrate the potential cost savings of using VR, the cost of VR equipment and a computer capable of supporting it can range from around 1K USD (Coyne et al. 2019) to 10K USD (Luo et al. 2021). On the other hand, the mean cost for the design, contracting, commission, and construction of a controlled experimental room are approximately 266K EUR or 287K USD (Pisello et al. 2021), excluding additional expenses for heating and cooling, sensors, or building management systems. The difference in cost is several orders of magnitude, with the costs of VR hardware being only a small fraction of the costs of building an experimental room. In recent years, several studies have examined the suitability of VR for research in human factors by comparing participant responses in real environments and in their VR counterparts.

Regarding the visual experience of the space, evaluations such as how pleasant, interesting, exciting, complex, or spacious the room is perceived (Abd-Alhamid et al. 2019; Chamilothori, Wienold, and Andersen 2019; Hong et al. 2019), or how pleasant and comfortable the lighting is perceived (Rockcastle et al. 2021) show no significant differences between real and VR indoor scenes. On the other hand, evaluations of the brightness of a scene in VR have shown conflicting results. Certain empirical studies show no difference in brightness evaluations between real and VR environments (Abd-Alhamid et al. 2019), while others show instances of brightness being overestimated in VR (Hong et al. 2019; Rockcastle et al. 2021), with mixed findings found even for different lighting stimuli within the same study (Rockcastle et al. 2021). Overall, these mixed outcomes stem from studies using real-world stimuli scenes with very different luminance ranges, ranging from daylit conditions to dimly lit LED lighting, and show that further work is necessary to delineate the limits of perceptually accurate VR representations. In addition to the aforementioned studies that compared participant responses in two environments, a recent study used an interactive and self-expressive approach where participants collected snapshots in a real daylit space or in the corresponding VR environment to mark and rate particularly dark or bright areas (Hegazy et al. 2021). Contrary to previous research, which mostly used physically-based renderings created in radiance or HDR photographs, the VR scenes were generated in real time using the game engine unreal engine 4. The collected snapshots were used to create perceptual light maps, heatmaps representing the perceived brightness of the investigated spaces. Results showed a strong positive correlation between responses in both environments, suggesting both the use of game-engine simulations and the collection of participant-driven input as promising tools to investigate brightness perception. In addition to the mixed findings regarding brightness perception, current VR technology appears to be problematic for assessing visual discomfort from glare. Empirical studies show either no differences in glare evaluations between VR scenes and real conditions (Chen et al. 2020), overestimation of glare in VR (Hong et al. 2019), or mixed findings with significant differences found only for the dimmest and most contrasted lighting conditions, the former showing higher and the latter showing lower glare ratings in VR compared to real conditions (Rockcastle et al. 2021). It is worth noting that in Rockcastle et al. (2021), where participants were exposed to a dimmable lighting system, the percentage of participants reporting glare in the scene was higher in VR compared to the real scenes for seven out of eight studied scenes, which is surprising given that the actual light intensity of the light sources was higher in the real environment and suggests possible effects due to the luminance and contrast of the VR display. Once again, differences in study outcomes might be explained by the variation in experimental conditions, equipment, and the exact measures used. In Hong et al. (2019), while evaluations of glare sensation were found to differ between real and VR conditions, this was not the case for evaluations of visual comfort, raising questions about the participants' understanding of the terminology and showing the importance of testing the perceptual accuracy of specific evaluations for a particular research application.

Beyond visual experience, effects of the environment on participant emotional responses seem to generally be conveyed in VR (Abd-Alhamid et al. 2019; Marín-Morales, Higuera-Trujillo, Greco, et al. 2019), with differences found between 360° and fully interactive VR scenes (Higuera-Trujillo, López-Tarruella Maldonado, and Llinares Millán 2017). Physiological responses of skin conductance and heart rate variability are similar under exposure to real and virtual environments (Higuera-Trujillo, López-Tarruella Maldonado, and Llinares Millán 2017). However, recent studies using Machine Learning showed that a participant's exposure to real or VR scenes could be identified through their electroencephalographic signals, indicating differences in brain activity in the two conditions (Marín-Morales, Higuera-Trujillo, Greco, et al. 2019). The resolution of current VR displays seems to influence visual performance: reading times in a visual acuity test are slower (Rockcastle et al. 2021), and text is seen as more blurry, less contrasted (Abd-Alhamid et al. 2019), and less clearly visible in VR (Hong et al. 2019). Mixed results have been found regarding task performance, with either lower speed found in VR (Abd-Alhamid et al. 2019) or no significant decrease in task performance or speed (Latini, Di Giuseppe, and D'Orazio 2023). When comparing the change in reading comprehension, reading speed, and object identification between bright and dark indoor scenes shown in real environments or in VR, no significant difference was found between the two environments (Heydarian et al. 2015). Lastly, studies comparing navigation patterns in real and VR environments found differences during the first two minutes of exploring the space, and thus recommend an adaptation period to reduce the effect of novelty from the use of VR (Marín-Morales, Higuera-Trujillo, De-Juan-Ripoll, et al. 2019). The authors note that adaptation in VR should take place in a virtual environment that is similar in level of detail and realism compared to the experimental conditions, and point out that this adaptation period might not be necessary in the future as people are increasingly exposed to VR technologies (Marín-Morales, Higuera-Trujillo, De-Juan-Ripoll, et al. 2019).

In recent years, VR has been used to investigate the visual experience of elements, such as shading system designs (Chamilothori et al. 2019; 2022), window size variations (Hong et al. 2019; Moscoso et al. 2022), wall color (Latini et al. 2021), or the view to the outside (Abd-Alhamid et al. 2020; Rodriguez et al. 2021). Beyond visual perception, VR has also been used to examine other aspects relevant to occupant behavior and experience, such as thermal and visual interactions (Chinazzo et al. 2021; Vittori, Pigliautile, and Pisello 2021), wayfinding (Sharma et al. 2017; Jiang, Allison, and Duchowski 2022), or interaction with lighting controls (Heydarian et al., 2017; Mahmoudzadeh, Afacan, and Adi 2021). In addition to self-reported ratings, studies also collect measures such as physiological responses (Chinazzo et al. 2021; Chamilothori et al. 2022) or gaze behavior (Rockcastle, Chamilothori, and Andersen 2017) in the virtual scene.

While VR has been shown to convincingly convey various aspects of a real-world indoor environment, it is important to also recognize its limitations and to be critical when generalizing user behavior and preferences in virtual environments to real-world scenes. For example, although the work of Heydarian et al. (2017) is valuable as one of the first to examine participant preferences toward electric lighting settings in VR scenes, reported preferred settings were later translated to real-world luminous conditions and not to those of the limited luminance range scene that the participants experienced in VR. Considering the limited luminance range of current VR displays, the limited interaction and exposure time of participants to VR scenes, as well as the lack of multisensory stimuli in current VR applications, it is essential to be cautious and to first examine the suitability of VR for specific applications. For example, the Ambiotherm wearable VR accessory, which can convey localized wind and temperature differences near the participant's head, was found to increase the realism of a scene (Ranasinghe et al. 2017). Sensing wind and heat in a VR environment, especially in a full-body experience, would be particularly useful for the field of building performance, conveying, for example, solar heat gains or airflow which are now absent from virtual scenes and leading to better-informed user decisions. Ongoing research endeavors focus on haptic devices that can convey sensory information such as texture, pressure, or vibration in VR (Biswas and Visell 2021), which could further increase the fidelity of the presented virtual scene. Another issue is the multitude of rendering workflows, equipment characteristics, and methodological choices used in the different studies, which might have unforeseen effects on the VR user's behavior and experience. For example, the presence of furniture and color in the VR scene, which varies widely in existing VR research, has been shown to affect brightness perception (Omidfar Sawyer and Chamilothori 2019). An important challenge is also the current lack of standardization regarding VR. To the author's knowledge, the only current standard regarding the measurement and reporting of VR characteristics is the IEC 63145-20-10:2019 (International Electrotechnical Commission 2019, 63145), which regards the measurement of optical properties of eyewear displays such as their luminance, luminance uniformity, contrast, or field-of-view. In order to broaden our understanding of the capabilities and limitations of VR, it is necessary to establish recommendations that guide the creation and display of VR scenes, the collection of user responses, as well as the reporting of the scene and equipment characteristics. Lastly, guidelines regarding documentation, data formats, and common open file repositories could greatly increase the transparency, comparability, and reuse of developed VR scenes, which are often expensive in terms of computation and effort involved.

Conclusion

To effectively address the current energy challenges, a vast amount of detailed information must be quickly and effectively communicated between various stakeholders. This is important in the realm of architectural design, particularly during the initial design phase, where timely feedback on design decisions and their impact on energy consumption is essential. At the same time, in order to make the most of existing resources, it is essential to aim not only for energy efficiency, but also for buildings that are pleasant and comfortable for their occupants. Therefore, innovative methods that can combine quantitative performance data and the experiential qualities of a design are necessary.

As presented in this chapter, VR technology has the potential to connect all aspects of design and provide a solution to these challenges. The use of VR in the architecture, engineering, and construction industry has many potential advantages. VR is an effective tool to represent the experiential qualities of architectural design, with the potential to greatly enhance the visualization of performance data by enabling immersive visual data exploration. VR can combine a first-person perspective of a design solution with the display of real-time building performance values, allowing designers and stakeholders to better understand the relationship between design choices and their impact on quantitative and qualitative aspects of building performance. Various methods that use VR have been developed to connect building performance simulation data to the experiential qualities of spaces. As highlighted by several studies in this chapter, the integrated data in immersive scenes can be easily understood by VR users and shows a positive impact on their decision making in the design process.

In architectural design review, the use of VR has been shown to assist designers in exploring design options, facilitate communication and collaboration between team members and stakeholders, and support informed decision-making. VR has also been shown to be beneficial in architectural education, improving student engagement and enhancing their understanding of spatial and visual information. However, the effectiveness of VR may depend on the students' familiarity with the equipment and the capabilities of the VR implementation. Moreover, the widespread and long-term use of VR raises questions about safety and equity in the classroom, for example, for visually impaired students, as well as its integration in established architectural education methods such as building and interacting with physical models. Initial evidence from the field of fashion design suggests that the designer's thinking process might be influenced by the different sense of scale and interaction with the design in VR, leading to a more global processing style, which can have important implications for the widespread integration of VR in building performance education and warrants further research.

VR technology has also been shown to be an effective tool for research on occupant responses to building design stimuli. The low cost, experimental control, mobility, and ease in presenting multiple stimuli offered by VR technology make it a suitable tool for research in human factors. As discussed in this chapter, empirical studies show that VR can generally accurately convey the user's emotions and visual experience, apart from brightness, and that physiological responses such as skin conductance and heart rate variability remain similar under exposure to real environments and the corresponding virtual scenes.

While VR technology has many advantages, it also has several shortcomings. Current challenges, such as the relatively high equipment cost, limited transferability of data from modeling and simulation software, and the lack of sensory information beyond vision must be addressed to fully realize the potential of VR in building design. There are also concerns about the practicality of using VR in daily design practice and the ease of creating VR scenes. Combining building performance data with indoor space visualizations in VR currently requires the use of multiple software, which can be time-consuming and limit the designers' ability to display complex data and geometries. Another important issue is the lack of recommendations regarding the creation, characterization, and accuracy of VR scenes, which can be problematic, particularly in the use of VR for research purposes. These challenges limit the generalizability of user behavior and decisions in VR to real-world conditions. Additionally, current VR displays are unsuitable for assessing discomfort glare, with significant differences found in glare evaluations between real and virtual scenes. Mixed results have also been found regarding task performance, and navigation patterns have been shown to differ between real and VR scenes, suggesting that users may need an adaptation period to reduce the effect of novelty from the use of VR. Lastly, especially considering the expected growing presence of VR in our work, education, and daily lives, it is important to be mindful of possible physical, physiological, and psychological adverse effects of using VR, such as cybersickness or users feeling isolated from others when using head-mounted displays.

Despite the limitations and challenges in using VR for design review, education, and research, VR remains a promising tool, providing a new avenue for investigating building design and performance. Further research is necessary to delineate the limits of perceptually accurate VR representations, to better understand the effects of VR on user experience and behavior, and to develop methods for simulating and assessing environmental factors that have not been well-represented in VR environments. While VR has demonstrated its potential in providing a portable, controlled, and flexible environment for architectural design, research, and education, we consider it a means to complement, rather than replace, existing real-world methods. The industry continues to explore ways to overcome these challenges and leverage the benefits of VR technology to improve the design process. As technology and research continue to advance, these challenges will likely be addressed and the use of VR technology in building performance design and research will become more widespread, with potential transformative effects on our understanding of the relationship between built environments and occupant behavior and experience.

References

Abd-Alhamid, F., Kent, M., Bennett, C. et al. (2019). Developing an Innovative Method for Visual Perception Evaluation in a Physical-Based Virtual Environment. *Building and Environment* 162 (September): 106278. https://doi.org/10.1016/j.buildenv.2019.106278.

Abd-Alhamid, F., Kent, M., Calautit, J., and Yupeng, W. (2020). Evaluating the Impact of Viewing Location on View Perception Using a Virtual Environment. *Building and Environment* 180 (August): 106932. https://doi.org/10.1016/j.buildenv.2020.106932.

Attia, S., Hensen, J.L.M., Beltrán, L., and De Herde, A. (2012). Selection Criteria for Building Performance Simulation Tools: Contrasting Architects' and Engineers' Needs. *Journal of Building Performance Simulation* 5 (3): 155–169. https://doi.org/10.1080/19401493.2010.549573.

Biswas, S. and Visell, Y. (2021). Haptic Perception, Mechanics, and Material Technologies for Virtual Reality. *Advanced Functional Materials* 31 (39): 2008186. https://doi.org/10.1002/adfm.202008186.

Bullinger, H.-J., Bauer, W., Wenzel, G., and Blach, R. (2010). Towards User Centred Design (UCD) in Architecture Based on Immersive Virtual Environments. *Computers in Industry*, Human-Centered Computing Systems in Industry – A Special Issue in Honor of Professor G. Salvendy 61 (4): 372–379. https://doi.org/10.1016/j.compind.2009.12.003.

Carneiro, J.P., Aryal, A., and Becerik-Gerber, B. (2019). Influencing Occupant's Choices by Using Spatiotemporal Information Visualization in Immersive Virtual Environments. *Building and Environment* 150 (March): 330–338. https://doi.org/10.1016/j.buildenv.2019.01.024.

Chamilothori, K., Chinazzo, G., Rodrigues, J. et al. (2019). Subjective and Physiological Responses to Façade and Sunlight Pattern Geometry in Virtual Reality. *Building and Environment* 150 (March): 144–155. https://doi.org/10.1016/j.buildenv.2019.01.009.

Chamilothori, K., Wienold, J., Moscoso, C. et al. (2022). Subjective and Physiological Responses towards Daylit Spaces with Contemporary Façade Patterns in Virtual Reality: Influence of Sky Type, Space Function, and Latitude. *Journal of Environmental Psychology* 82 (August): 101839. https://doi.org/10.1016/j.jenvp.2022.101839.

Chamilothori, K., Wienold, J., and Andersen, M. (2019). Adequacy of Immersive Virtual Reality for the Perception of Daylit Spaces: Comparison of Real and Virtual Environments. *LEUKOS* 15 (2–3): 203–226. https://doi.org/10.1080/15502724.2017.1404918.

Chen, C.-F., Yilmaz, S., Pisello, A.L. et al. (2020). The Impacts of Building Characteristics, Social Psychological and Cultural Factors on Indoor Environment Quality Productivity Belief. *Building and Environment* 185 (November): 107189. https://doi.org/10.1016/j.buildenv.2020.107189.

Chinazzo, G., Chamilothori, K., Wienold, J., and Andersen, M. (2021). Temperature–Color Interaction: Subjective Indoor Environmental Perception and Physiological Responses in Virtual Reality. *Human Factors* 63 (3): 474–502. https://doi.org/10.1177/0018720819892383.

Coyne, L., Merritt, T.A., Parmentier, B.L. et al. (2019). The Past, Present, and Future of Virtual Reality in Pharmacy Education. *American Journal of Pharmaceutical Education* 83: (3). https://doi.org/10.5688/ajpe7456.

Cummings, J.J. and Bailenson, J.N. (2016). How Immersive Is Enough? A Meta-Analysis of the Effect of Immersive Technology on User Presence. *Media Psychology* 19 (2): 272–309. https://doi.org/10.1080/15213269.2015.1015740.

Haefner, P., Seessle, J., Duecker, J. et al. (2014). Interactive Visualization of Energy Efficiency Concepts Using Virtual Reality. In: *EuroVR 2014 - Conference and Exhibition of the European Association of Virtual and Augmented Reality*, 6 pages. https://doi.org/10.2312/EUROVR.20141346.

Hegazy, M., Ichiriyama, K., Yasufuku, K., and Abe, H. (2021). Comparing Daylight Brightness Perception in Real and Immersive Virtual Environments Using Perceptual Light Maps. *Automation in Construction* 131 (November): 103898. https://doi.org/10.1016/j.autcon.2021.103898.

Heydarian, A., Carneiro, J.P., Gerber, D. et al. (2015). Immersive Virtual Environments versus Physical Built Environments: A Benchmarking Study for Building Design and User-Built Environment Explorations. *Automation in Construction* 54 (June): 116–126. https://doi.org/10.1016/j.autcon.2015.03.020.

Heydarian, A., Pantazis, E., Wang, A. et al. (2017). Towards User Centered Building Design: Identifying End-User Lighting Preferences via Immersive Virtual Environments. *Automation in Construction* 81 (September): 56–66. https://doi.org/10.1016/j.autcon.2017.05.003.

Higuera-Trujillo, J.L., Maldonado, J.L.-T., and Millán, C.L. (2017). Psychological and Physiological Human Responses to Simulated and Real Environments: A Comparison between Photographs, 360° Panoramas, and Virtual Reality. *Applied Ergonomics* 65 (November): 398–409. https://doi.org/10.1016/j.apergo.2017.05.006.

Hong, T., Lee, M., Yeom, S., and Jeong, K. (2019). Occupant Responses on Satisfaction with Window Size in Physical and Virtual Built Environments. *Building and Environment* 166 (December): 106409. https://doi.org/10.1016/j.buildenv.2019.106409.

Horvat, N., Kunnen, S., Štorga, M. et al. (2022). Immersive Virtual Reality Applications for Design Reviews: Systematic Literature Review and Classification Scheme for Functionalities. *Advanced Engineering Informatics* 54 (October): 101760. https://doi.org/10.1016/j.aei.2022.101760.

International Electrotechnical Commission. 2019. "IEC 63145-20-10:2019 - Eyewear Display - Part 20-10: Fundamental Measurement Methods - Optical Properties." TC 110 - Electronic displays. https://standards.iteh.ai/catalog/standards/iec/f01f1ff9-d5d1-4f5e-91ce-5a370b828d76/iec-63145-20-10-2019.

International Energy Agency, Global Alliance for Buildings and Construction (2019). 2019 Global Status Report for Buildings and Construction. In: *2019 Global Status Report for Buildings and Constructi on Towards a Zero-Emissions, Efficient and Resilient Buildings and Construction Sector*. Nairobi, Kenya: United Nations Environment Programme.

Jalaei, F. and Jrade, A. (2015). Integrating Building Information Modeling (BIM) and LEED System at the Conceptual Design Stage of Sustainable Buildings. *Sustainable Cities and Society* 18 (November): 95–107. https://doi.org/10.1016/j.scs.2015.06.007.

Jensen, L. and Konradsen, F. (2018). A Review of the Use of Virtual Reality Head-Mounted Displays in Education and Training. *Education and Information Technologies* 23 (4): 1515–1529. https://doi.org/10.1007/s10639-017-9676-0.

Jiang, S., Allison, D., and Duchowski, A.T. (2022). Hospital Greenspaces and the Impacts on Wayfinding and Spatial Experience: An Explorative Experiment Through Immersive Virtual Environment (IVE) Techniques. *HERD* 15 (3): 206–228. https://doi.org/10.1177/19375867211067539.

Keshavarzi, M., Caldas, L., and Santos, L. (2021). RadVR: A 6DOF Virtual Reality Daylighting Analysis Tool. *Automation in Construction* 125 (May): 103623. https://doi.org/10.1016/j.autcon.2021.103623.

de Klerk, R., Duarte, A.M., Medeiros, D.P. et al. (2019). Usability Studies on Building Early Stage Architectural Models in Virtual Reality. *Automation in Construction* 103 (July): 104–116. https://doi.org/10.1016/j.autcon.2019.03.009.

Latini, A., Di Giuseppe, E., and D'Orazio, M. (2023). Immersive Virtual vs Real Office Environments: A Validation Study for Productivity, Comfort and Behavioural Research. *Building and Environment* 230 (February): 109996. https://doi.org/10.1016/j.buildenv.2023.109996.

Latini, A., Di Giuseppe, E., D'Orazio, M., and Di Perna, C. (2021). Exploring the Use of Immersive Virtual Reality to Assess Occupants' Productivity and Comfort in Workplaces: An Experimental Study on the Role of Walls Colour. *Energy and Buildings* 253 (December): 111508. https://doi.org/10.1016/j.enbuild.2021.111508.

van Leeuwen, J.P., Hermans, K., Jylhä, A. et al. (2018). Effectiveness of Virtual Reality in Participatory Urban Planning: A Case Study. In: *Proceedings of the 4th Media Architecture Biennale Conference*, 128–136. MAB18. New York, NY, USA: Association for Computing Machinery https://doi.org/10.1145/3284389.3284491.

Lege, R. and Bonner, E. (2020). Virtual Reality in Education: The Promise, Progress, and Challenge. *JALT CALL Journal* 16 (3): 167–180.

Leontopoulos, M., Leontopoulos, S., and Knoop, M. (2023). Consideration of Blue Light Hazard for Virtual Reality Head Mounted Displays. *Lighting Research & Technology*, January https://doi.org/10.1177/14771535221145801.

Lombard, M. and Ditton, T. (1997). At the Heart of It All: The Concept of Presence. *Journal of Computer-Mediated Communication* 3 (2): JCMC321. https://doi.org/10.1111/j.1083-6101.1997.tb00072.x.

Loures Brandão, G.V., do Amaral, W.D.H., de Almeida, C.A.R., and Castañon, J.A.B. (2018). Virtual Reality as a Tool for Teaching Architecture. In: *Design, User Experience, and Usability: Designing Interactions* (ed. A. Marcus and W. Wang), 73–82. Lecture Notes in Computer Science: Springer International Publishing.

Loyola, M., Rossi, B., Montiel, C., and Daiber, M. (2019). Use of Virtual Reality in Participatory Design. In: *Blucher Design Proceedings*, 449–454. Porto, Portugal: Editora Blucher https://doi.org/10.5151/proceedings-ecaadesigradi2019_156.

Lucas, J. (2018). Immersive VR in the Construction Classroom to Increase Student Understanding of Sequence, Assembly, and Space of Wood Frame Construction. *Journal of Information Technology in Construction (ITcon)* 23 (9): 179–194.

Luo, H., Li, G., Feng, Q. et al. (2021). Virtual Reality in K-12 and Higher Education: A Systematic Review of the Literature from 2000 to 2019. *Journal of Computer Assisted Learning* 37 (3): 887–901. https://doi.org/10.1111/jcal.12538.

Mahmoudzadeh, P., Afacan, Y., and Adi, M.N. (2021). Analyzing Occupants' Control over Lighting Systems in Office Settings Using Immersive Virtual Environments. *Building and Environment* 196 (June): 107823. https://doi.org/10.1016/j.buildenv.2021.107823.

Marín-Morales, J., Higuera-Trujillo, J.L., De-Juan-Ripoll, C. et al. (2019). Navigation Comparison between a Real and a Virtual Museum: Time-Dependent Differences Using a Head Mounted Display. *Interacting with Computers* 31 (2): 208–220. https://doi.org/10.1093/iwc/iwz018.

Marín-Morales, J., Higuera-Trujillo, J.L., Greco, A. et al. (2019). Real vs. Immersive-Virtual Emotional Experience: Analysis of Psycho-Physiological Patterns in a Free Exploration of an Art Museum. *PLOS ONE* 14 (10): e0223881. https://doi.org/10.1371/journal.pone.0223881.

May, K., Walsh, J., Smith, R. et al. (2020). VRGlare: A Virtual Reality Lighting Performance Simulator for Real-Time Three-Dimensional Glare Simulation and Analysis. In: *2020 Proceedings of the 37th ISARC, Kitakyushu, Japan*. https://doi.org/10.22260/ISARC2020/0006.

Moscoso, C., Chamilothori, K., Wienold, J. et al. (2022). Regional Differences in the Perception of Daylit Scenes across Europe Using Virtual Reality. Part I: Effects of Window Size. *LEUKOS* 18 (3): 294–315. https://doi.org/10.1080/15502724.2020.1854779.

Natephra, W., Motamedi, A., Fukuda, T., and Yabuki, N. (2017). Integrating Building Information Modeling and Virtual Reality Development Engines for Building Indoor Lighting Design. *Visualization in Engineering* 5 (1): 19. https://doi.org/10.1186/s40327-017-0058-x.

Bahar, N., Yudi, J.L., Pére, C., and Nicolle, C. (2014). CAD Data Workflow toward the Thermal Simulation and Visualization in Virtual Reality. *International Journal on Interactive Design and Manufacturing (IJIDeM)* 8 (4): 283–292. https://doi.org/10.1007/s12008-013-0200-5.

Omer, A.M. (2009). Energy Use and Environmental Impacts: A General Review. *Journal of Renewable and Sustainable Energy* 1 (5): 053101. https://doi.org/10.1063/1.3220701.

Omidfar Sawyer, A. and Chamilothori, K. (2019). Influence of Subjective Impressions of a Space on Brightness Satisfaction: An Experimental Study in Virtual Reality. In: *Proceedings of the Symposium on Simulation For Architecture and Urban Design (SimAUD) 2019*. Atlanta, GA, USA.

Paes, D., Arantes, E., and Irizarry, J. (2017). Immersive Environment for Improving the Understanding of Architectural 3D Models: Comparing User Spatial Perception between Immersive and Traditional Virtual Reality Systems. *Automation in Construction* 84 (Supplement C): 292–303. https://doi.org/10.1016/j.autcon.2017.09.016.

Paes, D., Irizarry, J., and Pujoni, D. (2021). An Evidence of Cognitive Benefits from Immersive Design Review: Comparing Three-Dimensional Perception and Presence between Immersive and Non-Immersive Virtual Environments. *Automation in Construction* 130 (October): 103849. https://doi.org/10.1016/j.autcon.2021.103849.

Petersen, S., Strunge, J., Bryder, J., and Levinsen, K. (2014). Method for Integrating Simulation-Based Support in the Building Design Process. In: *Design in Civil and Environmental Engineering, Proceedings of the 3rd International Workshop*, 83–89. Denmark–COWI Fonden: Technical University of.

Pisello, A.L., Pigliautile, I., Andargie, M. et al. (2021). Test Rooms to Study Human Comfort in Buildings: A Review of Controlled Experiments and Facilities. *Renewable and Sustainable Energy Reviews* 149 (October): 111359. https://doi.org/10.1016/j.rser.2021.111359.

Podkosova, I., Reisinger, J., Kaufmann, H., and Kovacic, I. (2022). BIMFlexi-VR: A Virtual Reality Framework for Early-Stage Collaboration in Flexible Industrial Building Design. *Frontiers in Virtual Reality* 3: https://www.frontiersin.org/articles/10.3389/frvir.2022.782169.

Prabhakaran, A., Mahamadu, A.-M., and Mahdjoubi, L. (2022). Understanding the Challenges of Immersive Technology Use in the Architecture and Construction Industry: A Systematic Review. *Automation in Construction* 137 (May): 104228. https://doi.org/10.1016/j.autcon.2022.104228.

Purup, P.B. and Petersen, S. (2020). Requirement Analysis for Building Performance Simulation Tools Conformed to Fit Design Practice. *Automation in Construction* 116 (August): 103226. https://doi.org/10.1016/j.autcon.2020.103226.

Ranasinghe, N., Jain, P., Karwita, S. et al. (2017). Ambiotherm: Enhancing Sense of Presence in Virtual Reality by Simulating Real-World Environmental Conditions. In: *Proceedings of the 2017 CHI Conference on Human Factors in Computing Systems*, 1731–1742. CHI'17. New York, NY, USA: Association for Computing Machinery https://doi.org/10.1145/3025453.3025723.

Rockcastle, S., Chamilothori, K., and Andersen, M. (2017). Using Virtual Reality to Measure Daylight-Driven Interest in Rendered Architectural Scenes. In: *Proceedings of Building Simulation 2017*. San Francisco, CA, USA.

Rockcastle, S., Danell, M., Calabrese, E. et al. (2021). Comparing Perceptions of a Dimmable LED Lighting System between a Real Space and a Virtual Reality Display. *Lighting Research & Technology* 53 (8): 701–725. https://doi.org/10.1177/1477153521990039.

Rodriguez, F., Garcia-Hansen, V., Allan, A., and Isoardi, G. (2021). Subjective Responses toward Daylight Changes in Window Views: Assessing Dynamic Environmental Attributes in an Immersive Experiment. *Building and Environment* 195 (May): 107720. https://doi.org/10.1016/j.buildenv.2021.107720.

Rohde, L., Larsen, T.S., Jensen, R.L., and Larsen, O.K. (2020). Framing Holistic Indoor Environment: Definitions of Comfort, Health and Well-Being. *Indoor and Built Environment* 29 (8): 1118–1136. https://doi.org/10.1177/1420326X19875795.

Schnabel, M.A. and Kvan, T. (2003). Spatial Understanding in Immersive Virtual Environments. *International Journal of Architectural Computing* 1 (4): 435–448. https://doi.org/10.1260/1478077703773633455.

Sharma, G., Kaushal, Y., Chandra, S. et al. (2017). Influence of Landmarks on Wayfinding and Brain Connectivity in Immersive Virtual Reality Environment. *Frontiers in Psychology* 8: https://www.frontiersin.org/articles/10.3389/fpsyg.2017.01220.

Slater, M. (2009). Place Illusion and Plausibility Can Lead to Realistic Behaviour in Immersive Virtual Environments. *Philosophical Transactions of the Royal Society, B: Biological Sciences* 364 (1535): 3549–3557. https://doi.org/10.1098/rstb.2009.0138.

Spanlang, B., Normand, J.-M., Borland, D. et al. (2014). How to Build an Embodiment Lab: Achieving Body Representation Illusions in Virtual Reality. *Frontiers in Robotics and AI* 1: https://www.frontiersin.org/articles/10.3389/frobt.2014.00009.

Try, S., Panuwatwanich, K., Tanapornraweekit, G., and Kaewmoracharoen, M. (2021). Virtual Reality Application to Aid Civil Engineering Laboratory Course: A Multicriteria Comparative Study. *Computer Applications in Engineering Education* 29 (6): 1771–1792. https://doi.org/10.1002/cae.22422.

Vittori, F., Pigliautile, I., and Pisello, A.L. (2021). Subjective Thermal Response Driving Indoor Comfort Perception: A Novel Experimental Analysis Coupling Building Information Modelling and Virtual Reality. *Journal of Building Engineering* 41 (September): 102368. https://doi.org/10.1016/j.jobe.2021.102368.

Vorländer, M., Schröder, D., Pelzer, S., and Wefers, F. (2015). Virtual Reality for Architectural Acoustics. *Journal of Building Performance Simulation* 8 (1): 15–25. https://doi.org/10.1080/19401493.2014.888594.

Weytjens, L., Attia, S., Verbeeck, G., and De Herde, A. (2011). The 'Architect-Friendliness' Of Six Building Performance Simulation Tools: A Comparative Study. *International Journal of Sustainable Building Technology and Urban Development* 2 (3): 237–244. https://doi.org/10.5390/SUSB.2011.2.3.237.

de Wilde, P. (2019). Ten Questions Concerning Building Performance Analysis. *Building and Environment* 153 (April): 110–117. https://doi.org/10.1016/j.buildenv.2019.02.019.

Wolfartsberger, J. (2019). Analyzing the Potential of Virtual Reality for Engineering Design Review. *Automation in Construction* 104 (August): 27–37. https://doi.org/10.1016/j.autcon.2019.03.018.

Yang, E.K. and Lee, J.H. (2020). Cognitive Impact of Virtual Reality Sketching on Designers' Concept Generation. *Digital Creativity* 31 (2): 82–97. https://doi.org/10.1080/14626268.2020.1726964.

Yildirim, C. (2020). Don't Make Me Sick: Investigating the Incidence of Cybersickness in Commercial Virtual Reality Headsets. *Virtual Reality* 24 (2): 231–239. https://doi.org/10.1007/s10055-019-00401-0.

Zaker, R. and Coloma, E. (2018). Virtual Reality-Integrated Workflow in BIM-Enabled Projects Collaboration and Design Review: A Case Study. *Visualization in Engineering* 6 (1): 1–15. https://doi.org/10.1186/s40327-018-0065-6.

Zhang, Y., Liu, H., Kang, S.-C., and Al-Hussein, M. (2020). Virtual Reality Applications for the Built Environment: Research Trends and Opportunities. *Automation in Construction* 118 (October): 103311. https://doi.org/10.1016/j.autcon.2020.103311.

Zobel, R.W. Jr. (1995). The Representation of Experience in Architectural Design. *Presence Teleoperators and Virtual Environments* 4 (3): 254–266. https://doi.org/10.1162/pres.1995.4.3.254.

12

Digital Twin for Citywide Energy Modeling and Management

Narjes Abbasabadi[1] and Mehdi Ashayeri[2]

[1] *Department of Architecture, School of Architecture, College of Built Environments, University of Washington, Seattle, WA, USA*
[2] *School of Architecture, College of Arts and Media, Southern Illinois University Carbondale, Carbondale, IL, USA*

Introduction

The landscape of modern society is being reshaped by the growing phenomenon of urbanization. Currently over 50% of the global population is living in urban areas, and it is projected to increase to 70% by 2050 ("World Population Prospects - Population Division - United Nations" n.d.). However, this urban growth comes at a significant environmental cost, as cities are responsible for about 75% of greenhouse gas (GHG) emissions generated from global energy consumption (World Resources Institute (WRI) n.d.). Notably, buildings alone account for about 37% of the world's energy consumption and the associated emissions (International Energy Agency 2022). These are linked to the pressing issue of climate change. Despite the need to combat climate change, global energy consumption and its associated CO_2 emissions continue to rise (González-Torres et al. 2022). The collective impact of urbanization and the energy consumption of buildings necessitate prompt climate action (Intergovernmental Panel on Climate Change (IPCC) 2022). In this context, worldwide many cities have started setting goals to achieve net-zero carbon emissions by 2050, which demands substantial reductions in energy consumption from buildings at scale.

Simultaneously, the contemporary milieu presents a unique moment by growing technological advancement. Smart building and smart city innovations, Internet of Things (IoT) ubiquity, artificial intelligence (AI) progress, and the proliferation of infinite computing capabilities and multi-sensing technologies together underscore a remarkable era (Taylor, Bennett, and Mohammadi 2021; Ferré-Bigorra, Casals, and Gangolells 2022; Bibri et al. 2023). Compounded by the accessibility of big data and open geo-referenced datasets, this epoch offers an unprecedented capacity to understand and address the complex interconnected challenges within built environments (Chen, Mao, and Liu 2014; Ashayeri and Abbasabadi 2021). This convergence brings forth a paradigm of predictive information modeling and intelligence across various scales and domains, from energy to environmental quality, mobility, material behaviors, occupant dynamics and behaviors, and enabling a holistic understanding to situate cities for transformative changes.

Artificial Intelligence in Performance-Driven Design: Theories, Methods, and Tools, First Edition.
Edited by Narjes Abbasabadi and Mehdi Ashayeri.
©2024 John Wiley & Sons Inc. Published 2024 by John Wiley & Sons Inc.

As science and technology advance, Digital Twins (DTs) technology has emerged as an interactive tool bridging the real and virtual worlds (Guo and Lv 2022) and versatility in various fields, including industrial production, healthcare, smart cities, aerospace, among others. DT holds transformative potential for engineers across domains, aiding data-driven sustainability efforts, notably in decarbonizing the building sector (Francisco, Mohammadi, and Taylor 2020; Steindl et al. 2020; Agouzoul et al. 2021; Bortolini et al. 2022). The convergence of DT technology, big data, and emerging data-driven techniques including machine learning (ML) and urban building energy modeling (UBEM) holds immense promise in facilitating the transition toward net-zero at scale. This involves the imperative need for insights, primarily from data derived from DTs and cyber-physical and social systems.

This chapter delves into the relatively unexplored domain of Urban Building Energy Digital Twins (UBEDTs), addressing a critical gap in literature. Within this study, we comprehensively investigate UBEDTs, covering aspects such as their definition, framework, architecture, maturity level, and the range of enabling technologies employed, including AI, ML, and twinning and interoperability technologies. The chapter also emphasizes the implications for urban decarbonization efforts and urban building energy systems and management. Furthermore, this chapter examines the constraints and challenges associated with UBEDT development and implementation.

Urban Building Energy Digital Twins (UBEDTs)

Definition and Conceptualization

In this section, we provide definitions of DTs, with a specific focus on their applications within the Architecture, Engineering, and Construction (AEC) industry, civil infrastructure, urban planning and design, and urban building energy domains. We draw distinctions between the DT concept and other closely related technologies, including Building Information Modeling (BIM), City Information Modeling (CIM), City 3D Models, Urban Building Energy Models (UBEM), and Cyber-Physical Systems (CPS). Finally, we synthesize these definitions and concepts to formulate a comprehensive definition of an UBEDT.

The "Digital Twin" concept was born at National Aeronautical Space Administration (NASA) in the 1960s during the Apollo mission, where it was used to integrate physical and digital worlds for real-time analysis. NASA defines Digital Twin as an "integrated multiphysics, multiscale, probabilistic simulation of an as-built vehicle or system that uses the best available physical models, sensor updates, fleet history, etc., to mirror the life of its corresponding flying twin" (Glaessgen and Stargel 2012). As technology has advanced, the DT concept has found applications in various fields, such as aerospace, manufacturing, smart buildings, smart cities, healthcare, and commerce (Guo and Lv 2022). In 2002, Michael Grieves introduced the concept of DTs in product lifecycle management (PLM) during a presentation and later defined them in a subsequent article (Grieves and Vickers 2017) as "a set of virtual information constructs that fully describes a potential or actual physical manufacturing product from the micro atomic level to the macro geometrical level." This model comprises three essential elements: a physical space, a virtual space, and a data flow link that facilitates information exchange between them, enabling the convergence and synchronization of virtual and physical systems (Grieves and Vickers 2017).

While DTs are more mature in manufacturing and aerospace, the AEC sector is at initial to medium stages of maturity. In AEC industry, the definition of DTs is still evolving, and the concept remains somewhat ambiguous (Opoku et al. 2021). Within AEC, a DT is defined as a "real-time representation of the building or structure that is fully or partially completed and developed for the purpose of representing the status and character of the building or structure it mirrors... [utilizing] real-time or near real-time data" (Opoku et al. 2022). Urban Digital Twins (UDTs) are in the very early stages of development and limited by gaps.

UDTs, despite being in their infancy, can improve urban management by integrating city planning and management into a unified tool, allowing faster responses through autonomous actions and increasing efficiency by providing real-time insights into the city's state (Ferré-Bigorra, Casals, and Gangolells 2022). In the context of civil infrastructure, a Infrastructure Digital Twin (IDT) is described as "a virtual replica of a physical asset with bi-directional data flow (between virtual and physical worlds) that, solely or in integration with other IDTs as a part of system-of-systems, give a deeper understanding of how infrastructures truly work, enabling better performance of infrastructures" (Naderi and Shojaei 2023). Smart cities rely on a DT of the urban environment to sense, analyze, and integrate information from core urban systems by employing CIM models and urban DT technology for advanced simulations and predictions across various factors (economic, social, and spatial), dimensions (3D space, 4D time, 5D cost, and *n*-dimensional applications), and scales (macro, meso, and micro), ensuring sustainable development (Xia et al. 2022). Smart city DTs, through virtual city infrastructure coupled with IoT and virtualization technologies, such as Virtual Reality (VR), Augmented Reality (AR), and Mixed Reality (MR) facilitate data-driven decision-making and scenario analysis, aiding in the evaluation of smart city strategies and performance predictions across varying conditions (Taylor, Bennett, and Mohammadi 2021).

DTs hold promise for enhancing energy management. In their study, Bortolini et al. (2022) review Digital Twin applications in energy efficiency, categorizing them into four key areas: design optimization, occupant comfort, building operation and maintenance, and energy consumption simulation. A study by Agostinelli et al. (2020, 2021) explores the capabilities of DT-based methods to establish an intelligent system for optimizing and automating energy management. Their approach incorporates three-dimensional data modeling, IoT, AI, and ML, employing integrated analysis algorithms to assess various energy efficiency interventions while upholding comfort and climate conditions. Their research emphasizes the versatility of DTs, applicable at various scales, from districts to individual buildings, and highlights the role of real-time monitoring in bridging the gap between simulated and actual building energy performance (Agostinelli et al. 2020, 2021). In the context of energy efficiency and systems, DTs enable synchronization and monitoring of energy systems through virtual simulations grounded in data, information, and occupant behavior (Brosinsky, Westermann, and Krebs 2018).

To clarify the DT concept, it's important to distinguish DTs from BIM, Computer Aided Design/Computer Aided Engineering (CAD/CAE) models, CIM, 3D digital city model, Product Avatar (PA), simulation models, and CPS. Unlike BIM, which is a static representation of a building's design for understanding and communication but lacks bidirectional data flow between the physical and digital realms, DTs maintain this connectivity, providing continuous representation. A DT differs from CAD and CAE models by incorporating real-time data and providing dynamic, holistic representations, enabling monitoring, analysis, and decision-making beyond the capabilities of static CAD/CAE models (Barricelli,

Casiraghi, and Fogli 2019). while both CIM and DT technologies contribute to the development of smart cities, CIM provides a comprehensive view of urban areas for city planning and management, while DTs focus on creating detailed, real-time models of specific urban elements or assets for operational and optimization purposes (Xia et al. 2022).

There is also a misapplication of the term "Urban Digital Twin" to describe a 3D digital city model, partly fueled by the use of this 3D model as the basis for developing more comprehensive UDTs (Ferré-Bigorra, Casals, and Gangolells 2022). DTs and PAs differ in origin, capabilities, and purposes; while DTs can trigger actions on their physical twins, PAs focus on being precise virtual replicas of physical twins (Ríos et al. 2015). Simulation models rely on hypothetical scenarios and lack real-time data updates, while DTs constantly evolve with real-world data from their physical counterparts. The comparison between DTs and CPS is complex due to a lack of consensus on their distinctions, but literature offers three primary perspectives: DTs as alternative applications within space and manufacturing, DTs as prerequisites to CPS for specific use cases, and the acknowledgment of similarities in their focus on physical counterparts while emphasizing that DTs require a virtual model and a twin relationship with their physical entity, unlike CPS (Naderi and Shojaei 2023).

Based on literature definitions and examples as discussed above, we can synthesize a definition for UBEDT: A UBEDT is a dynamic, multiphysics, and multiscale virtual representation of a real-world urban building system, driven by real-time data through AI, IoT, and ML, enabling bidirectional data flow, continuous monitoring, modeling, real-time analysis, what-if scenario simulations, and optimization across its entire lifecycle to enhance decision-making processes for increasing urban building energy performance. This highlights the key attributes and functionalities of a UBEDT, emphasizing its dynamic nature, real-time or near-real-time data integration, reliance on AI, IoT, and ML, incorporation of intelligent functions such as automation, its lifecycle spanning design, construction, operation, and maintenance, and its role in decision-making, fault diagnostics, prediction, monitoring, and optimization within the realm of urban building energy management.

Implications for Citywide Energy Management

Decarbonization forms the essential foundation for transitioning to low-carbon practices, encompassing a range of actions from embracing renewable energy to integrate efficiency into all operations. DT technology finds versatile applications in power systems, spanning fault detection, load forecasting, operator behavior analysis, power control, and equipment health assessment (Jafari et al. 2023). DT technology holds great potential for monitoring, modeling, and managing urban building energy flows, and providing real-time feedback (Bortolini et al. 2022; Francisco, Mohammadi, and Taylor 2020; Huang, Zhang, and Zeng 2022). Particularly in the ACE/FM sector, DT has been utilized for energy demand forecasting, demand response, and grid stability improvements (Zhang et al. 2021), as well as predictive maintenance (Hodavand, Ramaji, and Sadeghi 2023) and data-driven fault detection and diagnosis (FDD) (H. Zhu et al. 2022). Furthermore, DTs have found application in various aspects of building energy efficiency, spanning design optimization, enhancing occupants' comfort, streamlining building operations and maintenance, and simulating energy consumption (Bortolini et al. 2022).

While the concept of city-level DT and digital ecosystems holds immense promise, its successful implementation faces certain challenges. A main limitation of current DT applications is their confinement to the individual building level, hindering their scalability across the entire city due to the novelty of the technology and lack of widespread smart infrastructure and data for all buildings (Lu et al. 2020; Agouzoul et al. 2021; Opoku et al. 2021). Notably, DTs are mainly employed where sensor data (e.g. for energy, occupancy, etc.) and smart infrastructure exist, which are currently confined to specific buildings and campuses. Future data-driven smart buildings envision reliable real-time data (Fierro and Pauwels 2022; O'Neill and Wen 2022), but challenges related to smart infrastructure, cost, privacy, and logistics hinder capturing data at the individual building level for large-scale urban exploration currently.

While a few DT models exist on a larger scale, such as at the campus level, their primary focus has been on operational and maintenance applications (Lu et al. 2020). DT technology has also found application in Positive Energy Districts (PEDs) (Zhang et al. 2021). Existing implementations at the city level primarily revolve around visualization and energy benchmarking (Francisco, Mohammadi, and Taylor 2020). Currently, it appears more feasible to implement DTs at the district or campus level for energy modeling and management compared to city-level implementations. However, it's worth noting that the initial investment and integration process may pose financial and technical challenges. In the article by Zhang et al. (2021), a review of existing PEDs is provided, encompassing key concepts, principles, tools/platforms, and practical applications (Zhang et al. 2021). In the power and energy sector, DTs find extensive utility across various domains, including electronic systems, wind-power farms, cooling systems, and fuel-related systems. Recent years have also seen a surge in energy consumption, especially for heating and electric vehicles. Control centers in smart transportation require real-time data on key components for efficient energy infrastructure management, particularly with the growth of electric vehicle charging, where DT architecture can provide vital real-time information. DTs act as bridges for faster, comprehensive decision-making. In microgrid and smart grid contexts, challenges involve remote data transmission and analysis, solvable through dedicated DT platforms. Distributed Energy Systems (DESs) offer a promising solution for increased renewable energy adoption; here, DT can unleash DES's potential in building decarbonization (X. Zhu et al. 2023).

Agostinelli et al. (2020, 2021) explored the potential of DT-based methods and approaches to create an intelligent optimization and automation system for energy management. The study combines three-dimensional data modeling with the IoT, AI, and ML. Integrated dynamic analysis algorithms are used to evaluate various energy efficiency intervention scenarios while maintaining comfort and climate conditions. The goal is to develop a cost-effective IT infrastructure for reliable data using edge computing, ultimately increasing renewable energy production from solar sources to meet near-zero energy building (nZEB) requirements. Utilizing BIM as-built models, IoT, and AI, they created a smart energy grid management system that generated an up-to-date city DT. Their study highlights the versatility of DTs, capable of application at different scales of district and building levels, and demonstrates how real-time monitoring can bridge the gap between simulated and actual building energy performance, facilitating advanced energy management techniques and revealing the impact of occupant behaviors. The project focuses on a residential district in Rome, comprising 16 eight-floor buildings with 216 apartment units powered by 70% self-renewable energy.

The potential of digital ecosystems becomes evident when the city's DT begins to collaborate with the DTs of individual buildings and energy infrastructure. This collective intelligence allows for the development of a comprehensive energy management strategy that takes into account various factors, including real-time energy demand, weather conditions, occupancy patterns, and energy prices, considering that digital transformation, including IoT, AI, advanced ML, optimization techniques, and Blockchain, will drive future smart cities.

Enabling Technologies

Twining Technologies

Twining technologies, encompassing a range of cutting-edge innovations, are shaping the future of various industries. Beginning with BIM, which creates digital representations of assets or objects (Javaid, Haleem, and Suman, 2023), Geographic Information Systems (GIS) facilitate the analysis and visualization of spatial data and Spatial Mapping (SM) augments this framework by imbuing it with real-world contextualization (Xia et al. 2022). The fusion of GIS data, which provides geospatial insights and spatial analysis capabilities essential for urban studies, with BIM, which comprises a digital representation of construction incorporating micro-level data presentation and active model utilization throughout the AEC lifecycle, offers a core technology for UDTs to support sustainable and intelligent city development. DT technology actualizes the vision of smart cities by creating CIM, encompassing modeling, monitoring, analysis, and simulation, which serves as a comprehensive framework derived from the integration of IoT, cloud computing, big data, and communication technologies, offering an innovative approach to realizing smart cities. The CIM digitally models physical urban features above- and belowground, indoors and outdoors, and their real-time conditions, providing a comprehensive representation of city-level building groups while standardizing management information and enabling data collection for future innovation and transformation into a city's intelligent model (Xia et al. 2022).

Few studies explore BIM integration with blockchain (Manzoor, Othman, and Pomares 2021), underscoring the need for more research in this rapidly evolving technology with growing relevance in both public and private sectors, leading to innovations such as smart contracts, automated code checks, and BIM-cybersecurity to enhance transparency and security, which can substantially benefit the AEC industry. Transparency, security, skills, government policies, cultural barriers, and costs are major challenges requiring solutions, including legal frameworks to promote a constructive AEC industry approach (Manzoor, Othman, and Pomares 2021). Mobile technology, driven by 5G, is vital for advancing DTs in the AEC industry, with potential applications beyond smart buildings (Chew et al. 2020). Anticipating the development of 6G technology, the AEC industry's growth and DT's role in it will be substantial.

The City Geography Markup Language (CityGML) from the Open Geospatial Consortium (OGC) is used to create a unified and interoperable data model within the DT system. CityGML is an open data model and XML-based file format as an internationally recognized standard for representing 3D city models, encompassing essential physical and semantic information about buildings, their surrounding environments, and energy systems (HosseiniHaghighi et al. 2022; Santhanavanich et al. 2022). To generate a CityGML file, several steps are undertaken. Initially, the scope and requirements, including the level of detail and coordinate system, are defined. Subsequently, the Data Acquisition and Extraction Layer collects data from various sources, including 3D models, terrain data, and other urban and building features in different formats such as shapefiles, KMZ, CAD, and CSVs. This data is then formatted into a single CityGML file. To ensure compliance with standards and specifications, the CityGML file undergoes validation through field surveys. CityGML files are typically available at the LOD-1 level for most cities, which only includes basic building volumes. CityGML data can be visualized using a range of 3D software applications, including GIS, BIM, and VR environments. CityGML is also integrated with other open standards, such as the Web Feature Service (WFS) and the Geography Markup Language (GML), enabling easy sharing and exchange of 3D urban data across diverse systems and applications.

Cities need to address the challenge of bridging the gap between urban building data, energy assessment, and end-user distribution in the context of low-carbon urban planning and retrofitting, with numerous *UBEMs* relying on non-geo-specified 3D building data as their inputs (HosseiniHaghighi et al. 2022). UDTs enable virtual representations of georeferenced building information using GIS and local data that evolves 3D modeling and data transformation into CityGML format. For example, (HosseiniHaghighi et al. 2022) developed a workflow for exploring district heating load validation and net-zero planning scenarios in Kelowna, BC. Creating realistic digital geographical models of real-world locations is crucial for DT applications, particularly for simulation and visualization. In another study, the authors (Azfar et al. 2022) focus on efficiently and conveniently generating a 3D digital model of a university campus, integrating terrain, buildings, and road networks into the CARLA project on Unreal Engine to support various DT applications, including computer vision, traffic simulation, and autonomous driving experimentation.

What sets a UDT apart from a mere model lies in the establishment of an interlinked feedback loop, one that fosters a dynamic symbiosis between the physical and DTs. In this context, live interconnection between these twins does not imply that data streams incessantly every second or decisions are instantaneously executed. Rather, this signifies a continuous supply of real-world data to the physical twin, mirroring the reciprocal flow of information that enriches the DT's virtual realm. Crucially, the applicability of UDTs extends to both existing and newly developed assets, offering a versatile framework for urban management and development. UDTs are typically processed on cloud servers for streamlined development and deployment, but as they expand to cover more city infrastructure and services with increased sensor deployments, some cities may shift to edge computing to manage bandwidth demands. These twins offer faster response times and enhance city management efficiency by providing real-time city status information (Ferré-Bigorra, Casals, and Gangolells 2022).

Currently, a limited number of DT platforms and simulation tools are available, which primarily target industrial applications, while feature manipulation engines provide versatile data integration capabilities across various sectors, including transportation, commercial, and utilities and the nexus of food, water, and energy. Some examples are Microsoft Azure (Nath, Schalkwyk, and Isaacs 2021; Wolf et al. 2022) and Bentley iTwin ("iTwin Platform, Bentley Systems, Infrastructure Software" 2022), which are employed for DT implementation. A literature review by (Zhang et al. 2021) explored the use of DTs for PEDs and highlighted various platforms and simulation tools. Some of these tools include the

Intelligent Communities Lifecycle (ICL) platform, which leverages open street maps and BIM interoperability to create digital models for assessing and optimizing building and energy systems throughout their lifecycle. The Building Minds tool employs a common data model, AI, and data democratization techniques to efficiently process and prioritize data from diverse physical systems, facilitating real-time feedback and interoperability with existing data sources for building entity representation. Ecodomus offers four submodules for asset DT creation, covering the entire building lifecycle, integrating building management software, BIM models, facility operational tools, and geographical data obtained through drones.

Key enabling technologies for Digital Transformation include simulation methods, such as Discrete Event Simulation and Continuous Simulation; communication protocols, namely OPC Unified Architecture (OPC-UA) and Message Queuing Telemetry Transport (MQTT); and core technologies of Industry 4.0 including IoT, Cloud Computing, and Big Data (Opoku et al. 2021). These DT platforms and simulation tools facilitate the creation of holistic digital replicas of environments, effectively bridging real-world entities with cloud-based solutions. NVIDIA's AI-on-5G solution strategically harnesses the potential of 5G networks, edge AI, and DT workloads to formulate hyperconverged systems for diverse applications. The integration of IoT devices and point cloud data, along with immersive technologies like VR, AR, and MR, enriched by the capabilities of 5G networks, revolutionizes interaction and data analysis. Smart city DTs, through virtual city infrastructure coupled with IoT and virtualization technologies like VR, AR, and MR, facilitate data-driven decision-making and scenario analysis, aiding in the evaluation of smart city strategies and performance predictions across varying conditions (Taylor, Bennett, and Mohammadi 2021). Additionally, ML and Computer Vision (CV), combined with Edge Computing and Distributed Ledger Technology (DLT), introduce intelligent decision-making, efficient data processing, and secure data sharing, further enhancing the potential of twining technologies.

Urban Digital Twin (UDT) and Data Sources

Data serves as the foundational ingredient of DT and there is a diverse array of data sources for the development and enriching of UDTs. These encompass data sources, including physical sensors directly integrated into assets such as buildings, bridges, roads, and vehicles, remote sensing technologies like laser scanners, unmanned aerial vehicles (UAVs), vehicle-mounted sensors, and satellite data, process data stemming from spatiotemporal analyses encompassing traffic patterns and construction studies, geo-tagged data from social media, mobile devices, GPS, and WIFI networks offering insights into infrastructure and energy loads as well as environmental issues, and a myriad of other data types, collectively enrich the canvas of urban infrastructure management (Figure 12.1). The required sampling rates and sensor densities depend on the modeled system, as static systems, such as a city's 3D digital model, evolve slowly and require lower sampling rates (yearly or longer), while dynamic systems, such as energy demand real-time monitoring with shorter intervals (hours to minutes).

An example study by (Botín-Sanabria et al. 2021) demonstrates establishing living interacting UDTs aligning with the United Nations' Sustainable Development Goals. It uses a network of vehicle-mounted sensors, edge computing, modeling software, and ML to

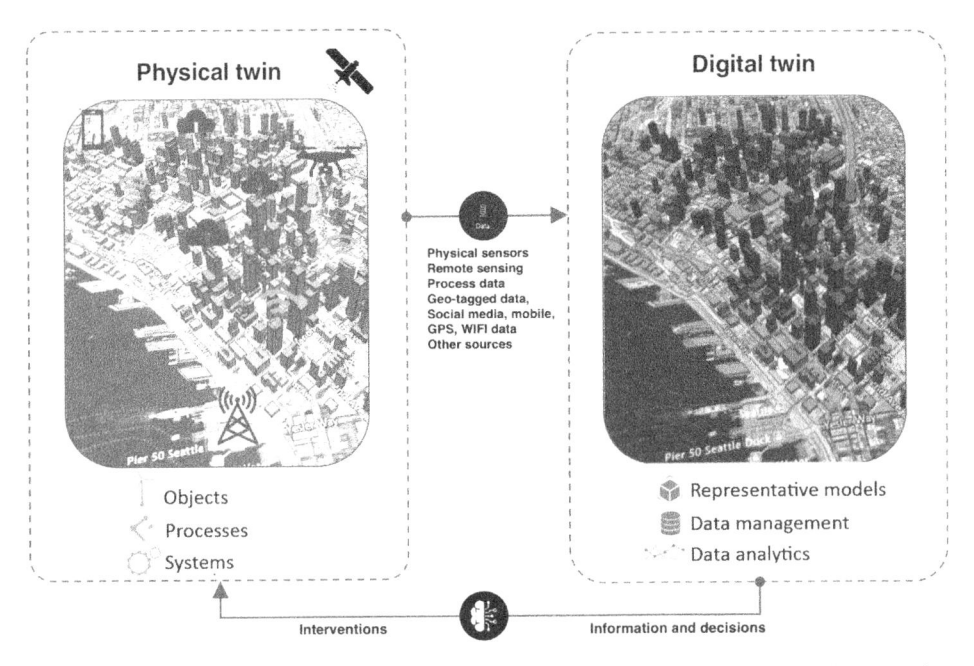

Figure 12.1 Urban Digital Twin and its corresponding Physical Twin with data flows between them.

process real-life data, enabling a 3D virtual representation of urban spaces and vehicles, and facilitating analysis of community evolution, mobility, vehicle dynamics, and urban infrastructure interactions. An analysis of modeled systems reveals a focus on meteorology, flood prediction, and mobility, likely due to the ready availability of data primarily collected from sensors and databases, which vary according to the specific DT application (Ferré-Bigorra, Casals, and Gangolells 2022). Furthermore, UDT development can significantly benefit from the integration of diverse data sources, including physical, cyber, and social sensing data, to support informed adaptation planning and enhance infrastructure resilience, as discussed in Ye et al. (2023).

Geo-referenced big data refers to vast datasets that are explicitly linked to specific geographical locations. These data are collected from various sources, including sensing technologies, mobile devices, GPS, and social media platforms. It offers real-time or near-real-time insights into human behaviors, mobility patterns, and environmental factors across urban areas. As cities and urban areas continue to grow, so does the complexity of managing energy efficiency across diverse building portfolios and infrastructures. When it comes to scaling DTs to campus and city levels, data scarcity becomes a major challenge. However, the abundance of geo-referenced big data, including information from social media and mobility sources, offers potential insights. For example, recent efforts using geo-tagged metadata show potential for occupant-driven energy efficiency (Stavropoulos et al. 2015; Yan et al. 2015), with a focus on IoT sensors, WiFi (Abolhassani et al. 2022), Bluetooth (Park, Dougherty, and Nagy 2018), and mobile phone data (Barbour et al. 2019). Several frameworks have been developed to quantify human activity patterns within built environments using geo-tagged metadata (Li et al. 2015; Pappalardo et al. 2015; Jiang et al. 2016; Mohammadi and Taylor 2017). Leveraging these data sources presents opportunities to address data scarcity, specifically regarding dynamic information such as human activity patterns, and offers insights into energy flows.

For creation and implementation of DT it is important to highlight the importance of data gathering approaches and the identification of relevant multi-dimensional data sets, such as meteorological, load profile, social, and geo-spatial data. In a campus setting, such as a university or large corporate campus, geo-referenced big data can be harnessed to create a holistic view of energy consumption across buildings and outdoor spaces. By analyzing mobility patterns, DTs can optimize campus transportation systems, lighting, and HVAC to align with occupant behavior and preferences. Scaling DTs to city levels opens up transformative possibilities for energy efficiency. With geo-referenced big data, DTs can analyze traffic flows, public transportation usage, and social events to anticipate peak energy demands and optimize citywide energy distribution. Real-time environmental sensing allows for immediate adjustments to energy systems in response to weather changes and environmental conditions. By leveraging this data with AI algorithms, DTs can make predictive analyses, anticipating energy demands, and optimizing resource allocation to meet future needs effectively.

Artificial Intelligence (AI) and Digital Twin

AI is a diverse field with applications in various domains, from autonomous vehicles to healthcare, and it continues to advance rapidly, enabling automation and enhanced decision-making in a wide range of industries. ML, a subset of AI, uncovers patterns in historical data to aid decision-making, with accuracy increasing as data volume grows (leveraging big data). It includes supervised learning (labeled data for regression and classification), unsupervised learning (unlabeled data for clustering), and reinforcement learning (feedback-driven). Examples algorithms for supervised are multi linear regression, decision trees, SVMs, naive Bayes, random forests, and for unsupervised are K-means, hierarchical clustering, mixture models, and for reinforcement are Monte Carlo, Q-learning. Deep learning, inspired by neural networks, employs multiple layers for data processing, optimizing connections iteratively.

Over the past decade, alongside the ongoing advancements in AI, there has been a proliferation of broadband and widespread connectivity, the integration of sensors gathering extensive descriptive data, and enhancements in big data processing and cloud computing. The convergence of these technologies has given rise to DTs, which are AI-driven virtual replicas of physical systems (Barricelli, Casiraghi, and Fogli 2019). Data fusion, AI, and big data analytics through IoT sensors enable communication and intelligent interaction between physical systems and their respective DTs, offering potential benefits in detecting inefficiencies and issues. AI plays a crucial role in managing data, automating processes, and enabling technologies like edge, fog, and 5G, merging physical processes with computing and network domains for DTs (Groshev et al. 2021).

However, it's important to note that DTs are not fully autonomous and often require human intervention, especially in scenarios involving testing, diagnosis, and treatment. Incorporating big data analytics and AI–ML methods into digital twinning increases its importance and expands its research horizons, presenting novel opportunities and distinct challenges (Rathore et al. 2021). Digital twinning entails constructing a cyber twin to digitally represent a physical entity or process, enabling a data-sharing connection for purposes like dynamic optimization, real-time monitoring, fault diagnostics, prediction, and health monitoring, with physical twins encompassing processes, humans, devices, or objects, replicated as either partial or complete twins (Rathore et al. 2021). AI is rapidly changing the AEC industry by enhancing automation for improved quality and efficiency (Manzoor, Othman, and Pomares 2021). Construction automation involves computerized frameworks and robotics, transforming traditional methods combining computer-aided design and on-site robotics for accelerated construction. Establishing a standardized approach and leveraging data-driven methods are essential to realize the potential benefits of automation in the built environment.

Relationship Between IoT, Big Data, AI–ML, and Digital Twins

The interconnected relationship between IoT, big data, AI-ML, and DTs unfolds as follows: DTs leverage IoT as their foundation, harnessing its capabilities to collect real-world data. This influx of data from IoT sources forms the bedrock of big data. Subsequently, the vast reservoir of big data undergoes transformative processes, powered by AI and ML techniques, ultimately culminating in the creation and refinement of DTs (Figure 12.2).

DTs build upon IoT, utilizing its potential for gathering real-world data. The process begins with IoT sensor technologies deployed in relevant settings, enabling real-time data collection. These data include information on physical devices, indoor asset tracking, and outdoor asset tracking. The collected IoT data are foundational element for creating DTs. It serves as the input required to establish a virtual replica of the corresponding physical components. This connection between the physical and virtual worlds is crucial for further steps. IoT generates big data. IoT data are often extensive in scale, making it a candidate for big data analytics. Big data analytics play a pivotal role in extracting valuable insights and patterns

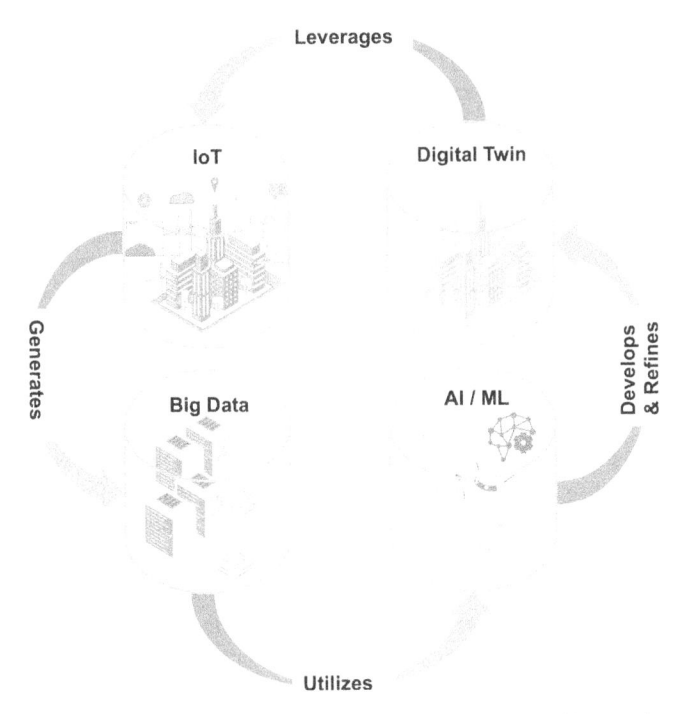

Figure 12.2 Interconnection of IoT, big data, AI–ML, and Digital Twins.

from this wealth of information. Big data analytics help identify potential issues early on, a task that traditional methods struggle with. An article by (Chen, Mao, and Liu 2014) provides a concise overview of big data, covering its background and current state of the art. It encompasses the general context of big data, relevant technologies (cloud computing, IoT, data centers, Hadoop), and the four key phases of the big data generation, acquisition, storage, and analysis. Additionally, it explores various applications such as enterprise management, IoT, social networks, healthcare, collective intelligence, and smart grids. The survey concludes by addressing open challenges and future prospects in the field. Cloud computing often emerges as the ideal platform for processing and analyzing big data efficiently. Its scalability and accessibility make it well-suited for handling the data generated by IoT devices in the context of DTs.

To enhance the capabilities of DTs, advanced AI techniques are applied to the data collected from IoT sensors. The extracted insights inform the creation and optimization of DTs using advanced AI techniques. Effectively managing and processing this massive amount of data necessitates advanced techniques, architectures, frameworks, tools, and algorithms. AI empowers DTs to detect critical factors (e.g. optimal processes, resource allocation, and fault detection), predict outcomes (e.g. health status and early maintenance needs), and optimize operations (e.g. planning, process control, scheduling, assembly line efficiency). These dynamic decisions are based on both physical sensor data and virtual twin data.

Interoperability Technologies

Interoperability technologies enable communication between various systems. Among these technologies, the Industry Foundation Classes (IFC) standards have emerged as key enablers for data interoperability. IFC 2×3 and IFC 4 have been foundational in representing and exchanging building and construction data, allowing different software tools to exchange information effectively. Moreover, the evolution of IFC 5 signifies advancements in data representation and semantic richness, enhancing the scope of complex modeling. CityGML, an OGC standard, complements IFC by focusing on the representation of 3D urban models. CityGML 2.0 and the more recent CityGML 3.0 contribute to the interoperability landscape by offering a standardized way to encode and exchange semantic 3D city models. These standards enable collaborative planning, simulation, and analysis of urban environments. The integration of IFC and CityGML standards has garnered attention for their potential in applications such as property valuation and urban modeling, facilitating collaboration and informed decision-making. The evolution of semantic web technologies further strengthens the foundation for achieving higher levels of interoperability, where meaningful data exchange and integration become paramount in realizing the full potential of interconnected systems.

Knowledge Graph (KG) is leveraged to represent structured knowledge and enable intelligent automation and decision-making. KGs have wide-ranging applications in information processing and management, including data integration, ML, and semantic applications (Sheth, Padhee, and Gyrard 2019). A KG is essentially a directed graph comprising nodes representing concepts and edges representing their relationships. This graph-based structure provides a robust framework for hosting, querying, and traversing data, as well as retrieving related information using Linked Data principles. To construct the dynamic KG, cutting-edge technologies from the Semantic Web stack, including Linked Data, are utilized. This approach allows for the automated incorporation of new data and the calculation of quantities of interest, ensuring that the DT evolves over time while remaining up to date. The construction of the KG involves several steps: defining the ontology and knowledge model specific to the DT, identifying relevant domains and subdomains, defining the concepts and relationships between them, and creating a formal ontology using standards like Web Ontology Language (OWL) or Resource Description Framework (RDF) Schema.

An article by (Akroyd et al. 2021) introduces a dynamic KG approach for DTs, utilizing Semantic Web technologies to enable a universal DT and extending the dynamic knowledge graph for developing decarbonization DT. The approach employs ontologies and computational agents to update the distributed KG, promoting interoperability and data connectivity. It accommodates real-time data, supports alternative designs, and showcases applications in geospatial, chemistry, simulations, and scenario analysis. KGs have gained significance as an integral part of DT architecture, enabling the representation of structured data, relationships, and contextual information in various domains. The utilization of knowledge graphs enhances the capabilities of DTs for improved analysis, decision-making, and automation. These KG approaches have been explored in recent years, with researchers and practitioners recognizing their potential to enhance the efficiency and effectiveness of DTs across different industries. The integration of KGs aligns with the broader development of Semantic Web Technologies, which aims to create a more interconnected and meaningful web by structuring and linking data in a standardized manner

Maturity Levels

In a recent study, Uhlenkamp et al. (2022) developed a classification framework to analyze existing DTs and support the development of current and future DTs. Using this approach, they identified seven key maturity model (MM) categories (context, data, computing capabilities, model, integration, control, human-machine interaction) crucial for characterizing DTs. They further segmented these categories into dimensions for detailed descriptions, providing an extensive set of characteristics to evaluate the maturity and usability of a given DT within a specific context. Usability and expected benefits of the DT depend on the application context and services it offers which is crucial when contemplating repurposing, redesigning, or reusing the DT for a slightly different purpose, necessitating an assessment of its nature and dimension maturity, with viability contingent on alignment with new requirements (Uhlenkamp et al. 2022). In another study in the context of model-based system engineering (MBSE) by (Madni, Madni, and Lucero 2019), four maturity levels of DTs is defined, including Pre-DT, DT, Adaptive DT, and Intelligent DT, based on four dimensions: physical twin existence, data acquisition, ML of operator preferences, and ML of system/environment, with the Intelligent DT representing the ultimate stage, featuring a virtual system model of the physical twin, an adaptive user interface, and reinforcement learning capabilities.

Guo and Lv (2022) provide insights into DT's practical applications in multiple fields (e.g. smart cities, healthcare, aerospace, and retail), interspersing core technology concepts and offer predictions for DT's future development based on its current status. In another study (Naderi and Shojaei 2023), the authors outline four stages of IDT development in the AEC field, beginning with information model technology having limited interaction with the physical world, progressing to integrated information models, data acquisition tech, and interoperability solutions for more complex interactions, and some employing four main technologies for IDT creation, representing levels 0 to 1; this trend continues toward predicting future IDT evolution (levels 2 and 3), culminating in a discussion of the current state (levels 0 to 1) and prediction of IDT's future evolution toward the Metaverse (level 3).

Adapting DTs for cities entails defining their content, orchestration, and enhancing urban efficiency. To ensure that DTs enhance urban and building performance by optimizing time, cost, and energy through improved design and planning, it's imperative that their applications are in sync with the needs, necessitating the alignment of city functions with DT techniques. While back-end city DTs store all data and front-ends offer visualizations and representations of that data, ongoing challenges exist, yet opportunities arise for AI-driven autonomous updates and delivering front-end advantages to the city ecosystem (Lehtola et al. 2022).

The concept of digital ecosystems is gaining traction, where multiple interconnected DTs collaborate and share data to optimize larger systems. For example, a city's DT can communicate with the DTs of individual buildings to create a cohesive energy management strategy for the entire city. Digital ecosystems are dynamic networks of interconnected digital entities, such as IoT devices, sensors, and virtual models like DTs, which collaborate and exchange information to achieve common objectives. In the context of energy efficiency and fault detection and diagnostics, digital ecosystems facilitate the coordination and optimization of various energy-related components within urban environments. Imagine a city as a living organism, with each building, infrastructure, transportation network, and energy system as vital organs working in harmony. Traditional approaches to urban energy management often involve fragmented solutions, with individual buildings and systems operating independently. However, the rise of digital ecosystems introduces a paradigm shift, where the city functions as an integrated and intelligent entity, leveraging real-time data and predictive insights to optimize energy utilization across its various components.

At the heart of the digital ecosystem concept are interconnected DTs that represent specific elements within the city. For instance, individual buildings, power substations, water treatment plants, and public transportation networks each have their DT. These DTs continuously gather data from their corresponding physical entities, feeding it into the larger ecosystem. Through secure data exchange and communication protocols, the city's DT can access and aggregate information from individual building DTs. This interconnectedness enables a profound level of data analytics, cross-system optimization, and collaboration that surpasses the capabilities of isolated DT implementations. However, it should be noted that the broader-scale adoption of these advancements remains in its nascent stages of development. Presently, the practical implementation of Fault Detection and Diagnosis (FDD) and self-correcting building control systems is largely confined to the realm of individual buildings and campus-level applications. This limitation stems from the relatively recent emergence of this technology and the scarcity of comprehensive smart infrastructure and data systems essential for citywide scalability. Large-scale applications, such as those within campus settings, are comparatively few and predominantly oriented toward operational and maintenance functionalities.

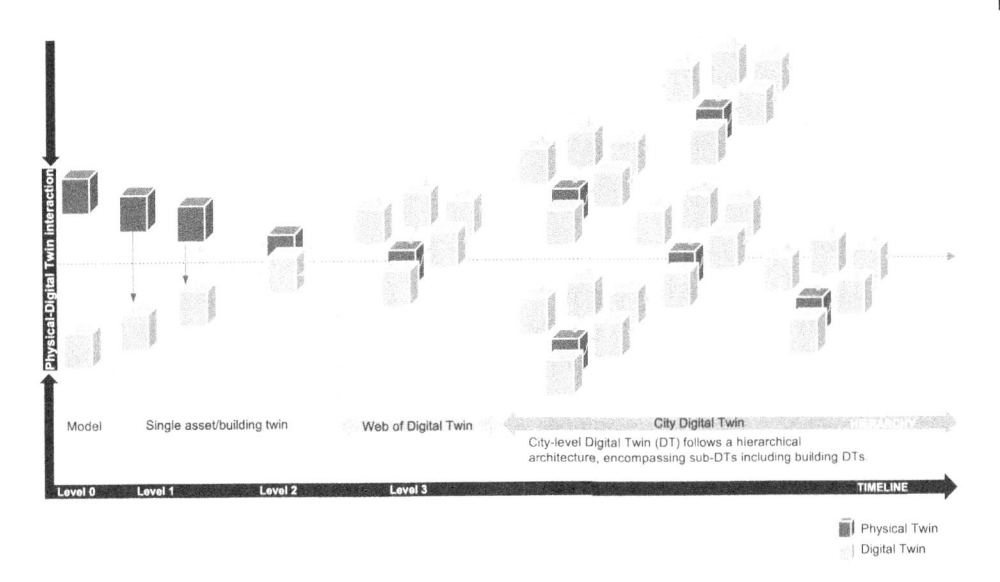

Figure 12.3 Urban building DTs evolution.

We adapt the four maturity levels of IDT as outlined by Naderi and Shojaei (2023) to formulate four distinct maturity levels for DTs in the context of urban building energy flows (Figure 12.3). Starting at level 0 as a basic digital model, it advances to level 1 with one-way data flow from the physical twin to the digital twin. More recent progress introduces a bidirectional relationship, allowing the digital twin not only to retrieve data from the physical twin but also to enact self-corrective functions. As we look ahead, the goal is to establish a closer and multifaceted connection between the digital and physical twin. This envisions a web of digital twins and a city-level network following a hierarchical architecture, encompassing sub-DTs including building DTs.

These levels represent a continuum of increasing complexity, integration, and application breadth of digital twins in the urban building sector and energy systems domain, emphasizing the transition from static models to dynamic, interconnected systems that leverage emerging technologies for real-time monitoring, analysis, and decision-making. Each maturity level signifies a step towards more complex and integrated systems, incorporating advancements in data acquisition, processing, and interoperability technologies to enhance the management, operation, and maintenance of urban building systems.

Architecture

The DT system architecture integrates physical, social, and technological aspects through ICT infrastructure, with the city serving as an integrated asset that incorporates sub-assets (e.g. buildings, utilities, infrastructure, and people) and the city-level DT acting as a dynamic digital replica for bidirectional interaction, information querying, stakeholder-responsive services, and data confidentiality. Zhang et al. (2021) identifies four crucial components:

virtual models, sensor integration, data analytics, and stakeholder engagement (Zhang et al. 2021). The city-level DT architecture consists of five major layers (Lu et al. 2020; Abdeen and Sepasgozar 2022): data acquisition, transmission, digital modeling, data/model integration, and service layer as follows (Figure 12.4):

Data Acquisition Layer

The Data Acquisition Layer is fundamental in every DT, particularly challenging given the diverse data in city environments. In the specific domain of urban building energy systems within a city-level DT architecture, this layer is pivotal for gathering essential data which is responsible for collecting all the necessary data related to building energy consumption and relevant parameters. It employs techniques such as contactless data collection (e.g. RFID, image-based), sensors, wireless communication, and mobile access (e.g. WiFi). Sub-DTs, tailored for various components such as buildings, adhere to the overarching city DT architecture with a focus on real-time data collection and integration. It captures real-time energy data through sensor networks and existing metering infrastructure, integrates external sources such as utility grids and weather data, and ensures secure data transmission to the DT platform via IoT gateways. Building DTs use methods such as IoT devices, wireless sensors, or QR codes. Additionally, it includes the acquisition of geospatial and semantic building data from public sources such as OpenStreetMap and 3D city models, and when such details are lacking, employs techniques such as imagery techniques to extract missing information (e.g. building materials and window-to-wall ratios). This comprehensive data foundation is fundamental for monitoring, analyzing, and optimizing urban building energy performance, enabling informed decisions and energy efficiency enhancements in the city.

Transmission Layer

The transmission layer facilitates the transfer of acquired data to higher layers for analysis and modeling. The transmission layer employs a range of communication technologies to achieve data transfer. These technologies may include short-range coverage access network technologies, such as WiFi, Zigbee, near-field communication (NFC), mobile-to-mobile (M2M), and Zwave. Additionally, it can utilize wider coverage options like 3G, 4G, long-term evolution (LTE), 5G, and low-power wide-area networks (LP-WAN). The choice of technology depends on factors such as data volume, coverage area, and energy efficiency.

Modeling and Simulation Layer

In this layer, mathematical and computational models are used to simulate the behavior of urban building energy systems. These models can include models such as thermal models, energy consumption models, renewable energy integration models, and energy grid integration. Thermal models simulate heat transfer within a building, taking into account factors such as insulation, heating, ventilation, and air conditioning (HVAC) systems, and external weather conditions. They help predict indoor temperatures and energy consumption. While, energy consumption models estimate energy consumption based on the behavior of

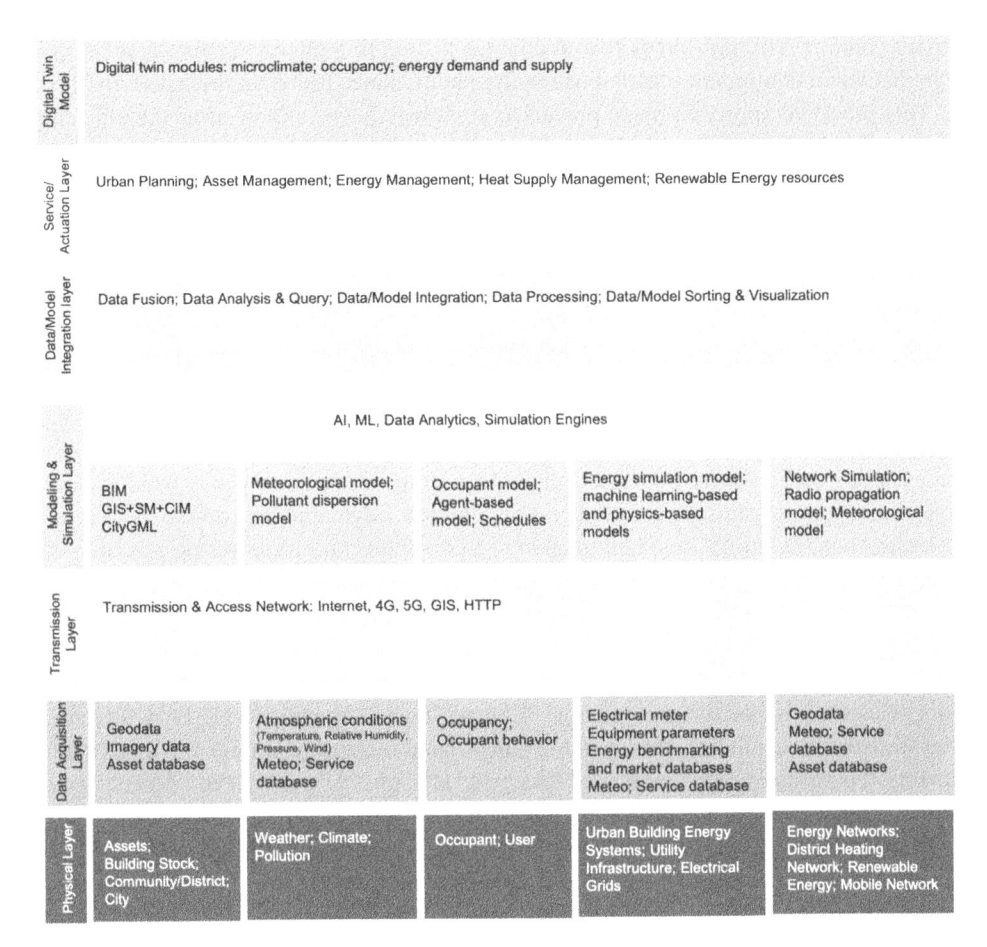

Figure 12.4 UBEDT architecture.

occupants, equipment, and building systems. They consider factors such as occupancy schedules, lighting, appliances, and HVAC operation. For buildings with renewable energy sources like solar panels or wind turbines, renewable energy integration models can predict how these sources generate electricity and how it interact with the grid and building energy demand. In addition to modeling individual buildings, the layer can also simulate interactions with the broader energy grid. This includes assessing the impact of demand-response strategies, grid integration of renewable energy sources, and the optimization of electricity consumption to reduce peak loads and lower energy costs.

The modeling and simulation layer allows various functions, such as scenario analysis, optimization, predictive maintenance, and energy performance evaluation. The layer allows for scenario analysis, where different "what-if" scenarios can be tested. For example, building managers or urban planners can simulate the impact of adjusting thermostat setpoints, upgrading insulation, or installing energy-efficient lighting to assess potential energy savings. Optimization algorithms can be applied to the simulation results to find the best configurations or strategies for improving energy efficiency. For example, algorithms can optimize HVAC scheduling or control to minimize energy costs while maintaining occupant comfort. Through predictive maintenance, building energy system simulations can predict when equipment may fail or require maintenance based on their performance data. This proactive approach helps prevent costly breakdowns and ensures the efficient operation of building systems. The layer provides tools to evaluate the energy performance of buildings and identify areas where improvements can be made. Key performance indicators (KPIs) can be generated from the simulation results to track progress toward energy efficiency goals.

Simulation engines or software tools are employed to execute these mathematical models. These engines use mathematical equations to simulate how a building's energy systems behave over time. Common simulation tools include EnergyPlus, TRNSYS, and Modelica-based platforms. Real-world data collected from the Data Acquisition Layer (e.g. temperature measurements, occupancy data) are integrated into the simulation. This real-time data can help refine and calibrate the models to improve their accuracy. These data streams can include aspects such as current indoor and outdoor temperatures, occupancy patterns, and energy consumption readings. This integration allows for dynamic adjustments and feedback loops, enabling the DT to adapt to changing conditions and improve the precision of predictions. For example, if a sudden change in weather is detected, the simulation can adjust HVAC settings in real-time to maintain comfort while optimizing energy use. Within this layer, mathematical models can vary in complexity and scope. For instance, thermal models can involve intricate equations that consider factors like heat conduction through building materials, convective and radiative heat transfer, and the impact of HVAC systems. Energy consumption models can be fine-grained, factoring in the behavior of individual occupants, their usage of appliances, and the energy efficiency of different equipment types. Such detailed models aim to capture the intricacies of real-world building energy systems, providing a highly accurate representation. In some advanced implementations, ML techniques can be integrated into the Modeling and Simulation Layer. ML models can analyze historical data to identify patterns, anomalies, and optimization opportunities. For instance, they can recognize trends in energy consumption and suggest changes to building system settings for improved efficiency.

DTs utilize real-time data and advanced analytics leveraging AI and ML algorithms for energy demand forecasting, demand response, and grid stability improvement (Zhang et al. 2021). They also support performance evaluation, predictive maintenance, and data-driven fault detection and diagnosis (FDD) for anomaly identification (Zhu et al. 2022; Hodavand, Ramaji, and Sadeghi 2023). Integration with external systems is crucial in the DT architecture. Energy Management Systems (EMS) used by building operators and facility managers are seamlessly integrated with the DT for communication and control. This integration enables coordinated energy management, load balancing, and demand response. Additionally, integration with renewable energy sources like solar PV installations and wind turbines optimizes their integration into the urban energy grid, considering building energy demands, solar potential, wind patterns, and other factors. Integration with the utility grid facilitates demand response, load forecasting, and two-way communication, enabling efficient energy exchange.

Additionally, the layer incorporates digital models of physical assets (e.g. BIM and CIM) and supplementary data like weather and socioeconomic factors, extending BIM concepts to city-scale applications for urban planning and decision support, necessitating a structured schema for diverse applications across buildings and cities.

Data/Model Integration Layer

The Data/Model Integration Layer is responsible for integrating data resources, facilitating data and model employment, storage, analysis, processing, and AI-driven knowledge learning for decision support. Real-time data analysis keeps city and building asset information up-to-date, with effective hierarchical data storage and query design ensuring performance in handling extensive data in city-level systems. Cloud storage, computing, and data/model visualization aid dynamic data management. Data fuels intelligent functions like AI, ML, and simulation for advanced decision support, driven by domain-specific knowledge engines (KEs) that describe dynamic asset conditions. Different KEs are developed based on domain knowledge and specific scenarios, playing a crucial role in enhancing services through robust data integration. Intelligent functions continually update algorithms for ongoing applications and future development.

Service/Actuation Layer

The service layer in the DT architecture facilitates knowledge interpretation and interaction between society and the data/model integration layer. Positioned as the highest level of the DT architecture, the service layer translates insights derived from knowledge engines (KEs) into tangible interactions between individuals or society and the data/model integration layer. It offers services, assesses DT performance, and enables energy management and smart infrastructure development. Importantly, user feedback serves as external knowledge that enriches KEs, contributing to overall satisfaction improvements. In this architecture, the service layer caters to FM professionals and end-users, offering decision-making support and interaction capabilities. To maintain operational performance, especially during early implementation, optimized decisions must undergo manual confirmation before execution. The design of smart buildings/cities enables a flexible decision-making process and facilitates interactions with FM professionals and users.

Challenges in Implementing Citywide Digital Twins

A review by Opoku et al. (2023) identifies and categorizes 30 barriers that hinder DT adoption in construction, with the top five being low knowledge, technology acceptance, unclear value propositions, project complexities, and static building data. While the concept of UBEDTs holds great promise, its practical development and application, especially within the complex urban building energy domain, encounter specific obstacles. Key among the existing limitations of UDT is interoperability, data quality, computing resources, budget constraints, and cybersecurity (Ferré-Bigorra, Casals, and Gangolells 2022). A noteworthy constraint in the current applications of UBEDTs for energy planning and management is their confinement to individual building levels, which hinders their scalability across entire cities due to the technology's novelty and the absence of widespread smart infrastructure and comprehensive data for all buildings (Lu et al. 2020; Agouzoul et al. 2021; Opoku et al. 2021). The key limitations can be summarized as follows:

Data Quality and Availability

Data quality concerns revolve around the accuracy, completeness, and reliability of the data used to build and update the DT. Inaccurate or incomplete data can lead to incorrect modeling and predictions within the twin, diminishing its effectiveness as a decision-support tool for urban management. In energy management, data quality issues can manifest as inaccurate or delayed data from sensors and meters. For instance, if a sensor providing real-time energy consumption data in a specific area malfunctions, it can lead to incorrect energy usage estimations within the DT. Consequently, the twin's ability to optimize energy distribution and identify areas for improvement is compromised. It's important to note that DTs are primarily utilized where sensor data (e.g. for energy, occupancy, etc.) and smart infrastructure are available, but these resources are currently limited to specific buildings and campuses. Future data-driven smart buildings envision reliable real-time data (Fierro and Pauwels 2022; O'Neill and Wen 2022), but challenges related to smart infrastructure, cost, privacy, and logistics hinder capturing data at the individual building level for large-scale urban exploration currently.

Required Smart Infrastructure and Associated Cost

Implementing and maintaining UBEDTs can be expensive, encompassing the acquisition of essential sensors, hardware, software, and expertise. Balancing these costs with desired functionalities is complex. For instance, establishing smart sensing infrastructure and advanced energy management features within an UBEDTs demands substantial financial resources. Presently, large-scale urban building DT projects may appear ambitious due to resource limitations, constraining the twin's energy management capabilities and its capacity to optimize energy efficiency citywide. Currently, it appears more feasible to implement DTs at the district or campus level for energy modeling and management compared to city-level implementations. However, the initial investment and integration process poses financial and technical challenges.

Interoperability

This refers to the ability of different systems and technologies to work together seamlessly. In the context of UDTs, interoperability issues arise when various data sources, sensors, and software systems used to create the twin struggle to communicate and share data effectively. Lack of interoperability limits the twin's ability to integrate and utilize data from different sources, reducing its effectiveness and potential. This challenge often becomes apparent in energy management applications. For instance, different utility providers and smart grid systems may use disparate data formats and communication protocols. When UBEDTs struggle to integrate data from these sources, it hampers their ability to provide a comprehensive view of energy consumption and distribution across the city, limiting the effectiveness of energy management initiatives. Additional research is required to further advance semantic interoperability in the context of sustainable development (Akroyd et al. 2021; Zhang et al. 2021).

Data Analysis

Adoption of IoT has created vast amounts of sensor data, big data, necessitating advanced architectures, frameworks, and tools for data capture, storage, processing, and analysis. Urban environments continuously generate big data and a vast amount of data in real time, from energy consumption to mobility, traffic, and environmental dynamics. The challenge lies in possessing sufficient computing resources to process and analyze this data in real time. Edge and cloud computing platforms can potentially handle DT data, with edge computing facilitating distributed processing at the network's edge while cloud computing handles aggregate processing. However, cloud data aggregation may introduce response time issues. Inadequate resources can lead to delays in decision-making and limit the twin's ability to respond quickly to changing urban conditions. Timely decision-making in energy management, such as load balancing and demand response, heavily relies on real-time data. If the urban DT lacks necessary computing resources for real-time energy data analysis, it can lead to delays in responding to energy demand fluctuations, resulting in inefficiencies and increased costs. For example, the smart buildings and smart grids deal with big data, necessitating technologies, such as cloud computing and IoT, and encompasses key phases of data generation, acquisition, storage, and analysis (Chen, Mao, and Liu 2014). While existing UBEDT implementations at the city level mainly center around visualization and energy benchmarking (Francisco, Mohammadi, and Taylor 2020). There are also large-scale energy DT models, such as those at the campus level (Lu et al. 2020), and PEDs (Zhang et al. 2021) that predominantly emphasize operational and maintenance applications and less focus on design and planning phase. AI algorithms in data analytics are central to DT decision-making as discussed in the literature (Rathore et al. 2021). However, choosing the best ML model and features among many configurations poses challenges, as their accuracy and efficiency vary across applications. The selection depends on DT objectives. Limited practical AI implementations in digital twinning add complexity.

Despite extensive research efforts to uncover the potential of DTs for industrial problem-solving, their adoption in the construction sector remains limited, as revealed by previous studies indicating a lack of widespread use of IoT-enabled sensor networks in the development of smart building DTs (Opoku et al. 2021).

Cybersecurity and Privacy Concerns

As UDTs rely on data and communication networks, they become potential targets for cyber-attacks. Ensuring the security and resilience of these twins are crucial to protect sensitive urban data and maintain the integrity of city operations. Cybersecurity measures must be robust and continuously updated to address evolving threats. As energy management systems are critical infrastructure, they are attractive targets for cyber-attacks. UDTs that oversee energy systems must be fortified against potential threats to prevent unauthorized access and protect against disruptions in energy supply. Additionally, privacy concerns arise in DT systems, particularly those associated with human related DTs, such as occupancy and health. These contexts require careful attention to protect sensitive data and preventing unauthorized access or breaches that could compromise individuals' or organizations' privacy.

These challenges underscore the importance of ongoing research and development in the UDT field to address limitations and ensure their effectiveness in enhancing urban management, particularly in complex areas like energy management, for improving sustainability and efficiency of urban energy systems.

Conclusion

This chapter has offered an exploration of the UBEDTs, shedding light on a topic that had previously received limited attention in the literature. We have defined UBEDTs and delved into their conceptual framework, architecture, and the enabling technologies that drive their development. By categorizing UBEDTs into different maturity levels, ranging from historical perspectives to envisioned future capabilities, we have provided a roadmap for understanding their evolution. Furthermore, we have addressed the limitations and challenges associated with UBEDT development, acknowledging the complexities involved in data quality, privacy, interoperability, and scalability. As we navigate the ever-evolving urban landscape, UBEDTs stand as a powerful tool to optimize building energy performance and contribute to broader urban decarbonization initiatives. This research calls upon researchers, policymakers, and urban planners to embrace and innovate in this transformative field, paving the way for more sustainable and energy-efficient cities in the future.

References

Abdeen, F.N. and Sepasgozar, S.M.E. (2022). City Digital Twin Concepts: A Vision for Community Participation. *Environmental Sciences Proceedings* 12 (1): 19. https://doi.org/10.3390/environsciproc2021012019.

Agostinelli, S., Cumo, F., Guidi, G., and Tomazzoli, C. (2020). The Potential of Digital Twin Model Integrated With Artificial Intelligence Systems. In: *In 2020 IEEE International Conference on Environment and Electrical Engineering and 2020 IEEE Industrial and Commercial Power Systems Europe (EEEIC / I&CPS Europe)*, 1–6. https://doi.org/10.1109/EEEIC/ICPSEurope49358.2020.9160810.

Agostinelli, S., Cumo, F., Guidi, G., and Tomazzoli, C. (2021). Cyber-Physical Systems Improving Building Energy Management: Digital Twin and Artificial Intelligence. *Energies* 14 (8): 2338. https://doi.org/10.3390/en14082338.

Agouzoul, A., Tabaa, M., Chegari, B. et al. (2021). Towards a Digital Twin Model for Building Energy Management: Case of Morocco. *Procedia Computer Science,* The 12th International Conference on Ambient Systems, Networks and Technologies (ANT)/The 4th International Conference on Emerging Data and Industry 4.0 (EDI40)/Affiliated Workshops 184 (January): 404–410. https://doi.org/10.1016/j.procs.2021.03.051.

Akroyd, J., Mosbach, S., Bhave, A., and Kraft, M. (2021). Universal Digital Twin - A Dynamic Knowledge Graph. *Data-Centric Engineering* 2 (January): e14. https://doi.org/10.1017/dce.2021.10.

Ashayeri, M. and Abbasabadi, N. (2021). A Framework for Integrated Energy and Exposure to Ambient Pollution Assessment toward Energy-Conscious, Healthy, and Equitable Cities. *Sustainable Cities and Society*, December, 103647 https://doi.org/10.1016/j.scs.2021.103647.

Azfar, T., Weidner, J., Raheem, A. et al. (2022). Efficient Procedure of Building University Campus Models for Digital Twin Simulation. *IEEE Journal of Radio Frequency Identification* 6: 769–773. https://doi.org/10.1109/JRFID.2022.3212957.

Barbour, E., Davila, C.C., Gupta, S. et al. (2019). Planning for Sustainable Cities by Estimating Building Occupancy with Mobile Phones. *Nature Communications* 10 (1): 3736. https://doi.org/10.1038/s41467-019-11685-w.

Barricelli, B.R., Casiraghi, E., and Fogli, D. (2019). A Survey on Digital Twin: Definitions, Characteristics, Applications, and Design Implications. *IEEE Access* 7: 167653–167671. https://doi.org/10.1109/ACCESS.2019.2953499.

Bibri, S.E., Alexandre, A., Sharifi, A., and Krogstie, J. (2023). Environmentally Sustainable Smart Cities and Their Converging AI, IoT, and Big Data Technologies and Solutions: An Integrated Approach to an Extensive Literature Review. *Energy Informatics* 6 (1): 9. https://doi.org/10.1186/s42162-023-00259-2.

Bortolini, R., Rodrigues, R., Alavi, H. et al. (2022). Digital Twins' Applications for Building Energy Efficiency: A Review. *Energies* 15 (19): 7002. https://doi.org/10.3390/en15197002.

Botín-Sanabria, Diego M, Jorge G Lozoya-Reyes, Roberto C Vargas-Maldonado, L Rodríguez-Hernández, Ricardo A Ramírez-Mendoza, Mauricio A Ramírez-Moreno, and Jorge J de Lozoya-Santos. 2021. "Digital Twin for Urban Spaces: An Application."

Brosinsky, C., Westermann, D., and Krebs, R. (2018). Recent and Prospective Developments in Power System Control Centers: Adapting the Digital Twin Technology for Application in Power System Control Centers. In: *2018 IEEE International Energy Conference (ENERGYCON)*, 1–6. https://doi.org/10.1109/ENERGYCON.2018.8398846.

Chen, M., Mao, S., and Liu, Y. (2014). Big Data: A Survey. *Mobile Networks and Applications* 19 (2): 171–209. https://doi.org/10.1007/s11036-013-0489-0.

Chew, M.Y., Lin, E.A., Teo, L. et al. (2020). Evaluating the Roadmap of 5G Technology Implementation for Smart Building and Facilities Management in Singapore. *Sustainability* 12 (24): 10259. https://doi.org/10.3390/su122410259.

Ferré-Bigorra, J., Casals, M., and Gangolells, M. (2022). The Adoption of Urban Digital Twins. *Cities* 131 (December): 103905. https://doi.org/10.1016/j.cities.2022.103905.

Fierro, G. and Pauwels, P. (2022). *Survey of Metadata Schemas for Datadriven Smart Buildings (Annex 81): Energy in Buildings and Communities Technology Collaboration Programme*. International Energy Agency, CSIRO https://pure.tue.nl/ws/portalfiles/portal/207017800/IEA_Annex_81_Survey_of_Metadata_Schemas.pdf.

Francisco, A., Mohammadi, N., and Taylor, J.E. (2020). Smart City Digital Twin–Enabled Energy Management: Toward Real-Time Urban Building Energy Benchmarking. *Journal of Management in Engineering* 36 (2): 04019045. https://doi.org/10.1061/(ASCE)ME.1943-5479.0000741.

Glaessgen, E. and Stargel, D. (2012). The Digital Twin Paradigm for Future NASA and U.S. Air Force Vehicles. In: *53rd AIAA/ASME/ASCE/AHS/ASC Structures, Structural Dynamics and Materials Conference*. American Institute of Aeronautics and Astronautics https://doi.org/10.2514/6.2012-1818.

González-Torres, M., Pérez-Lombard, L., Coronel, J.F. et al. (2022). A Review on Buildings Energy Information: Trends, End-Uses, Fuels and Drivers. *Energy Reports* 8 (November): 626–637. https://doi.org/10.1016/j.egyr.2021.11.280.

Grieves, M. and Vickers, J. (2017). Digital Twin: Mitigating Unpredictable, Undesirable Emergent Behavior in Complex Systems. In: *Transdisciplinary Perspectives on Complex*

Systems: New Findings and Approaches (ed. F.-J. Kahlen, S. Flumerfelt, and A. Alves), 85–113. Cham: Springer International Publishing https://doi.org/10.1007/978-3-319-38756-7_4.

Groshev, M., Guimarães, C., Martín-Pérez, J., and de la Oliva, A. (2021). Toward Intelligent Cyber-Physical Systems: Digital Twin Meets Artificial Intelligence. *IEEE Communications Magazine* 59 (8): 14–20. https://doi.org/10.1109/MCOM.001.2001237.

Guo, J. and Lv, Z. (2022). Application of Digital Twins in Multiple Fields. *Multimedia Tools and Applications* 81 (19): 26941–26967. https://doi.org/10.1007/s11042-022-12536-5.

Hodavand, F., Ramaji, I.J., and Sadeghi, N. (2023). Digital Twin for Fault Detection and Diagnosis of Building Operations: A Systematic Review. *Buildings* 13 (6): 1426. https://doi.org/10.3390/buildings13061426.

HosseiniHaghighi, S.R., Álvarez, P.M., de Uribarri, R., and Padsala, and Ursula Eicker. (2022). Characterizing and Structuring Urban GIS Data for Housing Stock Energy Modelling and Retrofitting. *Energy and Buildings* 256 (February): 111706. https://doi.org/10.1016/j.enbuild.2021.111706.

Huang, W., Zhang, Y., and Zeng, W. (2022). Development and Application of Digital Twin Technology for Integrated Regional Energy Systems in Smart Cities. *Sustainable Computing: Informatics and Systems* 36 (December): 100781. https://doi.org/10.1016/j.suscom.2022.100781.

Intergovernmental Panel on Climate Change (IPCC). 2022. "Climate Change 2022: Mitigation of Climate Change, Summary for Policy Making. Working Group III Contribution to the Sixth Assessment Report of the Intergovernmental Panel on Climate Change." https://www.ipcc.ch/report/ar6/wg3/downloads/report/IPCC_AR6_WGIII_SPM.pdf.

International Energy Agency (2022). *Roadmap for Energy-Efficient Buildings and Construction in ASEAN: Timelines and Actions towards Net Zero-Carbon Buildings and Construction*. OECD https://doi.org/10.1787/bda80fad-en.

"iTwin Platform, Bentley Systems, Infrastructure Software." 2022. June 6, 2022. https://www.bentley.com/software/itwin-platform/.

Jafari, M., Kavousi-Fard, A., Chen, T., and Karimi, M. (2023). A Review on Digital Twin Technology in Smart Grid, Transportation System and Smart City: Challenges and Future. *IEEE Access* 11: 17471–17484. https://doi.org/10.1109/ACCESS.2023.3241588.

Javaid, M., Haleem, A., and Suman, R. (2023). Digital Twin Applications toward Industry 4.0: A Review. *Cognitive Robotics* 3 (January): 71–92. https://doi.org/10.1016/j.cogr.2023.04.003.

Jiang, S., Yang, Y., Gupta, S. et al. (2016). The TimeGeo Modeling Framework for Urban Mobility without Travel Surveys. *Proceedings of the National Academy of Sciences* 113 (37): https://doi.org/10.1073/pnas.1524261113.

Lehtola, V.V., Koeva, M., Elberink, S.O. et al. (2022). Digital Twin of a City: Review of Technology Serving City Needs. *International Journal of Applied Earth Observation and Geoinformation* 114 (November): 102915. https://doi.org/10.1016/j.jag.2022.102915.

Li, L., Yang, L., Zhu, H., and Dai, R. (2015). Explorative Analysis of Wuhan Intra-Urban Human Mobility Using Social Media Check-In Data." Edited by Claudia Torres Codeço. *PLOS ONE* 10 (8): e0135286. https://doi.org/10.1371/journal.pone.0135286.

Lu, Q., Parlikad, A.K., Woodall, P. et al. (2020). Developing a Digital Twin at Building and City Levels: Case Study of West Cambridge Campus. *Journal of Management in Engineering* 36 (3): 05020004. https://doi.org/10.1061/(ASCE)ME.1943-5479.0000763.

Madni, A.M., Madni, C.C., and Lucero, S.D. (2019). Leveraging Digital Twin Technology in Model-Based Systems Engineering. *Systems* 7 (1): 7. https://doi.org/10.3390/systems7010007.

Manzoor, B., Othman, I., and Pomares, J.C. (2021). Digital Technologies in the Architecture, Engineering and Construction (AEC) Industry—A Bibliometric—Qualitative Literature Review of Research Activities. *International Journal of Environmental Research and Public Health* 18 (11): 6135. https://doi.org/10.3390/ijerph18116135.

Mohammadi, N. and Taylor, J.E. (2017). Urban Energy Flux: Spatiotemporal Fluctuations of Building Energy Consumption and Human Mobility-Driven Prediction. *Applied Energy* 195 (June): 810–818. https://doi.org/10.1016/j.apenergy.2017.03.044.

Naderi, H. and Shojaei, A. (2023). Digital Twinning of Civil Infrastructures: Current State of Model Architectures, Interoperability Solutions, and Future Prospects. *Automation in Construction* 149 (May): 104785. https://doi.org/10.1016/j.autcon.2023.104785.

Nath, S.V., van Schalkwyk, P., and Isaacs, D. (2021). *Building Industrial Digital Twins: Design, Develop, and Deploy Digital Twin Solutions for Real-World Industries Using Azure Digital Twins*. Packt Publishing Ltd.

O'Neill, Z. and Wen, J. (2022). Artificial Intelligence in Smart Buildings. *Science and Technology for the Built Environment* 28 (9): 1115–1115. https://doi.org/10.1080/23744731.2022.2125209.

Opoku, D.-G.J., Perera, S., Osei-Kyei, R., and Rashidi, M. (2021). Digital Twin Application in the Construction Industry: A Literature Review. *Journal of Building Engineering* 40 (August): 102726. https://doi.org/10.1016/j.jobe.2021.102726.

Opoku, D.-G.J., Perera, S., Osei-Kyei, R. et al. (2023). Barriers to the Adoption of Digital Twin in the Construction Industry: A Literature Review. *Informatics* 10 (1): 14. https://doi.org/10.3390/informatics10010014.

Opoku, D.-G.J., Perera, S., Osei-Kyei, R. et al. (2022). Drivers for Digital Twin Adoption in the Construction Industry: A Systematic Literature Review. *Buildings* 12 (2): 113. https://doi.org/10.3390/buildings12020113.

Pappalardo, L., Simini, F., Rinzivillo, S. et al. (2015). Returners and Explorers Dichotomy in Human Mobility. *Nature Communications* 6 (1): 8166. https://doi.org/10.1038/ncomms9166.

Park, Y., Thomas R. Dougherty, and Z. Nagy. 2018. "A Bluetooth Based Occupancy Detection for Buildings June." In https://www.semanticscholar.org/paper/a-bluetooth-based-occupancy-detection-for-buildings-park-dougherty/d8278818e68cbc14edd8dd449dba0d3af8fcca33.

Rathore, M.M., Shah, S.A., Shukla, D. et al. (2021). The Role of AI, Machine Learning, and Big Data in Digital Twinning: A Systematic Literature Review, Challenges, and Opportunities. *IEEE Access* 9: 32030–32052. https://doi.org/10.1109/ACCESS.2021.3060863.

Ríos, J., Hernández, J.C., Oliva, M., and Mas, F. (2015). Product Avatar as Digital Counterpart of a Physical Individual Product: Literature Review and Implications in an Aircraft. In: *In Transdisciplinary Lifecycle Analysis of Systems*, 657–666. IOS: Press https://doi.org/10.3233/978-1-61499-544-9-657.

Abolhassani, S., Soroush, A.Z., Ghourchian, N. et al. (2022). Improving Residential Building Energy Simulations through Occupancy Data Derived from Commercial Off-the-Shelf Wi-Fi Sensing Technology. *Energy and Buildings* 272 (October): 112354. https://doi.org/10.1016/j.enbuild.2022.112354.

Santhanavanich, Thunyathep, Rushikesh Padsala, Patrick Würstle, and Volker Coors. 2022. *The Spatial Data Infrastructure of an Urban Digital Twin in the Building Energy Domain Using OGC Standards. ISPRS Annals of the Photogrammetry, Remote Sensing and Spatial Information Sciences*. Vol. X-4/W2-2022. https://doi.org/10.5194/isprs-annals-X-4-W2-2022-249-2022.

Sheth, A., Padhee, S., and Gyrard, A. (2019). Knowledge Graphs and Knowledge Networks: The Story in Brief. *IEEE Internet Computing* 23 (4): 67–75. https://doi.org/10.1109/MIC.2019.2928449.

Stavropoulos, T.G., Kontopoulos, E., Bassiliades, N. et al. (2015). Rule-Based Approaches for Energy Savings in an Ambient Intelligence Environment. *Pervasive and Mobile Computing* 19 (May): 1–23. https://doi.org/10.1016/j.pmcj.2014.05.001.

Steindl, G., Stagl, M., Kasper, L. et al. (2020). Generic Digital Twin Architecture for Industrial Energy Systems. *Applied Sciences* 10 (24): 8903. https://doi.org/10.3390/app10248903.

Taylor, J.E., Bennett, G., and Mohammadi, N. (2021). Engineering Smarter Cities with Smart City Digital Twins. *Journal of Management in Engineering* 37 (6): 02021001. https://doi.org/10.1061/(ASCE)ME.1943-5479.0000974.

Uhlenkamp, J.-F., Hauge, J.B., Broda, E. et al. (2022). Digital Twins: A Maturity Model for Their Classification and Evaluation. *IEEE Access* 10: 69605–69635. https://doi.org/10.1109/ACCESS.2022.3186353.

Wolf, K., Dawson, R.J., Mills, J.P. et al. (2022). Towards a Digital Twin for Supporting Multi-Agency Incident Management in a Smart City. *Scientific Reports* 12 (1): 16221. https://doi.org/10.1038/s41598-022-20178-8.

"World Population Prospects - Population Division - United Nations." n.d. Accessed August 28, 2023. https://population.un.org/wpp/.

World Resources Institute (WRI). n.d. "GHG Protocol for Cities." Accessed August 28, 2023. https://ghgprotocol.org/ghg-protocol-cities.

Xia, H., Liu, Z., Efremochkina, M. et al. (2022). Study on City Digital Twin Technologies for Sustainable Smart City Design: A Review and Bibliometric Analysis of Geographic Information System and Building Information Modeling Integration. *Sustainable Cities and Society* 84 (September): 104009. https://doi.org/10.1016/j.scs.2022.104009.

Yan, D., O'Brien, W., Hong, T. et al. (2015). Occupant Behavior Modeling for Building Performance Simulation: Current State and Future Challenges. *Energy and Buildings* 107 (November): 264–278. https://doi.org/10.1016/j.enbuild.2015.08.032.

Ye, X., Jiaxin, D., Han, Y. et al. (2023). Developing Human-Centered Urban Digital Twins for Community Infrastructure Resilience: A Research Agenda. *Journal of Planning Literature* 38 (2): 187–199. https://doi.org/10.1177/08854122221137861.

Zhang, X., Shen, J., Saini, P.K. et al. (2021). Digital Twin for Accelerating Sustainability in Positive Energy District: A Review of Simulation Tools and Applications. *Frontiers in Sustainable Cities* 3: https://www.frontiersin.org/articles/10.3389/frsc.2021.663269.

Zhu, H., Yang, W., Li, S., and Pang, A. (2022). An Effective Fault Detection Method for HVAC Systems Using the LSTM-SVDD Algorithm. *Buildings* 12 (2): 246. https://doi.org/10.3390/buildings12020246.

Zhu, X., Xingxing Zhang, P., and Gong, and Yu Li. (2023). A Review of Distributed Energy System Optimization for Building Decarbonization. *Journal of Building Engineering* 73 (August): 106735. https://doi.org/10.1016/j.jobe.2023.106735.

Index

Note: Page numbers in "*italics*" represent figures and "**bold**" page number represents tables in text.

a

ACD *see* Augmented Computational Design (ACD)
addressing uncertainty   37–39
Agglomerative Hierarchical Clustering (AHC) algorithms   40, 44–46
airborne viruses   57
Ambient Intelligence (AmI)
   advancements and applications   196–197
   AmI-based EEF systems   197–201
   energy efficiency via AmI systems and DT technology   201–202
AmI-based energy efficiency feedback (EEF) systems   197–201
"Amusing Ourselves to Death: Public Discourse in the Age of Show Business"   162
ANN machine learning algorithm   214
ANSYS program   134
"archetypes"   34
architectural form   6
architecture, engineering, and construction (AEC)   129
architecture/structure, ANN   11
"argumentative consolidation"   236
Artificial Neural Network (ANN)   40, *42*, 58
   building envelope   101–104
   predicting IAQ-ESP   **60,** 60–61
"The Assault on Privacy: Computers, Data Banks, and Dossiers"   162
attention score visualization   172–173
Augmented Computational Design (ACD)
   Bayesian Belief Networks   17, *17*
   BBN meta-model   17
      augmenting   25
      backward inference   25
      build   20, *20*
      forward inference   24–25
      NTA 8800 simulation model   18
      parameter space sampling   18
      sensitivity analysis   18, 20
      toy problems   22, 24
      validation   21–22, *23*, 24
   case study   15–16
   design as decision-making   5–7, *7*
   design space exploration
      mapping   11–12
      navigation   12–13
   discrete design   9, 10
   generative design   7, *8*
   historical context   3–5, *4*, *5*
   meta-modeling   16
   relevance of AI   2–3
   spatial design variables   13–14
   statistical approaches to design
      possibilistic approach   14
      probabilistic approach   14–15
Auto Encoder   25
automated building control systems   190
Average Miles per Gallon (MPG) data   215

b

Bayesian Belief Networks (BBN)
  meta-model   17
    augmenting   25
    backward inference   25
    build   20, *20*
    forward inference   24–25
    NTA 8800 simulation model   18
    parameter space sampling   18
    sensitivity analysis   18, 20
    toy problems   22, 24
    validation   21–22, *23*, 24
  nodes and network architecture   17, *17*
BBN *see* Bayesian Belief Networks (BBN)
Bellman equation   121
bidirectional and auto-regressive transformers (BART) model   170
bidirectional encoder representations from transformers (BERT)   161
BIMFLexi-VR   237
Bing Liu's Opinion Lexicon (AFINN-111)   166, **166**
bi-objective minimization   152, *152*
"Biomorpher"   114
"black box" model   214
bottom–up UBEM approaches
  data-driven methods   *32*, 33–34, *35*
  physics-based methods   *32*, 34, *36*
Building Data Genome 2 (BDG2) Dataset   109
Building Energy Modeling (BEM)   15
building energy policy (BEP)   188
building envelope
  ANN   101–104
  CNN   105
  ensemble learning   107–108
  GANs   106–107
  machine learning and   101
  optimization frameworks   99, *100*
  optimization methods   99–100, *101*
  optimization routes and   98–99
  overview   97–98
  and performance   97
  RNNs   105–106
building performance
  ANN   103
  data   109
  DT leverages, DT
  GAN   106
  machine learning methods   101
  neural networks   108
  optimization   99
  real-time and predictive methods   81
  Virtual Reality
    architecture and engineering   236–240
    integration of   233–236
    occupant comfort and well-being   240–243
Building Performance Simulation (BPS)   81, 82
buildings façade systems
  building level and assembly level   129
  design optimization   130–131, **132–133**, 134
  environmental loads   129
  heating and cooling loads of   129
  multi-objective optimization   147–148
  Pareto front solutions   151–152, *152*
  surrogate models   145, *146*, 148–151, **150**, *150*, **151**
  UHP-FRC sandwich panels
    building level   141–142, *142*, **143**
    coupled structural-thermal model   138–140, *139*
    framework   135, **135**
    life cycle cost   136, 142–143, **144**

c

Cave Automatic Virtual Environment (CAVE) systems   232
CFD0   59
Chicago Building Footprints (CBF) GIS-based dataset   214
City Geography Markup Language (CityGML)   256–257
Classification and Regression Tree (CART)   40, 44
"Classifier" (CLS) token   170
Combinatorial Equilibrium Modeling (CEM)   114
Commercial Buildings Energy Consumption Survey (CBECS)   45
"Compas eplus"   118
Computational Fluid Dynamics (CFD)   58

Index | 279

COMSOL Multiphysics program   134
COMSOL software   148
Conditional Demand Analysis (CDR)   40
Conditional Probability Distribution (CPD)   17
Conditional Random Fields (CRF)   167
conduction transfer function (CTF)   134
CONTAM   59
conventional deep learning   167
Convolutional Neural Network (CNN)   42, *42*, 105
COVID-19   173, 179
  IAQ   161, 169, 173, 174
CubiCasa   88, *90*

d

data-driven methods   3*2*, 33–34, *35*
data/model integration layer   269
data sources   258–260
daylight performance prediction
  daylight simulation   84–85
  designers   92
  integration of   92, *93*
  research methods
    data acquisition   86, *87*, 88, *89*
    model training   88
    results and validation   88, *90*, *91*
daylight simulation   84, 85
Deep Belief Network (DBN)   46
Deep Learning (DL) models   82, 84, 85
Deep neural networks (DNNs)   41, *42*, 48
Deep-Performance (DP) method   83
denoising/decoding   15
design dashboard   123–124, *124*
Design of Experiment (DoE)   18
design space   9, 13
design space exploration
  advantages   125
  clustering design options   118
    adding weights method   119, **119**
    clustering method   120
    design space generation   116, **116**, **117**, *117*
    dimensionality reduction   118–119
    performance evaluation   118, **118**
  design dashboard   123–124, *124*

reinforcement learning-based recommender system
  constants/hyperparameters   121–122
  function determines beta (β)   122–123
  reward alteration with alpha (α) and gamma (γ)   122, *123*
  reward function   121
Digital Transformation encompass simulation methods   258
Digital Twin (DT) technology   190, 201–202
  see also Urban Building Energy Digital Twins (UBEDTs)
  NASA defines   252
Directed Acyclic Graph (DAG)   17
Discriminator (D)   85
DL-based surrogate modeling   85
domain-specific Lexicons   166
DT technology *see* Digital Twin (DT) technology
Dutch Normalization Institute (NEN)   15

e

embedding visualization   171–172
"Emergence: The Connected Lives of Ants, Brains, Cities, and Software"   162–163
emotion Lexicons   166
enabling technology
  AI and Digital Twin   260–261
  interoperability technologies   262–263
  IoT, Big Data, AI–ML, and Digital Twins   261–262
  twining technologies   256–258
  UDT and data sources   258–260
energy efficiency feedback (EEF) tools   189
EnergyPlus software   59, 134, 135, 149
energy-saving potentials (ESP)
  buildings dataset   61, **62**
  daytime/calendar characteristic   **60**, 61
  determine   67–68
  localize airflow on air paths   62–67, **67**
  meteorological dataset   60, **60**
  mobility patterns   **60**, 60–61
  physics-based simulation   70–73
  PM2.5 concentrations   60, **60**
  urban factors   60, **60**
  using machine learning   68–70
Energy Use Intensity (EUI)   214

ensemble learning   107–108
epistemic uncertainty   36
ESP *see* energy-saving potentials (ESP)
European Committee of Standardization (CEN)   15
European Energy Performance of Buildings Directive (EPBD)   15
Extreme Learning Machines (ELM)   41, *42*

f
Fault Detection and Diagnosis (FDD)   264
Federal Plaza   59
form-function dichotomy   2
frequency domain analyses   26
Functional Mock-up Interface (FMI)   59
"Function, Behaviour, Structure"   3

g
Generative Adversarial Networks (GANs)   82, 85, 106–107
generative design methods   7, *8*
Google AI in 2018   161
Grasshopper plug-in Human UI   114
Greenhouse Gas emissions   81

h
heating, ventilating, and air conditioning (HVAC) systems   57
Hebbian Learning   7
"Here Comes Everybody: The Power of Organizing Without Organizations"   161–162
High-Dynamic-Range (HDR)   105
Historical Mean Regression (HMR)   40
Huber M-estimation Regression (HMR)   40

i
IAQ *see* indoor air quality (IAQ)
Individual Load Profiles (ILPs) models   44
indoor air quality (IAQ)
   definition   57
   EnergyPlus software   59
   ESP
      buildings dataset   61, **62**
      daytime/calendar characteristic   **60**, 61
      determine   67–68
      localize airflow on air paths   62–67, **67**
      meteorological dataset   60, **60**
      mobility patterns   **60**, 60–61
      physics-based simulation   70–73
      PM2.5 concentrations   60, **60**
      urban factors   60, **60**
      using machine learning   68–70
   physics-based energy   59
   social media
      confidence distributions   175, *175*
      "elbow point"   176, *176*
      head-view visualization   177, *178*
      RoBERTa model   176, *177*
      RoBERTa sentiment analysis   173, **173**
      t-SNE visualization   176, *176*
      word cloud   173, *174*
indoor environmental quality (IEQ)   189, 231
Infrastructure Digital Twin (IDT)   253
"initial design process"   233
Intelligent Communities Life (ICL) Cycle platform   258
interactive evolutionary computation (IEC)   114

j
Joint Probability Distributions (JPDs)   17

k
kernelfeature detector   105
k-means (KM) clustering   40, 44, 45, *45*
k-Nearest Neighbor (k-NN)   40, 44, *44*
Kriging surrogate models   131

l
Lek's profile method   219–226
lexicons   165–166, **166**
"logical leap"   3
Logistic Regression (LR)   40

m
machine learning (ML)
   based surrogate UBEM   47–49
   building envelope   101
   data-driven approach   58
   daylight simulation   84, 85
   ESP   68–70
   NLP   167
   reinforcement learning   120
   in UBEM   32

reinforcement learning   46–47
supervised learning   39–44
unsupervised learning   44–46
maturity model (MM) category   263
mean absolute error (MAE)   119
Mean Absolute Percentage Error
    (MAPE)   21
Mean Squared Error (MSE)   102
ML *see* machine learning (ML)
model-based system engineering
    (MBSE)   263
Multi-Layer Perceptrons (MLP)   40, 41
multi-objective optimization   114, 147–148
Multiple Linear Regression (MLR)   40

n

National Human Activity Pattern Survey
    (NHAPS)   57
Natural Language Processing (NLP)
  conventional deep learning   167
  lexicons   165–166, **166**
  machine learning   167
  statistical approaches   165
  transformer deep learning   167–168
natural ventilation (NV)   57
Nearly Zero-Energy Buildings   16
Neuron Activation Heatmap   177, *179*
NLP *see* Natural Language Processing (NLP)
non-dominated sorting genetic algorithm
    (NSGA)   114
non-dominated sorting genetic algorithm
    (NSGA-II)   99, 104, 131, 134, 136,
    147, 148, 153
Nonlinear (Polynomial) Regression (PR)   40
Normalized Root Mean Square Error
    (NRMSE)   21
Noun–Verb Lexicons   166
NTA 8800 document   15–16
NV-operated buildings   58

o

occupancy-driven analysis   189
occupancy models   191
occupant-driven urban building energy
    efficiency
  occupancy and building energy use   191,
      192, 193

occupant monitoring methods
  via experimental studies   195–196
  via observational studies   194–195
  via Ambient Intelligence
      advancements and
      applications   196–197
    AmI-based EEF systems   197–201
    energy efficiency via AmI systems
        and DT technology   201–202
occupant monitoring methods
  via experimental studies   195–196
  via observational studies   194–195
occupant-related inputs   188
Ordinary Least Squares (OLS)   40
overfitting   103

p

partial differential equations (PDEs)   134
Perceptual Similarity (PS)   85
Performance-Driven Generative Design
    Systems (PDGDSs)   81
"performative AI"   83
physics-based methods   *32*, 34, *36*
"1138 PLYMOUTH"   60
PM2.5 concentrations   57, 58, 60, 68, *69*, 70,
    72, 74, 169
Policy-Driven design   7
"prediction error"   119
Probabilistic Graphical Models (PGM)   2
Probability Density Functions (PDF)   17

r

Radial Basis Function (RBF)   *42*, 104
Radius of Gyration (*rg*)   163, 164
Random Decision Forest (RDF)   40, 44, *45*
Random Forest (RF)   40
Rectified Linear Unit (ReLU) function   102
Recurrent Neural Networks
    (RNNs)   105–106
reinforcement learning   *46*, 46–47
reinforcement learning-based recommender
    system   115
  constants/hyperparameters
    discount factor (gamma (γ))   121
    exploration exploitation trade-off
        epsilon (ε)   121–122
    learning rate (alpha (α))   121

reinforcement learning-based recommender system (*continued*)
  priority trade-off (beta (β))   121–122
  design dashboard   120
  function determines beta (β)   122–123
  reward alteration with alpha (α) and gamma (γ)   122, *123*
  reward function   121
residential energy use   211–212
Resistor, Self-Induction Loop, Capacitor (RLC) circuits   26
RoBERTa model   169–172
RStudio software   59

s

SARS-CoV2 virus   57, 60
The Sciences of the Artificial   2
Scientific Architecture   2
Scikit-learn Linear regression model   119
SDPH   213
self-correcting building control systems   264
self-organizing maps (SOM)   114
Sentiment Lexicons   165
"Separator" (SEP) token   170
Simple Linear Regression (SLR)   40
Singular Value Decomposition (SVD)   12
Sobol's sequences   18
social dynamics in urban building and transportation energy behavior
  data   215, *216–218*
  explanatory model   214
  Lek's profile   219–226
  modeling framework   214
  occupancy and socio-economic factors   219
  variable importance (VI)   219, *220*
social health and occupancy factors   213
social media
  in environmental studies
    computing behavioral (mobility) patterns   163–165
    evolution of NLP analysis   165–168
    feedback and air quality   160
  IAQ sentiments
    confidence distributions   175, *175*
    "elbow point"   176, *176*
    head-view visualization   177, *178*

RoBERTa model   176, *177*
RoBERTa sentiment analysis   173, **173**
t-SNE visualization   176, *176*
word cloud   173, *174*
materials and methods
  co-occurrence matrix   170
  data query   168–169
  sentiment analysis and classification   170–171
  text preprocessing   169, **169**
  text summarization   170
  text tokenization   169–170
roles   160
and urban life   161–163
visualizations
  attention score   172–173
  embedding   171–172
social relations   212
"Space is the Machine"   6
Spatial Autoregressive (SAR) model   163–165
spatial configurations   2
spatial design variables   13–14
stochastic uncertainty   36–37
Structural Similarity Index Model (SSIM)   85
Subjectivity Lexicon   166
supervised learning   39–44
support vector machine (SVM)   40, *43*, 43–44, 84
Surrogate Models (SM)   82, 83

t

top-down UBEM approaches   *32*, 33
transfer functions   26
transformer deep learning   167–168
triple-objective minimization   152, *152*
TRNSYS tool   134

u

UBEDTs *see* Urban Building Energy Digital Twins (UBEDTs)
UBEM *see* urban building energy model (UBEM)
UDT *see* Urban Digital Twin (UDT)
UHP-FRC sandwich panels
  building level   141–142, *142*, **143**

Index | 283

framework   135, **135**
life cycle cost   136, 142–143, **144**
midspan displacement
   coupled structural-thermal
     model   138–140, *139*
   framework   135, **135**
   governing equations, structural–thermal
     finite element model   140–141
   thermo-mechanical properties of   136,
     137, *137*, 138, *138*
underfitting   103
Uniform Manifold Approximation and
   Projection algorithm (UMAP)   114
unsupervised learning   44–46
Urban Building Energy Digital Twins
   (UBEDTs)
   architecture   267
     data acquisition layer   266
     data/model integration layer   269
     modeling and simulation layer   266–268
     service/actuation layer   269
   definition and conceptualization   252–254
   enabling technologies
     AI and DT   260–261
     interoperability technologies   262–263
     IoT, Big Data, AI–ML, and Digital
       Twins   261–262
     twining technologies   256–258
     UDT and data sources   258–260
   implications for Citywide Energy
     Management   254–256
   limitations
     data analysis   271
     data quality and availability   270
     interoperability   270
     smart infrastructure and associated
       cost   270
   maturity levels of   263–265
urban building energy model (UBEM)   201
   bottom–up models
     data-driven methods   3*2*, 33–34, *35*
     physics-based methods   3*2*, 34, *36*
   machine learning (ML)   32
     based surrogate modeling   47–49
     reinforcement learning   46–47

supervised learning   39–44
unsupervised learning   44–46
top–down models   3*2*, 33
uncertainty in
   addressing   37–39
   epistemic   36
   stochastic   36–37
Urban Digital Twin (UDT)   258–260, *259*, 269
urban energy use   211
Urban Energy Use Modeling (UEUM)   214,
   216, *218*
urban-scale building energy models   212
Urban Transportation Energy (UTE)
   model   215
U.S. Energy Information Administration
   (EIA)   45
U.S. Environmental Protection Agency
   (EPA)   57
"user-generated content" (UGC)   162
U.S. National Institute of Standards and
   Technology (NIST)   58

v
variable importance (VI)   219, *220*
virtual environments   231
Virtual Reality (VR)
   ability of   233
   building design and performance
     evaluation   233–236
   in building performance
     architecture and engineering   236–240
     integration of   233–236
     occupant comfort and
       well-being   240–243
   illusion of   233
   use of   233

w
whole-building energy simulation
   programs   134

y
You Only Look Once (YOLO)   105

z
Zaha Hadid Architects (ZHA)   108

Printed and bound by CPI Group (UK) Ltd, Croydon, CR0 4YY
15/04/2024
14483480-0001